HEALING HANDS

By the same author

DANGER FROM MOSCOW

FROGMAN EXTRAORDINARY

SCHOOL FOR SPIES

STALIN—THE MIRACULOUS GEORGIAN

THE TRAITOR TRADE

OUT OF THIS WORLD

HEALING HANDS

J. Bernard Hutton

Introduction by
Edward Townley Bailey
M.B. B.S. F.R.C.S.

DAVID McKAY COMPANY, INC.
NEW YORK

HEALING HANDS

FIRST AMERICAN EDITION 1967

LIBRARY OF CONGRESS CATALOG CARD NUMBER: 67-11315

MANUFACTURED IN THE UNITED STATES OF AMERICA

I might have gone blind; I might have died. That neither happened is due to Pearl, my wife, who 'found' William Lang for me and to whom I dedicate this book in gratitude.

Contents

MIRACLE: a marvellous event occurring within human experience which cannot have been brought about by human power or by the operation of any natural agency, and must therefore be ascribed to the special intervention of the Deity or of some supernatural being; chiefly an act (e.g. of healing) exhibiting control over the laws of nature, and serving as evidence that the agent is either divine or is specially favoured by God.

The Oxford English Dictionary
(1961 *reprinted edition*)

Introduction

THIS IS a most unusual book written with the skill of an accomplished author about 'spirit healing', a subject which might be in danger of unenlightened dismissal without a preliminary introduction.

It is the true story of 'miracles' wrought by spirit healing through the devoted partnership of two men, a famous consultant surgeon William Lang, who lived in the nineteenth and early twentieth century, and who is known to a number of doctors living today, and his medium George Chapman, who is devoting his life to the mediumship by which Dr. Lang, as he likes to be known, and his spirit colleagues are able to apply healing forces which are not within the range of ordinary treatment. Most doctors know only too well the limitation of their ability to relieve sickness and suffering, and this book should indeed help to convince them of the reality of spirit healing and its potentialities.

The scope of this book, however, is much wider and brings a message of hope to all who are stricken and are without relief, despite the dedicated care of doctors and nurses.

I cannot stress too much that this is not a book on Spiritualism; it is a very human and touching account of 'miracles of healing'. The author includes his own miracle and admits that like many people he had never heard of the spirit body, which is nevertheless an integral though unseen part of us all. To many such a proposition seems unnatural, but knowing this, Dr. Lang conveys to all who visit him the simplicity of this idea, and the obvious reason why it is possible through the spirit body to receive treatment which helps the physical body.

There is nothing in this book which should offend any form of religious belief, or even the absence of it. Neither is there any intention of preying upon the emotions. All that is related is a presentation of *proven fact*.

I am convinced that the miracles described are not figments of the imagination. I know how hard it is for doctors to accept that which is not verifiable by the usual methods of assessment, but this book is one which should stimulate both doctors and patients to further unbiased enquiry. The greater the initial scepticism, the deeper will be the final conviction.

I have no hesitation in saying that from my own experience in my surgical career, I accept without question that 'miracles' can and do happen under the conditions so faithfully presented by Mr. Hutton in his book which I believe will in due course be regarded as a pioneer reference in a hitherto little known 'Science of Healing'.

EDWARD TOWNLEY BAILEY, M.B., B.S., F.R.C.S.(Eng.)
Consultant Orthopaedic Surgeon

Author's Note

When I first came across George Chapman's name, and read that his spirit doctor control was the late William Lang, F.R.C.S., of the Middlesex and Moorfields Eye Hospital, I knew little or nothing about spirit healing. It was difficult for me to accept any statements that spirit 'operations' and similar treatment could cure incurable (or serious) diseases which had not responded to orthodox medical attention. I did not believe in miracles. It was not really surprising then that, having made an appointment with George Chapman for January 6, 1964, I went to Aylesbury with certain reservations. I was 'to meet the spirit doctor, Lang'.

The visit turned out to be gratifying. For after I'd received healing from Mr. Lang, I was left in no doubt that his spirit operations had indeed brought about results which were not only stunning but convincing.

The more evident the improvement of my condition became, the stronger grew the desire in my mind to acquaint myself thoroughly with the intriguing subject of spirit healing. I made my first move and studied some of the available evidence about Mr. Lang's and George Chapman's work. I discovered that my own experience was similar to many thousands of cases where the spirit doctor had succeeded in bringing about wonderful successes.

There was, however, much much more I needed to know if I was to present an unbiased and authentic account of Lang's and Chapman's work. Both Lang and Chapman said they would help me in any way they could. The scene was set and I was able to go ahead with the tedious, though satisfying, task I had set myself.

There were many tape-recorded interviews with Mr. Lang while he was in control of his entranced medium. There were sessions with George Chapman during his waking state. These interviews frequently took the form of cross-examination, stubborn questioning, and requests for proof of any statements made. I travelled thousands of miles in Britain to interview those of Lang's patients I had picked out at random from Chapman's bulging case history files. As time went by, I had reel upon reel of tape-recorded statements from people who said that Lang had cured them. Some people claimed they had been cured completely by Lang from diseases which hospital doctors had said were incurable.

Apart from interviewing patients, I also checked their statements and medical histories. I wanted to be fully satisfied that I was in possession of *facts* and not highly coloured (and possibly inaccurate) emotional accounts.

Every patient's name and place of residence published in this book is authentic. I take this opportunity to thank each of them for their kind help and co-operation for, had these unselfish people not permitted me to record their individual cases and divulge their true identities, the authenticity and credibility of Lang's and Chapman's achievements would have been open to serious doubt.

I also want to thank William Lang and George Chapman for their untiring assistance, because without their invaluable help I would not have been able to write this book, and I acknowledge a special debt of gratitude to Liam Nolan for his advice and help with this book — travails which went far beyond the duties of a friend.

Being well aware that I have written an unusual book, I wish to make it abundantly clear that I have not the slightest intention of trying to influence or convert anyone to a new way of thinking. My task ends by having presented an objective account of the truth about the subject in question.

J. BERNARD HUTTON

Prologue

IT WAS an autumn day in 1963, and as the year died, the life seemed to be draining away from me too. The doctor standing by my bedside was quiet-voiced and serious. We were on friendly terms, and since I had never in my life felt as ill as I did now, I knew he would be honest with me when I asked him what was wrong with me.

'You've got a non-paralytic type of poliomyelitis,' he said. 'But I want some blood tests done.'

The words scared me. Poliomyelitis—could I really have it? The 'non-paralytic' part didn't ease my fear. I didn't know what to say. My head felt as if it was being split open. Aching pains throbbed in my legs and arms, and when I tried to stand up, dizziness engulfed me. Poliomyelitis. The word hammered and echoed in my brain. I went through a period then in which time and details fused. There was the hospital, blood tests, trolleys, sleep, weakness, confusion, pain. Antibiotics proved useless.

And then I began to go blind.

All my life I had suffered from poor eyesight, and from July 1958 onwards I had been under the care of a leading ophthalmic specialist, Mr. Hudson. Mr. Hudson had been perfectly frank with me from the beginning, and I had grown to accept the fact that there was precious little chance of my sight ever improving.

Now in 1963, having been diagnosed a polio case, I was also faced with the prospect of blindness. It became so bad that eventually all I could distinguish of a person standing ten yards away from me was an indistinct outline. Finally, there were signs of double vision.

One morning, at a time when I was feeling utterly desolate, my wife, Pearl, shoved a copy of *Psychic News* into my hands. 'Read the story on that man at Aylesbury,' she said.

I was short tempered at this period, continually snapping at Pearl and the children. The idea of forcing my eyes to try to pick out the words of small newsprint was too much. 'Don't be ridiculous,' I said. 'You know how hard it is for me to read even a book with large type in it, let alone this silly nonsense.'

'No, please read it Joe, please,' Pearl insisted.

Grumbling, I lifted the paper to the tip of my nose to try and get the words in focus. I was painfully sensitive to the fact that anyone looking at me in this position must be tempted to laugh. This, as much as anything, had prompted me to give up reading altogether except when I was alone. Even then the effort and the pain from my eyes made it a trial.

I had to search the page for the story Pearl wanted me to read, and I was just about to throw the paper from me in frustrated anger when I picked out a fragment about some remarkable happenings in Aylesbury. It had to do with eye operations which, it was claimed, were being carried out by some spirit healer.

I went back to the beginning of the story and started to struggle through it. It told of a Dr. Lang who had been a noted ophthalmic specialist in the latter half of the nineteenth and early half of the twentieth centuries. He died in 1937, but now, it was claimed, he was operating through a medium in Aylesbury.

I put the paper down with a derisive comment. Pearl, however, thought otherwise. 'Why don't you just give it a try, Joe?' she pleaded. 'We could drive up and at least *see*.' I was adamant at first in my refusal, but finally relented. I agreed to write for an appointment.

The medium was a man called George Chapman. Two days later I had a reply from him to the effect that Dr. William Lang would see me at 2 p.m. on January 6, 1964.

Well, I thought, if it is a game, at least this Mr. Chapman is playing it elaborately. I looked at the letter again. *Dr. Lang* would see me it said. Not Mr. Chapman, but Dr. Lang. I knew enough about Spiritualism to realise that this meant Mr. Chapman would be in trance, controlled by the spirit doctor.

On January 6 we left our Worthing home early. Because of my

eye condition, Pearl had long taken over the chauffeuring duties, and as it was going to be a long day out, the children had to come along too.

At about five minutes to two I knocked at the door of Mr. Chapman's house. I think that at the back of my mind was the idea that even if the whole set-up turned out to be phoney, there might be a feature story for one of the Sunday papers.

I was shown into the waiting room, and a few minutes later the receptionist said: 'Mr. Hutton, Dr. Lang will see you now.' There it was again, *Dr. Lang* would see me.

I peered through my thick lenses at the white-coated figure standing near the window in the consulting room. The face seemed lined and elderly, and the eyes were closed tightly. I just had time to feel surprised when, without opening his eyes, the man in the white coat said: 'Well, what troubles you, young man?'

I was surprised again. I was no young man; certainly not as young as the medium, Chapman, whose picture I had seen in *Psychic News*. Now that I was a couple of steps inside the room I could see the resemblance between the standing figure and the photograph of Chapman. But the face—it looked so much older. The wrinkles and lines were marks of true old age, but I knew Chapman was in his early forties.

The figure in the white coat moved towards me, eyes still shut.

'I am Mr. Lang,' he said. Even the voice sounded old, I thought. 'You wanted to see me, didn't you?'

'Yes,' I said.

He held his right hand out towards me and I lifted my own hand towards his, but only halfway. I was watching his face. His eyes didn't open. But his hand, with no groping or feeling around, found mine.

'I am pleased to see you,' he said. 'Sit here, please.' He gestured to a chair facing the window. Outside the day was grey and cold, and the light, such as there was of it, fell on my face. 'Your eyes, young man, are giving you trouble,' he said.

'Yes,' I answered, 'and during the past two months they have been getting worse. I find it almost impossible to read now. I can't type. My work has come to a stop and——'

'May I see these please,' he cut in, and removed my glasses. He still hadn't opened his eyes. He held the glasses before his face as though he were looking at them. 'Oh, dear!' he exclaimed, shaking his head slowly. 'Minus eighteen.'

He was quite correct—my lenses *were* minus eighteen, but I hadn't told him anything about them.

He slipped the spectacles into his breast-pocket, then bent down closer to me and brought his thumbs up and felt my eyes. Not once did he open his own. After a minute or so he straightened up.

'You had a squint operation on both eyes when you were a child. A very nice job.'

I was astounded. How could he have known this Not even Pearl, my wife, knew. I never spoke about it. In fact I hadn't even thought about it for years. It had happened a long time ago—when I was six years old. The surgeon who had performed the operation, Professor Elschnick of the Sanatorium Gottlieb in Prague, was dead.

He bent over me again, touching my eyes with his thumbs, and talking all the while. The stream of medical phrases and terms washed over me. '. . . and your sight is deteriorating all the time . . . lymph drainage system not functioning properly . . . diplopia. . . .' The words were only half caught, half heard. '. . . due to the derangement of the muscular balance of the two eyes . . . central scotoma. . . .'

I didn't know what to do or say or think. '. . . and some lesion of the retina as well as swelling of the conjunctiva due to the presence of the fluid . . . macula clouded over . . .'

Finally he straightened up once more. 'You are troubled with double vision too, young man, aren't you?'

By this time I could only nod.

'What is your profession?' he asked suddenly.

'I am a writer and a journalist,' I answered.

He pursed his lips and nodded three or four times. 'Well, you certainly depend on your eyes a great deal. I'll do my very best to help you.'

'Thank you, thank you very much,' I said. 'Anything at all that you might do would be most deeply——'

'That's quite all right, quite all right,' he said, dismissing my gratitude. 'Now there is something else—other than your eyes—troubling you. Let me give you a little examination.'

I expected him to ask me to take off my jacket and shirt, but he didn't. Seated where I was, he touched me gently with his hands. There was no sound in the room for what seemed like a couple of minutes. His eyes were closed the whole time. He hadn't opened them since I had come into his room.

'Now then,' he resumed eventually, 'the virus which brought about your illness, and which your doctor believed to be a non-paralytic type of poliomyelitis, has gone. But you have something which is very serious, a hepatitis virus which is upsetting your liver. Due to it, changes in your body temperature take place because the liver balance cannot be maintained. This hepatitis virus saps your strength.'

If I had been amazed before, I was speechless now. I had not told Chapman anything about my own doctor when I wrote to him, nor had I mentioned being ill. Yet here was the medium, telling me something that only my own doctor and my wife could possibly have known. And neither had been in touch with George Chapman. It was uncanny.

The temptation to accept totally everything claimed about the dead surgeon now operating through his medium Chapman, was suddenly very strong. But the journalistic instinct reasserted itself. Words like telepathy, thought transference, clairvoyance, and all that they meant, flashed into my brain. Somewhere in these could be contained the answer to the mysterious knowledge of facts about me the medium was quoting. And yet, the medical terms, what of them? He certainly could not have got those from me. I had never heard most of them before.

He was talking again in that peculiar old-sounding, denture-clicking way of his, in a voice both thin and ancient. 'In order to help you, I shall have to perform an operation on your eyes. You needn't worry, young man, you see everyone has two bodies—a physical body and a spirit body. Now I shall operate on your *spirit* body and attempt to produce a corresponding effect on your physical body. You may hear me talking, calling out names and asking for instruments. Don't be alarmed. I shall be assisted at the operation by my son Basil and various other colleagues of mine you won't be able to see because they too have passed into spirit. But you won't feel any pain. Now I want you to lie there on that couch.'

My impressions of that last little spiel were, to say the least, amused. It was getting more and more like an elaborate charade, but I thought I might as well play along with it.

When the medium asked me to lie on the couch I expected him to ask me to undress. He didn't. I lay back, fully clothed, with my eyes wide open.

He came across to the edge of the couch and then lifted his hands and started to move them, and flick his fingers just above my eyes. His own eyes stayed tightly closed. The fingers of his hands opened and shut as though taking and using instruments. Suddenly I had an almost uncontrollable urge to burst out laughing. The mime seemed so funny. I had to bite hard on my lip to hold back the guffaw that was struggling to get out. Then I forced myself to listen to that old voice again.

'I have drawn away slightly your spirit body from your physical body, and am now operating on your spirit body. . . . I am making an opening through the supra tarsal fold and am attending to the fluids and parts behind the eyes . . . the crystalline lens, retina and so forth . . .' And so it went on.

The desire to laugh suddenly left me.

'. . . I have dealt with your eyeball now, and the muscles themselves because I found that the ciliary muscles were tightened up. . . .'

Then, incredible as it may seem, I began to experience the physical sensation of incisions being made. They were painless, but none the less capable of being felt. The man's eyes never opened, and he did not touch me. And yet, a little later I felt as though he were stitching up the wounds. It was all very far from being funny now.

As soon as my eyes were dealt with, I heard him pointing out to his unseen and unheard assistants that if the hepatitis virus was not attended to, the eye operations might not be of much use.

'Now I am going to perform an operation on your spirit body,' he said to me. 'I'll attempt to dispose of the virus.'

Again I watched his hands hovering above me. Again they looked as if they were handling invisible instruments, and again I had those strange painless sensations as though incisions were being made in anaesthetised flesh. And when it was over, there was the selfsame sensation of a needle being inserted, drawn through, reinserted.

When I was asked to sit up, I felt dizzy and dazed. And then a full and terrible alarm hit me, because I found I could not see at all! I could only barely distinguish between light and dark.

It suddenly came back to me that Mr. Hudson, the eye specialist I had been attending since 1958, had once told me that the only remote possibility of an improvement in my eyesight lay in a complicated series of operations which might or might not succeed. He had stressed that if they were unsuccessful, I would be permanently blind. Other consultants had confirmed his opinion, and I had decided not to take the risk.

All this flashed into my mind as I sat sightless on that couch in Aylesbury. There was the frightful fear that the meddling of this so-called medium had resulted in what Mr. Hudson had warned me about.

In a panic I began to shout. 'What's wrong now? I can't see anything. Do something for God's sake!'

The voice, unruffled, denture-clicking as before, came to me. 'Don't worry, young man, it's only temporary, it'll soon lift and you'll notice considerable improvement.' He then added: 'I cannot promise to give you the sight of normal eyes, young man, but I can promise that I will improve your vision considerably.' His calmness was soothing. 'I shall continue to visit you during your sleep state, because I can then more easily detach your spirit body from your physical body and give you the necessary treatment. I assure you I shall do everything possible to improve your vision.'

'I only hope you are right,' I said in desperation.

'Don't worry; don't worry, young man,' he repeated. 'I would like to see you again in about three months. Do you think you will be able to come?'

'Oh, yes, I'll come,' I acknowledged. 'But now I can't even see where the door is.'

'Don't worry, young man,' he said once again, and I heard a buzzer go somewhere outside, and then the door opening.

'Yes?' a female voice said.

'Ah, Margaret, would you see to Joseph please.'

'Thanks, Mr. Lang, and I hope you are right and I'll be able to see.'

'Oh, you will, you will, it won't be very long.'

His voice was so reassuring.

I was led outside, and I asked to be shown to the front door.

It was with the greatest difficulty that I groped my way to where we had left the car. I had a splitting headache and felt dizzy, and all my body was shaking.

What a fool I had been to give in to Pearl's insistence on my coming here, I thought. I may not have been able to see very much, but at least I was able to see *something* before all this hocus-pocus rendered me blind.

I sat in the car. Pearl and the children had gone off somewhere for a walk to stretch their legs and have something to eat. I fumbled for my cigarettes and lighter, burned my hand trying to light up, and sat cursing and depressed.

And then it began to happen.

I was gazing blindly in front of me when very slowly the shape of a tree started to materialise. At first I thought it was imagination. But no, it was not imagination. Like one of those trick cinematic effects, the outline of the tree sharpened and came into focus, and then I was able to distinguish the large branches, then the smaller ones, and finally the winter-naked twigs.

I closed my eyes in disbelief. When I opened them again I noticed that the windscreen was dirty and needed wiping. *The windscreen was dirty and I could see it!* I nearly cried the words aloud. I looked out through the rear window, and away in the distance I could see some people approaching. And then, with a surge of emotion I recognised the people. It was my wife, Pearl, and my own children, and even at this distance I could make out their faces.

I wept then, fully and freely, as I sat there alone in the car and waited for them.

CHAPTER ONE

The Miracle

SITTING IN the front seat next to Pearl as she drove us back to Worthing, I found to my great joy that I was able to see much farther than ever before. And as early darkness crowded out the daylight, and street lamps and headlights were switched on, I discovered that they no longer dazzled me or hurt my eyes as they had done a little time ago.

My mind and heart were very full. I talked in long uninterrupted bursts, then became silent. Pearl understood and left me to my thoughts. It had been a day of happenings and mad emotional turmoil, and Pearl knew when to keep quiet.

On the following morning, a Tuesday, we were sitting quietly at breakfast, the familiar tones of Jack De Manio on his Home Service *Today* programme filling in the background. I was reading the morning paper. Presently I felt a hand being placed gently on my arm, and looked up to see Pearl standing there, smiling serenely down at me.

After a little while she said: 'Do you realise what you are doing. You are actually reading the paper. Isn't it wonderful? And you are holding it at least eight or nine inches from your eyes.'

She was right. I hadn't noticed, so rapidly does normality re-establish itself and come to be accepted without thought. Neither of us spoke after that. There was no need.

On the morning of the next day I woke up feeling oddly different. It took only a moment to understand why. The cruel headache and dizziness which had been my waking companions for so many weeks had vanished. Gone too from my body was the aching tiredness I had long endured and I was filled with such a surging sense of well-being that I decided there and then to go up to London for the day and show my colleagues and friends the remarkable new man Joe Hutton had become.

Now that all the aches and pains associated with my liver condition had fled, a certain conclusion repeatedly suggested itself to me. But consciously, time and time again, I drove it out of my thoughts. I was wary. I wanted proof. I didn't want to go overboard on an imagined metamorphosis.

My friends in London, when I told them the remarkable things that had befallen me, were at first disinclined to show any great enthusiasm, though they were obviously glad for my sake that I was in such good form. They too, I felt, wanted some proof. Until then they had known me as a pathetically short-sighted man, so I decided to let them judge for themselves.

I sat down at a typewriter and began to type, and they saw at once that no longer did I have to crouch over with my nose to the keyboard. Nor did I have to jack-knife forward in order to read what I had typed. I was able to sit as upright as the next man. They crowded round me excitedly, their congratulations bubbling into my ears. Then I knew.

That night, when I undressed for bed, I noticed a long mark, a thick line about five inches long, on my body. I moved closer to the mirror to see what it was. Pink in colour, it had a series of dots above and below the line. It looked exactly like the scar of a surgical incision. I ran my fingers over it, but it felt quite flat. And yet it was plain to see, just as if I had had an operation on my liver!

On January 22 I went back again to Aylesbury, this time with someone who was in need of help and who wanted to be seen by the spirit doctor. I myself was seen as well, and after an examination on the couch, I was told: 'The operation was a success, young man.'

But I didn't have to be told. I knew it.

It was a miracle, and it happened in Aylesbury on a cold January day in 1964.

CHAPTER TWO

The Spirit Doctor and His Medium

CAN ANYONE deny that what happened to me was a miracle? I don't know how this assertion can be refuted, and, without meaning to be impertinent, I don't care. I am satisfied that it was a miracle.

I had first gone to Aylesbury as a sceptic, prepared to scoff—full of derision and suspicion.

I went there as a man who was seriously ill. Seriously ill and teetering on the brink of blindness.

I came away with restored sight and renewed health.

These are the facts.

For me, the proof of a miracle is more than conclusive. I am satisfied also that the late William Lang, F.R.C.S., was instrumental in bringing about my cure. I had never heard of him before. The name George Chapman meant nothing to me. But I am convinced that when George Chapman goes into trance as a medium, his spirit control is William Lang.

I do not expect you to believe what I believe, nor is it my purpose to convert you to my way of thinking. I want this to be understood from the outset.

All I am doing is putting down in this book the things that I found out throughout a year of travel and research. I have met all those people whose evidence I intend to present, and the words they speak are theirs, not mine.

I am not offering you a rounded story. It is entirely without any formal plot, and while it has a beginning and a middle, it has no end because it is still going on. It is just that I feel these things deserve to be told, and now is the time to do so.

One other point I would like to mention is that I have decided, for the sake of convenience and *not* as an attempt to influence any reader, to refer to the in-trance George Chapman as Mr. Lang.

In March 1964 I went back to Mr. Lang for a check-up, and afterwards talked to him for a very long time. Our conversation embraced many subjects, and I found him to be a charming and knowledgeable speaker. Eventually I steered the talk around to the possibility of my writing about him and his medium, George Chapman.

When I put it to him he seemed slightly bashful. He smiled a small shy smile and dropped his head down on to his chest in thought. Then he said:

'Well, I suppose one day such a book is bound to be written, Joseph, and if it has to be done I'd like you to do it. Go on, young man, write it, but there is one thing I want you always to keep in your mind—that George and I are only God's instruments. It is through His aid and His aid alone that I am able to use my skill as a spirit doctor to relieve suffering.'

I knew, though, that the project could be carried out only if Mr. Lang agreed to talking to me fully and freely about his life on earth and in the spirit world, and of his association with his medium, George Chapman. I mentioned that such an arrangement could not but take up a great deal of his time.

'Oh, don't worry about that, young man,' he replied. 'Come any time. I love seeing you and your dear wife. It is good to meet people with whom one can speak so easily.'

I thanked him and said that there were many questions I wanted to ask George Chapman. 'I've never met him in his waking state,' I pointed out.

'That will be no problem. George is a nice man and you will like him, I feel sure. I suggest you write to him to enable him to make an arrangement with you.'

'Would there be any objection to my using a tape-recorder?' I asked. 'It is easier than having to make a lot of notes.'

'Of course not,' he said, 'I'm sure everything will work out satisfactorily.'

That was the end of our talk, and when I got back to Worthing I wrote immediately to George Chapman. It was much later (and then quite by accident) that I learned that many requests from well-known authors, journalists, television and film writers, had been received in the past. All had been turned down.

When my wife and I eventually met George Chapman at his house in Aylesbury, we found ourselves facing an extremely personable young man who looked to be in his late thirties. He was in fact then forty-three years of age.

During my three visits to the spirit doctor, I had had ample opportunity to study him closely. He had a distinctive way of holding his head slightly cocked in the listening manner of a much older man. Yet another indication of the seeming burden of years was an inclination to stoop. These were the characteristics of Chapman the medium but now they were no longer present. This was a person who walked easily and erect. His face was smooth and he was obviously a very shy individual.

The contrast in speech was equally striking. Chapman's voice, unmistakably Merseyside in accent, was that of a youngish man, and he spoke quietly because of an inherent diffidence, and Lang's on the other hand was cultured and assured, strongly Southern, peppered of course with medical terms, and high-pitched in the manner of the aged.

There were, however, certain attributes which were shared: exceptional friendliness and goodness, absolute unselfishness, and a powerful devotion towards helping those who, in medical terms, were considered incurable. Early on in my first meeting with Chapman I got the feeling that I had known him for a very long time.

CHAPTER THREE

Long before the Beatles

THE MISTS were swirling around Merseyside on February 4, 1921. They were carried in from the sea by a gusty wind which whipped around corners and bit to the bone anyone abroad on the streets. Down river there was the mournful cacophony of ships' hooters. Along the docks, donkey engines whined on wet slippery decks, cargoes swung precariously on the ends of protesting hawsers, and men with inflamed hands cursed the winter.

High on the dirty grey-black mass of the building that dominates the Pier Head and the whole river front, the Liver Bird, gilded and scrawny, looked down on the drenched and depressed city of Liverpool. Further along the river, in the county borough of Bootle, a woman strained in the pains of childbirth, and when her sweating and agony had ceased, there was beside her the pinched-up face of a baby who would be christened George William Chapman.

These were uneasy times. In Ireland there was unrest and poverty and the black shadow of civil war. In England there were many young men who were old because of what a world war had done to them, and there were many middle-aged men who looked like walking cadavers. The limbless and the disillusioned peopled the streets, and the poor, as always, were hit hard and often.

But George Chapman was too young to know. So he was suckled and grew strong and learned to crawl and walk and talk. And then, suddenly the baby was a baby no longer, but a six-year-old boy who saw and felt many things.

In the mean streets he saw toughness and poverty, stablemates at any time and place. He heard the accents of the Irish, lived through Catholic-Protestant brawls, and was eternally shocked at the things people would do to animals either in fun or in anger.

Whenever he saw a boy creeping up on a cat or dog nosing at a dustbin for food, George would scream a warning to the unsuspecting animal in an effort to save it the pain of a well-aimed brick. There were times when he was set upon as a spoil-sport. It would be false to say he didn't mind. He did, and was as scared as any back alley youngster would ever be, but he didn't seem to learn the intended lesson.

As he became bigger and stronger, the instinct for survival became even more dominant and, full of confidence, he learned to use fast hands and feet in a manner which came to be respected. But he fought only when necessary, and more often than not he had to only if a cat's life was at stake. Or a dog's. That was the way it was.

However, there were more injured and stray cats and dogs in and around Bootle than George Chapman could ever have hoped to save. And the Chapman living quarters were far too cramped to allow even a small number of those animals that George wanted to shelter inside.

He needed some sort of place to house the strays. Not only did he not have any accommodation, but there was no spare money either to buy food for the animals he loved. Then one day he hit upon an idea. Why not go around the doors and ask if they wanted any messages done?

The first five or six doors were slammed in his face. Didn't they have enough mouths to feed without trying to find coppers to give to a snotty-nosed ragamuffin for running messages? But George Chapman wasn't that easily put off, and when he turned to the homes of older women with grown-up families out at work all day, he found himself a handful of willing customers.

Not a halfpenny did he spend on himself. It all went on food for the animals. Then one magic day, a lady offered him the use of her cellar as a sanctuary for his pets. In return, she wanted him to do all her shopping and a fair proportion of domestic cleaning. To George Chapman it was a fine bargain.

Young George's animal sanctuary was soon well known in the district. People began to talk about the boy who undertook any errand or job to earn a few coppers to buy food for his stray cats and dogs, and who put splints on their limbs and nursed them when he found them injured. He did what he could, too, to help the neighbours' sick pets when they brought them to the 'child vet.' To this day, some of the people in Bootle talk about the unselfish boy who nursed animals with such tenderness.

George left school when he was fourteen. It was into the cold harsh world of unemployment that he went, and for longer than was good for his mind and body he stood at street corners and listened to the gutter talk of his companions. The future, such as it was, appeared grey and hopeless. He knew nothing, and didn't want to know. Why should he? What had the world done for him? He was a drifter beginning to drift, so what the hell.

But one day he heard of a job going, and almost before he had a chance to tidy his hair, he was running to the garage where they required a pump assistant and general labourer. He got there before any of his mates, and they gave him the job. It wasn't riches, but it was better than hanging about street corners. What was more, he liked the job. It made him feel that he had a place in the world. Until the day he was lying under a lorry trying to loosen a stubborn screw on the oil sump. The edges of the spanner were worn, the the corners of the screw rounded, and the spanner could get no purchase. Then it caught, held fast, and George pulled two-handed with all his might. The next moment the heavy spanner slipped and was pulled down on to his face with the full force of his strength.

The taste of blood running down his throat sickened the youngster, and he was hauled out with a badly lacerated nose. But there was scant sympathy from the garage proprietor, and the boy was sacked without wages. 'Bloody silly accident,' was all the owner said, and George Chapman was once again on the streets.

A few weeks later he was lucky enough to get a job as a butcher's boy, and though he often had to work from 6 a.m. to eleven o'clock at night, he liked the work. Soon, though, there was talk of another war and, when this became a reality, he told his boss that he intended to enlist. George had set his mind on joining the Irish Guards, and as soon as he picked up his wages, he took a bus to the Recruiting Office at Renshaw Hall. He looked at the guardsmen, tall and stiff and straight with their peaked caps low down on their foreheads, and tried to imagine himself in the same uniform.

But disappointment awaited him. As Chapman stood in front of a table, the recruiting officer glanced through his application form and then looked at the boy.

'You're too young, lad. You need another year to be able to join the army.'

George was just about to plead for a chance when he was told, 'Anyway, you're only five foot seven, and the minimum height for the Irish Gaurds is five foot eight. Sorry.'

But George's reputation as a boxer saved the day for him in an unexpected way. Across the hall, one of the N.C.O.'s, doing paper work, recognised him and called out to the officer. 'That's George Chapman, sir, isn't it? He's a useful boxer and would be a good lad to 'ave with us.'

The officer looked at Chapman. 'So you're a bit of a boxer, are you young man?'

'Yes, sir, I do a bit,' George said.

'Mm-mmm.' The officer glanced through the form again. 'Let's see. Stand against the wall will you.'

George hurried now to the wall behind the officer's table, and the officer measured him for height.

'Looks to me like someone made a slight miscalculation in your height,' he said. 'According to the way I read it, you're just five foot eight. And what did you say about your birth date being wrong? You were born in 1920 you say, and not 1921?'

'Yes, sir, that's right, sir,' George said, taking his cue smartly. So they gave George Chapman a shilling, sent him to the Q.M.'s Stores, and he was in the Irish Guards. In due course he was ordered to Caterham, given a regulation haircut, a meal of liver and bacon, and assigned to a training squad.

'But the first time I went on parade,' he recalled, 'and stood in the centre of a group of six-footers, I knew how small I was. I felt like a pygmy in the company of giants.

'A few days after going there I was among a crowd of fellows in the barrack-room when someone came in. Everybody jumped to their feet, but I was doing some chore or other and I remained seated. The next thing I knew was that a young officer was standing in front of me, looking down. "Are you tired, or sick or something?" he said. And I said "No." Well, he nearly hit the roof. He asked me if I knew I was talking to an officer, and carried on something alarming, then turned and stormed out. The sergeant had a go at me then and used language I could never hope to repeat for the sheer flow of its obscenity.

'Anyway, a couple of days later I was told I was being transferred to the Royal Irish Fusiliers, and I went along to headquarters to get my papers. The officer who saw me was not the same one who had bawled me out, but he looked me over and said, "Let me see now, you're—your name is George William Chapman?" I replied, "Yes, sir." He went on: "Your date of birth, Chapman?" And without thinking I said, "February 4, 1921, sir." He started laughing then. "Hah!" he said, "I thought as much. Well, I'm sorry Chapman, but you're under age. We could do with chaps with your spirit, but regulations have to be observed, you understand that. I'm sorry." And I was out.'

Back at Merseyside again Chapman managed to get a job on the docks, but his heart was still set on joining up, and after thinking things over for a few weeks, he decided to try to get into the R.A.F. By the time formalities were completed, his birthday had come around, and George William Chapman, civilian, became A/C Chapman.

Life in the R.A.F. was a crowded time for the young man from Bootle. His first posting was to Blackpool where he became a drill instructor. Then followed transfers to Tangmere and Merston. He met up with heavyweight wrestler Tony Mancelli, the Birkenhead boxer Jackie Parnell and several others who were useful performers in the ring, and as a squad they put on boxing exhibitions for the camps based around the South coast.

Then came a posting to Portsmouth for the purpose of gunnery training on H.M.S. *Excellent*. He buckled down to the tough practical tests and swotted hard at the theory, and eventually passed out as Instructor in Gunnery.

One day when a working party from Worthing arrived to lay a landing strip for Spitfires, one of the engineers, apparently in search of something to talk about, casually asked Corporal Chapman if he had ever considered the possibility of life after death.

Before he was able to reply, his mind was crowded with memories, many of which belonged to his childhood. He remembered, for instance, how one of his uncles, a solemn man, could talk of little else but life after death and Spiritualism. But his nephew declined to concern himself with questions that were beyond him.

'I'm not really interested in these things,' he told the engineer and left it at that.

The other man said: 'Yer oughta be, y'know.'

Chapman whirled on him: 'Don't give me any of that stuff, mate! There's enough happening here and elsewhere without my having to bother about what happens to me when I buy my lot. Get me? So drop it, eh?'

The engineer walked away.

In 1943 George William Chapman was transferred to R.A.F. Halton in Buckinghamshire, where he was promoted to Sergeant. And it was while stationed there that he met the girl who was to become his wife. A year after their wedding, Margaret presented her husband with a baby girl who was christened Vivian Margaret Chapman. The event brought the customary welling of pride in the hearts of the newlyweds, but their joy was all too soon tempered with tragedy, for the doctor called George Chapman aside and warned him that it was most unlikely the baby would live much longer than a month.

'I remember the tears I cried in the woods around the hospital at Ashbridge the day the doctor broke the news to me,' Chapman recalled. 'I wasn't a religious fellow or much of a believer in what religion teaches, but I'm sure nobody ever prayed harder to God than I did then. But when it was not possible to hope, I got to thinking that there just couldn't be a God who would let an innocent little baby die like that. Know what I mean? I was distracted.

'But she died. You know they say that tragedy never leaves us where we were originally. I found that to be true. We both did, Margaret and I. Somehow or other our baby dying drew us closer together, and when we had become reconciled to our loss, it kind of strengthened us spiritually.'

As the war drew to its grisly end, Sergeant Chapman became aware again of the problem of unemployment that would face him when he came out of the Royal Air Force. He had no special qualifications which would fit him for a civvy job, and he didn't particularly want to stay in the service. He was anxious to set up a permanent home for Margaret and himself and the children they hoped to have.

The coal mines were beckoning, but he had no yearning to spend the rest of his life below the ground hewing at the black seams and breathing in the black dust. The only two occupations that attracted him, even vaguely, were the police and the fire brigade. Nowhere else was there any hope of a job. Again his lack of height was against him, for the invitation to join the Aylesbury Police stipulated a minimum of five foot ten inches for would-be recruits. There was only one avenue left.

On May 2, 1946, Sergeant George William Chapman of the R.A.F. was demobbed. Within a few days he changed into a new uniform and became Fireman Chapman of the Aylesbury Fire Brigade.

CHAPTER FOUR

The Die is Cast

WHEN FINALLY the time came for my appointment to see Mr. Lang, I told Chapman, and he said I had better keep the tape-recorder plugged in as it would take him but a short time to go into trance. I did this, and kept my eyes on George Chapman.

He made himself comfortable in the armchair he had been sitting in during my interview with him, closed his eyes, and rested his head on the back of the chair as though in sleep. My wife and I watched closely. We saw the expression of the face changing into the look of an old man. The mouth gradually twisted into a new shape, and new wrinkles appeared about the eyes. One of the hands came up slowly into a position I had noticed in Mr. Lang. The deeper the medium sank into trance, the more he changed until he looked exactly the same as the person who had greeted me that first afternoon in January. Then he stood up and came towards Pearl.

'Hello, young lady, it is nice to see you again,' he began. He shook hands with her, then turned to me. 'And you, young man, it is good to see you too.'

'I am grateful that you have allowed us to come and talk to you,' I said, and I shook his outstretched hand.

'Yes, yes . . .' he said in that delightful vague way of his. 'Now let me see, it is Worthing you come from, isn't it? Yes. You know I used to rent a week-end house there once, in the early 'twenties I believe it was. Delightful, delightful. But I mustn't waste your time young man. You've come a long way to talk to me. I'll try to answer all your questions.'

On December 28, 1852, Isaac Lang—a prosperous and well-liked Exeter merchant—sat waiting in his splendidly furnished drawing-room while his wife lay in labour in an upper room. He was not worried. He said later that somehow he *knew* there would be no complications and that he knew, too, the baby would be a boy. When the family doctor appeared, at last, to announce, 'Your wife has blessed you with a bonny . . .' Isaac Lang coolly interposed and said, 'Yes, I know, with a bonny baby boy.'

'How do *you* know?' the doctor exclaimed. '*I* was quite certain it would be a girl, and told you and your wife so on several occasions. I am not often proved wrong in these cases.'

'I said all along that we would have a boy but you wouldn't listen,' the proud father reminded him.

'Yes, but *how*?' the doctor pressed.

'I can't explain it—I just knew.'

The doctor left the house a puzzled man.

The baby was christened William, and on the day of the christening Isaac Lang made another prediction for his child, his fourth-born: William would break away from family tradition and become a very successful doctor—a noted specialist. Isaac Lang's relations and friends refused to believe him. For generations the Langs had been successful merchants and it was unthinkable that a Lang would go into anything else. They laughed at Isaac and said he was indulging in day-dreams. But Isaac Lang spoke with such conviction of the child's future that he made many of them think again.

'My life was one of pleasure,' William Lang told me as we chatted about his happy childhood. The tape-recorder was switched on, and I sat facing him in his Aylesbury surgery. 'Of course we didn't travel a great deal, because travel was rather slow in those days. If we went to Plymouth, for example, or anywhere in Devon, it took a long time to get there.

'We spent most of our young lives in our large house in Exeter.

We never attended any school. No, we had a very capable tutor who used to come to the house. He was very strict but, although we liked and respected him, we used to play him up a lot because we were as mischievous as are most children. When we went too far, father would be called, because our tutor wasn't allowed to spank us. Father usually punished us much harder than the tutor might have done.'

At the age of twelve, William was sent to the then famous Moravian School in Lausanne to receive higher education. Although his tutor had prepared him well enough to justify his acceptance by the Swiss boarding-school, the youngster from Exeter nevertheless found it difficult at first to cope with Latin and several other subjects new to him. But, right from the start, the Senior Master, Pirie, took a liking to the small country boy from England and helped him to overcome his initial difficulties. The boy proved himself a keen student and soon went to the top of his class. He distinguished himself in chemistry, which was one of his favourite subjects.

'You may know that Swiss boarding-schools are very strict,' Mr. Lang recalled, 'but we had quite a lot of fun there. The standard of education was high and we had to work hard, but we were allowed to visit the town and the surrounding villages, and we also went to Germany on several occasions. My fellow students came from many different nations, and so we learned a good deal about the habits and life of our respective countries.'

While studying at Lausanne, William made up his mind to become a doctor. Knowing the family tradition as merchants, he feared opposition from his father. When, eventually, he felt bold enough to acquaint his father with his desire to study medicine, the old man's answer amazed him.

'It is your life, William, and I want you to have a profession which you'll really like. Become a doctor by all means.'

In 1870, at the age of eighteen, William Lang entered the London Hospital in Whitechapel as a medical student, and from the very start of his career studied with tremendous energy and enthusiasm.

'When I went to live in the East End of London,' he recalled, 'I met some very likeable people. In and around Stepney lived many people of diverse religion and race. Many were extremely poor—and somehow I became more friendly with them than with anyone else.'

The year 1874 was a notable one for the then twenty-two-year-old medical student. He qualified as M.R.C.S.—Member of the Royal College of Surgeons—and married his second cousin Susan. It had been an idyllic love affair for both of them, and the wedding was the commencement of a very happy union which only came to an end when Susan died in 1892.

The young surgeon was so devoted to medicine that he would spend many hours with his patients, talking to their relatives and doing all he could to discover more about the actual cause of disease; and, when he decided it was necessary to operate, he would arrange to have patients brought into the hospital an appreciable time beforehand, would visit them daily, gain their confidence and learn something about them as individuals.

'I always tried to touch a person's soul so that he or she had the *will* to get well,' Mr. Lang explained to me. 'My fellow-surgeons used to think I was wasting my time. Some of them even voiced the opinion that "William Lang spends too much time talking with his patients". Well, maybe I did, but thank God, my patients seemed to do remarkably well. I was . . . eh . . . quite successful —and I hope I don't sound boastful. I don't mean to be.

'I remember my wife Susan saying to me one day: "You know, William, you must have quite the longest list of lady patients of any surgeon in London!" I said it must be because of my good manners!'

In every surgeon's life there are cases which, despite all his tireless efforts, he finds himself defeated. I asked Mr. Lang what he had felt about this aspect of his work.

'Yes, you are quite right,' he answered. 'Sometimes when I examined a patient I knew immediately that he would die, that it didn't matter who operated, the patient would not survive. But as a surgeon, you never give up hope until the last heartbeat has long stopped.

'Now whenever I lost a case I became deeply, deeply depressed. It is an experience common to every doctor. You feel you have failed. Failed a human being. You feel responsible. Your rational mind will tell you that you were *not* responsible, that you did everything in your power, but you are still left with the feeling of having failed. And you look around at the heartbreak of those relatives who have to face life without the one who has died, and somehow their suffering becomes your responsibility too. Oh, I remember that so clearly. It was very hard. Very hard.'

He spent a great deal of his time on the sociological side of his work. One thing that always had an effect on him was when he heard that old people were about to be sent to the workhouse. Such a possibility would have him leaving the hospital or surgery at the first opportunity to beg and plead with the relatives of the old person *not* to send the old lady or old gentleman away. And when he succeeded (as he did on many occasions) he would go away happy that the old person would be able to live out the last few years in surroundings which were familiar and comforting, rather than in a poor-law barracks where human dignity was stripped away.

William Lang served as House Physician and House Surgeon at the London Hospital in Whitechapel for nine years. Late in his stay there he was Demonstrator in Physiology and Anatomy in the medical college, and it was then that he met and came under the influence of James Edward Adams, a famous ophthalmic surgeon. Such was the dedication and power of Adams' personality that Lang became engrossed in ophthalmology and began to study it. Adams encouraged him at every opportunity, and when Lang got his fellowship of the Royal College of Surgeons in 1879 and was offered a position at the Central London Ophthalmic Hospital, he accepted it.

His years at Whitechapel had been very happy ones, and when the time came for him to leave he was heavy in heart and rather afraid that he had made a wrong decision.

CHAPTER FIVE

A brilliant Career

William Lang, F.R.C.S. was appointed Ophthalmic Surgeon to the Middlesex Hospital, London, in 1880. Four years later, when an irony of fate forced his friend James Edward Adams to resign from the Central London Ophthalmic Hospital (later Moorfields Eye Hospital) in London's City Road because of increasing blindness, he succeeded Adams to his position at the hospital, and also took over his private practice.

Being a devoted ophthalmic surgeon, Mr. Lang realised that there was a vital need for a society of eye specialists and, together with colleagues and professional friends, founded the Ophthalmological Society in 1881. Despite his strenuous work at his private practice and at the Middlesex Hospital, he always found time to take a leading part in the activities of the Society. In 1903 he became its Senior Vice-President; later he held an additional post—President of the Ophthalmological Section of the Royal Society of Medicine.

'I haven't been a prolific writer—in fact I found writing and speaking in public quite difficult,' Mr. Lang told me. 'You know, I used to go through agonies of mind if I had to write a medical thesis, make a speech, or take part in a public function.'

Nevertheless, his output was considerable and his more important publications of great significance. The many cases he brought forward at the meetings of the Ophthalmological Society usually made the subjects of lengthy and fruitful discussions.

In 1882—when he was thirty—Mr. Lang published, with Mr. W. A. Fitz-Gerald, a study on the movements of the eyelids in association with the movements of the eye. It was his first contribution of importance in which he was able to pinpoint the function of the inferior rectus muscle in the downward movement of the lower lid.

The publication created considerable controversy. He was accused of 'availing himself of unconventional methods', since Sir William Gowers had previously stated that the lower lid was depressed by the pressure of the limbus upon the margin of the lower lid. Sir William was eventually proved wrong, and Mr. Lang's theory accepted by ophthalmologists throughout the world ever since.

He was for many years the editor of *The Royal London Ophthalmic Hospital Reports*, and contributed, in collaboration with Sir James Barrett, some very important studies.

Among other notable contributions to ophthalmology was that entitled *The Retractive Condition of the Eyes and Mamalia* and was published in 1886. This study was the conclusion of extensive examinations on a great variety of animals—185 pairs of eyes in all—which established that the majority were hypermetropic. At this time Mr. Lang was a member of the committee which reported on 211 cases of sympathetic ophthalmitis, and he published an elaborate study on *The Action of the Myotics on the Accommodation*.

Greatly impressed by Mr. Adams Frost's suggestion of a then revolutionary operation—the insertion of an artificial globe into Tennon's capsule after excising the eye—Mr. Lang investigated the possibility very thoroughly and wrote his own account of it in 1887. In the same year he also published, in collaboration with Sir James Barrett, *The Action of Myotics and Mydriatics on the Accommodation*—a work that had considerable practical importance and led, ultimately, to the use of cycloplegics in refraction work.

This study was a record of a patient supported by careful investigation, and was introduced as an enquiry into the action of a mixture of homotropine and cocaine—often known as 'Lang's Drops'—and of the extremely ingenious oily solution of these alkaloids. It was shown in this work how easily and safely the action of these drugs could be controlled by the subsequent use of eserine.

These listed are only a few of Lang's published works.

Mr. Lang was at all times concerned with the practical side of ophthalmology and here he was a master. He improved many of the instruments in common use.

The McHardy Perimeter, for instance, was ameliorated by Mr. Lang in many ways, and his modification was extensively used everywhere until it was surpassed by better models. His speculum with solid blades is still in use, and his twin-knives for dividing anterior synechiae marked an epoch in the improvement in cataract extraction because, by using them, he drew attention to the importance of avoiding the inclusion of lens capsule in the wound.

As a clinical observer and all-round ophthalmologist, Mr. Lang was at his best. His operating technique and resource in difficult cases was admired and remembered by those who were his House Surgeons. The delicacy, certainty and speed with which he worked, made him a surgeon to be remembered. His students (he called each of them 'dear boy') were always loath to leave him for he had so much to impart, and did so with brilliant fluency. This I found out for myself in doing the preparatory work for this book. Mr. Lang, they said, was extremely patient, the essence of courtesy, and rarely showed himself to be of short temper. Indeed, when driven to the limits of his patience, the most violent expletive he was known to use was 'Dash my wig!'

Lang married again, and with his second wife Isabel and his son Basil, once again found the contentment that he thought had deserted him forever when his first wife died. It was a matter of deep satisfaction to him when Basil, as a young scholar, revealed interest in medicine. It was an interest which was to develop into a vocation, for Basil Lang, too, became a distinguished surgeon.

During one of our tape-recorded interview sessions at Aylesbury, Mr. Lang suddenly interrupted his train of thought and said: 'You do smoke, young man, don't you?'

I said: 'Yes, I do, but I was asked not to smoke while I was with you.'

He passed no comment on this but went on:

'Today they say that smoking causes cancer of the lungs. In my days they used to say that central scotoma—the blind area in the field of vision—was caused through smoking. Although I never smoked myself, I couldn't believe that smoking would cause central scotoma and, being the kind of person who liked to get to the bottom of any problem, I decided to put my distinguished colleagues' theory to the test.

'I chose a young doctor, who was one of my patients, as my first "guinea pig". He was ideal for my research work because he had been troubled with central scotoma for a number of years and also smoked quite heavily. I outlined to him my colleagues' theory about the relationship between smoking and scotoma and said: "Let's try something, shall we? Now I want you to stop smoking." He agreed to collaborate and stopped smoking completely. He received the same treatment as before but his eyes did not improve—in fact they became worse.

'This was sufficient for me, but I realised I would have to offer much thorough proof if I wanted to substantiate my findings and convince my stubborn opponents. I made many other tests on different patients who were troubled with central scotoma and finally got together enough evidence to show conclusively that smoking could not cause central scotoma. I wrote quite a lot about the extensive research I had done, and my papers on the subject started a controversy.

'My learned opponents attempted to brush aside my findings and said: "Lang can't be right, it can't be as he says." This was because they had accepted their own theory for so long that they did not like to be proved wrong by anyone, and especially not by "a know-all", as they put it. However, some of them decided to carry out their own experiments on a number of patients, and as you know, they eventually admitted that central scotoma was *not* caused through smoking.

'I was of course grateful at having been proved right because I always tried to make a point of it that there can be *many* causes for *any* disease. If a person has a central scotoma it can be caused by so many factors. If you have an irritation of the eye, then smoking can make it worse of course but it *can't put* the disease there—as it *can't* put cancer in your lung—the disease must *be* there, and then smoking can make it worse. . . .'

Lang's father, Isaac, had been at the centre of many a strange happening at their home in Exeter. The word 'psychic' would have meant nothing to the children. It was never used. What did impress them were the unaccountable sights and sounds in a room they knew to be empty of people. And it was always their father who sought to reassure them by explaining the phenomena.

'They are spirits,' he would say, 'and there is nothing to be afraid of. Spirits won't hurt you. They just come to visit us, to be around and help us.'

So it was that early in his life William was made aware of an unseen world. Life after death was a topic he had heard much discussed. As he grew to manhood certain beliefs grew strong in him, but of course as an eminent man of medicine he realised that it would be unwise to advertise too much what was, after all, a very personal thing to him. In any event, his beliefs were unpopular then, as they are now, and he didn't want unnecessarily to lay himself open to derision.

Three men who came into his life provided him with the outlet he needed to discuss these matters. They were distinguished medical men, knights all of them—Sir John Bland-Sutton, Sir Arnold Lawson and Sir William Lister.

'They were splendid people,' Mr. Lang said to me at Aylesbury. 'We would talk with each other about everything—everything you can think of—but our favourite subject was life after death. I remember, I used to say to them: "The knowledge of life after death is very consoling, because we know that even if we do our best for a patient when we operate on him but nevertheless fail, he will live on." They agreed, but whenever any of us had to reckon with a case in the operating theatre when the pendulum could swing either way, we forgot that line of thought and did everything humanly possible to save, or at least prolong, the patient's life. . . .'

One of the great joys of Mr. Lang's life was the pleasure he derived in the career of his son Basil who had followed in his footsteps and become a surgeon. Father and son often operated together, and nothing gave the senior Lang greater pleasure or satisfacton than watching Basil engaged in very difficult and complicated surgery and bringing many an 'impossible' operation to a successful conclusion.

Then Mr. Lang's happiness was dealt a cruel blow. Basil fell ill with pneumonia and, although the best medical skill did everything that could be done for him, it was not possible to save him.

'All my hope went then, all my hope,' Mr. Lang said, reliving the tragedy. 'My world collapsed, and with it all my dreams of Basil's brilliant future. He was my son. He was also a wonderful, a very wonderful surgeon, and I could not bear the thought that he would never again be seen in the operating theatre. I lost interest in everything, and went to Crowborough in Sussex because I wanted to get away for a little time from my house in Cavendish Square—it held too many painful memories for me. . . .'

Many of his famous colleagues and friends came to see him and offered help, but there was really not much they could do. Mr. Lang was then already in his eighties.

One of the doctors who came to see him was a Dr. Alexander Cannon—a very capable medical practitioner who was not, however, looked upon with favour by the profession because of his views about life after death. Dr. Cannon believed in the projection of the astral body and spoke to Mr. Lang at great length about it as well as about many other psychic aspects.

'We became rather well acquainted,' Mr. Lang told me. 'I did not accept *everything* Dr. Cannon said and, at times, I thought he had quite mad ideas. But I rather liked the way he stuck to his guns if he believed a thing and his never giving up what he was doing, even though it sometimes landed him in trouble.

'When Dr. Cannon came to see me one day he said: "I could cure you by drawing away your spirit body a little and giving you treatment." He was very kind and went out of his way to help me but, I suppose, I had grieved too much and no longer had the will to pull through, so he couldn't really do much.'

On Tuesday, July 13, 1937, William Lang's heart stopped beating. He was holding the book *The Life of Jesus** in his hands.

* By Ernest Renan, Member of the French Academy (Mathieson & Company).

CHAPTER SIX

The Moment of Death

COUNTLESS TIMES during our interview sessions I sat and peered intently at the figure seated in the chair opposite me. My thoughts occasionally wandered into wondering just what I was doing. But it was not a fantasy I was experiencing. The constant muted hum of the tape machine kept me reminded of where I was. This was reality and I was doing a straight job of hard interviewing for what I hoped would ultimately turn out to be a bit of good factual reportage.

There was one question I wanted to ask, but wasn't quite sure if I had the courage. Suddenly, I felt I had to know.

'Can you remember exactly what it was like when you died?'

'Oh yes, yes. It is perfectly clear to me. You see on that day—July 13, 1937—I knew my time on earth was up. I said to my dear friends who were sitting around my bed that I was going to die. One of them said: "Well, William, we shall all meet one day in the spirit world, and when that happens we shall have the privilege of watching you operate once again." I nodded my head. I was unable to talk because suddenly I felt very very tired and began to drift into a deep sleep.

'I knew a good deal about life after death, that somehow or other I would continue to exist. But I didn't know what to expect when I drifted off into sleep and passed into spirit. I was not aware of the fact that my heart had stopped beating. I felt somehow content, free from troubles and worries and I thought I'd suddenly got better.

'Then I saw my two dear wives, Susan and Isabel, dear Basil, my son, and quite a few of my best friends standing around me. It didn't dawn upon me at that moment that spirit people know when a person ends his time upon earth and so gather around him, to be near him, to help him. I thought it was just a dream. And, as I asked myself, "Where am I? What am I dreaming about?" I saw myself lying lifeless on my bed with my surgeon and doctor friends sitting around it. I could distinguish strange sounds, but not voices. Obviously they could neither hear nor see me. It was all quite worrying and I did not know what to make of it. Then I fell into another deep, dreamless sleep and was spared from worrying.

'I do not know how long this period lasted—whether it was seconds, hours, or even days? I never attempted to find out because it was not really important to me, but I did find out that during this period of unconsciousness spirit doctors and helpers attended to me, that they relieved me of this ailment and also of the worries that had been on my mind.

'Quite suddenly everything changed, and I could clearly see my two dear wives, Susan and Isabel, standing there with outstretched arms; dear Basil was of course with them, as well as the rest of my family and some of my closest friends. We could speak with each other, and I was no longer kept in doubt as to whether I had left earth or if everything was only a strange dream, because one of my medical friends said: "William, you are with *us* now in the spirit world." I then saw many of my patients whom I knew on earth and who, I'm afraid, passed on before me. They came to thank me and I felt happy, very very happy.

'My wives and friends told me they would show me round this new world, give me a holiday, so to speak. It was all very beautiful with magnificent flowers and lovely scenery, and I felt a deep peace at being able to talk with my dear family and friends again.

'As a child I used to wonder, "What is God? Who is God?" I was brought up in the Church of England faith but, throughout my life got on well with most people—Church of England, Catholics, Jews, and those of other faiths. I wasn't what you would call a very religious man because I didn't spend much time in church praying, but I used to give an awful lot of thought to God. When I used to see my patients before an operation, I always prayed for them.

'When I was ill and knew my time on earth was running short, I expected that the moment I passed into the spirit world I would be brought before God to account for my life. Nothing of the sort happened, When we pass over here, we see God every day of course, but no one is brought before Him. He is not an imaginary legendary figure. God is what I see in you; God is what I see in everything that is good; and when I am healing I am doing the work of God. God is simply a Great Love, a great feeling of doing good. You see, God is a very good, a wonderful God—that is if we understand this God, and *I* feel I do understand Him. We are here to do God's work—you, George, I, anyone else; and by doing this, we get near God and are given God's favours.

'When you pass over here, you retain the same personality as you had on earth. Some people who come to see me, say: "You are such a wonderful spirit person, Dr. Lang," and I tell them: "Now, look here, young lady, or young man, when I lived on earth, I liked to live my life to the full. I tried to do good and not to wilfully harm anyone, but I was *never* the *perfect* being. And now that I have passed into the spirit world, I am still the *same* William Lang as I was upon earth. I know a little more about my work, but as for changes in myself—there are none, I am still the *same* person." You see, people believe that when you pass over here you become very wonderful, but you do not. You remain the same.

'Well, having passed into spirit, I soon had a yearning to once again do something positive. I told my friends who were with me. I said: "Medicine was my whole life. I knew little else, and I would like to use my knowledge and my experience once more to help people. Can you help me?" It was then they showed me into the hospitals here, which are quite similar to other hospitals I have known. I was able to see how patients who had passed over in an imperfect state received treatment from spirit doctors and nurses. I immediately noticed that treating patients in the spirit world is very different from the way which we employed on earth and I was eager to learn this specialised technique as early as possible.

' "You won't find it difficult to learn to operate on the spirit body, William," my dear friend Bland-Sutton, who had come over here a year prior to my arrival, enlightened me. "We all had to go back to student days to acquire this new method which is vastly different from working on a physical body, but it is the only way for a spirit doctor to help his patients over here."

'I was very interested and keen to return to some work and at once started studying the art of spirit surgery. Although the spirit body is more or less identical with the physical body, it is none the less rather difficult to explain to anyone living on earth exactly *how* a spirit doctor operates upon a spirit body or engages in any other form of treatment, because it would not be understood *fully* anyway.

'Together with a number of medical friends I operated on many people who had passed over in an imperfect state, and helped to free them from all their troubles. It was very rewarding work, but I thought eventually: "I am not *really* needed here as a doctor. There are plenty of highly skilled surgeons and physicians here who are quite able to look after the spirit people. Perhaps I could help people suffering from serious ailments on earth." I spoke about this to my friends and, having considered my idea carefully, they said:

' "The only way in which your ambition can be realised is to find a medium for you through whom you could reappear on the earthplane. It is very hard to find the *right* medium, but it is possible."

' "Well, let's try to find one," I suggested.

' "You must be perfectly certain that returning to the earthplane and giving medical help to the people living there is really what you want to do, *before* the *right* medium is found and trained for you," they went on. "The reason for this is that when you find your medium, it means that you will have to stay with this medium, complete your work, and then, when the medium's lifespan on earth is finished, your work as a spirit doctor will be finished as well."

' "Well, I have made up my mind that I want to return to earth as a spirit doctor and I am perfectly willing to carry on the work as long as possible," I assured them. "Will you now assist me to find the *right* medium?"

' "You can rest assured, William, that everything will be done to help you," my friends promised. "You must be patient of course because, as we told you before, it is difficult to find the *right* medium. Don't forget that there are many doctors over here who have the same ambition as you, and who desire to return to the earthplane to work as spirit doctors through mediums; for very few of them has a medium been found. You may, however, be luckier than the others. There is a young man living on the earthplane who could be trained to become your medium. But it is an involved business and full of imponderables. For the time being you must continue your work at the hospitals here. Perfect your skill as a spirit doctor. *We'll* do our best to have experiments carried out with this young man so that he can be trained for you." '

CHAPTER SEVEN

A Transformation

NOT LONG after George Chapman joined the Aylesbury Fire Brigade, one of the officers was complaining about pains in his back.

'What you need is some Yoga,' Chapman said, believing it might help.

His colleague looked up in surprise and said: 'I didn't know you were interested in Spiritualism.'

Chapman replied: 'What has Spiritualism got to do with it?'

The other man then began an explanation that was almost a minor lecture, the nub of it being that it was possible to receive spirit messages if people sat round a table, put their fingers lightly on an inverted tumbler and waited for it to spell out words. Chapman was interested enough in what his fellow-officer told him to decide to try it one day just to find out what would happen.

Shortly afterwards he made friends with another man in the station who claimed he knew all about the reception of messages from spirits via the inverted glass method. It turned out that this person had taken part in Spiritualist seances while serving in the forces during the war, and consequently he knew how to conduct a glass seance. Chapman proposed to a few of his fellow-officers that they should try a seance. At first there was a laughing reluctance, but a few days later they gathered together in a group and held a successful meeting. The inverted tumbler moved from letter to letter on a sheet of paper on which the alphabet was written in a circle, and spelled out general messages for all those sitting around the table.

From then onwards the urge to give Spiritualism a try became stronger in Chapman's mind and prompted him to attend Spiritualist meetings and sit in circles. Time and again he was given messages from spirits. The most recurring one was that he would become a healer.

'I found I did not get anywhere in the circle and only wasted my time as far as my own Spiritualist development was concerned,' he told me. 'Consequently I came to the conclusion that the only way to really find out anything was to try sitting on my own. I thought, "well, nothing can happen to me because I know I am master of my own mind, I know what I want, and if any spirit comes, he certainly won't frighten me. Might perhaps even help me to find out more about it."

'So I started sitting on my own in my bedroom—every day, Saturdays and Sundays included—and I meditated for hours on end. I found my psychic development coming on in leaps and bounds, and one day I decided to try something new. I now know it to be astral travel. I just lay down and it happened straight away—I seemed to know what steps I should take and no one needed to tell me, "you ought to do this or that or study books about the other".

'At first I used to watch myself moving about in different parts of the house while my body remained lying on my bed—I used to let myself look in different rooms downstairs. Then I tried to send myself farther afield.

'Another stage in my development was that I used to go to sleep, and when I woke up, I knew consciously where I had been. As I matured still further, I would find myself falling into a very heavy sleep, but when I awoke I didn't know anything of what had happened. This was the start of my being able to go into deep trance.'

Most people without mediumistic faculties are interested to know what a medium feels when going into trance, so I interrupted Chapman to ask him.

'Well,' he said, 'I sit down, and after a short while I feel a heaviness on the head. A strong pulling sensation appears to take place at the base of my skull. Soon I feel very tired and fall asleep—or so it seems. In this state I experience all kinds of dreams—some quite ridiculous and fantastic, and others instructive and interesting. I have, however, no recollection whatever of what my spirit control is doing when he takes full charge of my physical body.'

I took this opportunity to enquire if it was *always* easy for him to slip into the state of trance whenever required and wherever he was or if there were instances when he encountered difficulties of some sort or other.

'To get into trance doesn't ever create *any* difficulty for me,' he said. 'It doesn't make the slightest difference to me where I am or under what circumstances I have to do it. I just sit down, make myself comfortable, and the rest you already know.

'There was only one occasion when I experienced some difficulty and could not slip into trance with my usual ease. This happened ten years ago in the Midlands—in the autumn of 1954.

'A woman there had been given distant healing for some time for internal trouble, and one day she wrote to me and asked me to visit her to give her contact healing. In those days I was able to visit patients in urgent need of contact healing, so I made an appointment and drove to where she lived.

'When I arrived she asked me if I could wait until her husband arrived, as he was also in need of help but refused to have anything to do with Spiritualism or spirit healing. She hoped that by watching William Lang giving her treatment, her husband might be convinced and, perhaps, agree to receive healing. I'd had requests of a similar nature previously, and as she assured me that her husband would arrive home very shortly, I agreed to wait for him.

'When he came in and his wife told him what she had in store for him, he was quite adamant and determined not to have anything to do with spirit healing. He was a highly intelligent man, but of stubborn determination. I remember wondering what his job was, but I was not told and was not inclined to enquire. Anyway, he eventually yielded to his wife's persuasion—probably out of courtesy to her and because of his curiosity about what would happen—and he led me into the lounge. He said he'd "have a go first". He had a spine injury, and I noticed that he walked with considerable difficulty.

'When we retired to the lounge, I endeavoured to go into trance, but for the first time in my association with William Lang, I experienced difficulty. As soon as I felt near to it, unknown faces materialised and a strange odour—which reminded me of death—pervaded the room.

'I mentioned this difficulty to my patient, who had not had the chance to have his customary bath and change of clothes since arriving back from work. He smiled and stood up. He walked to the door, and, as he went out, said, "I'll be back shortly."

'When eventually he returned to the lounge, I again composed myself to go into trance. This time I succeeded without difficulty and very shortly William Lang was able to take full control of me. He attended to the patient, performed an operation on the spirit body and succeeded in curing the man almost instantaneously. Afterwards the wife was operated on and her internal trouble disposed of.

'A little later, when we were having a cup of tea, the husband mentioned my difficulty in going into trance. "As I told you," I said, "I kept getting a most peculiar smell, and all these faces kept materialising. And it was a smell of—I hope you'll excuse me—a smell of death."

'The husband inclined his head slightly and smiled. "I think I can explain why," he said. "You see, I'm a surgeon. Today I was doing post mortems." The conditions which I'd picked up in the first instant were undoubtedly those of the dead bodies the surgeon had examined that day.'

But this carries us ahead of George Chapman's development as a medium.

The process was slow, and at first very far from spectacular. There was little of the sensational associated with it which might have convinced the easily-swayed into instant acceptance of the extraordinary.

But one day in 1946 Chapman was hurrying along a street on his way to the fire-station. As he rounded a corner he came across an old man whose ragged clothes betrayed the fact that he had seen better days. Apparently, the old fellow had been standing at the kerb for some time trying to cross the stream of traffic. High Street was crowded, and he was standing there isolated and helpless.

George Chapman stopped when he saw him and said: 'Trying to get across, are you dad?'

The man turned rheumy old eyes at him, and nodded, mouthing frustrated curses at the traffic and his own lack of mobility.

'Here, I'll get you across,' Chapman said taking hold of the man's arm.

They moved slowly forward, Chapman once or twice holding up a hand to restrain the speeding vehicles.

As he held the stranger's arm, Chapman realised that the old man could hardly have any use of the limb, so locked did it feel on its bent position. He made no comment, however, but laid his free hand on the fixed joint. When the reached the other side of the road, the old man suddenly shouted:

'It's free! It's free!'

Chapman did not say anything. He left the stranger, and walked quickly away. When he had gone some little way, he looked back and saw the old man still standing on the edge of the pavement, moving his arm up and down and crying excitedly:

'He's made it move! It's free! It's free!'

There were other people in the Aylesbury district who, as time went by, were helped by the fireman with the soft voice and the Merseyside accent. And since Chapman was fully conscious on these occasions he, too, was often amazed at the things that happened.

It was raining outside in the Aylesbury streets and a cold wind was whipping the freezing drops against the windows. It was one of those treacherous days when driving demanded great care and concentration. All the way from Worthing, Pearl, my wife, had listened while I talked but had said nothing. She was keeping her eyes on the road. It was only when we got into Aylesbury at last, and had to slow down, that she relaxed. We were both hoping that the weather would clear by the time the interview with Mr. Lang was concluded.

He was sitting in his usual chair, back to the window over which the venetian blind had been drawn shut. The red wall lights made a soft warm glow in the room. The reels on the recorder were revolving at their slow 15/16 speed. Lang was talking, and his words were being preserved on the thin brown tape.

'. . . and so Joseph, my friends in the spirit world came to me and said they had been successful in finding the right medium for me. They had prepared and tested him and were quite confident that we should be able to work perfectly together.'

'This testing and preparing, how long did it go on?' I asked.

'Oh, I think five years or thereabouts. But you can check that. Yes, my friends told me that my medium was a young man named George Chapman who was living in Aylesbury. He was a member of the local Fire Brigade. Well, of course I found George to be an extraordinarily nice chap.'

'Can you tell me what it was like the first time you worked through George Chapman?' I said.

'Yes, yes of course. You should know, by the way, that in his period of preparation George had been the instrument of a number of cures.* These were carried out by some of my colleagues from the spirit world, notably by two Scotsmen. One of them was Dr. McPherson who, I understand, attended to George's mother in Bootle in the 1920's. The other was my Scottish-born surgeon friend McEwen. I think I told you on a previous occasion that he was a noted bone specialist.

'But now to the first time—I remember it well. As soon as I was told: "You have completed your training and your medium is ready", I went to take control of George. He just went into trance (it has always been easy with him, he can sit and go into trance anywhere as if he is going to sleep) and I was able to control him straight away. My colleagues, the other spirit doctors, had done an excellent job and enabled both George and myself to embark on a working association which has always been ideal.'

'Is George Chapman your only medium, or do you work through others as well?' I asked.

'Only through George,' Lang said decisively. 'I couldn't work through any other medium. Why do you ask this question?'

'Because certain healers and mediums have said that you are also working through them when you are not using George.'

'That's nonsense!' the spirit doctor exclaimed emphatically. 'I have *never* worked through any other medium but George, and indeed I wouldn't be able to. I told you a little while ago that George and I were trained for each other and that before George's training as my medium started I had to make up my mind once and for all whether or not I wanted to stay with him throughout

* I checked this and found out that George Chapman had become well known around Aylesbury at this time. It was known that he frequently travelled at his own expense to patients who could not come to him, or who could not afford the fares. So, while still a serving fireman, he was winning a reputation as a healing medium.

his life span on earth. I made my decision to do so, so you see, even if I wanted to leave him and work through someone else I couldn't. But of course I don't ever want to leave him. I am very fond of him as I've told you already, and our association is ideal.'

'I can't understand how people dare state for a fact that you're working through them if it isn't true.'

'Well, you know how it is,' Lang said. 'George and I are by now well known, so other individuals try to enlarge their numbers by pretending that I am working with them—that they are in good hands, so to speak. But that doesn't worry us. It is sufficiently well known that my *only* medium is George and that's all that matters.'

I also asked George Chapman what it was like the first time the spirit doctor took full control of him.

'Well, he conveyed to me that he had been a man named William Lang,' George Chapman told me. 'Said he'd been a surgeon working in London in the last part of the past century and right up to some years before the Second World War.'

I said: 'What was your reaction to this?'

'Don't get my meaning wrong,' he said, 'it wasn't that I didn't believe it, you know, but I wanted to, well, put it to the test. So the next time I went into trance, I got one of my mates from the Fire Brigade to come along and get all the details down. I can't remember anything that goes on and is said when I'm in trance, and I wanted to have some details to check on.'

CHAPTER EIGHT

'There's no doubt about it'

FROM THE day in 1951 Mr. William Lang, F.R.C.S., returned as a spirit doctor, he endeavoured to establish that he was *the* William Lang who had been born at Exeter on December 28, 1852, and passed away on July 13, 1937. In order to satisfy his medium of his true identity, he revealed many episodes from his life on earth—things that could only have been known to a circle of intimate friends—and requested that his information should be corroborated.

When George Chapman studied these revelations which his colleagues had recorded for him while he (Chapman) had been in deep trance, he was pleased that his spirit doctor control had given him something to go on. As an ordinary layman he had not heard of a surgeon named William Lang. This was not surprising, because during his life Mr. Lang had not been what one could call either 'famous' or 'fashionable' and his name was consequently not bandied about in the popular press. Although he had distinguished himself in many ways as an outstanding ophthalmic surgeon, he had been far from a spectacular figure, and his skill was more familiar among the profession itself.

Chapman was satisfied that his control was highly skilled because he had already had ample evidence. A number of patients who had come to Chapman's house to be treated by Mr. Lang had already been classed 'incurable' by their own doctors and specialists. Lang, working through Chapman, cured these 'incurables'. But Chapman was eager to know as much as possible about the past life of the man who controlled his body while he himself was in deep trance. To corroborate what had been told to him by his control Chapman asked his friends to look up details about Mr. William Lang, F.R.C.S., in the public libraries. This was done to the best of their ability but the searchers drew a blank.

Unaware of the fact that details about Mr. Lang could not be found in this way, they jumped to the conclusion that corroboration did not exist. Was this evidence of fakery somewhere? One of Chapman's helpers said to him: 'It would appear that your spirit doctor has given us fictitious information about himself because we can't find a single book or pamphlet that contains any reference to a surgeon named Lang around the time he claims he was alive.'

Mr. Lang was disappointed with the 'poor' attempts that had been made to authenticate his statements. He said to George Chapman: 'Of course you won't find anything about me in the books published for the general reader; look up literature which was published for members of the medical profession and you'll find out that everything I've told you is correct.'

The British Medical Association was then approached with an enquiry as to whether anything was known about a Mr. William Lang, F.R.C.S., born on December 28, 1852, died on July 13, 1937. No further details were given. In due course, a reply from the B.M.A. was received, and it confirmed all the details the spirit doctor had revealed about his medical career. Chapman and his friends then accepted as a fact that the spirit doctor was the same Mr. William Lang, F.R.C.S., who had started his medical career at the London Hospital, and who had later distinguished himself as an ophthalmic surgeon at the Middlesex and Moorfields.

Some time later even more striking proof was furnished that the spirit doctor controlling George Chapman during his trance state was indeed *the* brilliant William Lang, F.R.C.S. This unsolicited evidence was supplied by a number of people who had met Mr. Lang either at the Middlesex or Moorfields Hospitals, or at his private practice. These were people who vividly remembered the dapper, kindly ophthalmic surgeon.

When going to George Chapman's sanctuary to seek the spirit doctor's help, Mr. Lang's ex-patients and friends just expected to be seen by *a Dr.* Lang.* As soon as they met and talked with him, they were astonished by old familiarities in speech and manner. Here was someone they hadn't seen in years, someone who had died before the Second World War! And, yet, he was able to recall instances from long ago meetings, matters known only to themselves. They were more certain than ever that no possibility of mistaken identity existed.

One of the personalities to identify the spirit doctor as Mr. William Lang, F.R.C.S., in 1961 was Dr. Kildare Lawrence Singer, M.R.C.S. (Eng.); L.R.C.P. London, 1917, Middlesex; Capt. I.M.S., who remembered Lang well. He had first met him while a student at the Middlesex Hospital, where he received instruction in ophthalmology from him. Later, after he had qualified as a doctor, a friendship with his distinguished senior developed, and their devotion to each other continued until Lang's death.

Dr. Singer's recognition of his old friend was entirely unexpected. Singer suffered from cancer and when he found out that a spirit doctor named Lang had cured some patients also afflicted with the malady he decided to consult him. It never occurred to Dr. Singer that there could be any connection between this *Dr.* Lang and the *Mr.* Lang, his old mentor and friend, but when he entered George Chapman's sanctuary and the spirit doctor greeted him with the familiar: 'Hello my dear boy, I *am* happy to see you again,' Singer knew immediately he was facing William Lang, F.R.C.S.

Mr. Lang talked with his 'young' friend for some considerable time and sometimes about long-forgotten episodes from their past.

'I have been given ample evidence that he is, without a doubt, the Mr. Lang I met at the Middlesex Hospital for the first time in 1914,' Dr. Singer said immediately after the confrontation. His next visit strengthened this conviction.

Mrs. Katherine Pickering of Aylesbury identified, in 1952, 'Dr.' Lang as Mr. William Lang, F.R.C.S., with as much certainty as Dr. Singer had done nine years later. She had first met Mr. Lang almost sixty-one years ago, had been under his care for fifteen years and

* The spirit doctor is generally known as 'Dr.' Lang although as a surgeon his correct description is Mr.

consequently was able to claim she knew him fairly well.

'I was four years and nine months old when I had a serious attack of measles and German measles which affected my eyesight and were suspected of having contributed to my alarming myopia,' Mrs. Pickering told me when I visited her at her Aylesbury home on August 26, 1964. 'I was taken to the Ophthalmic Department of the Middlesex Hospital and became Mr. Lang's patient.

'I was a rather shy child and was usually frightened of strangers, particularly doctors, but as soon as Mr. Lang sat me on a chair and started talking to me, before even looking at my eyes, all my shyness and fears were gone and I felt as though I was speaking to an uncle or a relative.

'He was not tall, like some of the other doctors there, and he spoke so kindly that I took to him right from the start.'

'It's extraordinary that you can remember all these details,' I cut in. 'It's over sixty years ago.'

'Well, not quite,' Mrs. Pickering explained. 'I *was* Mr. Lang's patient for *almost fifteen years*—till I was nearly twenty. You would be surprised how clearly one remembers things in one's life if they made a sufficient impression at the time. Mr. Lang made a very great impression on me. I was shy and frightened, as I told you; and this is doubtless the reason why a childhood memory of a man who was so kind and gentle is so deeply engraved in my mind.'

'What made you so sure that the spirit doctor is the same Mr. Lang under whose care you were at the Middlesex Hospital?'

'Well, as soon as I walked into Mr. Chapman's sanctuary in 1952, Dr. Lang greeted me with the words: "It's nice to see you again after all these years, Topsy. I remember you when you were so high," and he held his hand out. Now, he'd always called me "Topsy", as a child, and the way he said it now and put his hand on my shoulder—well, I mean who could possibly have known a thing like that about me from over sixty years ago? I'd not met Mr. Chapman before. I'm convinced that it was, is, Mr. Lang.

'He examined my eyes and the way he said: "Oh dear, they are still not too good," made me remember that he frequently used this very same phrase when I went to see him as a teenager. I really felt myself back at the Middlesex Hospital. To have found Mr. Lang after all these years was quite astonishing.'

Mrs. Pickering told me that Mr. Lang had performed a spirit operation on her eyes and that, as a result of it, her vision improved to such a degree that she can now read without spectacles—something she could not do before her visit to George Chapman's sanctuary. She added that she had not told Chapman or Mr. Lang about her suffering from internal trouble for which she had gone to see him to receive help; Mr. Lang had nevertheless diagnosed her complaint precisely without asking her anything about symptoms. He had performed some additional spirit operations, given her spirit injections, and had relieved her from her complaint and suffering.

'I was brought up of old Quaker stock—my people have lived in Buckinghamshire for three hundred years—and my father always instilled in me the obligation to speak the solemn truth,' Mrs. Pickering went on. 'I'm mentioning this to make it absolutely clear that I never say anything in public without being perfectly certain of my facts. When I say that I believe the spirit doctor and Mr. William Lang are one and the same person, I am absolutely sure of it.'

Mrs. Pickering is indeed very much concerned about checking everything before making any statement. Since childhood she has kept diaries, concise but descriptive accounts of the people she has met and the things and events that have impressed her. Before answering any of my questions, Mrs. Pickering consulted her records. She didn't, she said, want to rely on recollection which can be fallible.

At the time of Mrs. Pickering's treatment, George Chapman had no idea of what William Lang looked like. He had been unable to find any photographs, and all he had to go on were the descriptions given him by Mrs. Pickering. Then one day he came across a reference to a Mr. McDonald who called himself a Psychic Artist. It was a description which intrigued George Chapman.

Mr. McDonald, it appeared, claimed that he could paint portraits of people who had died, with no more help than the signature of the person who required the portrait. Wondering just what he would get back, George Chapman wrote a simple letter which said: 'I should like a portrait of my spirit control.' Apart from the address and his own signature, there was nothing else on the plain sheet of note-paper.

In due course a thin oblong parcel was delivered at Chapman's house. When he opened it, he was to see a picture in colour of an elderly man wearing wing collar and cravat. A note accompanying the painting explained that the spirit control's name was William Lang, and that he had been a medical man.

Chapman had never met this Mr. McDonald. He had never spoken or written to him, other than to send the request for the portrait. Yet here was McDonald's note already identifying the spirit control as William Lang. George Chapman, for the umpteenth time in his life, was astounded. Nevertheless, the exchange remained incomplete. Chapman wondered how good a likeness had the Psychic Artist managed to make.

A few days after the portrait arrived, Chapman met Mrs. Pickering. As soon as he could decently interrupt her conversation, he said: 'Oh by the way, someone sent me a picture the other day. It's of an elderly man. Very nice picture too. It's an original. Would you like to come and have a look at it?'

Mrs. Pickering looked mystified at this strange request, but returned with Chapman to his home to see the work of art. As soon as she saw it, she put her hand to her mouth in an involuntary gesture of surprise and said: 'Oh but this is Mr. Lang! Didn't you know?'

'Mr. Lang, you say?' Chapman said by way of reply.

'Yes, yes, of course it is.'

'Look Mrs. Pickering, how sure are you that this really is Mr. Lang?' Chapman pressed.

'My dear Mr. Chapman, how could I ever mistake him? I *knew* the man, attended him for fifteen years, right through my childhood and teens until I was twenty! Don't you understand? One doesn't forget a face you've known all that time, you know.' She turned away from Chapman to look back at the portrait. 'Why I even remember that cravat he's wearing. Extraordinary. Quite an extraordinary likeness.' She stood there looking at it for some minutes. When she left, it was with a strange quizzical stare at George Chapman.

Some months later, after persuading friends to search all sorts of unlikely as well as likely sources, Chapman managed to get hold of an old medical publication which carried a photograph of William Lang at the height of his career.

He brought the book with him, found the page with the picture of Lang, and then compared it with the portrait.

The similarity between the painting and the photograph was remarkable.

The success achieved by George Chapman as the medium of a spirit doctor quickly became known and marvelled at not only in Aylesbury and throughout Hertfordshire but all over the country.

His achievements were startling. Many persons suffering from incurable diseases visited him and were able to leave his house and pass on the news of miraculous cures affected by the 'dead' doctor—the spirit doctor named William Lang. Soon the number of patients who sought out George Chapman to be treated by Mr. Lang became enormous.

CHAPTER NINE

The Voice of Authority

PERCY WILSON, M.A. (Oxon)—Technical Editor of the journal *The Gramophone*; former Vice-President of The College for Psychic Science; one of the world's leading authorities on psychic research and phenomena; and Chairman of Psychic Press Ltd.—is one of the few who not only met George Chapman in the early days of his mediumship, but who also continued to meet him and the spirit doctor at frequent intervals. But, unlike the others, Mr. Wilson did not, in the first instance, seek out the medium for the purpose of healing. As a critical but fair-minded investigator, his object was to establish whether George Chapman's claim to being controlled by a spirit doctor was genuine or whether the young man was a victim of self-deception.

'I first met George Chapman some twelve years ago in London and we sort of gravitated together,' Mr. Wilson told me when I interviewed him on December 11, 1964. 'He was one of the people I wanted to meet because I was anxious to establish by means of serious research whether or not this young man was indeed controlled by a spirit doctor and, if that being so, he was sufficiently developed to enable his spirit control to work efficiently through him.

'Of course I did not really suspect the young man of any consciously fraudulent intention, but there are so many people who so much want to be trance mediums that frequently they are apt to fall victims to involuntary self-deception; they trick themselves into the belief that their imagination is fact. Although there may be no calculated imposture, they are nevertheless as dangerous as deliberate frauds because they mislead, and often greatly disappoint, those who come to them in good faith. In this way they throw a stigma on spirit healing and Spiritualism as a whole. One can therefore never be too careful when investigating trance mediumship.

'Now, in the case of George Chapman, I had to be particularly thorough because he not only claimed to be a trance medium who was controlled by a spirit doctor, but even stated that his control was a certain William Lang, F.R.C.S., who had died in 1937 and who, during his lifetime had been a surgeon and consultant specialist at a number of well-known London hospitals. Well, if the result of my investigation satisfied me that this was a fact, it would be a wonderful and significant contribution to spirit healing and Spiritualism in general, and I would do everything I could to help the young man and his spirit control in every way. However, if my research convinced me that the claim was unfounded I would of course have to make it known that in my view this was not a bone fide case of spirit healing. A step like this would, indeed, have been my duty, because, in spirit healing in particular, every possible precaution must be taken that only those people are accepted as spiritual healers whose bona fides have been proved beyond all possible doubt.'

'Having been an active Spiritualist for over half a century and having engaged extensively in psychic research, are you satisfied that you could not be tricked in any way by a very clever and cunning impostor?' I enquired.

'Well, I believe I am qualified to carry out these investigations quite competently. During the past fifty years or so I have studied the phases of mediumistic trance through many notable exponents,' Mr. Wilson replied. 'I should think it is true to say that I have more direct experience of trance mediumship, and more knowledge of its different aspects, than any other person alive today. That may sound rather strange because there are plenty of trance mediums who have more direct experience of *being in trance*. But a person who goes into trance doesn't necessarily know the intricacies of trance mediumship and the variety of it, or its peculiarities or even techniques. If I investigate a form of trance—or supposed trance—I can tell quite quickly whether it is genuine or whether it is just self-deception, or perhaps even deliberate fraud. Quite a lot of so-called trance is self-deception.'

'Did you investigate George Chapman's claim when you first met him?'

'Well, no. I met him in London as I said, and at that time he was in his normal state of consciousness. To be able to investigate his claims, I needed to see him in trance. So, all I could do at our first meeting was to arrange to meet him when he was under spirit control.

'I talked with him of course about his mediumship and work, and I was in no doubt that he was a sincere young man who was imbued with the desire to be of service to suffering humanity. Unfortunately this was no guarantee that he was indeed a genuine trance medium—his desire to help suffering people could well have been the root of involuntary and quite innocent self-deception. But of course I didn't make up my mind either way, because if I was to engage in serious research I couldn't afford to arrive at any conclusions before I had unearthed all the relevant facts by careful investigation.'

Mr. Wilson kept his appointment with George Chapman, and when he entered Mr. Lang's consulting room he found the medium already in trance.

'When I first went to Aylesbury and saw Dr. Lang, I got a most favourable impression,' Mr. Wilson said. 'I could tell at once—and anybody who is experienced in trance mediumship can do this—that it was not only a genuine trance, but one of a very high order.

'I got a definite impact that I was meeting an entirely different personality—entirely different from George Chapman—an old man, a wise old man at that, whose medical background stood out a mile so to speak. I should have taken him for a Harley Street specialist straight away, you see, both from his general attitude and from the fluent and almost casual way he spoke about medical things.

'After I'd carried out a very thorough investigation which furnished me with conclusive proof that this was definitely a case of a very high-grade mediumistic trance, I once more met George Chapman as soon as he had regained his normal state of consciousness. Though I had already collected all my evidence that here was a really outstanding medium who was controlled by an identifiable surgeon, I cross-examined him very searchingly once again in his normal state of consciousness. There were lots of things I wanted to know from him.

'In these early days of his mediumistic association with Dr. Lang it was clear that George Chapman's own medical knowledge was very much less than mine, and that, apart from this, he was a very simple, genuine and honest character. Yet Dr. Lang was unquestionably an expert. The difference was marked.

'Moreover, in those days George Chapman was not what you could call an intellectual type of man—he was quite simple in some respects, and indeed was perhaps inclined to be a little *gauche*; but as his healing mediumship developed and he came more and more under Dr. Lang's influence, he's become more and more cultured and more intellectual. He's learned a lot through Dr. Lang, but even now, after thirteen long years of close association with his spirit control, he's still as entirely different in personality from Dr. Lang as he was when I first met him in his normal state of consciousness.

'When I left Aylesbury that particular evening in 1952, my considered verdict was: It is one of the most interesting and thorough forms of trance mediumship that I've ever seen. And the more I met George Chapman and Dr. Lang in these later years, the more I have confirmed the verdict I'd arrived at thirteen years ago.'

Mr. Wilson also met Mr. Lang as a patient when he went to consult him ten years ago to receive help from the spirit doctor, help which he could not get through orthodox medical treatment. The complete cure of his ailment was so speedy and striking that whenever he felt in need of medical advice he went to consult Mr. Lang as well as his own doctor or specialist. And he was so impressed with Mr. Lang's abilities and achievements that he took a considerable number of relatives and friends to Aylesbury for spirit operations and healing.

'One of the people I took to Dr. Lang was my niece, who'd been a medical problem ever since she was born,' Mr. Wilson said. 'When she was sixteen weeks old she started suffering from tummy trouble and couldn't keep any food down. The hospital doctors operated on her three times to try and find what the trouble was. They didn't reach any definite conclusion, but fortunately the operations seemed to have the desired effect and for some years she was free from trouble.

'Then, five years ago, she suddenly had a recurrence of it. Her parents took her back to the hospital. The same specialist who'd performed the operations before was still there, and after he'd examined her again, he said it was the old trouble and that they'd have to operate again to try to detect the cause.

'At that stage, however, I took my niece to Dr. Lang. As soon as he examined her he said: "Oh, this is a very peculiar inflammation of the stomach, a very peculiar one. It's an inflammation of the interior walls. I'll operate myself and we'll put that right." He performed an operation on her spirit body and she has not had any recurrence since.

'That was five years ago. The specialist at the hospital, who'd had her under observation for years, was—and still is—puzzled by the miraculous recovery, which occurred before he'd had the chance to operate. Well, there she is. She's a highly intelligent child who is doing very well at school. I asked her only about a month ago whether she'd had any further trouble, and she replied: "No, nothing, not the slightest little bit." Well, I've taken quite a few people like that to Dr. Lang. Not a single one has failed to have considerable relief from Dr. Lang's spirit operations and healing.'

Mr. Wilson also recalled the following case of a lady whom he had taken to Mr. Lang but who was already beyond help even through spirit healing:

'When he'd examined her, Dr. Lang told me candidly that he did not think he would be able to save her earthly life because he'd been consulted too late. This is one of Dr. Lang's unique qualities. If he knows he cannot help, he never misleads anyone by lulling them into false hopes, though of course he says it diplomatically so as not to upset or frighten the patient. This candidness is very important because one knows that if, on the other hand, he says he can help a patient, it's not just a frivolously made statement.

'Well, according to the family doctor's prognosis, the lady was expected to live another two or three weeks. When I spoke with her the day after Dr. Lang had seen her, she told me: "I'll have breakfast with Dr. Lang next Monday or Tuesday." I said: "Why do you think so?" She looked at me with one of those knowing looks and said: "Dr. Lang is very cute."

'On Monday evening she passed away calmly and peacefully.'

During his many visits to Aylesbury over the past twelve years Mr. Wilson has had ample opportunity to study Mr. Lang's behaviour and healing techniques, and he summed up his findings as follows:

'I am always impressed by the fact that Dr. Lang goes out of his way to explain things to a patient—and especially a new patient—and by the way in which he almost immediately gains everybody's confidence. I am equally impressed by his explanation of how he detaches a person's spirit body so as to be able to perform his operations on it or give it other forms of healing treatment, and particularly by the clear-cut words with which he makes it understandable to everyone that there is a difference between the spirit body and the spirit itself.

'Still another thing about Dr. Lang that impresses me is his sure touch on *everything*, his sure touch in every way. Mind you, I have good reason to know that when he's doing his diagnosis and explains things to a patient, he's quite diplomatic about it. It's one of his great subtleties that he never blurts out things on impulse which would give the patient a shock or even a wrong impression of any kind. And he only promises to be able to cure a complaint if he is completely sure of himself. Even then he usually only says "I think we might be able to help you" and that's, generally speaking, as far as he goes.

'Apart from his healing, I think even more striking is his uncanny power of diagnosis—his X-ray eyes, as I put it. His description of a patient's symptoms and even the medical history is always accurate, and so is his prognosis of the effect his operations and treatment of the spirit body are to have on the physical body.

'One is never in doubt when listening to Dr. Lang that here is an old and learned and experienced medical man. And this is not merely my own opinion, but also that of many members of the medical profession, some of whom indeed were his friends and pupils when he was at the Middlesex Hospital in his earth life.'

Mr. Wilson's testimony as to the genuineness of George Chapman's mediumship carries with it an immense amount of authority. Those involved with psychic research are only too keenly aware of the stringent tests they are required to set up to prove the veracity of the claims made by those who think themselves gifted with psychic qualities. In the area of psychic science and research, the name of Percy Wilson is a very considerable one indeed.

CHAPTER TEN

A Policeman's Lot

REGINALD ABBISS of Aylesbury—a retired Superintendent of Police who spent thirty years in the force—was one of the people who went to George Chapman's sanctuary during the early stages of his association with Mr. Lang.

I wanted to know how it came about that a senior police officer with a sceptical mind went to seek a spirit doctor's help instead of consulting his own medical practitioner?

'Well, I'll tell you,' Mr. Abbiss said when I saw him at his Aylesbury home on September 16, 1964. 'A friend of mine who'd served with me in the police force since 1929, and who knew that my wife was in poor health, told me about how wonderfully Dr. Lang had helped a friend of his who had been hopelessly ill. He thought the spirit doctor might be able to do more for my wife than orthodox medical treatment which had not, frankly, shown too good results. Actually I found out later that this friend of mine had been thinking about it for some time before approaching me. He was afraid I'd blow up at the mention of unearthly things. At the same time he didn't want my wife to be deprived of something that might bring about a cure. So, first he told me all about the remarkable things that Dr. Lang was doing.

'I'd never come in contact with anyone or anything connected with Spiritualism or spirit healing before, but I was interested to learn from my friend that Dr. Lang worked through his medium, Mr. George Chapman, and how the spirit doctor actually worked and helped his patients. I was so intrigued with what my friend told me that I decided to visit Dr. Lang to find out for myself what it was like to meet the spirit of a "dead" man.

'My friend arranged an appointment for my wife to be seen by Dr. Lang at Mr. Chapman's sanctuary and I went along with her. From what I had learned by then I had some idea of how things were but I did not really know exactly what to expect.

'When my wife and I entered Dr. Lang's consulting room, a courteous old gentleman, or so it seemed to me, with his eyes shut, welcomed us and extended his hand in greeting. He conversed with us for a while and we spoke of all sorts of things. When he learned that I was a retired Superintendent of Police, he said I was his first patient of this sort and spoke with me about how very much easier police work was in his day.

'It was an unusual, in a way overwhelming, experience. It was the first time in my life that I had ever seen anybody in trance. In fact, when I spoke with the spirit of a "dead" man through the medium as freely as with any person, I thought, "I wonder what I've missed by not having attempted to find out about these things before." '

Mr. Lang requested Mrs. Abbiss to lie on the healing couch and, as he touched her fully-clothed body lightly with his hands, he diagnosed her complaint in every detail. He then explained to both Mr. and Mrs. Abbiss that every person had a physical and a spirit body, that he treated the spirit body only, in an attempt to achieve a corresponding effect on the physical body.

Then Mr. Lang performed some spirit surgery on Mrs. Abbiss, her husband the whole time looking on and noting what was happening.

'I was surprised when he wanted to examine *me* because I had not arranged to see him myself—I'd just come to accompany my wife,' Mr. Abbiss continued. 'As a matter of fact, I had been troubled for some time with a little internal discomfort but hadn't bothered about it, and I had certainly not mentioned anything about it to anyone. I wondered how Dr. Lang could know about it.

'I did of course as I was told and, as soon as I lay on the healing couch and Dr. Lang—his eyes still shut—touched my fully-clothed body lightly with his hands, he told me exactly what was wrong: that I had been suffering from something to do with my pyloric opening which needed attention because of the constipation and discomfort it caused. He then explained that he would perform a spirit operation which would relieve me of the trouble.

'I must say that I felt a most pleasing sensation as he did his work.

'Dr. Lang was perfectly right in everything he said. The day after he'd operated on me, I felt a slight improvement. Don't think that this was brought about by wishful thinking or willpower. Anyway, within about a fortnight I was in the clear, proof enough that Dr. Lang had indeed cured me.'

'Are you telling me then that you accepted the whole thing right from the beginning?' I asked.

'Well, when I first entered Dr. Lang's room you know, not knowing exactly what to expect, I must confess that I was on the alert to see if everything was above board,' the ex-Superintendent replied. 'You see, it is only natural that during my thirty years of service in the police force I had become accustomed to looking at things critically in an endeavour to differentiate between the genuine and the fraudulent. I watched every movement Dr. Lang made closely.

'Any possible suspicions of any sort which I may have harboured were quickly dispelled and, in a way, I became ashamed of having been suspicious at all. The whole atmosphere in that room was one of sincerity and desire to help anyone in need.

'Yes, I was convinced that I was facing a genuine spirit doctor who spoke and worked through his medium. What is more, I was—and am—greatly impressed with Dr. Lang. I felt I was talking to an old doctor whose mannerisms and demeanour proclaimed his profession and I had no hesitation in saying that I accepted him absolutely. My speedy recovery confirmed my faith in him.'

Ex-Superintendent Abbiss accompanied his wife to George Chapman's sanctuary for continued treatment from Mr. Lang. On one occasion he met George Chapman when the medium was not in trance.

'What a marked contrast there was between Mr. Chapman and Dr. Lang!' Mr. Abbiss said to me. 'Physically Mr. Chapman was a much younger man, and his speech too was entirely different. The older doctor always spoke as an elderly consultant, but Mr. Chapman spoke with a distinct Northern accent. Their mannerisms were very different and I was left in no doubt whatever but that I was indeed meeting two completely separate individuals. Incidentally Mr. Chapman was then still an officer in the Aylesbury Fire Brigade.'

Mr. Abbiss regularly accompanied his wife when she went for treatment. On one occasion, a long time after the first visit, Lang unexpectedly asked him to lie on the healing couch.

Abbiss was surprised at the request, as he told me.

' "There's nothing wrong with me, Dr. Lang," I said. "You've cured me completely of my trouble." Dr. Lang answered: "I'd like to have a look at your eyes, young man." Well, I did as I was asked and Dr. Lang performed a spirit operation on my eyes. He told me he had rectified the weakness and, to be sure, I soon noticed a considerable improvement in my vision. I used to wear glasses when driving, but since Dr. Lang's operation, I no longer need to wear them.

'I am by no means an exceptional case—I know many others who have benefited from Dr. Lang's operations and treatment just as strikingly as I did.

'It would not be right to assume that all Dr. Lang's patients are convinced Spiritualists prepared to accept everything without questions. Quite the contrary. The patients in Mr. Chapman's waiting-room come from all walks of life. A substantial number of them are not Spiritualists at all. I remember hearing a patient being asked by another whether she was a Spiritualist and her prompt reply was: "No, I am not. But, what on earth has that got to do with healing? I am receiving wonderful help and I don't need to know or believe any more than that." '

CHAPTER ELEVEN

The Knife is cheated

DURING GEORGE CHAPMAN'S earlier association with William Lang he agreed to visit patients in need of help whenever he could find the time. Sometimes it meant making long trips which he paid for himself. One such visit took place in 1954, when he set out to see Mrs. Winifred Holmes at her home in Chester.

Mrs. Holmes had been suffering from gall stones for a considerable time. Having failed to receive noticeable relief from orthodox medical treatment, and being reluctant to consent to an operation (like so many people, she had an inordinate fear of the surgeon's knife) she decided to try spirit healing. She had heard of some of Mr. Lang's successes and wrote to George Chapman to arrange distant healing from the spirit doctor. This was arranged but failed to produce any noticeable alleviation and Mrs. Holmes then asked if she could undergo contact healing and if it was possible for Chapman to come to Chester. He agreed and arranged to visit her on September 3, 1954.

When he arrived at Mrs. Holmes's house, she asked him if he would wait until her husband returned home from work.

'He too is in need of treatment,' she explained. 'He is not a believer in spirit healing—in fact he has no time for Spiritualism or anything of the sort—but I am hoping that if he witnessed my treatment he can be convinced of its worth and agree to being treated himself.' She added thather husband was receiving medical attention at the hospital but didn't appear to be improving.

While they waited, Mrs. Holmes told George Chapman about her husband's trouble.

'He had an accident some time ago, and ever since he's been in a very bad state—often in agony,' Mrs. Holmes said. 'The X-rays disclosed it was a slipped disc, a condition from which he has suffered on three previous occasions without being able to secure any permanent relief. He's a steel worker and you can imagine how difficult it is for him having to wear a terrible steel corset. The doctors have now decided that a plaster jacket might be better for him. I pray that Dr. Lang may be able to relieve him of his suffering and put him right. . . .'

'I am sure he will do everything he can,' Chapman replied.

When John Holmes arrived, he was introduced to George Chapman, and immediately showed strong antipathy towards anything connected with spirit healing. He said he wanted nothing to do with it, but Mrs. Holmes was a persuasive wife and broke down his resistance. Reluctantly, he agreed to undergo treatment by the spirit doctor, although he remained very sceptical if somewhat curious. But he made it plain that he had yielded simply to please his wife.

The two men then retired to another room where the medium went into trance with his usual ease. Shortly afterwards Mr. Lang was able to take full control of him.

'I am pleased to meet you, young man,' Mr. Lang greeted Holmes. As he touched the patient's fully clothed body with his hands, he added: 'I am very happy that your dear wife wanted you to see me because I think I'll be able to put your slipped disc permanently into its right place. There won't be any need for you to wear a steel corset or a plaster jacket afterwards—you'll be perfectly all right, young man, and will be able to work with the same ease as you did before your accident. And when you go to the hospital for your next examination, the doctor will confirm it.'

Holmes was surprised that the spirit doctor had not found it necessary to question him but knew at once the nature of his illness. He began to feel much less sure that nothing would come out of the strange experience.

Mr. Lang performed a spirit operation and, as he flicked his fingers and gave orders to his son Basil and other invisible assistants, John Holmes felt a sudden sharp pain.

'It was remarkable,' Mr. Holmes stated afterwards. 'Dr. Lang did not actually touch my body—his hands were all the time hovering just above it. When I felt the stab of pain during the "operation", I realised his hands were still an inch or two away from me.'

At first the so-called spirit operation appeared to be a failure. Far from feeling better, Mr. Holmes was convinced that his condition had worsened. He thought himself all sorts of a fool for having allowed himself to be persuaded into something he had disbelieved from the start. Why hadn't he stuck to his own convictions? Women—they were always meddling! Now look at the condition he was in!

Holmes was about to give vent to his feelings when he was told: 'Very well, young man, you can try to walk and move about now if you wish.'

Holmes restrained his anger and raised himself up on the couch. Amazingly, it was easier than he expected. He slid his legs down over the side and pushed himself into a standing position on the floor. No twinge. He took a tentative step. It was painless. Then he walked across the floor to the other side of the room, and back again, and could feel himself starting to laugh with sheer relief.

But there was still one thing he wanted to try. Memory of past pain inhibited him. But he knew that if he didn't try it, he'd never know whether what he thought had just happened had *in fact* taken place. He summoned up courage, then slowly, expecting every moment to lock stiff with agony, he began to bend down as far as he could reach. He made it without the semblance of a twinge and then, as successfully, made the return journey. He had done it! There was no pain! He was cured!

John Holmes stood staring at the hunched figure watching him. 'Well, there you are young man. Feel better now?'

Holmes couldn't talk. He nodded his head.

'Now I want to see your good lady. Would you ask her to step in here please?'

Holmes went out and called his wife. When she saw his face there was much that she wanted to ask him—particularly about the inane grin he was wearing. But there wasn't time for that now. Mr. Lang was waiting.

John Holmes stood and watched while the spirit operations were performed on his wife. And when they were done, he saw his wife sitting up, a smile on her face, pain lines already appearing to smooth away. She walked across to him after thanking the spirit doctor, and held out her hands. 'John,' she said, 'I feel much better. No pain any more, and I won't have to have an operation. Isn't it wonderful?' She turned back from her husband. 'Oh Dr. Lang, thank you so much. Thank you, thank you,' she said.

John Holmes never wore a steel corset again.

When he visited the hospital a few days after his cure by Mr. Lang, he was told that his slipped disc had gone back into place. The examining doctor expressed amazement, and also confirmed what Mr. Lang had said—that there would be no further need for the steel corset or a plaster jacket. Mr. Holmes kept quiet about the spirit doctor.

In January 1965 I located the Holmeses. Neither had been in touch with George Chapman or William Lang since that single occasion some ten years previously.

'There was no need to contact them,' Mr. Holmes told me. 'I have worked at my old job as a steelworker ever since without a day's illness. It's many a year since I have felt so well.'

Mrs. Winifred Holmes too has been in good health since that September day in 1954.

CHAPTER TWELVE

Miracle Girl

OF ALL the cases I investigated, that of the Amersham housewife, Mrs. Dorothy James, was the most astonishing and moving. Apart from wartime, I have never come across anyone so appallingly injured; fractured skull, shattered limbs, loss of sight, loss of memory—her condition appeared so hopeless that a priest had been called to administer the last rites.

But on a June day in 1964 I met Mrs. James and heard from her and her husband of what had happened on November 12, 1954. Mrs. James was a lively and delightful person.

'I remember getting off the bus on the way to work,' she recalled. 'And as usual, I waited until it pulled away from the stop, and I could see in both directions. I was always over-careful when crossing—in fact it was a joke with my two sisters. They always said that I never would be killed by getting knocked down by a car, because I was "too much of an old woman!" Anyway, as I say, I waited till the bus pulled away, and I must have been pretty certain nothing was coming before I took a step forward. That is all I am able to remember.'

Mrs. James's husband took up the story:

'Dorothy was hit by an Aston Martin whose driver was trying it out for the first time. It was a present to him on his twenty-first birthday and he admitted to the police that he had been doing eighty miles an hour. He said he had looked away for a moment at the lovely autumn fields he was passing and when he saw the road again Dorothy was right in front of him. He slammed on his brakes but hit her. She was tossed on to the bonnet and her head went through the windscreen before she was finally flung over the top of the car and on to the road behind. She lay there broken and covered in blood.

'When the ambulance arrived, a cottager who had covered her body over with a blanket, told the crew: "You've come too late, she's ready for the mortuary, not the hospital." But the ambulance driver pulled the blanket away and, after a quick look, answered: "No, there's still life in her, let's get her to the hospital at the double." This much was told to me later.

'When Dorothy arrived at the hospital, the doctors found she had a fractured skull and that both her legs were broken. She was terribly lacerated and her condition so critical that she was not expected to survive longer than a few hours. They bandaged her head, put her legs in plaster and called the priest.

'I was practically demented at this stage,' Mr. James told me. 'I mean, I could hardly think straight. All I knew was that my wife was smashed up and dying. And then I was listening to some woman talking about a spirit healer who could save my wife. I cannot remember ever having given Spiritualism a thought. But I told myself, "anything, anything at all that might help." And I said to the woman: "No, I have no objection. But if he can do anything, for God's sake get him to hurry."'

George Chapman was contacted, informed of the plight of Mrs. James, and asked if Mr. Lang could commence distant healing as soon as possible. Meanwhile, at the Bucks Hospital, Mrs. James was dying.

'The nurses,' she said, 'told me afterwards that there was an orderly from a men's ward nearby who used to come in at least once a day, sometimes twice, and again during the night, and would look at the chart at the end of the bed and ask the nurse questions.' Mrs. James continued. 'When they asked him to explain his interest in me he replied, "It's all right, it's for Mrs. James's good. I have to tell a friend of mine exactly how she is." Afterwards, a long time afterwards, Mr. Chapman told me that a friend of his who had been working in another ward provided him with a daily account of my condition. This enabled Dr. Lang to give me the most effective distant healing. But of course I knew nothing at all about it at the time. In fact it was ages before I knew anything.

'The hospital doctors were of course not aware of my being

given distant healing and they couldn't understand how it was that I was alive. First they said I would never live. When I didn't die they said I would never see, or talk or walk again, and if I did indeed survive, I would have to face a future in a Mental Home. You see, the specialists had diagnosed that my brain was damaged, my whole nervous system affected, and that this damage would result in mental deficiency and permanent blindness; apart from this, my right leg and ankle were crushed.'

'Dorothy was semi-conscious for nearly six weeks,' Mr. James put in. 'At times she came round, but she had no idea where she was or what had happened.

'The doctors and nurses used to refer to her as The Miracle Girl. She was taken on several occasions to the operating theatre where her wounds were stitched and where the amputation of her crushed right leg was considered. And, had the surgeon not refused to operate because he feared that she would die on the operating table (he thought the injuries to her brain too serious to subject her to such an ordeal) she would have lost her leg.'

Mr. James was repeatedly told by the hospital's medical staff that he must be prepared for the worst to happen at any time. When some weeks passed and Mrs. James slowly gained strength, it was the opinion of the doctors that if Mrs. James survived she would be blind, possibly severely mentally affected and would have to be found a place in a mental hospital.

Distant healing was given continuously by Mr. Lang, and although Mrs. James still remained only semi-conscious and on the danger list, she slowly grew stronger. Five weeks after the accident she recovered full consciousness for the first time. Let's take up Mrs. James's story again in her own words:

'When I first woke up, I asked a lady in the next bed to tell me where I was, but instead of replying she called the ward sister who explained that I'd had a very bad accident and had been there for almost six weeks. She called me Mrs. James but I told her that my name was Dorothy Danielson* and that I wasn't married. She then went to the locker beside my bed, showed me a photograph of a little boy and said he was my son Martin. She put the photograph in my hand and helped me to hold it, because my right side was completely paralysed. I looked at the photograph and thought:

* Mrs. James's maiden name.

"What a lucky person a woman would be to have two such lovely boys." I remember saying what lovely twins they were. Sister told me that there was only one little boy in the photograph and I told her I could see two.

'Sister then called the staff nurse and another young nurse to stay with me while she went to the telephone. I asked the staff nurse to give me a looking-glass so that I could see if I was Dorothy Danielson, but she said, no, the doctor had said it wasn't time to see my face yet (because it was ugly with all the stitches and raw skin). She also told me not to touch my face as otherwise my wrists would have to be fastened to the sides of the bed. My husband told me later that, during the first weeks, my bed had been like a baby's cot—sides had been fixed to the bed to stop me trying to get out, and my wrists had been tied because I had kept trying to pull the stitches from my face.

'Sister came back with some doctors, and one of them said he was so pleased that I had awakened and could see. He asked me to look at the clock on the wall and tell him the time. I did as I was asked and I also remember saying that it was rather silly having two clocks so close together, and he said: "Thank God, sister, she's told us the correct time." Then they walked away, talking about half a battle being won.

'I was trying so hard to think things out after they left my bedside, but I just couldn't remember anything. I remember my father kissing me on the forehead and saying: "God bless you, my dear, there are others who need you more than I," so when he'd gone I asked the patient in the next bed what he'd meant. She told me *no one had been at my bedside* since the doctors had left. As I was to realise, much later, my father had died some years before.

'My fellow-patient also told me that Jeff had almost lived at the hospital for nearly four weeks—he'd stayed day and night and had fed me—and that the photograph of the little boy was really my own son Martin. She told me that my sisters and my mother frequently came to see me, and many other relatives as well. I asked her when was visiting time and she said: "You needn't worry, your family and relatives can visit you when they choose." I didn't understand what she meant. I wanted to know why *I* was so special that I could have people coming in at any time. She told me then that I had been on the danger list.

'Then sister came back. She had a person with her whom she said was a priest. I don't know his name. Sister said: "Here's a friend you'll be very pleased to see, Mrs. James," but I didn't know him. For some unknown reason I was afraid of him and, as soon as he began to speak, I didn't want him to come near me. I expect I subconsciously knew that he was the priest who had given me the last rites, I don't know. Anyway, every time he came again and I heard his voice, I used to pretend I was asleep.

'But on the day I was going home, he and sister between them caught me. Sister had ordered a special dinner—chicken, etc. and Christmas pudding—and I had a wishbone on my plate—I still have it at home as a souvenir. For the first time I was allowed to be propped up in my bed to feed myself. We were all ready to start and then two nurses pushed a little trolley on wheels to the bottom of my bed. The trolley was made like an altar with candles and a cross in the centre. They lit the candles and in came the Dean with sister and he said: "Oh, I've found you awake at last!" We all laughed about it, the whole ward. Then he conducted a little service and it was really lovely.

'There are just a few things I can remember while I was in hospital.

'One was that a very kind man used to be nearly always there with me—he used to feed me—and he had loving eyes. I found out afterwards that it was Jeff, my husband.

'Another time, I can remember, the surgeon telling a lot of other doctors that it was *his* case and he did *not* intend taking off my leg—he was going to patch it up, and if one was a little shorter than the other, I could always have a special shoe built up. The ward doctor told me that I hadn't been quite unconscious in the operating theatre.

'Then, on another occasion, I can remember being on a stretcher and it seemed as though my right leg was put into an oven in the wall. The ward doctor was standing beside me and I could hear his voice saying to someone: "She's coming round, shall I give her the needle now?" The next thing was that I was in the ward and all the screens were drawn around my bed. Sister and the ward doctor were on each side of me. I was in most awful pain and the doctor said something to sister about having the plaster sawn off and a new one put on. I don't remember anything after that. Later the nurses told me that the house-doctor was at my bedside all through that night.

'I also remember once seeing my sister-in-law, but they told me later that she came every day. You see, I was not quite aware of everything that was going on around me.

'One incident I remember clearly. A very old lady in a bed opposite mine cried because the nurses said she was to get up and sit in a chair. It was for her own good they said, otherwise she would never get better. I called out to sister to let me get up in her place and not to worry the old lady, but sister called across the ward to me not to be a silly girl, as it would be months before I would be allowed up. I then tried to push the clothes back, but found I couldn't move my right arm. I pushed some of the clothes away with my left, but could not move my legs.

'Sister then came to my bed and showed me the plaster around my legs. She sat on my bed and told me that there was a great possibility that I'd never walk again. But I just laughed at her and said: "Oh yes, I will, even if the doctors have to cut both my legs off. I'll have artificial ones." Sister then said: "Yes, my dear, if it ever comes to that, and please God it won't, I am quite sure you will be able to master it." She told me that in her whole nursing career she had never come across anyone with so strong a will to live and such a determination to do just the opposite of what was expected.

'After I'd been in hospital six weeks I was just beginning to realise who I was, and to know that Jeff was my husband. I longed to go home and find out if I could remember my son. It was almost Christmas and I asked the surgeon if I could possibly go home for the holidays. The doctors talked it over and the next afternoon Jeff arrived and I was taken home by ambulance by the same men who had rushed me to hospital. They just could not get over the fact that I was still alive.'

Mrs. Dorothy James was released from Buckinghamshire Hospital just for Christmas 1954. It was made clear that after New Year's Day she would have to return.

On arriving home she discovered to her dismay that she could not recognise anything. She was not convinced Martin was her son and not even sure whether or not she was Mrs. James.

George Chapman called to see Mrs. James immediately after Boxing Day during his off-duty time at the Aylesbury Fire Brigade. He talked with her for a little time about her accident and about the hospital but, while he was still talking, she fell into a deep sleep. Only when she woke up after a long and refreshing slumber did she find out from her mother, who had been in the bedroom, that George Chapman had gone into trance, and that Mr. Lang had performed a number of spirit operations and had then ordered that the patient was not to be wakened, but allowed to sleep on.

'When I awoke I asked my mother: "Where's the gentleman gone?" ' Mrs. James continued. 'Instead of telling me, my mother said: "Don't try to pull yourself up in bed, you'll hurt yourself!" I told her: "No, don't touch me, I can do it myself." I remember putting my right arm down—the arm that I couldn't use or feel before—and I cried out, "I can lean on my arm!" And oh! there can be only one explanation—the gentleman must have done it. Why isn't he still here? Where is he? He must think me very rude going off to sleep in the middle of a conversation. You see, I didn't know who he was or what he could do, or anything. They hadn't told me about it—my mother had just introduced him to me as the gentleman who wanted to enquire about my health. It was now that my mother told me about the spirit doctor, Dr. Lang, who had performed spirit operations on me while I had been asleep.

'The next morning Mr. Chapman came again—straight from the fire service and still in his uniform. He hadn't been home to have his breakfast. He wanted to see what progress, if any, I had made since the previous day. I said to him: "I'm very sorry that I fell asleep yesterday—I'm not really as rude as that." He only laughed and said: "You didn't fall off to sleep, Dr. Lang put you to sleep." He then explained that he was Dr. Lang's medium and assured me that he and Dr. Lang would do all they could to help me.

'On this occasion I saw Mr. Chapman go into trance. He took off his wrist-watch and put it on the side-table, and then went over to the corner and muttered a prayer. I watched him and noticed that his body went down a little bit. I thought that my eyes must be playing tricks on me again, and I felt upset because since his first visit the previous day I had had no eye trouble at all.

'When he spoke to me a few moments later, Mr. Chapman's

voice had changed completely. It was not Mr. Chapman's quiet voice, it was a deep husky voice and it seemed to me as though the words were sort of blurred. He came over to me, moving his hands and flicking his fingers and I had the impression he was talking to doctors and nurses, asking for instruments and things. He never touched me, but was obviously working on my head and I felt a strange sensation. Then he started working on my shoulders. My arms had been pulled out from my shoulders during the accident, and the right one hadn't been set back properly. Again he didn't really touch me, but I could feel the bone moving inside the socket. It didn't hurt, it went sort of numb.

'He was talking the whole time, and moving his hands, and he moved right down my body. When he got as far as my knee—you must remember my legs were still in plaster—he suddenly said: "I'll say goodbye for today, young lady, but I shall see you again in two day's time." I don't remember any more—suddenly I fell into a deep sleep. When I woke up, my mother was sitting by my bed, knitting, and she told me that Mr. Chapman had left two and a half hours ago.

'During that afternoon and the following day I improved rapidly. I felt so much better—my speech was better, I could move my arm much more easily and my vision was so much clearer. For the first time since my accident I really started feeling on top of the world.

'When Mr. Chapman came again—that was on the day before I was due to go back to hospital—I saw him go into trance for the second time, exactly in the way he had done so on the previous occasion. And when Dr. Lang operated, I noticed something very interesting. When he was Mr. Chapman, he used his right hand; but when he was Dr. Lang he used his left. In fact, when I first noticed it I said to him: "Have you hurt your right hand, Mr. Chapman?" and he replied: "Dr. Lang you are speaking to—I have the honour of Mr. Chapman allowing me to come through him to you to help you."

'We talked for a little while and out of the blue he said: "You do believe that I am going to make you better?" I assured him that I did, but I told him that I had to go back to the hospital next day. "I've no intention of staying there," I said. "No, you won't have to, young lady," he said. "I shall see you again next week—here in this house." He then went on performing further operations and suddenly said: "I'm afraid you won't be able to say goodbye to me today either because I am going to put you to sleep."

'After this I don't remember any more. I can't tell you what operations he performed this time. I'd slept longer than ever that day and when I woke up it was already afternoon. And again I felt very much better.'

Mrs. James was taken back to hospital the following day but she was convinced that she would not be requested to stay. When the doctors examined her it was to find an improvement in her condition that was beyond their capacity to explain. They agreed to her request that she should be allowed to return home, because, they said, they believed the home atmosphere might be beneficial.

From then onwards Mrs. James was taken to and from Buckinghamshire Hospital twice, sometimes three times a week. The hospital doctors invariably greeted her with 'Ah, the Miracle Girl!' or 'How's the Miracle Girl today?' Mr. Lang continued to visit her regularly at her home.

'When they took the plaster off at the hospital, my right leg was three-quarters of an inch shorter than the left, and they said that I would have to have a special surgical shoe built,' Mrs. James told me. 'Well, I didn't want to have this, and I fervently hoped that Dr. Lang could do something. So I told him about it when he came again through Mr. Chapman, and of my dread. I could see he understood my feelings. While he was operating on me that day, I suddenly had this funny feeling, as if someone was lifting my leg and putting weights on the end of it.

'Next thing was someone slapping my face lightly. It was Mr. Chapman himself. He said: "Come along, come along, Dr. Lang didn't want you to sleep all day, wake up. I've put the kettle on for a cup of tea. Are you feeling all right? What happened?" Evidently he doesn't know what happens, so I told him as much as I could remember, and he said when I finished: "Come on then, let's try your legs." He measured them. The right one was still a little shorter than the left, but it was longer than when they'd measured it at the hospital. Anyway, when I returned three days later to the hospital, the doctors were flabbergasted when they measured my legs and found that they were both the same length!

'There was another remarkable thing. When they set the ankle and put pins in my bones they set the ankle-bone too far forward. When they took the plaster off and discovered it, they made arrangements for me to be operated on in April 1955 so that they could try and correct it. I told Mr. Chapman about it when he came the next time and I said: "You know, Mr. Chapman, I feel I just can't stand any more operations." He said: "Well, I don't know anything about such operations—I expect they did their best for you under the difficult circumstances."

'While we were talking, he changed in his chair and Dr. Lang came through. Almost immediately he started operating on my ankle, moving his hands and fingers and talking, and truly I could feel things being done. As soon as he had finished, I could see that the ankle-bone had been moved into its proper place. Before he left, he told Jeff to 'phone the hospital in four days' time and tell them that the proposed operation was no longer necessary. Well, Jeff did as Dr. Lang had asked, but the hospital didn't take much notice of what he said. They insisted that I come in for the operation, but when they examined my ankle, they were speechless. They said they just couldn't understand how my ankle-bone could have gone back into its right position without an operation or treatment. And they said that they wouldn't need to have me in to do anything on my ankle at all.'

When the Aston Martin tore into Mrs. James and did its grisly job on her body, it did not neglect her face. Her features were ripped and crosshatched by scars. When she was strong enough she was sent to the famous Stoke Mandeville Hospital for plastic surgery. This is what she told me about that episode in her life:

'Having had all those operations at the Buckinghamshire Hospital, I was frightened of what lay in store for me again, and the next time Mr. Chapman came I told him about it. To cut a very long story short, Dr. Lang performed a plastic surgery operation on my face. When he'd finished he wanted to know exactly when I had to go to hospital, and I told him that it was to be in a fortnight's time. He then said: "Oh, by then it'll be cleared up. Don't forget to bring that to the doctor's notice, and ask whether you can have your name taken off the list." Well, I did, because my face became as it is now—with powder on you can't see a thing—and when the lady doctor from the Stoke Mandeville Hospital examined me she was stunned. She couldn't understand it. She said there was no need for plastic surgery now. Once again Dr. Lang had performed a miracle.'

It was a long time before Mrs. James fully recovered from the injuries she had sustained in the accident. Although Mr. Lang and his specialist colleagues in the spirit world had restored her brain and nervous system, there were no *immediate* results—she regained her full mental self only step by step. However, barely six months after her terrible accident, she was able to go out. She had to learn to use crutches, but slowly her strength and co-ordination improved. She picked up once more the threads of social life. The doctors at the hospital kept a continuous watch on her and then, on the anniversary of her accident, they classified her 'almost normal'. The Miracle Girl had lived up to her descriptive nickname.

'When Dorothy was fit enough, I used to take her to Mr. Chapman's house in Aylesbury to save him coming to us,' Mr. James told me. 'I was present when Dr. Lang performed his operations, and several times I actually watched how Dr. Lang took control of Mr. Chapman. Mr. Chapman himself used to more-or-less shrink slightly; the features, the whole body seemed to change, and the voice changed. Mr. Chapman's quiet soft voice became, well, gruffish and old, if you know what I mean. Mr. Chapman is very shy when he is himself, but Dr. Lang knows exactly what he wants. He has an authority that you'd expect from a man used to handling a staff of assistants, nurses and doctors.

'What Dr. Lang has achieved for my wife is really wonderful. He improved her eyesight with every operation. She had three changes of spectacles. Now she doesn't need them at all. His operations brought back the smell in her right nostril, he took away her awful headaches and relieved her of the dizzy spells—she used to have complete blackouts and did not even know they were coming on. . . . I could go on and on telling you all the many, many things Dr. Lang did for her.

'When she came home from hospital, she was really in a terrible state. I remember one occasion when she had made a trifle after she'd learned to cook again, and when the door-bell rang, she just dropped the bowl with the trifle on the floor, just like that, so that she could open the door! Another time, when she wanted to put coal on the fire, she went to the pantry, got a handful of eggs and threw *them* on it. This shows you how mentally disturbed she was—in those days there was no telling what was going to happen.

'Look at her now—she is as well as she was before the accident. If it had not been for Dr. Lang, and she still survived, it would only have been to spend the rest of her life in a mental hospital.'

CHAPTER THIRTEEN

Birth of the Birmingham Healing Centre

THE NEWS of incredible healing successes spread slowly but steadily through patients who had first contacted the fireman-cum-medium in despair, and had experienced the 'dead' doctor's painless spirit operations and treatment. The number of patients grew from day to day. Consultations with Mr. Lang were free of charge to *any* patient.

Despite the fact that there was hardly any time left which Chapman could call his own, he never refused to travel any distance if a sufferer from ill health genuinely required the spirit doctor's help. It came about that he embarked on such a journey to Birmingham in the early part of 1956, and this was in fact the first step towards the setting up of the Birmingham Healing Centre.

For a considerable time, Mrs. Joan Smith—crippled with arthritis and bed-ridden—had no other alternative but to accept the doctor's and specialists' verdicts that nothing could be done to get her on her feet again. Then she learned about how the spirit doctor William Lang had cured a patient suffering from an almost identical ailment, and Mrs. Smith hoped that she, too, might benefit from spirit healing. She wrote to George Chapman, explained her circumstances, and asked if he could come and see her at her Birmingham home. To her surprise and delight she got a reply saying that he would visit her.

A frequent visitor to Mrs. Smith's home at the time was Mrs. Hilda Carter, a kindly woman living at King's Heath, Birmingham. When I met Mrs. Carter in June 1964, she told me about the concern she used to feel for Mrs. Smith. On her regular Tuesday visits she would try to be outwardly cheerful for the patient's sake, but inwardly sorrow at the plight of her bed-ridden friend. And the fearful thing about it was that nothing could be done.

'Then one day she told me about what she had learned of Mr. Chapman and his spirit control,' Mrs. Carter said. 'And she told me she'd asked Mr. Chapman if he could come to Birmingham to try and help her. I was most interested in all this because I hadn't heard a thing about Mr. Chapman or his spirit doctor Lang at this time. I knew of course that Mrs. Smith had tried a lot of healers in the past but didn't get any real benefit because here in Birmingham we are very short of good healing mediums. Well, I hoped that Mr. Chapman might be able to extend proper spirit healing in Birmingham, and I asked Mrs. Smith whether she thought he might be willing to take a small group here, because I knew of quite a few people in urgent need of help. Mrs. Smith approved of my idea and suggested: "Well, if you like I'll give him your address and then he can write to you and see what arrangements he can make."

'In due course Mr. Chapman wrote and told me that Dr. Lang agreed he would like to help patients living in Birmingham. We arranged that when he came to visit Mrs. Smith he would also attend to some patients whom I would have waiting for him at her house.'

From the moment George Chapman set foot in Birmingham and went into trance at Mrs. Smith's house, Mr. Lang stood up to the great expectations the sick woman had had. He diagnosed immediately that Mrs. Smith suffered from rheumatoid arthritis and performed a number of painless operations on her spirit body. But, although he made it clear from the start that he could not bring about quick and striking results, and that improvement would be rather slow with regular long-term treatment essential, Mrs. Smith none the less felt the first signs of relief straight away.

After Mr. Lang had concluded his treatment to Mrs. Smith, he attended to the group of twenty patients Mrs. Carter had waiting for him. The visit was an astonishing success and Mrs. Carter asked Mr. Lang whether he would agree to give a public healing demonstration. The spirit doctor readily consented.

The public exhibition of his unique skill and ability to help the gravely ill made Mr. Lang and his medium the talk of Birmingham —and not just among grateful patients and believing Spiritualists, but among those people who had witnessed his public display and passed the word on. In the Press, although some correspondents expressed their doubts about Spiritualism and allied subjects, it was recorded that 'the "spirit healing" which a number of patients received from the fireman-cum-psychic-healer, who claims to be controlled by the spirit of a dead doctor while in trance, was striking and convincing.'

After his first visit to Mrs. Smith's house in Birmingham in the early part of 1956, George Chapman revisited the city frequently. Mrs. Carter received so many SOS calls for spirit healing from people suffering with serious complaints that Mr. Lang found it necessary to attend to his new patients at Birmingham itself.

The more the contented patients talked about the wonderful help they had received from the spirit doctor, and the better Mr. Lang and his medium became known in the Midlands, the more often reports about their activities—and especially about the spirit doctor's public healing demonstrations—appeared in the Press. On September 17, 1956, for instance, the following report appeared:

'Last week-end was a very busy one for Mr. George Chapman, the Aylesbury fireman-spiritual healing, who came to Birmingham to demonstrate in public how his spirit Dr. Lang attempts to help sufferers of various illnesses by means of "spirit operations" and treatment.

'These healing demonstrations were conducted at the Birmingham districts of Moseley and King's Heath.

'The first healing demonstration was held last Saturday afternoon at the newly erected Queen's Bridge School, Moseley, and had a large attendance. Among the audience were some people who had travelled from as far as Leamington Spa, Stafford, Walsall, and other distant places.

'Dr. Lang selected cases and, after describing the condition of the patient, commenced spirit treatment. In every case the patient confirmed that the diagnosis which the "spirit doctor" had given by merely touching his fully clothed body with his medium's hands, was correct and corresponded with the diagnosis his own or hospital doctor had expressed. Quite a few patients attested that they felt considerable improvement after having received treatment.

'Dr. Lang maintained interest by his remarks both to patients and the audience throughout the demonstration, and kept every one in a happy frame of mind. Many remained after the meeting to speak to the healer who speedily regained his natural state.

'Sunday morning and afternoon were fully occupied with healing given to those who required it privately, but a further public demonstration was given at the evening service of the Silver Street Christian Spiritualist Church, King's Heath. The Spiritualist Church was packed and some people who did not want to miss the performance stood in the porch outside throughout the meeting.

'Both on Saturday and Sunday, I interviewed a considerable number of people—some of whom had received spirit healing from Dr. Lang and Mr. Chapman's previous visits to Birmingham. They testified to the benefit they had received from spirit healing.

'Mr. Chapman gave a promise that he would come again in the very near future.'

The promise was kept.

One of the people healed by Mr. Lang in that autumn of 1956 was Mrs. G. Fletcher of Birmingham, who had suffered since 1949 from stones in the kidneys. She was rarely free from pain, which was accompanied by vomiting, bouts of colic and the acute discomfort of passing stones. Regular morphia injections kept her from becoming crazed with pain.

Mrs. Fletcher was under permanent medical care. It was eventually decided at the hospital that there was possibly a growth on the parathyroid gland which upset the calcium output and distribution in the body. This caused the calcium to crystallise in the kidneys and form stones. The surgeon and doctors responsible for the diagnosis believed that surgery was the only way in which the condition might be corrected, but nevertheless a positive result was by no means certain unless the surgeon succeeded in dealing with the parathyroid gland, from which excess calcium could affect the whole body, lungs, chest, skeletal structure, etc., and lead to a fatal result.

Having been informed by the surgeon that, 'if the proposed operation fails to produce the result based on the tentative diagnosis, further complications are to be expected', Mrs. Fletcher decided against the operation. Instead she went to a friend who was a healer and underwent treatment. Improvement was minimal. Suffering remained her bedmate. And yet, at the back of her mind, somewhere, was a conviction that spiritual healing would one day cure her.

Then, after seven years of suffering, Mrs. Fletcher heard of George Chapman and his spirit control, William Lang, and decided to find out whether he could do anything for her. She was first seen by Mr. Lang in October 1956, and was greatly impressed by his accurate diagnosis of her complaint. Mr. Lang made it clear to her that it would take a long time to relieve her of her complaint and this would only be possible if she received regular treatment. When she told him she was determined to co-operate, he performed the first of several operations.

Immediately after this very first confrontation, Mrs. Fletcher felt better. Eight years later I read her case history at Aylesbury. Her name had come up at random and I wanted confirmation of the claims made in pen and ink. I jotted down the address alongside many others I had entered in my note-books. On November 16, 1964, I finally got around to contacting Mrs. Fletcher. Here is what she had to say:

'I have not consulted the medical profession since receiving healing from Dr. Lang, although I did pass several stones after my consultation with him. The last was in 1961. It was painful, yes, but I didn't suffer nearly as badly as during my previous attacks when X-rays showed my kidneys were full of stones. I have visited Dr. Lang in recent months and he informed me that I have no stones now or any disease whatsoever. I know this must be so because since 1961 I haven't been troubled with this painful and depressing complaint.'

In March 1957 Mrs. Hilda Carter suggested to George Chapman that he should come to Birmingham every Saturday at five to six weekly intervals; Chapman agreed to a trial period of twelve months. On one occasion, when Mr. Lang spoke with Mrs. Carter before starting his healing session at Silver Street Christian Spiritualist Church, he predicted that 'a house very near the Church will become vacant and will be our permanent Healing Centre'.

Mr. Lang's prediction came true.

At a time when the number of patients had reached such large numbers that it was difficult to deal with them at the Spiritualist Church, the house next to the church became vacant. It was turned into George Chapman's Birmingham Healing Centre in 1958. To this day it is being run with remarkable success.

CHAPTER FOURTEEN

Killing a Cancer

NORAH OSBURNE of Folkestone, M.O.A.T., S.R.N. and Matron, fell ill in 1943 while working at Guy's Hospital during her training as a nurse. Three specialists confirmed the hospital doctors' verdict that her condition was due to gland trouble in the throat. They advised her against having an operation.

'Cancer was never mentioned,' Miss Osburne told me when I saw her at Folkestone in September 1964. 'At the same time I became most frightfully worried and depressed. One of the specialists told me: "I don't know what you're worrying about, it will clear up." It was obvious that the doctors thought I was making a fuss about nothing. But I was the one who was in great pain.'

For ten years Miss Osburne bore her suffering. Then, in 1953, her father—a doctor and superintendent of a mental home in Cork, in the south of Ireland—fell ill and asked his daughter to come home and help. She went back to Cork.

'Then my illness really flared up because, after my father passed away, I was working too hard,' Miss Osburne continued. 'The doctor I saw in Cork aspirated the gland in my neck, but it got steadily worse.

'For the next two years it was "grin and bear it" for me. The pain became harder to endure and I knew I had to get some sort of treatment. It so happened that I got hold of a copy of the *Psychic News* while over in England for three days' holiday, and I looked at the column containing "Spirit Healers". For some reason I picked out the name of George Chapman and wrote to him, asking if he could arrange distant healing for my pain and nervous apprehension. He answered my letter immediately, told me that he was controlled by a spirit doctor named William Lang, and assured me that distant healing had commenced on receipt of my letter and Dr. Lang would do all he could to help me. I found it rather interesting and gratifying.

'When distant healing commenced, there was a very slight relief, but I couldn't honestly say that I felt really better. I was pleased when Mr. Chapman wrote to me that Dr. Lang considered contact healing necessary. It meant that I would have to travel from Cork to Aylesbury—a long and costly journey—but I decided I'd go anyway. That was in April 1957.

'I arrived at Mr. Chapman's house half an hour early, and met him and his wife while he was still his own self and not yet in trance. He seemed a very pleasant, sincere person and very quiet. You sometimes see mediums who are rather talkative, but Mr. Chapman seemed a very ordinary type of man—he hadn't a lot to say really. And from what conversation we had, he didn't appear to have a clue about medicine.

'I saw him going into trance after he'd taken me into the sanctuary. He was sitting down, and suddenly I saw him look up and smile. I had a queer sensation, a shiver—probably due to excitement, I suppose.

'Then he stood up and greeted me. "How are you, young lady?" His voice was very different from Mr. Chapman's. He struck me as rather old-fashioned—a type that one doesn't meet nowadays, a type I still remember from my grandfather.

'After we'd chatted with each other about all sorts of things, he said: "What a dreadful mark on your neck." I told him the doctor in Cork had aspirated it, and he commented that the doctor had made a mess of it. He asked me to lie down on the healing couch, and after he'd examined me, he gave me his diagnosis. Listening to it, I decided he possessed vast medical knowledge.

'He performed a spirit operation and it seemed that he was cutting the invisible spirit body with unseen instruments. I could almost see myself in the operating theatre with him. I mean, I could visualise the operation he was doing—he was draining the thing out. You see, I'd put in a lot of duty in the operating theatre during my time at the hospital. . . .

'After he had finished the painless spirit surgery, he told me that he would attend to my eyes because there was a weakness there. This was quite true. Things used to get blurred a bit if I was looking at bus numbers or anything else in the distance.

'Dr. Lang performed an operation on my eyes, and when this was done I asked him if I would have to wear glasses. I had worn them for years. He replied: "No, it won't be necessary, but avoid bright lights and just use your glasses for reading, and perhaps when you go to the cinema or theatre." He really succeeded in achieving something extraordinary. Since the operation on my eyes, identifying buses at a distance or anything else, is no longer a difficulty. I no longer wear spectacles and am able to drive a car.

'But to go back—when I left Dr. Lang on that first occasion I felt terribly ill. I returned to Ireland with pains worse than ever. I hoped that my next appointment in May would show greater benefit. I did not blame Dr. Lang for my being worse than before I saw him—quite the contrary—for some inexplicable reason I felt convinced that he would eventually be able to help and cure me.

'I was so sure of his ability to do this that I spoke at length about him to my mother. You see, she had serious trouble with her eyes—she had been complaining of seeing floating objects before them, and a specialist diagnosed an early cataract and gave her six months before her sight failed altogether. To cut a long story short, my mother welcomed my suggestion to see Dr. Lang when I went to Aylesbury for my next appointment in May.

'When Dr. Lang examined my mother, he said: "This is not a case of cataract, it is scotoma—black spots interfering with the vision. I'll soon put this right." And, as he performed his spirit operation on my mother's eyes (having asked me to stand behind the healing couch), he told me exactly what he was doing. I felt once again as if present in the operating theatre, watching intricate surgery being performed. It was all so real, all so true to life.

'Dr. Lang kept his promise and cured my mother—on the spot. When we left Mr. Chapman's sanctuary, mother suddenly exclaimed: "My eyes are all right, no more floating objects!" And when she went back to Cork and went with me to the eye specialist, I was enthralled by the look on his face. Utter amazement when he examined her eyes. He kept testing and testing them, and in the end looked across at me and said: "They seem to have cleared up—

extraordinary! Your mother is all right now!" I'll never forget the look on his face!

'My mother thought Dr. Lang was wonderful—he was of the same generation as her father who'd been a surgeon. I come from a medical family—five generations—father, grandfather, great-grandfather, and so on, were doctors and surgeons and the mental home in Cork was handed down through the family.

'But to return to my own case, when Dr. Lang had finished his operation on my mother, he asked me to occupy the healing couch and, having examined me, said: "Oh dear, this is very bad, I am sorry about this. I'll have to drain the poison off again from the gland." Then he operated on me and I distinctly felt some very slight pain—as if incisions were being made. Afterwards he asked me to go upstairs, and rest in the sitting-room for about ten minutes without talking. When I came down again, he performed still another spirit operation.

'When he was finished he said: "Don't do anything, don't go to any doctor now, don't have an operation yet; wait for me to tell you when it is safe to operate." He explained that the gland at the back of my neck was full of poison, that he wanted to dispose of it and was doing his best to drain it into a carbuncle-like thing down the front so that it could be easily dealt with. He didn't tell me anything about cancer, but when my mother re-visited him for a check-up on her eyes two days after her operation, he told *her* I had cancer. He made it clear, however, that if given time he could cure me completely.

'I went back to Ireland immediately, leaving my mother behind, and still knowing nothing of cancer, to return to my duties at the mental home. The train journey from Dublin to Cork nearly finished me off. The pain—I'd never experienced such agony in my life!

'Within a week, the gland on my neck started to work down—it came from the back to the front and was hanging down like a carbuncle. In the end I had to send an express letter to Mr. Chapman to ask his advice because Dr. Lang had impressed upon me not to do anything. Dr. Lang replied through Mr. Chapman that I had reacted so well to the spirit operations that I could go and see my doctor and have the gland opened. But he added I must not have it *removed* at this stage. I must wait for him to tell me when it would be safe to do so. I was still unaware of the fact that this was due to the cancer not yet being cured—my mother kept this secret from me.

'I saw my doctor, who was quite amazed by the transformation. He said: "I've never seen anything like it happen before." He made a slight incision into the carbuncle-like gland, and the pus just poured out. The pain lessened and lessened.

'During the following three months progress was very slow and pain sometimes drove me to near madness. I received distant healing from Dr. Lang and knew that he came to visit me. I couldn't see him of course, but I sensed his presence time and again. Sometimes I used to say to my sister: "Dr. Lang is here." She'd ask: "How do you know?" and I'd reply: "I just know he is here." He told my mother that I had psychic faculties and knew when he was there. And, sometimes when I meditated, I felt a strange tingling in my body. All this proved to me that regular contact was being maintained between Dr. Lang and myself.

'One of the things Dr. Lang insisted I must do to help him cure me was to rest as much as possible, and to go to my bedroom not later than eight o'clock in the evening for ten minutes' quietness. I did as I was asked, but one night, instead of going up to my bedroom at eight o'clock, I remained sitting in the drawing-room longer than usual. Suddenly I heard a loud clicking of fingers—the same sound I knew so well from my visits to Aylesbury when Dr. Lang clicked his fingers while operating and asked for the invisible instruments. I knew immediately that Dr. Lang was there and thought: "My goodness, I'm late." I flew up the stairs. My mother and sister, with whom I had been talking, also heard the clicking sound, but they didn't think anything about it at the time because none of us could see Dr. Lang. I realised, however, that it was a sort of reminder from Dr. Lang for me to go upstairs. . . .

'In August 1957 I saw Dr. Lang again. There was another spirit operation and, when he had finished, he said: "It's cured now, you can have your operation for the removal of the gland at the hospital. Don't be annoyed with me because of the time it has taken and all the suffering you had to endure, but it was malignant." I had gathered that, and I assured him that I was most grateful to him for what he had done for me. It was only then that I found out that I had suffered from cancer, but that now I was completely cured.

'In September I entered hospital and had the operation for the removal of the gland. When they operated, it became septic—I had an awful time with it. Afterwards I was completely paralysed in my left arm, and the physio-therapist confirmed the doctors' and surgeon's opinions that the paralysis would remain because there was nothing that could be done to remedy it.

'When I saw Dr. Lang again in October, he told me I was a very lucky person. Anybody else in my condition would have been in the next world by now. He told me: "You may wonder why *I* didn't remove the gland? I'll tell you. After my spirit operations and treatment, it was only like a dead growth, which had to be removed, and it could be done easier and speedier at a hospital." He went on to say that he was not competing with the earthly medical profession—that he liked nothing better than to co-operate with his "living" colleagues as much as possible.

'He then said that the paralysis of my left arm was due to the nerve and muscles having been damaged during the operation. He performed a spirit operation and afterwards I asked him whether I should go to a physio-therapist and have heat treatment. "No," he said. "Not heat treatment, but gentle massage and exercises. And take a hot bath daily." I went to the physio-therapist and did the exercises.

'A month later, I visited Dr. Lang again. I felt very much better, and he was quite pleased with me. "Oh, the muscles will come back," he assured me, and he was right. You can see for yourself that my arm and hand are completely normal. They are perfect, and they were so after Christmas 1957. I've had no trouble of any sort ever since and I have worked very hard. I can truly say that I have seen a miracle take place before my eyes.'

Miss Osburne looked in splendid health. She is a fine matron, respected and admired. Her case impressed me profoundly. There is no dubiety about the details.

CHAPTER FIFTEEN

*Mirabile dictu**

THE CASE of Mrs. Barry Miron of Saltdean, Sussex, is in my opinion the most important contribution to this book. Hers was undoubtedly one of the most difficult and trying cases which Mr. William Lang ever encountered—not only during his distinguished career on earth, but also throughout his practice as a spirit doctor.

When I met Mrs. Miron in October 1964 to obtain details of her illness and treatment, I had the good fortune also to meet her husband, Mr. S. G. Miron, L.D.S., R.C.S. (Eng.), who agreed to explain to me all the complex aspects of this unusual case in medical terms. Indeed, Mr. Miron was possibly the best person qualified to give me a full medical account, because he was not only a dentist of considerable experience but had also engaged extensively in oral surgery at hospitals during his long professional career.

Trouble for Mrs. Miron started in the late summer of 1957 when her upper left first molar was removed. The extraction had been difficult and, due to the fact that a small piece of bone adhered to the root of the tooth, a perforation into the antrum occurred which led to an infection of this hollow—a complaint considered by the medical profession to be one of the most difficult things to clear up. But let the surgeon give us his interpretation of how such an unfortunate mishap could have occurred.

'The roots of this particular tooth are in very close proximity to the floor of the antrum. The roots of the tooth don't project directly into the sinus, but the bone covering the roots often comes

* Latin 'Marvellous to relate'.

up in waves into the floor of the sinus, as you can see on X-rays. Well, in removing the tooth it can happen that a small piece of the bone adheres to the root and causes a perforation into the sinus. If this perforation is very tiny it can heal up under its own volition.

'In my wife's case, however, it was unfortunately not a very tiny perforation, but was what is known as an antro-oral fistula—a great hole from the mouth into the antrum. This was in consequence of a so-called dry socket after the extraction of the tooth—a very painful affair which brings with it a certain amount of bone infection. As this was attended to, a mistake in treatment had been made in so far as a type of dressing had been used which set rather hard and forced the tissue to open to such an extent that I could have put my finger in the hole. This gives you an idea of how extensive and serious the opening was.

'Now, when you have an acutely infected antrum, any doctor will tell you that it is one of the most difficult things to clear up. An antral operation is a gamble, a toss of the coin. You never know the result. In about fifty per cent of cases people with antrum trouble suffer some types of recurring discomfort for the rest of their lives. It is one of the most unsatisfactory operations you can possibly think of.

'I was on the hospital staff myself at that time, and from my experience of oral surgery—surgery in the mouth—I knew that this was a job for plastic surgery. So I took my wife to the Churchill Hospital in Oxford where she was seen by the maxillo-facial people who suggested flapping the soft tissues together and sewing them up. Owing to my experience in this field which I had acquired from years of hospital work, it was my considered opinion that trying to stitch it up was just a waste of time because too much of the bone was missing and there was nothing to support the soft tissue. I was, however, not in charge of the case and could not very well argue with the surgeon, who was of a different opinion. To cut a long story short, they had a go at it, but it was unsuccessful. It was just impossible to tackle the problem this way—the hole was too big for closing it by flapping the soft tissues together and sewing them up. It was a clear case for plastic surgery.

'Two days after the futile sewing-up my wife was released from hospital. She was in great pain. In the end she was seen by a leading plastic surgeon, who stated at once that a graft was the only way to close the opening to the antrum and suggested the operation should be carried out as soon as they had a bed available at Stoke Mandeville Hospital.

'This type of graft operation is the same type as a skin graft. They take a flap of tissue from inside the cheek, turn it back over the opening and then stitch it up inside the palate. The flap of tissue has got to have a blood supply from the live tissue to stay alive until it has grafted itself on, and is consequently only severed from the live tissue when the grafting has proved successful. It is a lengthy and unpleasant process, but it is the only means of closing up an opening in the antrum of such size.'

Having been advised that this operation could not be carried out for another three weeks or so, because a bed was not available, Mr. and Mrs. Miron decided they would meanwhile consult Mr. William Lang. They knew a good deal about him and his successes as a spirit doctor and hoped that spirit surgery and treatment might put the trouble right, or at least lessen Mrs. Miron's suffering until the hospital bed was available.

'I had a rotten time,' Mrs. Miron told me. 'It was extremely painful and throughout I had to have the hole stopped with large cotton-wool plugs. If you have a thing like this you have to have it plugged, you can't have it open, because if it is unplugged it feels as though you are underground in a huge cave—everything echoes and reverberates in your own head. If you swallow anything, it immediately goes into the hole and down through your nose. I know only too well.

'Anyway, I went to see William Lang, and after he'd examined me he stated: "I *think* there is a very good chance that I may be successful." He did not *promise* success, but pointed out he would know whether or not he was able to help me after he performed the necessary spirit surgery. This seemed fair enough and I asked him to go ahead with what needed to be done.

'He performed the operation on the spirit body. After he'd finished, he said that he had been successful and added: "The hole will heal. Ask your husband to watch it." He then made it clear that I must come back to him frequently for observation and further spirit operation.

'A most interesting thing happened while I was on my way home from Dr. Lang. I told you I had the hole plugged with a large wad of cotton wool. Well, as I was about half-way home—it took about three-quarters of an hour to get to William Lang's door from where we lived then—I began to feel pressure on the cotton-wool plug. In other words, there was a tightening up process going on from either side, a distinct feeling of a growth of some sort going on, and it continued, slowly but steadily. As this continued, the plug had to be made smaller and smaller, till the opening to the antrum closed down to the size of a pin point. But I am ahead of events—all this took quite some time.'

Mr. Miron had this to say. 'I watched it and treated it day by day—by treating I mean I saw to it that it was kept clean and covered with the smooth plastic plate we had made for this purpose,' he said. 'I examined it daily, X-rayed it myself at least once a week and, well, the soft tissue gradually flapped over it—I mean it just closed up.

'There was not a shred of doubt in my mind that this was due to the spirit surgery William Lang had carried out, because during the time of waiting for the hospital bed and the graft operation to be carried out, my wife did not receive medical attention from *any one*. William Lang's prognostication that it would close up was correct. If in ordinary surgical practice a specialist had said anything of the sort to me I'd probably have thought, "the chap is a bit round the bend, he's probably overworked", because no one could say things like that and, in fact, no one *would*. William Lang, however, had said that the hole would close up and that I should watch it, and *it did close up!*

'I accompanied my wife several times when she went to see William Lang, and I saw him perform his spirit operations. He worked an inch or so *above* her face, at the floor of the sinus and around the site of the wound. He was asking for instruments which were handed to him by his son Basil and a large number of assistants and I knew the instruments he was using because I used them myself.

'Quite apart from the fact that he was telling me exactly what he was doing—he was building up the tissue, not in the physical sense but on the spirit body—I knew precisely the type of surgery he was performing from the movement of his hands and from the various instruments he asked for. I mean, had he been carrying out a physical operation, as a physical man in an operating theatre, everything would have been the same in every detail—the only difference would have been that I'd have seen it. Everything he was doing was a hundred per cent correct—it was the correct technique for flapping tissues over a great hole, for building a plastic graft over it.'

Before Mrs. Miron went to see the plastic surgeon at the end of the waiting period, she saw Mr. Lang. He was very pleased with her progress and declared that a graft operation would not now be necessary as the hole was closing up. 'I'll do my best to impress upon the surgeon to leave it alone,' he said. 'He is a sensitive man and we might succeed in influencing him.'

'We do not know of course whether William Lang succeeded with the plastic surgeon or not, but it is an irrefutable fact that when the gentleman examined me prior to my entering Stoke Mandeville Hospital, he decided to give it a further chance,' Mrs. Miron recalled. 'He told me that under the unexpected circumstances he would postpone the operation for another three weeks so as to find out whether the progress had continued. If it had, a plastic graft operation might not, after all, be necessary. He made it clear, however, that if there was even the slightest setback I must see him immediately.'

Mrs. Miron continued her frequent visits to Mr. Lang. Additional spirit operations were performed. The opening to the antrum continued to get smaller and smaller.

After the expiration of the second waiting period, Mrs. Miron again saw the plastic surgeon and he was amazed to discover that the opening to the antrum had become even smaller. He decided: 'We'd better let it go and see what happens to it.' He did not know that the patient had been receiving spirit treatment—Mrs. Miron did not consider there was any purpose in telling him.

'I wanted to know what he would say, so I asked him how he explained that such a large opening suddenly grew smaller and smaller, because one must remember that he had asserted all along that *only plastic surgery could close up the hole,*' Mrs. Miron continued. 'He replied: "Well, of course very occasionally nature does take over and it is possible that these two separate bits of skin could grow together, but cases like this are *very, very rare.*" He added candidly that during his long career as a plastic surgeon he himself had not met with a similar development in a case where there was such a large opening.'

'With all due respect to the plastic surgeon, who is a specialist with vast experience and skill, I whole-heartedly disagree with his explanation and affirm that it could not have happened by nature having taken over,' Mr. Miron told me. 'Let me be a little more specific about this. There is no point in my humbly saying he knew more than I did because he didn't. He is of course a plastic surgeon of the highest repute and experience, performing countless plastic operations on various parts of the body, but I specialised in *oral* surgery at the hospital and, therefore, I know more than he does about what can or cannot happen in the *mouth*. I say this with all modesty but it is true. If one realises that the skin that covers the body is much harder and tougher than the soft tissue in the mouth, it will be understood that there is considerable difference between graft surgery on any part of the body and graft surgery in the mouth, though the operating technique is very similar.

'Taking everything into account, I say most emphatically that the tissue just could *not* have grown together by the normal laws of nature as we know them. Look, I watched the opening close up. I plugged it, X-rayed it regularly and we made a little plastic dental plate to cover it, and I recorded every stage of the progress until the opening was covered with a thin floor of skin. If one remembers that the hole at one time was so big that you could put your finger up it, as I've already told you, you'll appreciate how considerable the opening was. *Nobody* who has the least knowledge of medicine or surgery can tell you that where there is such a great loss of bone, soft tissue can span nearly half an inch and grow firmly together. It is just not possible. However, it *happened*, and that *is* a fact.'

After a short pause, Mr. Miron added:

'I am by no means trying to belittle the plastic surgeon's experience or skill. He had no knowledge of my wife having received spirit healing and was faced with the fact that something like a miracle had happened. Having been asked to explain rationally how the closing of the opening in the antrum was possible, it is understandable that he attributed it to nature having taken over. Quite frankly, had I not known that it was the result of William Lang's spirit operations and treatment, I don't know what I would have thought had I come across a similar case. I would probably have said that something inexplicable had happened.'

As Mr. Lang continued treatment, and the opening grew together to a minute hole which became almost invisible to the naked eye, he warned Mrs. Miron:

'You must exercise great care. Owing to the floor to the antrum being very thin and having no bone structure to support the tissue, there is at this early stage the danger of breaking it open again. Until sufficient time has elapsed for the tissue to grow stronger, you must be terribly careful how you blow your nose when you have a cold, because the force of the pressure could break the tissue down again.'

This is what, unfortunately, did happen.

Quite apart from the antrum trouble, Mrs. Miron was at that time very low in health and became the victim of endless colds and attacks of influenza. She fought a losing battle and developed a further infection in the antrum. Because of this, the healing broke down and, although the hole did not get nearly as large as it had been formerly, the trouble started all over again.

'If you can get over here every day, I can prevent this getting worse,' Mr. Lang then told his patient. When she replied that the best she could do was to come to Aylesbury once a week, he comforted her: 'Don't worry, I'll do all I can to keep this accumulating poison at bay.'

For a long time his efforts were successful, but suddenly Mrs. Miron became much worse.

'During the next six months I became progressively more ill, because, due to the hole having opened again, I was swallowing poison,' Mrs. Miron described. 'It was physically a most revolting and filthy ordeal because I was aware all the time of an endless trickle of poison which I tried to spit out. The taste was awful and made me feel ill. It was draining into my stomach and poisoning my entire system. I became extremely distended, my skin turned a peculiar yellow, and I became exhausted. However, I carried on to the best of my ability and even went with my husband on a summer holiday we had planned. I felt the only thing I wanted to do was to rest in bed.

'By agreement with William Lang we went to see an ear, nose and throat specialist at Oxford, but on no account was he to be allowed to operate. Dr. Lang explained his reasons as follows: "The poison has got into the marrow of your bones and your system, and if the specialist is permitted to operate, the poison will still remain in your system, and regardless of how successful the actual operation might turn out to be, it will still gravely affect your health. I am doing my utmost to remedy this by giving you contact healing here every week and working on your spirit body every night during your sleep-state. I am trying to localise the poison. This will take time, but when I have succeeded, you can ask the specialist to operate because it will then be safe to carry out surgery." I realised how very difficult, if not impossible, it would be for me to tell the specialist what he should or should not do, but I was determined to comply with my instructions as closely as I could.

'To give the specialist his due, he was not awfully keen on operating. The X-rays showed that pus had spread out everywhere under the orbit of the eye, and he said quite candidly that an operation did not appear advisable. He gave me several wash-outs, which William Lang did not like at all (he said they did a lot of damage to his treatment) but *I* couldn't stop him doing it.

'Eventually Dr. Lang succeeded in collecting the poison into a localised area and it felt as if a terrific weight was under my eye. He told me then that I was to see the specialist without delay and tell him to operate.

'I called on the specialist and said: "I am sorry to have to say this, but I feel terribly urgently that I ought to have this operation now." I felt awkward telling an eminent surgeon what to do. He didn't say anything as he examined me, and for some time he just walked about the room. Then he turned round and said: "Do you know, I don't know why I am saying I will operate because I don't think it will be a success. The normal thing I should say should be: 'No, I won't operate,' but I will." He did. After the operation he told me that it was the worst case he had ever encountered.'

'My wife had a Caldwell-Luc operation, which is a bad thing because the result is generally fairly indifferent in fifty per cent of cases,' Mr. Miron explained. 'It is a crude operation and one which is only performed because it is the only thing that can be done, but no real surgeon likes having to do it. Very often the result is a chronic sinus which doesn't completely clear up and is always giving trouble. In my wife's case, however, it was completely successful. I saw the ear, nose and throat surgeon after the operation and he told me that he was highly delighted and a little surprised at the completely satisfactory result.'

'The usual thing after this kind of operation is that the pain is so terrible that the patient is given morphia for twenty-four hours,' Mrs. Miron told me. 'Well, I was sitting up in bed and eating a meal within six hours and smoking quite happily, which they thought was extraordinary. They all came to look at me in astonishment and said: "How is it you are so cheerful and free of pain?" In the end I said to the sister: "It is because I am having spiritual healing." Her remark was: "Oh, no wonder."

'After my comparatively speedy release from the nursing home where the operation was performed, I was to come straight away back to William Lang, and of course I did. For another week I received regular treatment from him, and then rapidly started to recover my full health. He succeeded in effecting a complete cure—I had no return of any sort since William Lang's spirit treatment terminated in April 1959.'

'If you take into consideration the various stages of this case, you'll arrive at the conclusion that William Lang actually cured my wife in record time,' Mr. Miron summed up. 'During the first part of his treatment he successfully closed up the oral fistula. During the second stage came the complication of the infected antrum which was due to my wife's lowered health. The third period saw the breaking down of the tissue that he had built up, and this occurred because of the infection. Finally, he succeeded in gathering the poison from all over the body into one central point and was then able to rebuild the tissue a second time.

'In my considered opinion he succeeded in making the impossible possible.'

CHAPTER SIXTEEN

Full-time Healing

George Chapman found it increasingly difficult to continue his dual occupations and the time came when a decision had to be made. He could continue in the secure and pensionable career of a public servant, which had already earned him his Long Service Medal as an acknowledgment of ten years' service, or become a full-time spirit healer, acting as medium for Mr. Lang. He had his wife and family to think about. Would they be able to live without a steady, guaranteed income? He pondered long over the problem and on October 31, 1957, resigned from the Aylesbury Fire Service.

With plenty of time now for spirit healing, Chapman was not only able to cut down the waiting list of Mr. Lang's patients, but to accept many more sufferers as patients. The regular journeys to the Birmingham Healing Centre no longer created difficulties. In the past he had frequently been obliged to ask colleagues to change duties with him so that he could travel to the Midlands. Now that particular form of worry was at an end. And, above all, he could now fulfil his desire to make Tuesday the day for a Free Clinic where anyone in need of spirit healing could receive attention from William Lang without being involved in any payment.

From the day George Chapman became a 'professional' medium, his sanctuary never lacked patients. Quite the contrary. So many sufferers from every type of disease requested consultations with Mr. Lang that he was often required to stay in trance from 10 a.m. till 5 p.m. Indeed there were many occasions when the crush of patients in need of lengthy spirit operations and healing was so great that Chapman remained under Mr. Lang's control until well into the evening. Yet, even the longest working hours were never too much for the dedicated medium—the thought that he was compelled by his spirit control to spend an excessive amount of time in trance never entered his mind. He had devoted his life to healing and accepted wholly whatever conditions were necessary.

On November 1, 1957, he spent his first day as the full-time medium of William Lang, F.R.C.S.

One of the early patients to come to Chapman on his first day was Mr. Cyril G. Woodley of Brill. I got in touch with him to learn how his illness had fared under the treatment of William Lang. This is what Mr. Woodley told me:

'Around about seven years ago (in 1950) I began having pains in my legs. After trying every known embrocation and ointment to no avail, I was finally forced to go to the doctor, who said it was fibrositis, and suggested a period of rest. As time went by the complaint got steadily worse, however, and I was sent to hospital for X-rays. They then said I had inflammation of the spine. I had eight weeks' heat and massage treatment with no apparent benefit. I was X-rayed again and finally told that I had a serious complaint called spondylitis.

'In 1953 I had a spell in Mount Vernon Hospital where I was given deep ray treatment. When I was discharged, to be frank, I felt even worse!

'After two years on National Insurance, I had another eight weeks' heat and massage treatment, but again, it seemed useless. I started work again in my shop, but I found it hard to stand for any length of time. I was attending a hospital clinic the whole time, and all they could do for me was to give me some tablets which I was supposed to take every time the pain got bad.

'Then my wife Jessie, who'd heard from Mr. Maurice Barbanell about Mr. Chapman and Dr. Lang, persuaded me to try spiritual healing. I agreed in the end and made an appointment to see Dr. Lang in November 1957.

'When Dr. Lang saw me and examined me, he diagnosed exactly what was wrong with me. He was quite frank with me and said he'd be able to help me get right enough, but that it would take some time, and that I'd have to be patient and come to see him often. I told him that I was willing to do as he said. After all, I had been suffering for seven years and didn't expect a cure to happen overnight. In fact, I thought, if he succeeds in curing me, he'll be doing something doctors have failed to do.

'Dr. Lang then carried out what he called an "operation on my spirit body" and, although I didn't feel a thing at the time, I was a heck of sight better by the time I got home.

'I kept every appointment Dr. Lang made for me, and each time I went, he did something for me that made me feel much better afterwards. By February 1959 I felt nearly one hundred per cent again, and since I was due for a check-up at the hospital, I was very curious to learn what their verdict would be. I can tell you the doctor was flabbergasted, and that's no exaggeration. He muttered something about "inexplicable things sometimes happening". I told him then about the treatment I had had from the spirit of Dr. Lang. He listened and didn't say anything. He asked me to call again in two years' time. I did of course—in February 1961—and, after examining me again, most carefully and thoroughly, he said I needn't come any more as I was completely cured. Oh and he said something to the effect that it was an extraordinary occurrence and hard to believe that anything of the sort could happen.'

On December 6, 1964, Mr. Woodley kindly gave me the following information about the present state of his health:

'I'm happy to say that though it is now more than seven years since I first consulted Dr. Lang, I am practically one hundred per cent fit again. Since we moved to our present house, I have managed the upkeep of our garden which is two hundred feet at the back and thirty foot at the front. With the help of my son I have managed the heavy digging—it's clay, and that speaks for itself!'

When Mr. Woodley first visited Mr. Lang on November 1, 1957, his wife Jessie accompanied him. She was equally impressed with Mr. Lang and his effective spirit healing, for she had been suffering from high blood pressure and accompanying ailments for many years, and the doctors had not been able to do more for her than prescribe tablets. Her regular visits with her husband to Mr. Lang enabled the spirit doctor to cure her completely of her complaint, and she, too, confirmed in December 1964 that she had enjoyed good health ever since Mr. Lang had given her treatment.

'You may be interested to know that I spent more time in bed in winter before I went to see Dr. Lang, than I was able to be up and about, owing to bronchial asthma,' she stated. 'It's wonderful now to be active in wet weather and fog with only an occasional wheeze! My usual bronchitis would start any time after September, but all that belongs to the past now. I guess you can imagine how glorious it is to breathe freely and deeply—thanks to Dr. Lang's cure.'

When Mr. and Mrs. Woodley came to George Chapman's sanctuary in August 1958, a leaflet was handed to them as well as to other patients. It was a request for notification to be given if any phenomenon was noticed arising out of treatment by Mr. Lang.* Mrs. Woodley complied with the request and sent George Chapman the following letter:

'I am writing to let you know of some of the experiences my husband and I had when consulting Dr. Lang.

'During our consultation with Dr. Lang in January this year, he told me that he had injected deeply into my chest in two places and warned me not to become alarmed if marks appeared on my body. I didn't feel anything and I didn't think any sort of mark could appear. I was quite wrong. Two marks did appear on my body! Quite distinctly. And they remained there for four days.

'Twice during the winter I was unable to visit Dr. Lang and he told my husband on both occasions that he would visit me. Each night I was awakened by a kind of electric shock. It was a tingling sensation from my head down to my feet, as one gets from stinging nettles, and lasted for perhaps a minute. On both mornings I felt fine and was able to get up.

'After Dr. Lang had treated my husband and myself on our visit to him last June, he explained to us that he had drawn some fluid from my husband's spine. There sure enough was the wet patch on the cover of the healing couch! This was most remarkable because, as you know, Dr. Lang *only* performs *spirit* healing and *never touches* the actual *physical* body. I always watched him very closely and saw his hands every time some short distance *above* the *physical* body.'

When George Chapman received Mrs. Woodley's letter it pro-

* A considerable number of Mr. Lang's patients also complied with the request expressed in the leaflet and notified George Chapman. Some of these discoveries of phenomena are included in patients' case histories.

vided the explanation to a puzzle that had irked him for the past two months. When he regained consciousness on a day in June 1958, after Mr. Lang had attended to the last patient, George had noticed a wet patch on the cover of the healing couch. He could not find any explanation as to how this had come about and, without thinking a phenomenon could have occurred, he just changed the soiled cover for a clean one. But Mrs. Woodley's letter provided the answer.

CHAPTER SEVENTEEN

'I shall not look back in anger'

As I sat opposite Miss Ilse Kohn and listened to her account of an accident that had befallen her seven years previously, in 1957, I could feel again the horror that wells up in me whenever I think of human beings being catapulted into physical trauma. About this accident there was the appalling familiarity that characterises so much of the slaughter and near-slaughter that takes place daily on our roads. A hospital matron on her bicycle, a car, a crash, twisted steel, and the maimed body of a woman lying, head bleeding, on the road. Then the mercy dash to Amersham Hospital, the examination, and the cataloguing of its findings—fractured skull, right eye gravely injured, fractured nose and fractured ribs.

'I was unconscious for ten days and nights. When I came round I didn't know where I was or what had happened. You see I'd had concussion, and after it one usually has no recollection of what has happened,' Miss Kohn told me. 'I couldn't lift my head off the pillow—I didn't want to. And I felt completely exhausted. I was really glad to be in bed.

'A few days after I'd regained consciousness, a number of doctors were standing around my bedside talking, discussing my case. I heard one of them saying quietly to another that he was concerned about my eyesight. One of his colleagues said something to the effect that he doubted whether I'd ever be able to see again. They didn't know I could hear what was being said. I had it on the tip of my tongue to say, "*I know* I'll be able to see again." They had replaced an eye which had been torn from its socket and had then closed the lid for protection. But they had left a part of it open in the centre, and through this I could see a fraction of the sky.

'I was determined to get better. When I heard a specialist express his doubts on whether I would fully regain my mental balance, and explain that it would take a long time before I could resume my duties as Matron, I regarded it as a challenge to get well quickly. I think the doctors were amazed to see how soon I recovered. Within three weeks I had learnt to sit up straight, to stand and walk again, to look after myself and talk with other patients. Then I was discharged and allowed to return home.

'A very trying time followed. I was terribly weak and my right eye was still closed. I frequently suffered from intolerable pains in the head and it was very alarming to find out that I was unable to think clearly and logically. At times I wondered whether the hospital specialist had been right after all when he'd said it would take a long time (if ever) until I was fit enough to resume my duties as Matron. And when a psychiatrist friend said: "She'll have to start from the very beginning, as if she'd just been born, and go through every period of her life again," I was shocked. I thought: "My God! That's something to hear at the age of 33!" I found it terribly difficult to swallow this bitter pill, but eventually I accepted it.

'After a month at home I had to return to hospital to have my right eye opened. It was frightfully painful, almost like experiencing another accident. When I returned home, I had a relapse and felt weaker and worse then ever.

'Shortly afterwards I went to a convalescent home at Farnham and made good progress. I wanted to show that I was well enough to resume my duties as Matron, but apparently my mind was still not quite normal.

'As much as I tried, I couldn't meet my own challenge and everything I attempted seemed to fail. I couldn't understand it. Looking back I'd say it was because I was trying to rush things all along the line. And you can't *force* the pace of getting better beyond what nature will accept.

'There were times when I gave way to depression and the nights were bad, too. Unable to sleep, I could only weep and felt terribly alone, despite the sympathy and love of friends who cared for me as much as my parents would have done had they been alive. But I couldn't appreciate it. I felt as if I were in a prison, with no one to talk to. Deep within myself I think I knew that the misery was of my own making. It was like being in a cruel trap and feeling you'd never get out and would die.

'There was little change in my condition until after the New Year when it was suggested to me that I should consult the spirit doctor William Lang to see if he could help me in any way. Not being a Spiritualist, however, I wondered if anything could come of it, but I was curious and very willing to try anything.

'When I eventually met Dr. Lang in February 1958, it was a very pleasant experience. There was so much friendliness about him that I felt at ease immediately.

'As he walked towards me, he reminded me of a German professor with whom I had enjoyed working in hospital. I at once thought: "I'm in good hands, here's someone who understands." I realised I had done right in coming to see him.

'Dr. Lang talked with me for a while about all sorts of things. He wanted to know from where I came, what was my work and how the accident came about. He then asked me to lie down on the couch and examined me by touching my body very lightly with his hands. He said very little about my condition, but somehow gave me the feeling that I could rely upon him to help me.

'While I lay there, he explained that he would perform a number of painless operations on my spirit body. He talked to invisible assistants and asked for surgical instruments. His hands hovered an inch or so above my body as if delicately holding some instruments and performing an operation, but I didn't feel a thing. I knew instinctively that he would help me, though I wondered *how*.

'When I left I felt much easier, so much lighter and gayer. I felt that something had happened, though I didn't know exactly what. It was as if somebody had opened the door of my imaginary prison.

'At first I didn't know how to enjoy my new-found freedom. In my subconscious mind I feared that this wonderful feeling of being free, of being myself again, might not last, but I consoled myself with the thought that in a fortnight's time I would be seeing Dr. Lang again, and he would then be able to help me still further. As the days went by, I was delighted to find that the freedom of mind neither vanished, nor even diminished, but, in fact, grew more real and permanent every day. I felt I was no longer alone.

'When I went to Aylesbury on the second occasion, I met Mr.

George Chapman before he went into trance. He was a much younger man than Dr. Lang, and I noticed that he spoke differently. Being a trained nurse, I naturally spoke about medical matters, and particularly about my case. He had no knowledge of medicine, and was anything but a doctor.

'Dr. Lang again performed some operation and gave me spiritual healing, and again I felt better. This improvement was, in fact, so remarkable that I became fully capable of resuming my duties as Matron.'

After her third and final visit to Mr. Lang, Miss Kohn knew she had at last reached the stage of well-being when she could carry out her onerous duties with the same proficiency she had been able to show before her accident.

'I didn't feel on top of the world all the time, but Dr. Lang somehow succeeded in implanting in my mind the sure confidence that I would get better,' Miss Kohn told me. 'Of course, there were difficulties still to be met, but in the end I managed to overcome them.

'For years now I have felt very well—I could not wish to be better. I enjoy life and I enjoy meeting people. I am reading and writing more than ever before.

'I shall never look back in sorrow and anger. When sometimes I think of all that happened to me I wonder whether, in fact, I should have found the road to happiness had I not met Dr. Lang. I pray that God will preserve the strength in me to help those who need me, as once I needed help.'

CHAPTER EIGHTEEN

The Quest for Co-operation

ONE OF the first things I became aware of in my talks with William Lang in the preparation of this book, was his earnest desire to establish greater co-operation between himself and members of the medical profession. It was a subject he touched on often. This longing was not prompted by the idea that help from earthly doctors would enable *him* to achieve even more striking results. The catalogue of these spoke for themselves. But he wanted to impart, in some way, something of his own unique ability and knowledge to man whose horizons were limited in the field of healing.

The ambition was fulfilled to some extent. A number of his patients who attended their own doctors or hospitals for periodic examinations spoke about the spirit doctor and his painless operations which had cured, or improved, their ailments. Many members of the profession of course would have none of it, or would refuse any comment, but there were some doctors and surgeons who agreed that divine or spiritual healing should not be dismissed or pooh-poohed. Some of them, in fact, went so far as to advise their patients to continue to receive treatment from Mr. Lang, and also to attend at regular medical check-ups so that their state of health could be observed clinically.

One such gentleman was Mr. G. S. Miron, L.D.S., R.C.S.(Eng.), whose co-operation with Mr. Lang has already been told in the chapter '*Mirabile Dictu*'. He also co-operated with the spirit doctor whenever he believed it would help the patient.

Other instances involving both doctors and distinguished

consultant specialists could be cited.

Although this co-operation with certain members of the medical profession was a remarkable and most welcome achievement, it only partly satisfied Mr. Lang's great ambition, for he aimed at working closely with as many doctors as possible.

He made his first decisive move in this direction in 1958, for while controlling George Chapman one day, he dictated the following letter and asked it to be sent to the Registrar of the Royal Ophthalmic Hospital (Moorfields Eye Hospital):

> 'I know that this is a strange letter for your hospital to receive, but both I and my son Basil were active members of your staff for many years.
>
> 'If you will look into my past records you will find much about me, e.g. I wrote a book entitled "The Medical Examination of The Eye" and my son wrote a number of books on the examination and approach to a patient.
>
> 'It is my wish to invite members of your active medical staff, or indeed past members, to contact my medium, George Chapman, with the view to having appointments with me.
>
> 'I know that in eye surgery and technique I can be of great help and I am sure that many of the staff who are so interested and love their work will enjoy meeting me.'

No reply was received. When I asked Mr. Lang during one of our interviews if he'd been upset by the Registrar ignoring his letter, he replied: 'Ooh no, I wasn't upset, no. I didn't really expect the Registrar to reply—it's perhaps too much to ask a gentleman in such a position to correspond with a "dead" man—but I just felt I had to write the letter to let them know I'm back and always willing to help in any way I am allowed to, but I don't consider it a wasted effort. I didn't receive a reply to my letter, but as a consequence of it some of the dear boys came to see me.

'A fortnight after George sent off the letter he received a communication from ———, I must not mention his name, it was a private consultation; but I can tell you that he is a very capable and skilled specialist. I didn't know the dear boy personally, he was one of Basil's colleagues, but I enjoyed talking to him.

'At first he marched into my room like a prize fighter,' Mr. Lang continued. 'From the questions he hurled at me it was obvious that he intended to establish that I couldn't be the William Lang I'd claimed to be in my letter. He asked me very intricate ophthalmological questions and I answered each one in detail and also spoke about various treatment approaches. At the end the dear boy apologised for his hostile attitude and then enquired if I would permit him to consult me if ever he was faced with a problem he did not quite know how to tackle. Of course I said I would.

'Over the years we became quite good friends and he visits me quite often. In fact, he saw me only a few weeks ago about a case in which, I am pleased to say, I was able to assist him.' He looked at me in a mischievous way and added with a smile: 'I helped him of course in my own way. I was present in the theatre as he performed the operation and was able to guide him. Afterwards I visited the patient during his sleep state and attended to his spirit body. Of course the dear boy doesn't know any of this and I prefer him to believe it was his own care and skill that saved the patient's sight.'

During this interview it came to light that a number of specialists from various ophthalmic hospitals come to see Mr. Lang now and then to discuss complex cases.

These visits to Mr. Lang resulted in news of the spirit doctor spreading to other specialists and practitioners in other fields of medicine. George Chapman has a considerable file marked 'Confidential'. It contains letters from hospital and private doctors—some of them well-known specialists, others less notable practitioners. Many of them had asked for appointments with Mr. Lang because they wanted to discuss with him some of the cases which worried them and which they hoped might be cured, or at least improved, by treatment from the spirit doctor; every letter showed that the patient had not reacted to orthodox medical treatment and was, as far as could be judged, incurable. There are letters openly requesting appointments for patients to be seen by Mr. Lang so that spirit surgery and treatment can be tried. Since these communications are all marked 'Private and Confidential' the identity of the writers cannot be revealed. But I assure you I have seen them all and read them. And the names of these correspondents would probably startle you.

One prominent Harley Street specialist wrote: 'I am relinquishing my practice which will be taken over by ——— who was trained at Guy's Hospital and was a ——— prizewinner. ——— spent a year at a Clinic in Canada, specialises in industrial injuries and polio cases, and has spent further periods at two hospitals (names stated) in London. I hope that ——— will call and see you, and that you will afford him all the help you can.'

The specialist's successor in fact came to see Mr. Lang to discuss with him a particular case which was causing him considerable concern. Mr. Lang gave his advice and, unknown to his visitor, commenced distant healing for the patient. It was successful.

George Chapman continues to receive letters from members of the medical profession. One of the most recent—written in December 1964—said: 'Next month I open my new department at ——— Hospital. Please ask Dr. Lang to give this medical department his blessing and to give me the strength, awareness, calmness and confidence to run it. I will look to Dr. Lang for his help.'

Ultimately, Mr. Lang's letter to the Registrar at Moorfields served its purpose, though not officially. But Mr. Lang is never concerned with officialdom or public acclaim—his sole aim is to assist any sufferer in need of help. If he can obtain support from the medical profession and, through medical co-operation, bring about a patient's recovery, he is quite content.

Some years ago journalist Desmond Shaw wrote: 'The day will come when no great medical man, physiologist or pathologist, will dream of attempting to cure diseases without speaking to the spirit world, any more than he would dream of going into the operating-room without his scalpel.' Perhaps Mr. Shaw's prophecy is on the brink of coming true.

CHAPTER NINETEEN

Open the Doors of the Mind

DOCTORS ARE just as self-opinionated as anyone else. Because they have qualified in university and medical school, presumably they are reasonably intelligent people. But when it comes to the expressing of opinions, they are peculiarly hesitant. The most vociferous and the least vociferous share at least one quality—a massive inhibition centred on the public use of their names in connection with their views on certain subjects.

I spoke to many doctors in the cause of preparing this book. Some of them went in off the deep end at the mention of spirit healing. They laughed, they denigrated, they dismissed, they scorned. Others smiled condescendingly or shrugged their shoulders, or offered unfinished phrases such as: 'Yes, well, you know how it is . . .' or 'Well, people are entitled to believe what they like, but I, well, how should I put it . . .'

One was left with the impression that as far as the main body of the medical profession is concerned, spirit healing was beyond the pale. Not only was it a thing they either didn't understand, or plainly disbelieved, but it didn't even warrant objective investigation.

Only a fraction of those doctors with whom I spoke would agree to allow me to quote their names together with their opinions. This is something I don't pretend to understand. Why the fear?

Even those doctors who had come in contact with George Chapman-William Lang showed some reluctance. And it wasn't as if I was simply in search of favourable opinion. I would have been pleased to quote the 'anti' spirit healing (or anti-Lang) opinions as well as the 'pros'. But the response I encountered was almost a wholly 'VERBOTEN' attitude.

One of the doctors who met the spirit doctor on several occasions, and kindly permitted me to name him, was Dr. Theodore Stephanides. After half a lifetime's experience as a doctor, he served during the Second World War as a Major in the R.A.M.C. and afterwards joined the staff of Lambeth Hospital, London, where he worked until his retirement from hospital service in 1961.

'I first met Dr. Lang at the beginning of 1958,' Dr. Stephanides told me at his Chelsea flat. 'A friend of mine, Mr. Eric Raymond who comes from Haddenham, and who suffered from deafness (he had progressive sclerosis of the tympanum—hardening of the ear-drum), asked me to go along with him to Aylesbury. He'd decided, he said, to go to a spirit doctor, and he wanted me to hear what the spirit doctor would have to say and see what he might do.'

'Had Mr. Raymond had any medical treatment before he went to Aylesbury?' I asked.

'Oh yes, he'd tried orthodox medicine for a long time, without getting any results at all,' Dr. Stephanides said. 'Unfortunately, Dr. Lang was unable to improve Mr. Raymond's deafness either. But this, I think, may have been an unfair test as far as Dr. Lang is concerned, because you see sclerosis of the tympanum is known to be a progressive condition, practically impossible to cure by orthodox medicine. It goes on and on until a person becomes quite deaf. Practically nothing can stop it.

'Anyway, when we went to see Dr. Lang at the beginning of 1958, he rightly diagnosed Mr. Raymond's condition. He *didn't promise* that he'd heal him; he said he *hoped* that he might improve his hearing. He performed what he called an "operation" on Mr. Raymond's "spirit body" which he said would result in virtual surgery on the ear-drum. This "operation" was of course performed without any visible instruments or assistants.

'Immediately after the treatment Mr. Raymond's deafness did seem a little improved, but this didn't last. I saw Mr. Raymond about a fortnight ago in fact and there's no appreciable improvement there I'm sorry to say. But, as I have said before, this wasn't really a fair test and Dr. Lang's failure was no indication that he lacked success with other cases. To take this view would be manifestly unfair—and of course illogical.'

'Speaking as a doctor, what impression did Mr. Lang make on you?' I enquired.

'Oh, competent, kindly, slightly pedantic. Like a medical practitioner of the old school,' Dr. Stephanides replied. 'During my talks with him—I accompanied Mr. Raymond about eight or nine times to Aylesbury—he never made any medical mistakes. But as I was present as a guest and not as a scientific investigator, I never asked him any test questions of any kind.

'It appeared to me that there was vast medical knowledge there but of a time gone by, if you understand me. He didn't seem to mention any of the modern developments—things like penicillin, etc., but that may of course have been coincidence. But what he spoke about at various times clearly indicated that he had a great deal of medical experience and knowledge.

'I have personal knowledge of an incident during one of my meetings with the spirit doctor which made quite an impression on me.

'In February 1958 I had an operation at Lambeth Hospital for retinal detachment of the right eye. The following June I visited Dr. Lang with Mr. Raymond. On that occasion Dr. Lang came up to me and stood in front of me (with both eyes firmly closed as usual), and told me that he was pleased that my operation for a "retinal disorder" (he didn't use the term "retinal detachment") had been so successful. There were no outward signs of any kind which would betray the fact that I had had the operation, and I hadn't at any time mentioned it. Nor had Mr. Raymond; I confirmed this with him afterwards.

'Of course, there is no absolute guarantee that the information in question could not have come from some person connected with the Lambeth Hospital, but I don't think this probable because, as far as I know, Mr. Chapman hasn't any connection there.

'Another possibility is, of course, telepathy; but here again I don't think telepathy comes into my case because I certainly wasn't thinking about the operation when I went to Aylesbury. There was no reason why I should be thinking about it. The operation had been performed four months before my June meeting with Dr. Lang and I had no trouble afterwards.

'When Dr. Lang told me about the operation, I was surprised, most surprised. I myself incline to the opinion that Dr. Lang made or sensed the diagnosis by what I would term "super-normal" means.'

During my interview with Dr. Stephanides it came to light that he had met George Chapman in his non-trance state during one of his visits to Aylesbury. I asked him about his impressions.

'Well, they seem to be two entirely different people,' Dr. Stephanides said. 'Of course I never knew Dr. Lang—or Mr. Lang to give him his right title—in real life, but I think that people who had known him and spoke to Mr. Chapman in trance, when he was under the influence of Dr. Lang would recognise him and find a resemblance. His manner of speaking and the way he holds himself, among other characteristics, were quite different from Mr. Chapman's.'

'Do you believe that George Chapman is in fact controlled by Mr. Lang?' I asked.

'This is a very difficult question to answer. Let me put it this way: Either Mr. Chapman is an extraordinarily good actor or he *is* controlled by Dr. Lang.'

'If Mr. Chapman was just an extraordinarily good actor, how could he achieve his wonderful healing results?'

'Well, there of course I can't speak from *personal* knowledge because the only case I saw for myself was the inconclusive one of Mr. Raymond,' Dr. Stephanides replied. 'But let me say this: I believe that spirit healing actually takes place. The only thing is that, so far, we don't know the laws of spirit healing or how it works.

'Although I haven't had any first-hand experience, I have read a good deal about spirit healing. So far we haven't discovered enough about its laws. Very often, people who don't believe in spirit healing are cured, and yet others who do believe in it find that the effects are sometimes negligible, even negative.

'The healer himself appears, too, to have his ups and downs. Over a period he may have a long chain of successes and then suddenly, and for some time, lose some or all his power. Even if he doesn't do this, another curious phenomenon may occur in which, sometimes, he may treat three patients in succession and achieve good results with two of them while the third, whose case seems exactly similar, will show no improvement. And that's the reason why it's difficult to assess exactly what the overall results of spirit healing are.

'There is also the great difficulty of knowing how far auto-suggestion comes into it. This is a very important force indeed, because it can make a person better or worse. I mean, a person can imagine himself to be far worse or better than he actually is.'

'Is it possible to cure cancer, for instance, by auto-suggestion?' I cut in.

'Personally I don't know of any case myself where it has been done or tried, but so little is known of the forces of the body itself as it were, that one really cannot say what auto-suggestion can or cannot cure.

'Auto-suggestion seems to be a very strong force. Cases have been known—let's say for instance in an epidemic of plague in India—when people die of fear because they convince themselves they have indeed got the plague. Incredible as it may seem, these victims of auto-suggestion die with many of the symptoms of the disease, although post-mortem examinations prove that the bacillus is absent.

'It is also well known that where a patient has an illness—practically any illness—and the doctor tells them, "Oh, you'll soon be better," the patient has a much better chance of recovery. But if the doctor were to shake his head and say: "I don't think much can be done, you'll be dead in a few days," the chances are that the patient will get worse almost immediately.

'There is a huge gap in our knowledge of what exactly influences the human body. There's where I think research ought to be done to try and find out what I'd call the *laws* of spirit healing. Then one would know more about it and could assess easier which patients would benefit from spirit healing and those who would not.'

'Generally speaking, do you accept that spirit healing might help a patient who doesn't respond to orthodox medical treatment?' I asked.

'Yes, I think so,' Dr. Stephanides said. 'I think there is ample evidence of the great effectiveness of spirit healing. Take Lourdes, for instance. No one can deny that countless cases have been treated there with most remarkable success. And not only at Lourdes, but also at the Island of Tinos in Greece, where the Virgin of Tinos has achieved, and daily achieves, most wonderful healing results. My father lived many years in India and he said that similar healing results were obtained by people who bathed in the Ganges. It is not just a case of a particular religion being able to bring about miraculous healing results. Lourdes is the healing grotto of the Roman Catholic Church; Tinos is the healing island of the Greek Orthodox Church; and the Ganges is the healing river of Hinduism. Here alone we have three different religions practising spirit healing and I believe there are others who bring about exactly the same sort of fantastic healing results.'

'If you had a patient who didn't respond satisfactorily to orthodox medical treatment, would you advise him to seek William Lang's help?' I asked.

'I'd advise him first to try orthodox medicine and then, if that didn't succeed, to try spirit healing.'

'I am sure you realise that your views are quite exceptional,' I said. 'Because my own experience with members of your profession is that they refuse to entertain the idea of the existence of a spirit body. They see nothing beyond their own sphere and find it inconceivable that spirit healing, which they don't understand, can succeed where medicine often fails.'

'Well, I am of the opinion that orthodox medicine, however advanced in the light of scientific discoveries, knows very little of the forces of the body,' Dr. Stephanides replied. 'There seem to be a lot of things which influence the human body and which have not so far been proved or recognised. This is the reason why I would like to see full research into spirit healing so that an assessment could be made of the assistance it could render orthodox medicine.'

'So you would welcome co-operation between the medical profession and spirit doctors?'

'Yes, if I knew that a patient had tried orthodox medical treatment without success, I'd certainly be only too pleased to advise him to try spirit healing, to consult Dr. Lang. And you can take it from me that I am not by any means the only doctor who believes in the vast possibilities of spirit healing. Have you read, for instance, the books on the subject by Professor Charles Richet and Dr. Alexis Carrel? They were both orthodox medical practitioners, but they believed it was possible to get amazing results from spirit healing. They didn't profess to know *how* the results were obtained, but that they were obtained they were certain.'

I am grateful to Dr. Stephanides for allowing me to publish his views. I only wish that more members of his profession would cultivate his attitude, if only for the reason that any form of treatment, orthodox or unorthodox, which ultimately benefits mankind, is worthy of consideration. Perhaps a more embracing interpretation of the Hippocratic Oath would help them to open the doors to those parts of their minds which remain so tightly shut.

CHAPTER TWENTY

A Matron's unexpected help

THE FOLLOWING case is different from others in as much as the details of the medical history and the spirit healing by Mr. William Lang were not revealed to me by the patient, but by the Matron of the Seven Gables Nursing Home where the spirit operations and treatment were carried out. The matron is Mrs. D. M. Williamson, S.R.N., S.C.M., of Winslow, and the value of her testimony is enhanced, I believe, not only because of her extensive medical knowledge, gathered during a lifetime devoted to nursing, but also the fact that she was present on every occasion Mr. Lang came to visit his patient. Mrs. Williamson was thus able to satisfy herself about the spirit doctor's unique abilities.

'Mrs. Jo Brown, who had been transferred to us from Stoke Mandeville Hospital in early September 1958,' Mrs. Williamson told me when I saw her at Winslow on October 26, 1964, 'had sustained a broken neck and other multiple injuries in an accident. She had been at Stoke Mandeville Hospital for several months but her condition was regarded as hopeless. It defeated the best that medical science could do. The patient was completely paralysed from her neck down. She was unable to lift her head off the pillow, or even turn it, and had difficulty in taking in food when being fed. There were certain functional disabilities.

'When Mrs. Brown was admitted here, her husband told me that he had arranged for a Mr. George Chapman of Aylesbury to call and see his wife to try and help her. He explained that Mr. Chapman was the medium of the spirit doctor William Lang. Mr. Brown was concerned about my reaction to the news and to pacify me and secure my help, he emphasised that his sole purpose was to try *anything* that might possibly help his wife.

'I must admit I felt somewhat lost for words. Having been so closely connected with the medical profession all my working life, it was only natural that I had never given a thought to spiritual healing or spirit doctors—to be quite frank, I did not even know that either existed. Although I was far from convinced that it could achieve any benefit, I could well understand the anxious husband being ready to try *anything* to help his wife. Knowing the doctors' verdict on this patient and her pitiable condition, I had to admit that nothing could be lost by trying spiritual healing—although it was hard to understand what could be gained. In the circumstances I told Mr. Brown that I thought he was right to try.

'When Mr. Chapman arrived at the Nursing Home, for a reason I cannot explain, I immediately felt that here was an honest and sincere man. Before taking him to Mrs. Brown's bedroom I talked to him for a moment about her condition and explained to him that the doctors at the hospital were of the opinion she would never again walk or be able to move about. It was obvious to me, though, that he had no medical knowledge at all, and I couldn't help feeling that his visit was going to be a waste of time, and, worse, a shattering disappointment to poor Mr. Brown, not to mention his wife.

'As soon as we went into Mrs. Brown's room, Mr. Chapman told her in a very reassuring manner that Dr. Lang would do everything possible to help her. As he sat at the bedside, I watched him closely and noticed that his eyes were closed, as though going to sleep. It seemed to me that his face changed and became older. His body too seemed to shrink. After a time he stood up, stretched out his hand in greeting to me and said: "Good morning, young lady, I am grateful to you for having allowed me to come." His voice was entirely different from Mr. Chapman's. It was gruffer, the voice of an old man, and the way he spoke was very cultured. It was a remarkable experience for me I assure you.

'Mr. Chapman introduced himself as Dr. William Lang, and walked over to Mrs. Brown's bedside. While touching her head, arms and body lightly with his hands, he correctly diagnosed her condition. I was stunned. I am a trained nurse of considerable experience and I was astounded by the accuracy of his diagnosis. Incredible as it may seem, when he said he was sure he would be able to help, I half believed him. I don't know why, but I did. His warning that the process of recovery would be long increased my confidence in him because, if Mrs. Brown could be helped at all, it was obvious that it could only be done step-by-step.'

Mrs. Williamson remembered Mr. Lang's explanation about the spirit body and the physical body, and how operating on the former would transfer its effect to the latter. 'It was a little bit much for me to digest,' she said. 'I had never before heard anything like it. He radiated so much confidence that I could not take my eyes away from him. I have had a lot of experience in the operating theatre, and the way his hands moved a little above the patient's head and body was so real as to suggest that a most delicate operation was being carried out. I tell you, I was transfixed.

'Afterwards Dr. Lang told me he was quite certain the effect of his surgery would transfer from the spirit body to the physical body, and he said he would come again in two days' time to perform further operations. He asked me if I would co-operate with him, and when I assented, he told me exactly what he wanted me to do—gentle massage of the patient's neck at the site of the vertebrae.

'He then went back to his chair, and very soon I was again facing Mr. Chapman. He was once more as tall and upright as when I'd first met him, his face having changed to that of a youngish man, and his voice having reverted to the normal timbre before going into trance. I was left in no doubt that I had in fact met two entirely different people.

'Dr. Lang continued visiting Mrs. Brown once or twice a week, and every time he performed his spirit operations I was present. During each visit he instructed me exactly on what he wished me to do, and of course I did it. He was very grateful for the co-operation. But you should have seen Mrs. Brown!

'Gradually, she was able to use her fingers; then she began to lift her arm a little and also her legs; she could turn her head from side to side and make other movements. It was really marvellous the way she recovered, and all this after what the doctors had said.

'I saw to it that Dr. Lang's instructions were carried out in every detail. The gentle massage on Mrs. Brown's vertebrae improved the placement of that part of the spinal column and enabled the spinal fluid to flow more normally. We used to encourage her to push, move and draw her legs up, and use her hands. With help, she began to feed herself and eventually was able to do this quite comfortably. Her next victory was to comb her hair, very unsteadily at first, but with perseverance she managed. It was a case of co-operation between the spirit doctor and medicine.

'Then one marvellous day Dr. Lang decided we should try and get her to stand. I remember him saying to her: "Now you really can stand up, you can do it, you are all right and you'll soon be able to walk." She was terribly nervous, but we gave her all the encouragement we could, and told her it would be all right. With a little help she stood up, very slowly and shakily, and then she straightened up and stood there, unable to believe it, trembling with excitement and her eyes shining. Afterwards, we were present at the side of her bed twice a day to give her confidence while she stood up. It took about six months until she could, with help, walk about her room.

'Three months after Dr. Lang had first visited Mrs. Brown, we were able to drive her to Bletchley station to meet her husband each week-end when he came to visit her. I remember the first time. We had not told Mr. Brown what we intended to do, we just got her ready, put her into the car, and she was at the station waiting for him. He was so excited, he couldn't believe that it was his own wife waiting there for him.

'Mrs. Brown stayed at our Nursing Home for a year, and throughout that time Dr. Lang came to visit her each week. He was as pleased and thrilled with her wonderful progress as were all of us.

'When she left us, she was able to walk—with someone at her side because she was still nervous but she could stand unaided. It was just a matter of time and of gaining confidence.

'During his visits I spoke to Dr. Lang in what you might call medical jargon—as I would talk in my capacity as matron to any consultant specialist visiting a patient. Over the months I came to have a great admiration for this gifted man, and having seen the results of his treatment, I found myself seeking him out whenever either myself or my daughter needed treatment of any kind.'

I asked Mrs. Williamson about her own indisposition and she said:

'I had suffered for a long time with bladder trouble, and I also had trouble with my legs. I had had medical attention, but it didn't do me any good and I thought I just had to accept the situation.

'When I consulted Dr. Lang he told me he would help me. It was completely painless and I am not exaggerating when I saw that he indeed succeeded in curing my trouble.

'With regard to my daughter Chérie, her eyesight deteriorated considerably after an attack of measles. We first noticed it when her piano teacher told us that she was unable to read the music. She was seen by an eye specialist who tried to correct her impaired vision by prescribing spectacles for her but, even so, her eyesight remained poor. The specialist said that there was nothing else he could do for her.

'I took Chérie to see Dr. Lang. He attended to her eyes and the result was that her vision improved tremendously. She no longer has any difficulty and, in fact, passed her driving test. Before she went to Dr. Lang her vision would not have been good enough. From having to wear spectacles regularly she is able to take them off whenever she wants and can see quite well without them. Chérie is an actress, and this relief is quite important to her, especially when she appears on television. In fact when she has any part that calls for a girl with normal eyesight she can act it.

'We are not what you would call "convinced Spiritualists", but we take a great interest in it since we met Dr. Lang. He does an excellent job in this world, and I only wish that many more members of the medical profession would work with him. By doing so, they would help him to help people who otherwise might be destined to die before their time, or are condemned to live in misery and pain.'

CHAPTER TWENTY-ONE

Drama on the A–41

SATURDAY, SEPTEMBER 6, 1958, started like any other ordinary working day for George Chapman. He left his house as usual in the morning to drive his car from Aylesbury to Birmingham to enable Mr. Lang to keep his appointments with his patients at the Healing Centre. It was an uneventful journey—George Chapman knew the road well and drove at his customary speed so as to arrive at the Midlands town in good time.

And, as on most occasions, there were so many patients at the Centre that it was rather late in the day when the last visitor left, and George Chapman was able to become his own self again.

George was obliged to stay overnight in Birmingham, because appointments had been made for some patients to be seen on Sunday morning at Brownhills Spiritualist Church.

The return journey to Aylesbury early on Sunday afternoon was once more one of those routine trips. Chapman, travelling at a speed of about 85 m.p.h. on the straight stretches of the A–41, soon had Solihull, Warwick and Banbury behind him. If conditions remained favourable, he expected to cover the next twelve miles to Bicester in under ten minutes, and reach his home within half an hour.

He was about four miles north-west of Bicester when it happened.

The nearside front tyre burst while the speedometer needle was climbing towards the nineties. The car went out of control, and then began to roll over and over. The driver of a car behind saw the whole thing. He told police later that the speeding Citroën must have turned over ten times before it came to rest. His wife verified this.

When I asked George Chapman to tell me what he thought and did at the moment of accident, he replied:

'When the car became uncontrollable and started to roll over, I thought: I must get out quickly. I had my tank almost full of petrol and feared it might explode and engulf the car in flames. Almost at the same moment I could see myself lying on the rear seat as though asleep and the thought occurred to me that my spirit body was in fact examining my physical body.

'Then I saw myself suddenly standing outside the car and looking at the wreck. At that time I didn't know whether I existed in my physical or spirit body. I actually wondered if those who spoke to me were discarnate, but the feeling gradually grew upon me that I was still on earth.'

The motorist who witnessed the accident said that, almost immediately after the car stopped turning over, he and his wife saw its driver standing beside the car looking at it as it rested on its roof.

'How did you manage to get out?' I asked Chapman.

'I have no recollection of leaving the car,' he answered. 'In my dazed condition I assumed that I must have crawled out through the broken windscreen, but I couldn't have done so because it was intact, and so were the other windows.'

'Could you perhaps have crawled out through your open offside front window?'

'It was open, but only about five inches,' he said. (The police report confirms this.) 'Yet, although I don't know how I got out, I found myself outside without being seriously hurt,' he went on. 'The only injury I had was a cut on my head.'

'What about the doors?' I persisted, trying to get an explanation of how he managed to escape. 'Couldn't you have opened a door and . . .?'

'That's no good either,' Chapman replied. 'Neither the driver behind me, nor the police and insurance surveyor, could explain how it had been possible to get out of the car. Not a window was broken but they could not be opened, and when the police patrol arrived on the scene they found that every door was still *locked from the inside!* I couldn't have opened a door and got out through it, and the windows, too, were jammed.'

The car was so badly damaged that the insurance company

considered it a write-off. Yet neither the windscreen nor any of the windows were broken or even cracked!

The incident was investigated by the Bicester police (Oxfordshire Constabulary), and the facts recorded by the officers who probed the accident confirmed every word George Chapman told me. The police report stated: Doors locked from inside. Doors and windows immovable due to damage. Windscreen and windows unbroken and shut with exception of front offside window which was lowered 5 inches from top. Driver cannot explain how he left wrecked car. . . .

'How do you think you got out?' I pressed.

'Well, I don't know really. All I can say is: I feel that although this incident demonstrates a good example of involuntary spirit projection, it also goes much deeper and shows that in circumstances of absolute extremity spirit power can apparently overcome physical laws. One could perhaps also say it is materialisation in reverse or something like that.'

One other unexplainable thing needs to be recorded.

'The following day, in the company of a former Superintendent of Police, I visited the scene of the accident,' Chapman recalled. 'We both carefully examined the wrecked vehicle, and then the surface of the road. We were surprised to find that it bore no signs of an accident—not even a tyre mark was to be seen.'

I should perhaps add that the cut on his head which he had sustained during the car accident was completely gone after a full day of trance healing on Monday, September 8, 1958. Mr. Lang attended to his medium so perfectly that not even the slightest sign remained of a bloody wound he had carried that morning as he went into trance.

CHAPTER TWENTY-TWO

The End of a Twenty-year Hell

PATRICK P. CALDER of Ballinger suffered for twenty years from spondylitis. Yet, although he was under constant medical care and everything known in medicine was done for him, he found no relief from his ailment.

'I suffered with spondylitis from 1942 until 1961,' Mr. Calder told me in December 1964. 'During these years I had hospital treatment for it in 1944 while I was in Italy with the Forces and again in 1948 when I was in Scotland. Later, when I came south, I received regular treatment at Lambeth Hospital in London. The orthopaedic specialist was Dr. Robb, and he did everything he could to help me. I was receiving radio-therapy at regular intervals, but it didn't help.

'Ten years went by, and I had become worse. The doctors could do no more than they were doing already and made it plain that it was one of those cases in which the patient had to reconcile himself to the fact that no other alternative treatment was possible.

'My health deteriorated so alarmingly in 1958 that I became really desperate, but fortunately for me someone told me about spiritual healing, and in particular about the spirit doctor William Lang who worked through the mediumship of a Mr. George Chapman in Aylesbury. I was told Dr. Lang had cured many people whom doctors and hospitals had classed as incurable, and I was advised to find out if I, too, could be helped. I had nothing to lose—throughout my illness my only relief was codeine tablets—so I decided to give Mr. Chapman and his spirit doctor a try.

'Well, I met Dr. Lang on October 27, 1958. Although I was a little nervous—and naturally also somewhat sceptical—the elderly spirit doctor with his kindly approach and his reassuring way put me at my ease. We had a little talk and then he asked me to lie down on the healing couch.

'While he examined me, we spoke about the radio-therapy treatment I had received at Lambeth Hospital; he told me he did not approve of it as it dried up the natural fluid in the joints and left them without any natural lubricant. He told me he would operate on my spirit body and was certain he could cure me of my complaint if I was prepared to undergo treatment from him at regular intervals for a considerable time. I was willing to do anything that would help me to get rid of the spondylitis which was crippling me.

'It was a strange experience. Although he was not using visible instruments, I used to feel the inoculations as the spirit needle was inserted into my spine. It was a sensation I can hardly describe because I had a sort of champagne feeling when I got off the couch.

'Dr. Lang asked me to come and see him again in six months' time for further contact healing, and asked me in the meantime to regularly report my state of health to Mr. Chapman, so that contact could be maintained and I could continue to receive spirit treatment during my sleep state. I did this and began to improve slowly but surely.

'I saw Dr. Lang at six-monthly intervals—in April and October every year—and at every visit he performed additional operations. After six visits—the last one was in April 1961—my back was completely cured and I was free of it and never experience even the slightest twinge. I am a self-employed garden contractor and get through a lot of hard and rough work every day. I would certainly have been unable to do what I do but for Dr. Lang.'

Apart from freeing Mr. Calder from spondylitis, Mr. Lang also attended to a cyst on his right wrist by means of an operation on his spirit body. This cyst had troubled Mr. Calder to such an extent that he had planned to see his doctor about it. However, Mr. Lang noticed it and dealt with it in his usual painless way.

Mr. Calder recalled the occasion: 'The cyst on my right wrist was about the size of a pigeon's egg, very painful, and Dr. Lang got rid of it without fuss or bother.

'A few days after he performed the spirit operation, a small red scar appeared on the wrist. As the days went by it disappeared, and I then noticed that something strange was taking place on top of the lump. The skin seemed to be dying and withering and then a small blister began to form between the layers of the skin.

'Then, one day when my wife and I were out in the car, my wife suddenly asked me what was on my wrist. Out of the top of the lump a clear jelly-like stuff was oozing. With the help of my wife I pressed the lump until it was free of fluid. It didn't hurt at all, and afterwards the cyst disappeared.

'All that I'm left with is a small red scar about the size of a sixpence. Actually I'm rather proud of it and show it off whenever I get the chance.'

CHAPTER TWENTY-THREE

The doubting Oculist

TEN YEARS ago, Mrs. Joan D. Harris, M.A. (Oxon) of Maidenhead, had to face up to the unpalatable fact that she would have to wear a steel jacket. The reason for this went back many years, to a time when a serious injury caused a crushed disc in her spine. The back injury was eventually remedied, but, as Mrs. Harris told me in November 1964, there was another distressing side effect.

'My sight was affected,' she said. 'Whenever I took up a book, I could only manage to read a single page, and then everything became terribly blurred. I was not very old and to be unable to read was really a dreadful blow. I went to see the ophthalmic consultant under whose care I'd been for years, but when he examined my eyes, particularly the left one which was the troublemaker, he asked me if I had been accustomed to doing much fine work. I told him that I had taken a degree in mathematics which entailed doing a lot of fine drawing at one time. I had also done considerable embroidering. He said: "Well, there is no question of doing any more, you must drop it, because I can't correct your eyes. I can't do anything for you. You'll have to be content with reading a little at a time, and when your vision gets blurred, put the book down, look around the room and take a break before starting again. But don't read too much." He consoled me by saying that he didn't think my eyesight would get any worse, and said he'd give me some spectacles for long distance and reading. The idea, I think, was that they would help just a little, but that I couldn't expect any radical change for the better. He left it at that.

'Then, fortunately for me, I was given a copy of the *Psychic News* by a friend containing an article about Dr. Lang in which it was revealed that he was once a Moorfields man. I came to the opinion that I ought to see him. There was, I realised, nothing any eye specialist could do for me, and I had nothing to lose by seeking help elsewhere.

'My appointment with Dr. Lang was for the early afternoon of June 17, 1959.

'When I arrived at Mr. Chapman's house and his wife admitted me, I thought what a lovely atmosphere there was in the house and how charming Mrs. Chapman was. Then Mr. Chapman came in and I found I liked him enormously. He was a really genuine sort of man, very much interested in healing, and very kind. In meeting certain people one may have immediate reservations, even regret, but it was exactly the opposite with Mr. Chapman. I trusted him at once and thought, "Everything will be all right."

'Having talked with him for some little time about ordinary things, we went into Dr. Lang's consulting-room where he sat in a chair, a very healthy, virile and upright middle-aged man. And as he sat there with his eyes closed, I saw him changing—he shrank into an aged man in a most extraordinary fashion!

'When he got up a minute or two later and greeted me with "Good afternoon, Mrs. Harris," his voice was entirely different. In Dr. Lang's voice there is not the slightest resemblance to Mr. Chapman's, none whatever. Dr. Lang's voice is cultured, very old and rather tired. His choice of words and manner of speaking was most striking. Listening to Dr. Lang's speech, it struck me how much faster we talk these days.

'That afternoon was perhaps one of the most astonishing occasions throughout my life. I was surprised when Dr. Lang said to me: "You have come about your eyes, haven't you?" When I indicated this was so, he told me reassuringly, "Oh, we'll see to that." I had not mentioned in my letter to Mr. Chapman the reason for the appointment I asked for, and when I talked with him before he went into trance, we did not discuss my disability.

'When Dr. Lang told me: "There is something else, you know, that must be dealt with as well," I looked at him questioningly and thought immediately of my back. But I dismissed the thought, because everything that could be done for it had been done.

' "You know, don't you," he said, "that you look as if you are overweight? You are somewhat, but a lot of you is puffed up." I replied: "Yes I know I'm a bit plump, but I didn't realise that I was 'puffed up', as you put it." He said: "It's not so much your overweight that worries me, it's that you *are* puffed up. It must be put right. It is very bad for you."

'I looked at him in some surprise as he said: "I'll give you a diet that will put you right, but you must keep to it under my guidance for not longer than a month. You must not pass it on to anybody else, or use it again unless I tell you to do so."

'He then said: "We'll do your eye now. You needn't worry, it will be painless and all you need to do is to lie still, relax and keep your eyes shut—don't open them." Usually I don't find it easy to follow this advice, because I am very highly strung. I know this. Lying on the healing couch, however, I felt relaxed in a quite extraordinary fashion, almost as if I had been helped by someone else, rather like the feeling you have when you are given injections before surgery. I didn't open my eyes, but I think he must have seen from my expression that I was wondering what he was doing. He said: "Oh, Basil is my son and he is helping me and he knows what I mean when I click my fingers."

'The operation was completely painless, but I could feel something like cold metal above and beneath my eye. The whole thing took very little time.

'When he told me that everything was finished, Dr. Lang said: "Just a moment, keep your eyes shut and rest." And as I remained lying on the couch he continued operating. He explained that I should wait a month before seeing the ophthalmic consultant again and he advised me to have them tested every year. Until then I used to see the specialist every two years, but I was more than willing to take this advice.

'Before I left Dr. Lang, he told me that he regretted he was unable to make my eyes well enough to dispose with spectacles altogether, but that doesn't worry me now because I can see well enough with this aid. Dr. Lang said: "You will have no more trouble with your eyes. You will see clearly and you will not again be troubled by distorted vision. Nor will there be for the rest of your life."

'He asked me if by any chance I had paper and pencil with me, or a pen, because he wanted me to write down a note to my oculist.

Luckily I had, but I asked him if he really wanted me to pass on a message to the oculist. I mean it does strike one as a bit odd, doesn't it?

' "Yes, I want you to tell him what I have done," Dr. Lang said, and began to spell out for me the word "chemosis". "It means," he explained, "the aqueous fluid is not clear. That's why when you try to read everything looks as if it is under water." I'd never heard of "chemosis" and "aqueous liquid" before! Dr. Lang continued by spelling out the words "occipito frontalis", explaining: "This means that the muscle has dropped and therefore there is pressure on the retina; these two things combined made it difficult for you to see but I have now put everything right. I want you to pass on these details to your oculist." I promised I would.

'When I returned home to Maidenhead in the late afternoon, I felt rather tired and disinclined to do anything. I decided I would not attempt to read and, in view of the operation, to give my eyes a rest. But the next morning, when I picked up the newspaper from the breakfast table, I found I could read the newsprint easily without the small letters clouding.

'It hit me all of a sudden. "Good gracious, I haven't had to look up and blink once!" You know what I'm getting at, don't you? It meant my sight was all right. And, since that afternoon of June 17, 1959, when Dr. Lang performed his spirit operation on my left eye, I have never had the slightest trouble.

'I carried out to the letter the instructions Dr. Lang had given me regarding diet. The regimen was severe, to say the least and normally I'd have found a great deal of difficulty in keeping to it. For some unknown reason I took it in my stride, and the enormous puffiness just fell away from me during that month. And it disappeared for good, just like pricking a balloon. I've never put it back since and as a result I feel much better.

'I went to see the ophthalmic consultant a month after I'd seen Dr. Lang. He examined my left eye and confirmed that the impossible had happened—that my eye was completely cured. I told him about Dr. Lang and read out to him the message which had been dictated to me. He looked at me with raised eyebrows and said: "Well, of course you don't see mistily any more." I replied: "No, I don't," but he had nothing further to say, then or subsequently, when I've seen him each year. I've often thought it was a pity that he didn't respond in any way, because I felt Dr. Lang would like to have drawn him into it.

'Four years passed, and during this time I received distant healing from Dr. Lang. I have had arthritis, particularly in my hands and in my knee, and I also suffered from asthma and hayfever. I felt considerable relief from the distant healing, but last year I was in real trouble with bronchitis, asthma with hayfever, sinus, catarrh, the whole works—I was full of it. I decided to see Dr. Lang again and made an appointment for June 12, 1963. Again I didn't say exactly what was wrong with me. I only wrote that I wished to come and see him.

'When I entered the consulting room, Dr. Lang said: "Good afternoon, Mrs. Harris, I am happy to see you again." Almost immediately he added: "You know, you are very full of catarrh, both in your head and chest." Well, I was dumbfounded, all I could say was: "That's what I have come to see you about."

'Dr. Lang then asked me to lie on the healing couch and he worked on my left lung which is always the one that fills first. I could feel how the gummed-up feeling, as I call it, just went. He snapped his fingers and asked Basil for some injection—I wish I could remember what he called it—and I could almost feel the injection by the pressure. "That will relieve you a lot," he told me, and he was right. Until then I had had to breathe through my mouth and the pressure was as if I had a welt across my eyebrows from the swollen sinus, but he moved it all. It was wonderful how speedily he relieved me.

'After the spirit operation and treatment, Dr. Lang explained to me that he couldn't cure asthma and hayfever, or prevent the onset of these complaints. The most he could do was to keep them under control by continuing to give me distant healing. This is being maintained and it undoubtedly helps me.

'I haven't been back to see Dr. Lang since June 1963, the distant healing keeps my arthritis, asthma and hayfever at bay. However, as far as my eye and the overweight are concerned, I have never had any trouble since he performed his spirit operations during that remarkable afternoon in June 1959.'

CHAPTER TWENTY-FOUR

The mending of a former Conservative M.P.

THE CASE of Mr. Norman Bower, M.A.—a non-practising barrister-at-law and former Conservative Member of Parliament for Harrow West—is remarkable because he had been suffering from liver trouble and spastic colon for almost thirty-five years. It was his state of health that forced him to give up his career in Parliament. He was told about Mr. Lang—at a time when he needed help most urgently, and decided to go to Aylesbury. Mr. Lang performed a painless operation on his spirit body, and as a result of it and subsequent healing, Mr. Bower was completely cured of his ailment within ten months.

George Chapman mentioned Mr. Bower's case history to me in the summer of 1964, and told me that this ex-patient might be willing to give me full details about his experience. I contacted Mr. Bower and a few days later was invited to his London flat in Mayfair. First reactions on meeting him pointed to the fact that he was a highly literate man with a lively mind and a rational way of thinking.

Norman Bower was born in 1907 in Hampstead, the son of a prosperous businessman. He was educated at Rugby and Oxford.

'From about the time I was twenty I suffered with my liver,' he told me. 'To be honest I did not know what the deuce was wrong with me until I came across a doctor in the South of France on an occasion when I was visiting my mother. She used to winter out there. Well, I was talking to this chap, telling him how I felt and all that, and he told me that my liver was enlarged and I ought to diet. I was not to eat anything fried, avoid all alcohol except claret and leave things such as eggs, pastries, chocolate, etc., alone.

'I must admit that while I observed this diet, I felt quite all right, but if I deviated from it at all, I became ill again. Of course at that age one tends to forget medical advice. I'm afraid I did, and in fact after about a year I became very lax indeed. Forgot all about it, didn't stick to the instructions at all. But by golly I paid for my stupidity. I got some really nasty attacks again.'

Mr. Bower studied law and although he became a barrister, he did not take up the profession and instead went into business. His interest in politics was aroused from the time he was at Rugby and Oxford. It was a subject constantly in his mind. 'But there was the question of getting an opening, and that's not always easy. It takes time if one has no particular influence, and I had none at all. My father had no political connections and party affairs did not appeal to him. Well, I simply went about it in the only way I knew. At Oxford I took part in its various political activities with some enthusiasm, and did a certain amount of speaking at the Union and other meetings. When I came down, I went along to the Conservative Party Central Office, in London. I'd decided by this time that this was the party I wanted to belong to. I got my name put down on their list as a candidate. Eventually I was put on a short list, and I don't remember how many times I tried to get adopted. I used to go all over the country, trying various constituencies, and I got turned down times out of number.

'At long last I got the opportunity to fight a more or less hopeless seat in the General Election of 1931. I was defeated, and again in 1935 in similar circumstances. But I hadn't done too badly, not badly at all.'

When the Second World War broke out, intensified political campaigns came to an end. The outbreak of war also brought about the closing down of Mr. Bower's successful business venture and he joined the army.

'I practically put politics out of my mind then,' Mr. Bower continued. 'Then, by an extraordinary chance, a by-election occurred in Harrow during the war, and my application for adoption was accepted. My political luck had turned. I had the experience of course, and having fought previous seats, I had a good deal of political knowledge and acumen, and that happened to appeal to them. And

I was the right age—thirty-four. They quite liked the idea of having someone from the army. So there it was, I became an M.P.'

Mr. Bower's activities as a Conservative Member of Parliament for Harrow West seemed to mark him out for a prominent political career. He was not only liked and respected by his colleagues in the House, but became also fairly well acquainted with Winston Churchill. But Norman Bower's ascent to political prominence was prematurely cut short.

'It was the spastic colon that finally compelled me to give up my political career,' Mr. Bower recalled regretfully. 'This unpleasant and serious condition so affected my health that both my doctor and my specialist warned me that I was unlikely to recover unless I led a less strenuous existence. And the specialist warned me that my illness was partly accentuated by a nervous condition and it was imperative for me to lead a very quiet life if I wanted to avoid still greater trouble. So I had no other alternative but to give up my seat in the House of Commons.'

Neither antibiotics nor any other treatment improved Norman Bower's health, and towards the end of 1961 he began to suffer from a distressing type of distension after meals. Fearing that it might be a growth or some other serious condition, he consulted his doctor and was advised that until an X-ray was made no diagnosis was possible. Before this took place, the doctor decided to try a course of tablets but they were of no help.

Mr. Bower viewed the forthcoming test with some apprehension. He had had previous experience of barium—the sulphate powder that the patient has to take in liquefied form prior to an internal X-ray.

'It is terrible stuff,' Mr. Bower recalled. 'And I was afraid it might make me ten times worse. I was terrified.

'Fortunately Miss Yeatman of the College of Psychic Science had in the meantime told me about Dr. Lang and Mr. Chapman, and I thought I would like to go and see him. I was pretty desperate and had great hopes that spiritual healing might help me.'

On February 20, 1962, Mr. Bower wrote to George Chapman, requesting a consultation with Mr. Lang. He was particularly careful not to disclose any details about his condition and just stated: 'I feel very unwell. My doctor suggests a form of examination which I am anxious to avoid. Due to my serious condition, I should be obliged if an early appointment could be arranged.' George Chapman arranged for Mr. Bower to see Mr. Lang on February 27. This was how Mr. Bower described his visit to Aylesbury:

'When I went into the consulting room, I wasn't prepared for what I encountered. I anticipated seeing Mr. Chapman to begin with, and was surprised to find he was already in trance. I thought it very strange. I had seen his photograph and he didn't resemble it in the slightest way. I knew that Mr. Chapman was about forty but the gentleman I faced was unmistakably an elderly man.

'It only dawned on me then that I was meeting Dr. Lang. He greeted me and introduced himself. He talked to me about the Middlesex Hospital and Moorfields, and he spoke in a way I imagine a Victorian or Edwardian doctor would speak. I was staggered, really.

'I saw that his eyes were closed and that seemed to me to be peculiar. Nevertheless, he was capable of walking about the room without any difficulty and was able to avoid anything in his way. He asked me how old I was, and when I told him, he remarked that I looked younger.

'He told me a number of things about himself and his son Basil who had also been a surgeon. He said Basil was now helping him with his spirit operations. Then he started examining my spectacles and remarked, "My goodness, don't they make them big these days." In his days, I imagine, spectacles were either rimless or had thin silver or gold frames.

'He passed his hands over my eyes—gently, without really touching—and told me at once that the fluid at the back of my eyes had become disturbed some years ago when I had suddenly lifted some heavy weight, and that ever since I had periodically seen little black spots floating across my vision. They didn't actually impair my sight. *I* knew this of course. But how did he? I don't think it could have been through telepathy because nothing was further from my mind. I had come for help for another reason and was certainly not worried about my eyes.

'Then he passed his hands all the way down my fully clothed body, and almost immediately started telling me about my illness. He mentioned the various symptoms I had and explained how they affected each organ. These symptoms were of course familiar to me and I wondered if his knowledge of them could have been obtained through telepathy. But there was one thing which finally convinced me that it had *not* been telepathy. These were the terms "intestinal diverticulum" and "diverticulosis", which he went to the trouble of spelling out for me. I can absolutely swear that I'd never heard them before and, consequently, they could not have been in my mind. Later, I asked a doctor if he had heard of these terms and he confirmed that he knew them.

'I told Dr. Lang that my doctor wanted me to have an examination which I was anxious to avoid, and he replied, "Well, the X-rays would not have shown anything, because what you are suffering from would not reveal itself in this way. No doubt they would then want to carry out an exploratory operation. It is just as well that you didn't have it." I accepted all he said as reasonable.

'Dr. Lang then told me that in the past I had had an enlarged liver and this was now causing inflammation. He said he would perform a spirit operation.

'While I lay on the couch, he told me: "I've got my son Basil here—he's going to assist me," and then he called for various instruments. And each time he used one he flicked his fingers. I imagined that when he did this he was using the instrument in a certain way, but I didn't feel anything, not a thing. After about five minutes, he went through the motion of sewing up.

'He then told me that it was all over, and asked me to sit up again in the chair. He told me that he would give me distant healing, but he said that he felt that my condition would improve only gradually. "I think you'll be quite all right," he said. "It won't be an instantaneous cure, but I feel confident that you are on the right road and you'll find that there will be a steady improvement."

'He instructed me what I was to do so far as diet was concerned, and what he advised was much the same regimen as my French doctor had suggested many years ago. He asked me to write once a month about my state of health.

'When I left Dr. Lang's, or Mr. Chapman's, consulting room, I felt I must not be hostile, or sceptical, but rather to take it for what it was, because only later would I be able to judge by the results. Should these prove successful, I'd have proof of the unique power of spiritual healing. I ought to say, however, that I was very hopeful of the results, and in a sense thankful that—whatever the explanation of this phenomenon—I had been given the chance of recovery.

'The more I thought about my visit to Aylesbury—and cogitated on the possibility of Dr. Lang really being a secondary personality of Mr. Chapman the firmer grew my conviction that I had indeed met the old doctor. I was sure I would have liked him as my medical adviser. He was very forthright and kindly and had a great store of medical knowledge and experience.

'I went home and the same night, after dinner, I felt there was a slight improvement. I could feel the trouble in some way resolving itself in the form of wind which I was able to get rid of. And the distension began to lessen. It was less painful than it had been for some months past.'

Mr. Lang continued giving Mr. Bower distant healing, and four months after his visit to Aylesbury, on June 25, the patient was able to write the following letter:

'I am glad to report a further very pronounced improvement in my condition during the past month. I have since been pretty well one hundred per cent normal—better than at any time since the start of the trouble last October. I feel that provided I continue to be careful about my diet, which is clearly very important, my recovery is now so well established that no further distant healing is necessary.'

Complying with Mr. Bower's wish, distant healing was discontinued, but the result was the following letter which the patient wrote to George Chapman the following month:

'I think perhaps that the distant healing I had received was terminated prematurely, before my recovery was properly consolidated, as I have not been feeling so well this month. I have again been getting intermittent attacks of intestinal inflammation causing a certain amount of pain and distension, though they are not nearly as bad as they were when I visited Dr. Lang in February.

'Do you think a resumption of distant healing for a further period of, say, a month or two might be beneficial, or is a complete and absolute recovery from this sort of condition too much to hope for? I should be most grateful if it is possible for you to obtain Dr. Lang's opinion on this point.'

William Lang's opinion was: 'This condition can be cured completely', and he recommended distant healing. Mr. Bower's next letter to George Chapman, written on August 26, 1962, read as follows:

'I am glad to say that I have been considerably better again during the past month. Much of the time I feel quite well, but I still get occasional setbacks if there is any irregularity in the action of the bowels, which is sometimes hard to avoid. However, they are almost invariably short-lived, and the symptoms are very much less severe than they used to be.

'I feel that perhaps one more month of distant healing should bring me to the point where it can be permanently discontinued without my suffering any further setbacks of a major character. I am indeed thankful for the great improvement which has taken place in my condition since I visited Dr. Lang, when I was almost in despair.'

Another month later, on September 23, Mr. Bower wrote again to George Chapman:

'I am pleased to be able to tell you that there has again been a great improvement in my health during the past month. Almost from the day I last wrote to you, my bowels have been acting with much greater ease and regularity than for years past, with the result that I have been able to avoid even the mildest aperient and have consequently experienced no further distension or any other form of intestinal discomfort.

'In fact, I appear to be right back to normal again now. Let me say over again how very grateful I am for all Dr. Lang has been able to do for me from the moment of his remarkable diagnosis to the truly wonderful effects of the distant healing. It would seem that the time has now come for the healing to be discontinued, but I prefer to leave this decision to you.'

Mr. Lang, advised by George Chapman about Mr. Bower's report, decided: 'His ailment responded wonderfully well but I'd like to keep an eye on him for three months longer.' Mr. Bower, however, was not advised about Mr. Lang's decision and believed that the distant healing was no longer given. Indeed, when I spoke to him some two and half years after his visit to Mr. Lang, he told me:

'Despite the fact that distant healing was stopped in the early autumn of 1962, I was completely all right after another three months. My illness cleared up and I've never had any more trouble.'

Mr. Bower is genuinely grateful to Mr. Lang and George Chapman for the painless and complete cure. He says that if ever he becomes ill again, he will immediately turn to George Chapman and his spirit control, William Lang.

CHAPTER TWENTY-FIVE

A Surgeon here and a Surgeon there

MANY OF those who dismiss out of hand the entire concept of spirit healing, do so from a basis of the sketchiest knowledge of the extent of its significance. Prejudice is perhaps the commonest of human failings, as much in this century as in earlier times, and an open mind a rare virtue.

How refreshing is it then to come across an example of clear judgment free of all bias among a profession which has its share of Philistines and closed minds. This story concerns a nurse and a Harley Street surgeon. It is true in every detail and can be verified.

The nurse is Miss Evelyn B. Habershon of Lindfield, Sussex, the surgeon Mr. Vincent Nesfield, F.R.C.S. Eng.; L.R.C.P. Lond.; Major L.M.S. retired.

Evelyn Habershon was born an astigmatic with a blind spot in her left eye. At one time it appeared that her future would be imperilled because of deficient sight, but with the help of spectacles she was able to pursue her studies and eventually qualify as a nurse. Then, in 1958, her vision deteriorated alarmingly. A well-known ophthalmic surgeon told her: 'You have got a cataract which will have to be operated at some time in the future.' This prospect was four years in coming, but in 1962 Evelyn Habershon's sight became so poor that she knew something would have to be done quickly.

'I tried to make an appointment to see the ophthalmic surgeon late in 1962,' she told me, 'but I was told that the earliest date he could see me was the beginning of the following year.

'I already knew Mr. Nesfield's name as an eminent ophthalmologist, and I telephoned him and arranged to see him on November 15, 1962. When he examined me, he confirmed that I was astigmatic, had a blind spot in my left eye, and added: "You have an advanced cataract in the right eye and traces of one in the left. An operation is necessary. I can do it for you at the end of December. Would that suit you?"

'Mr. Nesfield must have known how greatly I feared the operation because, when I saw him again in December and he again examined me, he said: "There's no immediate hurry for this you know. I'm going away at the end of January so suppose we leave it until some time in March or April, when the weather is warmer? I'll let you know. Meanwhile, there's no need to worry." And he left it at that. Needless to say, I was very happy with the unexpected reprieve.

'During Mr. Nesfield's absence I had spiritual healing from Mrs. Catherine Sheppard, a psychic healer, at her sanctuary. In the first week of April 1963 I knew that the cataract had suddenly begun to separate and, as I hadn't heard from Mr. Nesfield, I wrote to him and asked if I could see him because I thought the cataract was separating. Rightly or wrongly I was sure that it was due to my having received spiritual healing. Mr. Nesfield has told me it was an advanced cataract. As a nurse I knew something about these things, and I was certain that a cataract doesn't begin to separate just like that, on its own.

'Mr. Nesfield arranged an appointment for me, and after he looked at my eyes he said that the cataract was indeed separated. He said, simply, "The improvement of your eyes is due to divine healing." I hadn't told him that I had been receiving spiritual healing. And yet he made this observation unhesitatingly.

'Shortly afterwards I heard through the *Psychic News* about the spirit doctor William Lang who had been an outstanding ophthalmic surgeon during his lifetime. I felt that he might be able to help me even more than Catherine Sheppard who, at that time, was very ill. I wrote to Mr. Chapman for an appointment to see Mr. Lang, and went to Aylesbury on May 28, 1963.

'Mr. Lang immediately diagnosed precisely what my trouble was by touching my eyes lightly with his fingers. "A physical operation is not for you, young lady," he said. "I'll perform a spirit operation now," which was what he did. I could hear him asking for scalpels and other instruments, talking with someone he called Basil. After the operation Mr. Lang asked me if I would be returning to Lindfield that same day. I told him I would stay overnight at a hotel in Aylesbury because I was afraid the long train journey back might prove too great a strain for me and undo what God had done for me, working through the doctor. You see, after the operation I felt desperately tired. Mr. Lang was very pleased to hear of my intentions and said: "Go to bed at nine o'clock after a light meal, and I'll come to visit you during your sleep state to see whether anything needs clearing up."

'When I left Mr. Chapman's house, I was astonished at the extent of the improvement the spirit operation had brought about. I had only been able to get about in taxis because of the mist that always swam before my eyes. But now I could suddenly see things around me. I felt I would be able to resume my usual life using a stick as before. Of course I used common sense, I had to be careful of steps, but I *could* see. After that I even started going up to London on my own.

'In June—three weeks after going to Mr. Lang, I went to see Mr. Nesfield. I admitted to him that I had had a spirit operation, and he seemed very interested. He tested my eyes and said he found an enormous improvement, though the centre, the lenses, were not clear yet. But he repeated that part of the cataract was much improved. He knew of course that I hadn't had any physical operation and repeated what he had said two months earlier: "The improvement of your eyes is due to divine healing." He also added: "You have additional sight developed in your left eye." I was so grateful to him for not being annoyed with me for having undergone spirit surgery and treatment, and very moved by his desire to help his patients in every way—even if someone went behind his back to a spirit doctor to seek additional help.'

Miss Habershon saw Mr. Lang again in July 1963, when he performed further operations on her spirit body. There was again an improvement in her vision, and when she went to see Mr. Nesfield afterwards, he confirmed this fact.

These alternate visits to the spirit doctor and the eminent Harley Street specialist continued.

'When I saw Mr. Lang again last July,' Miss Habershon told me in November 1964, 'he told me that my eyes had improved to a quite remarkable degree and were now requiring different glasses. "You can now ask Mr. Nesfield to prescribe glasses for distance," he said, and asked me to give his "colleague", of whom he thought so much, a message: "Tell Mr. Nesfield when he gives you the glasses to have special regard for the macabus muscle." (As I had never heard the term before, or knew what its function was, it is unlikely that I could have made up the message.)

'Now put yourself in my position—a *nurse* was to give an *eminent surgeon* a message from a spirit doctor what to do! I felt very uneasy about it but I knew I must pass on the message. When I saw Mr. Nesfield, I said somewhat uneasily, "I have a message from the spirit doctor William Lang to give you. I can only pass it on, Mr. Nesfield." He was quite marvellous, honestly. He said that those who are in spirit know more than we do. "The surgeons won't accept the fact that there are more things than man understands—they may know it but they will not accept it," he said. And when he tested my eyes and wrote out the prescription for the new glasses for me, he said that Mr. Lang's message made sense and that he was paying attention to it.

'When I saw Mr. Lang again in September, he told how very pleased he was with the progress I had made and he asked me to tender his congratulations to Mr. Nesfield on the spectacles he had prescribed. Mr. Nesfield, however, was away, so I had to tell Mr. Lang, when I saw him again in October, that I would do it when I saw Mr. Nesfield in November. I enquired from Mr. Lang whether I could now have reading glasses. "No, I don't want you to have them yet because for the present it may lead to strain," he said. "Ask Mr. Nesfield what he thinks about the idea. But don't worry, young lady, you won't have to wear those you now have very much longer, you'll get ordinary ones when the time is suitable."

'When I saw Mr. Nesfield a few days ago, on November 13, 1964, I gave him, at long last, Mr. Lang's message about the very good work he'd done with my glasses. He smiled in acknowledgment and, after having examined me thoroughly, he said he was very pleased with my condition which had greatly improved since he last saw me. He endorsed all that Mr. Lang had said. I still haven't got reading glasses. But I'm not worried. I know I'll get them when the time is right.

'Words can hardly express my gratitude to the power of God and to the two distinguished ophthalmic surgeons who have helped me to see again—which means that I am alive once more. And although I know that Mr. Lang gave me back my vision by his numerous operations on my spirit body, I am equally aware of how important to my recovery was Mr. Nesfield's skill and understanding. It was he who prescribed the right glasses for me and co-operated with his spirit doctor "colleague", William Lang.'

CHAPTER TWENTY-SIX

An unexpected Reunion

MRS. ETHEL J. BAILEY of Streatham Hill knew Mr. William Lang in his days as ophthalmic consultant at Moorfields. And when she went to see the spirit doctor William Lang in the autumn of 1963 at Aylesbury, she was left in no doubt but that she was facing the same specialist.

Here is Mrs. Bailey's personal recollections.

'My right eyelid has been completely closed since birth, and every doctor my mother took me to said that it might right itself as I grew up or, failing that, a small operation could be performed in later years to correct it.

'In 1915, when I was twenty-one, I went with my mother to Moorfields in the hope that the time had now come for the long-awaited operation. I was engaged to be married and anxious to be given normal sight before my wedding.

'I was seen by Mr. Lang and, after he'd examined me, his verdict was that he couldn't do much for the "child's" eyelid (he called me "child") because, as he explained, if he operated, the eyelid would remain permanently open. We decided to think matters over before deciding whether or not to go on with the operation. I did not want to have to make my own decision, and therefore wrote to my fiancé, who was in the trenches in France, and asked what he thought about it. I shall always cherish the letter he wrote to me in reply. It ended by saying: "Remember Ethel, I chose you as you are, so leave things well alone." I did. I had nothing at all done and was happy that is what he wanted.

'Years later I became interested in Spiritualism and divine healing.

Then I had a car accident and so seriously injured my back and legs that, for a time, the doctors doubted if I would ever walk normally again. I had always been very active, and suddenly finding I was unable to get out and about, and suffering pain most of the time, my health began to go. Prior to my accident, I had been a patient of Mr. J. J. Thomas, a spiritual trance healer, but he had moved to Brighton, and in view of my condition further visits were out of the question. Fortunately a friend suggested I should visit Mrs. Durrant—Mr. Harry Edward's sister—who lived near me in Streatham. I couldn't walk, and had to have a taxi wherever I went, so, as you can imagine, it cost me quite a bit getting there and back. But it was worth it, because after a time I was actually able to walk again.

'It seemed strange to me though that no one ever spoke about my "lazy" eye and permanently closed lid, or that the spirit guides had not thought it right to help me with this. But one day in 1963, I read about a Dr. Lang who worked through the mediumship of a Mr. George Chapman. I thought that this Dr. Lang must be the late Archbishop of Canterbury and might perhaps be a brother of *my* Mr. Lang from Moorfields, so I decided that if indeed he belonged to the Lang family, I'd like to meet him and wrote to Mr. Chapman for an appointment.

'When I arrived at Aylesbury and went into the surgery, Mr. Chapman, who was Dr. Lang of course, greeted me by saying: "Oh, come along my child, we have met before."

'I recognised his voice immediately and said: "Yes, sir, we have met. I came to Moorfields in 1915 and you told me you couldn't do very much for my closed eyelid. It was the last time I saw you."

'He put his arm around my shoulder and said: "Oh, how big you are now. You were such a little thing and very frail when we met. What were you then—twenty-one, twenty-two?"

'I said: "Twenty-one."

' "You were about seven stone two or three, weren't you?"

'I said: "Well, I was about that in those days, but I've got stouter since I had a family."

'The longer I talked with Mr. Lang the more certain I was that he was the same person I had gone to see with my mother at Moorfields. I would have recognised him if only for the way he spoke. And when he showed me around the room, pointing at photographs of himself, his son Basil (who was of course alive in those days) and his colleagues, I had a peculiar feeling that time had been put back and I was again at Moorfields talking to him.

'Mr. Lang then told me to lie on his healing couch so that he could perform an operation on my spirit body which, he said, would put my eyelid right. He called Basil to assist him, asked him for instruments, and I had the odd notion that I was not even present although something marvellous was being done for me. And I didn't feel a thing. I just lay there and said a prayer, I think.

'When he told me that he had finished spirit surgery and that my eyelid was all right now, I prepared to get up from the couch, but he held me back and said: "Oh no, you stay where you are, we've something further to do for you." and then he did another operation—on my liver this time. When it was all over he asked me to get up and rest for a while in the chair. And while I sat opposite him, he described my dress in detail, the colour, pattern and even the large buttons, and then talked about all sorts of things. I just sat there thinking how wonderful it was meeting him again after forty-eight years and still remembering him so vividly.

'When I went out to my husband, who'd been waiting for me, I said to him: "Well, how do I look?" He stared at me but was unable to say a word. But our friend Frank Hill, who'd been kind enough to drive us to Aylesbury in his car, said: "Thank God, oh thank God!" You see, my eyelid was open. Remember it had been closed permanently all my life—for sixty-nine years! Yet, from the moment Mr. Lang performed his spirit operation, I was able to open and shut my eyelid as easily as I can now—as if nothing had ever been wrong with it.

'This in itself would have been a miraculous thing, and I'd have been more than thankful. But Mr. Lang did very much more for me. You see, due to the fact that my eyelid had been permanently closed all my life, I had very little vision in my right eye—it was what they call a "lazy eye". But Mr. Lang didn't just operate on my eyelid alone, he also attended to the sight.'

Mrs. Bailey visited Mr. Lang again for a check-up in the late Spring of 1964.

'Mr. Lang was very pleased with the progress I had made. He decided an additional operation was necessary to improve the vision of the right eye still further and I am happy to say he was able to accomplish this.

'Afterwards he discovered that a bone in my thumb was displaced. It had been painful for some time but I hadn't mentioned it to him because I didn't want to take up too much of his precious time, especially as I thought it was nothing serious and would eventually right itself. Anyhow Mr. Lang operated on it and stitched the joint. Afterwards he asked me to grip his hand to prove all was well. From that time domestic chores such as polishing and ironing were done more comfortably.'

Mrs. Bailey told me that she was due to see Mr. Lang again on November 20, 1964. I got in touch with her after her visit to Aylesbury and she explained:

'When I saw Mr. Lang a fortnight ago, he was very pleased with the progress I had made since last visit and again performed some operations on my once "lazy" eye.

'I can say my vision is much better for it—in fact I can read your manuscript. When one considers that I had practically no vision in this eye, I think you'll agree that what Mr. Lang did for me was quite wonderful.'

CHAPTER TWENTY-SEVEN

A Man from West Germany

IT WOULD be wrong to think that those who came to Aylesbury seeking help do so from near-by countries. While working on this book, I came across a distinctly German name in George Chapman's files. As much out of curiosity as anything, I traced the address, and though I found the case was far from finished, I decided it deserved a mention here if only to show that the spirit doctor's fame has spread far from the shores of Britain.

In 1938, when he was eighteen, Alfred Prehl, a West German clerk of Würzburg, noticed that an alarming tremor had developed in his right arm. It had come on without warning and grew worse with time. At the end of five years he had lost almost entirely the use of his main muscles.

During this period Herr Prehl consulted doctor after doctor. He was seen by distinguished specialists at the University Clinics at Würzburg and Freiburg, but none of them was able to help him. They were unable to comprehend the nature of his illness.

'Take medicaments containing belladonna and keep to a strict raw-food diet'—this was the sum total of the advice he received. But it had no effect and he became worse. As the years wore on, Alfred Prehl's loss of muscle control became pitiful. The Second World War had ended, and everywhere in Germany the ravages of war were being obliterated. But Alfred Prehl slipped further into misery. He was forty-five-years old when a specialist told him bluntly: 'As a normal man, you are finished. You'll never walk normally again.'

Further complications appeared in the autumn of 1963. Herr Prehl began to suffer from intense pain in the lower part of his body and to pass blood. In April 1964 the pain increased to such a degree that a specialist had him admitted to the Urological Clinic, where X-rays revealed a stone in the kidney. He was given the orthodox treatment for his condition, salines and infusions, and a loop was also fixed. He failed to respond, however, and the persistence of renal colic became so distressing that he was given drugs to alleviate the pain.

During this time, Herr Prehl read in *Die Andere Welt*, a German magazine, an account of the activities of George Chapman and his spirit control, Dr. Lang. He was impressed and began to consider the possibility of consulting the spirit doctor. But, he asked himself, would he be justified in spending so much money on a journey which might prove futile? What made matters still more difficult was the fact that for the past twenty-five years his illness had prevented him from working and he was unable to travel anywhere without his wife accompanying him. Eventually, Herr and Frau Prehl decided to undertake the journey together and, on September 15, 1964, travelled by air from West Germany to England.

When I heard about Herr and Frau Prehl's visit to Aylesbury, I was anxious to find out what had given them the confidence to assume that Mr. Lang might be able to help them. Consequently I contacted Herr Prehl at his home in Würzburg and he kindly gave me the information I had asked for.*

'I knew that no practising doctor could help me, so when I read about Dr. Lang and Mr. Chapman, I felt an overwhelming desire to find out whether these gentlemen could do for me what it was said they had done for others,' Herr Prehl told me.

'I worked out that the air journey and the stay in England would cost about a thousand West German Marks—an enormous amount of money for someone in my position. You see, due to my illness, I have been unable to follow my occupation as a clerk, and we live on the earnings of my wife who is a nursing sister at a hospital. But what wouldn't a man do to regain his lost health, even par-

* All questions and answers were put in the German language and are a true translation.

tially? My wife showed great understanding and that made my decision to travel to Aylesbury easier.

'We arrived at Mr. Chapman's house on September 15 and at the moment when another patient was just leaving by car. As we had come on the off-chance, having no appointment, my visit came as a surprise to Mr. Chapman who had just come out of trance because he thought he had finished for the day. Nevertheless he was willing to accept me as a patient and invited us in in the friendliest manner.

'After a brief conversation in the consulting room, he told us he would now go into trance. Sitting comfortably in the chair opposite me, his eyes closed, and, resting his head as if going to sleep, he remained in this state for a time. Then he introduced himself as Dr. Lang. His way of speech was now more difficult for me to understand than when he had been in a waking state before. I think I ought to point out that my knowledge of the English language is rather limited and, naturally, I did not understand every word he said.

'When he started talking with my wife and I told him that she worked as a nursing sister at the hospital, Dr. Lang, in the person of Mr. Chapman, seemed very pleased to meet her and he went across to her and welcomed her cordially. His behaviour was very different from what Mr. Chapman's had been during his wake state, older, more deliberate, and old-fashioned.

'Dr. Lang examined me and gave me his diagnosis. I am not a medical man, and my knowledge of the English language is insufficient to understand everything correctly. But because I considered his diagnosis of great importance, I asked him if he could confirm his findings to me in writing so that I was sure I had it right. He agreed, went to the dictaphone which stood at his desk, and recorded exactly what he thought was wrong with me and the reason for it. His diagnosis, which Mr. Chapman sent me three weeks later, was as follows: "Virus infection at an early age. This caused a condition of slowly spreading disseminated sclerosis which is scattered in patches of degeneration in the white matter of the brain."

'Still in trance, Mr. Chapman asked me to lie on the couch which stood by the wall so that he could start giving me treatment. For about fifteen minutes he attended to me. Mr. Chapman's hands hovered along my body from feet to head. He came back several times to attend to my abdomen because he obviously felt that here additional treatment was required.

'This was indeed perplexing, because he kept coming back to that part of the body where I had had the most violent and painful colics. I hadn't spoken about these pains at all, nor had my wife. The fact is, we considered them to be of far less importance than the other complaint I was suffering from, and which had been the reason for our flight to England. So, as I say, nothing about those pains was mentioned to Mr. Chapman.

'When he had finished treating my body, Dr. Lang asked me to sit on the couch, and he attended to my spine in the same manner as I described before—again never really touching me. I was told later that he had performed an operation on my spirit body. I did not feel a thing, but then, I must add that, due to paralysis, my body is rather unreceptive to all feeling.

'And I can't claim to have felt an immediate improvement when I left the surgery that day. But within a few hours, the difference was appreciable. I was able to walk with greater confidence and with more strength than at any time during the past twelve months or so. And after our return to Germany, the improvement continued. But ten days after my visit to Aylesbury, I became subjected to a sudden and violent colic, caused by the kidney stone and I wrote at once to Mr. Chapman, asking him to inform Dr. Lang of my unexpected trouble. A few days later the stone left the ureter and entered the bladder!

'Now, I thought, as did my doctor, that a kidney stone in the bladder would not cause any further trouble, and that I would eventually be rid of it. But this particular kidney stone was probably too big for the bladder to eject without trouble. As a result every time I urinated, I suffered acute pain.

'A fortnight later, I wrote again to Mr. Chapman and informed him about this condition. Within a few days the kidney stone promptly left the bladder! We were astonished at the size and shape—it is approximately fifteen by five millimetres big and has sharp edges. I keep it as a souvenir! The steady improvement of my major disease continues to this present day.'

Only three months had elapsed from the time Herr Prehl first received spirit treatment from Mr. Lang to the time he gave me the information I had asked for. In view of the serious nature of his illness, and the fact that at the time of writing this book he has been under Mr. Lang's care for so brief a period, albeit successfully, I kept in touch with Herr Prehl. His frequent reports recorded an uninterrupted chain of success—his health improved steadily, though he was still far from being a healthy man.

A year after he had performed the first series of operations on Herr Prehl's spirit body, Mr. Lang considered that the time had come for the patient to undergo further contact healing at Aylesbury. Though this meant another £100 or so travelling expenses (which Herr Prehl could ill afford) the German and his wife nevertheless decided to fly to England. The improvement of Herr Prehl's overall condition had been so marked that they believed additional spirit operations could only mean further considerable progress. And when Herr Prehl informed me about his decision to see Mr. Lang, he asked whether I could be present—to see for myself what was taking place and to act at the same time as intepreter. Herr Prehl's knowledge of English was still poor and naturally he wanted to know *everything* Mr. Lang had to say.

On November 29, 1965, I met Herr and Frau Prehl at George Chapman's house in Aylesbury. Alfred Prehl was still a wreck. His speech was only a little less impaired than a year earlier, his hand was still unable to grip mine firmly as he greeted me, and he walked weakly. From his written reports to me I had imagined that his state of health was much better than in fact it turned out to be. Knowing his financial state, I remarked: 'I'm surprised that you undertook the costly and strenuous journey to England.'

'I don't quite understand,' he said.

'Well, it doesn't look to me as though your improvement is as great as all that. . . .'

'But *it is*!' he said emphatically. 'It may seem to an outside observer that there isn't much improvement because I still look an invalid, but *I* know how very much more strength I've built up during this past year. And if Dr. Lang succeeds in bringing about a similar additional improvement, then all the expense and physical strain of our journey will be more than worth it.'

When we entered Mr. Lang's consulting room, he greeted all of us with his usual cordiality. He quickly got down to examining Herr Prehl, and within minutes was saying: 'I am very pleased with the progress you've made, young man. You have reacted admirably to treatment.'

He then performed, with his unseen colleagues and assistants, a number of operations on Herr Prehl's spirit body, keeping Frau Prehl, the hospital sister, and myself informed about what he was doing.

'Do you think I'll ever get better, Dr. Lang?' Herr Prehl said when the last operation was concluded.

'You *will* be cured,' the spirit doctor replied with firm conviction. 'Due to the very serious nature of your complaint and the fact that you consulted me rather late, it will take some considerable time before you are cured of your disease, but I can promise you that you *will* regain normality—provided you *don't* give up and that you *do* continue co-operating with me.'

Tears of gratefulness and happiness streamed down Prehl's cheeks. 'You can be sure that I'll never give up,' he whispered.

Mr. Lang then demonstrated how and where Frau Prehl should massage her husband, the kind of exercises Herr Prehl should do daily, and told him what food to eat.

'He hardly eats any food,' Frau Prehl cut in. 'He doesn't listen to me when I tell him he must have proper meals, and insists that he can't eat anything else but a few slices of dry bread a day. . . .'

'It is imperative that your physical body is kept well nourished,' Lang told him, 'because, if this is not done, the strength which I am putting into your spirit body cannot transfer efficiently into your physical body. You must realise this and comply with my advice if you wish to be cured.'

'Oh, I will, I will,' Prehl muttered.

'I promise you, Dr. Lang, I will see to it that my husband will do *everything* you want him to do,' Frau Prehl pledged.

'I shall continue visiting you during your sleep state, young man, and you will find that in a month you will experience further improvement,' Mr. Lang said at the end of the consultation. 'I hope you'll have a pleasant journey to Germany—actually, I know you'll have a good journey home.'

Ten days after his visit to Aylesbury, Herr Prehl contacted me and said he had already experienced a very marked improvement. At the time this book was in proof form and ready to be printed (in January 1966), he gave me the latest up-to-date details about himself:

'My wife complies religiously with Dr. Lang's instructions and massages my spine exactly as he showed her; I do all the exercises Dr. Lang asked me to do; I am also eating regular nourishing meals.

'The improvement of my condition during the past two months is very much greater than the improvement was which I experienced during the year between my two consultations with Dr. Lang. I feel very much stronger and am able to use my limbs much better than when we met at Aylesbury on November 29, 1965. My own and my wife's gratitude to Dr. Lang and Mr. George Chapman is too great and overwhelming to be expressed adequately in words. This good spirit doctor has pulled off a miracle because he has already enabled me to get about, whereas all the other doctors and specialists under whose care I was made it abundantly clear that I was beyond help.'

CHAPTER TWENTY-EIGHT

*'. . . and there shall be no more death, neither sorrow, nor crying . . .'**

JONATHAN BELL was five years old and as lively as any child of that age. The family lived in Worksop and to Mr. and Mrs. Bell, though they would only say it to one another, there never was a child like Jonathan.

They would catch a glimpse of him playing with his friends, or see his grubby face impish and mischievous after some prank, and look meaningfully at each other. They had watched him grow from babyhood, had marvelled at the arrival of his first tooth which stood out from his gums like a tiny white tombstone and they hugged and cuddled him the day he took his first steps. And as he developed into a little harum-scarum boy, they stood by, the proud and protective onlookers. That rare happiness that only children can bring belonged to the Bells, until late in the summer of 1964.

It was then they began to become a little uneasy but not alarmed. At that time it was difficult to sense the change slowly taking place in their little boy. He played a little less vigorously one day than he had on other occasions. But children were creatures of mood and whim. Perhaps he was over-tired in the way children exhaust themselves.

The next day Jonathan Bell was still tired. But you never can tell with children. In a day or two he would be his old self again.

Jonathan did not regain his high spirits. He didn't want to go out and play, he just wanted to rest. The day the child's face began to

* Revelation of St. John.

puff up, his parents decided to call in a doctor. After the examination he turned to the parents and said:

'I'm afraid, Mr. and Mrs. Bell, that Jonathan is suffering from advanced leukaemia.'

What he told afterwards they scarcely heard. They knew enough about leukaemia to realise that anyone who contracted it was in the grip of a fatal disease. They had, from time to time, read the heart-rending accounts of children who had been 'condemned to death' by it. And, now, it had struck at themselves, the Bells, and their little boy Jonathan.

The doctor wanted to be certain of his diagnosis and arranged for a blood test and a second opinion by a specialist.

The boy was taken to Kilton Hill Hospital, Worksop, where the doctor's diagnosis was confirmed. It was leukaemia. The disease was particularly rife in the spinal fluid and was so advanced that the little chap was given only about two months to live.

Mr. and Mrs. Bell became desperate and refused to accept the sentence of death on their little boy. Mistakes had occurred before in hospitals and they told themselves that the diagnosis could be wrong. Why should Jonathan have to die? He'd always been so healthy and full of life. It was unthinkable that he could be taken from them now. They had heard of the famous Hospital for Sick Children at Great Ormond Street in London. There, they hoped, perhaps the doctors might prove the local hospital wrong. Or, if the boy did have leukaemia, maybe they'd find it was only in the early stages and be able to cure it.

Jonathan was taken to the famous hospital. But the verdict was the same:

Advanced leukaemia.

Mr. and Mrs. Bell were given tablets which Jonathan had to take daily, and the family returned to Worksop. Arrangements were made for the child to be seen again.

Back home, the parents cherished their dying child. The few weeks of his life that remained, they knew, would see the ebbing away of his strength, and they wanted to be with him for every precious hour that was left to them. If there was anything the child wanted, they would do everything within their power to give to him.

In their desperation they went through periods when they

rejected the cruel truth and hoped that the tragedy which had invaded their home might remit itself. They prayed for a miracle. Was it too much to ask for? That one small life be spared. But when further visits to the London hospital convinced the parents that nothing could be done for Jonathan they decided that all that was left to them was to try and keep him happy—until the end.

This then was the situation when Mr. and Mrs. Rose, Birmingham friends of the Bells, made a hesitant suggestion to them. Mr. and Mrs. Rose were deeply moved by the grief of their friends at Worksop, and the thought of what yet lay before them. The Roses themselves knew of William Lang and his medium George Chapman. They were aware of some of the startlingly successful cures that had been brought about in the house called St. Brides and at the Birmingham Healing Centre, and yet it was with reluctance that they suggested to the Bells that Jonathan might yet be saved by the spirit doctor. It was a reluctance born out of knowledge of the distrust felt by so many people towards anything connected with spirit healing. Under *ordinary* circumstances the Bells would hardly have consented to go near a spirit doctor. They were far from convinced that anything other than medical skill could be of any value; but what was there to lose? Their son was dying. This was the brutal truth. On Saturday, December 19, 1964, Mr. Rose took Jonathan to see William Lang at the Healing Centre. The boy, of course, was too young to know the purpose of the visit. As far as he was concerned he was going to see another doctor, one of the many who had examined him, looked serious, jotted down notes and talked quietly to his Mum and Dad.

When Lang examined Jonathan, he confirmed that he had advanced leukaemia, and said it was particularly heavy in the spinal fluid. He then told Mr. Rose that he needed to operate in order to help the boy.

William Lang operated on Jonathan's liver and opened up the heart valve to increase its blood count. It was all very mysterious and strange to the child who felt nothing and wondered why this man in a white coat with his eyes closed, talked to people who weren't there. Then there was the funny business of this doctor washing his hands even though Jonathan had not seen him do anything to soil them. But he liked the way the funny man did those things with his hands and fingers. It was, he thought, a curious game, but was amusing.

Mr. and Mrs. Rose watched William Lang attending to the boy. The minute hand of the clock moved round with agonising slowness. Was there any hope? Even a shred? They hardly exchanged a whispered word. There was so much to say, and yet so little that could be put into words. What was happening? Anything? And then there was Lang standing up, his operations finished. Jonathan got up from the couch and was quietly, calmly smiling. And as Mrs. Rose led the child out of earshot, her husband faced the man in the white coat.

'Well,' Mr. Rose said, 'do you think there is any chance of doing anything?'

'Oh, yes,' Lang answered. 'Quite a good chance. I want to see Jonathan again in six weeks' time, and then I'll be able to tell you more. To what extent the operations were successful and so forth. But I can tell you *now* that there's nothing much to worry about. We are doing all we can for the boy and I'll be visiting him during his sleep state to give him additional treatment.'

Mr. Rose spent a few minutes talking with Lang, asking many questions and trying desperately to establish some sort of basis for confidence from which he and his wife could draw and transmit to the boy's parents. There was much that was consoling in what Lang said, but at the same time Rose knew the Bells' fears were now so deep-rooted, and their suspicions of spirit healing so strong, that he hardly knew how to convince them that there was hope for Jonathan.

Within three weeks after Lang's operations, Jonathan was due at Kilton Hill Hospital for the customary blood test. But within *two* weeks, the boy had improved so much that his parents could scarcely believe it. The doctors were amazed at his blood count.

Five weeks after Lang's operations, Jonathan kept his appointment at Great Ormond Street Hospital. The examination tests established that the spinal fluid was clear of leukaemia. The medical staff appeared astonished and said quite frankly that they didn't know how the change could have happened.

Six weeks after Lang's operations, Jonathan had his second appointment with the spirit doctor. It was at the Birmingham Healing Centre. The date was Saturday, January 30, 1965. Lang was very pleased with the progress the boy had made since he had first seen him. He told Mr. Rose that the operations on the spirit body had been successful. 'Jonathan is going to be perfectly healthy again—now there's nothing to worry about any longer,' he explained. He requested that the boy be brought to him again in three weeks.

The third appointment with the spirit doctor—on Saturday, February 20, 1965—was of course kept. William Lang was delighted with how well his young patient reacted to treatment and confirmed: 'Everything is now working perfectly, the spinal fluid is clear and there remains only a slight trace in the bloodstream, but this will clear. Jonathan will be a perfectly healthy little boy again, but treatment must be continued for some time.'

The improvement in Jonathan's health condition was remarkable. He felt well, was full of energy, and had lost all blown-up appearance about his face.

Any small doubt that may have lingered in the minds of the boy's parents was stamped out of existence. At the beginning they were of course keenly aware that in many instances a seeming improvement comes before deterioration and death; indeed the first months added up to a time of almost unbearable breath-holding.

But, bit by bit, stage by stage the signs of improvement came, were consolidated, remained. The visits to William Lang's Birmingham Healing Centre were maintained, and the young body of Jonathan Bell became stronger as the days went by. There came a day when it was felt he could return to school, then another day when the most rigorous blood test showed that the child was free from leukaemia. Today (in November 1965) he runs and jumps and shouts and plays pranks like any other schoolboy. And his progress at school is enough to cause small stirrings of pride in the breasts of two people who thought his school days were over.

On November 29, 1965, I spoke to William Lang about Jonathan Bell. The face of the old man smiled with inner contentment. After a while he said: 'Thank God he was brought to me just in time.'

And the parents who were stalked by tragedy no longer look grey with sorrow. The shadow of death has gone from their home and they are able to marvel at a reprieve that has given them back their little son and richly restored their faith in the future.

CHAPTER TWENTY-NINE

More things in Heaven and Earth

DURING THE extensive research I carried out into every aspect of Mr. Lang's spirit healing, I decided to discuss his cures with an eminent physician who was a senior member of a famous London hospital.

The doctor in question agreed to meet me, on the strict understanding that under no circumstances would I disclose his identity or the name of his hospital. He explained that he had no desire to get into trouble with the British Medical Association for 'co-operating with an unregistered practitioner', or lay himself open to a charge of 'unprofessional conduct'. I gave him this undertaking, indeed I could not do otherwise, but I can assure those who read this book that the account of this interview is genuine and based on a verbatim transcription of a meeting which took place in the late autumn of 1964.

I had brought along a number of Mr. Lang's most striking case histories together with particulars of evidence from doctors, hospital authorities and distinguished specialists who confirmed that the patients in question had not reacted to the treatment that had been given them; that in their opinion there was nothing further medical science could do for them; and that they were incurable.

As against this was the evidence that these incurables had *not* died and had, in fact, got better after treatment from William Lang. And their improvement and cures were verified by those same doctors who had previously had them under their care, indeed in some cases had written them off.

This, perhaps, was the most valuable evidence of all. After having examined the patients most thoroughly and subjected them to all forms of clinical tests, these medical experts had confirmed that the diseases had been cured completely, and that no trace of any hidden or dormant signs could be found.

When I presented the physician with this well-authenticated evidence and asked him for his comments, he examined the papers very carefully and after much thought replied:

'Well, speaking from a strictly medical point of view. I have no explanation to offer on how it is possible for patients, who are found to be beyond hope, to recover from time to time. If cures of this kind happen, it is usually assumed that nature itself somehow brings about what is otherwise inexplicable. On more than one occasion I've heard eminent physicians and surgeons say that "a miracle has happened". They are of course right in one sense, because with some incurable diseases it is quite evident that only a miracle—something beyond our comprehension—could have brought about the cure of a patient, regarded from the viewpoint of orthodox treatment, as beyond hope of recovery. One finds in quite a few medical institutions the inscription, "We dress the wound, God heals it", which is benevolently tolerated by our very strict association. But I think in reality an awful lot of us accept the truth of that inscription.'

'Having examined the evidence of Mr. Lang's successes in curing incurable people, would you agree that they were the result of his spirit operations and other forms of healing?' I enquired.

'Well, the evidence you have presented is certainly most convincing. What else can I say?' He paused for a moment, and added: 'If I were to consider these cases simply in the light of the medical code we observe, I'd be forced to dismiss any possibility of spirit operations and healing being able to achieve *anything*. According to our way of thinking, only qualified medical practitioners and medically trained staff are able to treat patients properly. But . . . well, I personally am not so sure about this tenet.' He paused again, and after a while said: 'But to answer your question. Yes, I believe that the complete and confirmed cures of the patients whose case histories you've shown me *are* due to spiritual help—to Mr. Lang's spiritual operations and treatment, I should really say.'

'You accept then that by performing invisible and painless operations on the spirit body of a patient Mr. Lang is able to bring about a corresponding effect on the physical body?'

'I did not say that,' the physician asserted. 'You see, I'm not at all convinced that there is such a thing as a "spirit body", and therefore I cannot accept that treating a so-called "spirit body" brings about *any* effect on a patient's physical body. I may of course be wrong—perhaps there is such a thing after all—but I haven't come across it during the many years I've practised medicine.

'But don't let's argue as to whether there is or isn't a "spirit body", because neither of us can furnish conclusive proof of our beliefs. Let us instead consider the issue of spiritual help objectively and rationally. As far as I am concerned, I do not really care *how* Mr. Lang cures his patients; the significant thing to me is that he *does* cure them. I am prepared to say I accept this.'

When the question of distant healing was mentioned I regretted not having brought along the documentary evidence of the successes achieved by Dr. Lang with many patients, but I was able to tell him about a number of cases I had investigated. The physician heard me out, his eyebrows rising occasionally, but he made no comment until I had finished.

'Well, I am not suggesting that what you've told me is incorrect or exaggerated,' he said. 'But it is difficult for me to believe that healing from a distance, just by means of letter-writing produced the results you have suggested. Although I don't know exactly how spiritual contact healing can work, as it apparently does, I still believe that something happens, and extraordinary things take place. Maybe by actually touching a patient's body and establishing direct physical contact, Mr. Lang somehow succeeds in harnessing some kind of spiritual power, I don't know. Healing rays maybe. To accept, however, that the same thing is possible from a distance, through a sort of correspondence course, is really too much to expect from a member of the medical profession.'

'Would you like me to offer you the same kind of evidence of Mr. Lang's achievements as I have given you in regard to his contact healing?' I asked.

'Well, yes, I would be most interested,' he replied. 'But don't send it to me care of the hospital. I don't want to risk having the letter opened by mistake. Send it to my private address please.'

I kept my promise.

A few days later the physician returned the case histories relating to distant healing. He did not say what he thought of the evidence and his letter consisted only of the following lines written in a determined hand:

'It is astonishing, to say the least!

'I hope you don't consider me banal quoting William Shakespeare but, as usual, he said the most appropriate thing to fit the situation: "There are more things in heaven and earth, Horatio, than are dreamt of in your philosophy".'

CHAPTER THIRTY

How effective is distant healing?

THIS QUESTION is best answered by recording some of the many cases of distant healing which I picked out at random from George Chapman's bulky filing cabinets.

Mrs. Marjory Hemsworth of Hull requested distant healing from Mr. Lang and wrote to George Chapman in March 1959:

'Will you please help me with my throat? My doctor says it is a nervous one, but I am constantly having to clear my throat every few seconds. I may add that I have been troubled with this condition for over five years.'

Distant healing commenced on receipt of the letter, and two weeks later Mrs. Hemsworth reported:

'I am very puzzled; at about 11 a.m. I went to make the beds, and on nearing the top of the stairs, I could smell violets; on reaching the small landing and front bedroom it was overpowering, it was a lovely smell. I sat on the bed wondering where it was coming from; after a few seconds it gradually faded leaving me with a wonderful feeling I can't explain. I only wish someone had been there to share the experience with me.'

Seven weeks after distant healing commenced, Mrs. Hemsworth was cured. On April 29, 1959, she wrote to George Chapman:

'I should like to say how well I am feeling now. My throat condition has completely cleared up.'

Mr. Lang's cure was a lasting one. I ascertained this when I contacted Mrs. Hemsworth in December 1964.

Marjorie's husband, George Hemsworth, also became a patient of William Lang and gave me the following account of his own experiences.

'My wife wrote for distant healing for me in December 1962,' he told me. 'I had developed cataracts in both eyes, and as I had heard of people sometimes having to wait a very long time before it was deemed advisable to operate, I was naturally worried. I gave up my driving job in November 1962, and by the end of August 1963 both eyes were so bad that I had to be led about.

'One cataract was removed in October 1963, and the other in May 1964, and although I wear thick spectacles I now have splendid vision. In fact my optician says I have better eyesight than he has!'

I enquired from Mr. Lang about the type of distant healing he had given to Mr. Hemsworth, and he explained: 'It is true that it would have taken many years for the cataracts to grow sufficiently to be removed successfully, so my spirit helpers and I accelerated the growth to enable the patient to have his operation at the hospital as speedily as possible.' William Lang could have brought about a complete detachment of the cataract, he explained, but this would have necessitated contact healing and would have been a lengthier process than if the cataract was operated on in hospital. Consequently he had decided to concentrate on forcing the cataract to grow speedily to be ready for removal.

In February 1962 Mr. Joseph C. Manuel of Hoylake suffered from pain in the rectum and consulted his doctor who diagnosed external piles. He prescribed the known treatment, but the condition slowly got worse. He then sent the patient to a specialist who diagnosed a fistula in the rectum, and at the end of April 1962 Mr. Manuel went into hospital for an operation for its removal. This was done, but the wound would not heal and the whole area became inflamed and swollen to such an extent that the patient could not sit down and could only lie on his side.

'I went back time and again to the hospital to see the specialist but the pain and discomfort persisted,' Mr. Manuel stated. 'I felt sure that they had not got to the root of the trouble in the first place. I became more and more depressed and it seemed as if I should never be rid of the condition.'

In September 1962 Mr. Manuel learned about George Chapman and his spirit doctor Lang and, hoping spirit healing might possibly help him as much as it had done in a case of which he had heard he decided to 'give it a try'. So he wrote the following letter to George Chapman:

'I am writing to ask you if you would be good enough to give me distant healing for the rectal trouble from which I am suffering. The doctors diagnosed it as a form of fistula and have, following an operation, been treating me for the past six months without success. They have now told me there is nothing more they can do. As the condition appears to be getting very much worse, I wonder if you can help me.'

Distant healing commenced on September 25, 1962, and a week later, Mr. Manuel sent the following report to George Chapman:

'I am pleased to say that in the last three days there has been an improvement in my condition. I have had far less pain and irritation, and I am hoping it will continue to improve.'

Then, on November 26, 1962, the patient wrote again:

'I should like to say that you and your spirit control (Dr. Lang) have done a wonderful job of healing in my case, as I am sure you have done for many others. Thank you, Mr. Chapman, for your marvellous work.'

Mr. Manuel's last report, which he sent the following month, stated:

'I am very glad to say that all the pain has now gone, and that the swelling and irritation have disappeared. I am most grateful to Dr. Lang and yourself, Mr. Chapman, and I wish every success in the future to you both.'

Exactly two years later—on December 5, 1964—I contacted Mr. Lang's ex-patient to find out from him his present state of health. He kindly told me the following about himself:

'I am glad to say there has been no recurrence of the trouble and I should like to say once more how grateful I am to Dr. Lang and George Chapman for the healing I received from them which completely cured me.'

William Lang's successful healing activities in the Hutton household were not confined to myself. What was accomplished for my twelve-year-old son Harold was, from a medical point of view, insignificant. But who can tell with certainty what is important or of little account? To some people the slightest feeling of illness causes concern; others, suffering from a serious ailment, often try to convince themselves it is not half as bad as it appears.

But let me tell you about Harold.

For many months my son had looked forward eagerly to mid-December 1964, when he was to go on a cruise to the Holy Land for Christmas with some of his class-mates. If the prospect of visiting Jerusalem and other places was truly exciting so, too, was the idea of a cruise—the first in his young life. The voyage would take him to Italy and Greece as well as the Holy Land, and being the youngest member of the grammar school party, he was, perhaps, more keyed up than most.

The party was to leave Worthing on the morning of December 16, a Wednesday. But on the Sunday evening before, Harold suddenly developed a very heavy cold with severe bouts of coughing and a temperature of 101·3°.

In the past, similar attacks had always developed into bronchitis or influenza which dragged on for a week or two before he was passed fit by the doctor to return to school. It became quite obvious that Harold would be confined to bed until some time after the departure of the school party and he became very dejected. We knew only too well how much the holiday meant to him, and some of his depression rubbed off on Pearl and me.

What could we do to help our son? It was Sunday evening and there was no point in dragging out the doctor because, as we knew from past experience, he could do no more at this stage than advise keeping him in bed until it could be seen what course the illness would take. As night approached, however, Harold's temperature rose still higher, his cough became more persistent and breathing became difficult for him.

Lying awake in bed and listening to the spasmodic bouts of coughing coming from Harold's bedroom across the landing, it suddenly occurred to me to ask William Lang for help. From my many interviews with the spirit doctor I knew what to do—just send out positive thoughts to him, telling him what was wrong with my son and requesting him, or one of his colleagues, for assistance. I sent out a thought message to William Lang—without the boy's knowledge of course.

The alarm clock at my bedside table continued ticking the minutes away but no help came. The boy continued to cough, chokingly, and it seemed to me that, if anything, he was worse.

When almost ten minutes had gone by since I had first sent out my thought message to William Lang, I began to wonder if for some reason or another he had not received it. As I lay there trying to decide whether to make a further attempt I sensed the presence of someone at my bedside. I strained my eyes in the semi-darkness but could not see anyone. Then, almost immediately, I distinctly felt a soothing cool hand stroke my forehead. But there was no one there, at least no one I could see! A moment after the invisible hand had touched my forehead, the alarm clock was picked up by an unseen hand and gently put face down. Then it flashed through my mind that this was meant to be some sort of proof that William Lang or one of his spirit colleagues had received my thought message and that my call for help was being answered.

Minutes later Harold stopped coughing. He had no more difficulty with his breathing. I got up and went to his room. He was sleeping soundly and breathing easily and his temperature had dropped.

Next morning the boy was perfectly normal. His temperature was down and there was not the slightest trace left of the cough. On Tuesday he returned to school and, as planned, left Worthing with his school party on Wednesday morning for the cruise.

It may of course be argued that the sudden improvement of his condition could have been brought about by mere laws of nature. Well, everyone is entitled to his own opinion, but both my wife and I are convinced that this unexpected recovery was brought about with the help of William Lang or one of his colleagues. The connection between the phenomenon that I had experienced while fully awake and the immediate improvement in Harold's condition was too striking to induce us to seek any other explanation.

An 'insignificant' case? Perhaps. To Harold, and us, it was most significant. It enabled the boy to fulfil his dearest wish, and it gave us at first-hand an insight into the healing power that can be exercised unseen by spirit doctors.

CHAPTER THIRTY-ONE

Saved from a Wheel-chair

IN THE realm of spirit healing are to be discovered many diverse groups of people. So far I have given accounts of most of them, from the scoffer to the sceptic, to those prepared to take a last chance and those who avow a willingness to try anything. One group, however, which I have hardly dealt with are the confirmed believers, those people who embrace fully all the faith and its tenets, its ritual and teachings.

Mrs. Barbara Haines, a State Registered Nurse from Canterbury, is a confirmed Spiritualist. So is her husband. On April 27, 1960, Mrs. Haines wrote to George Chapman as follows:

'Four years ago, in the playground at school, my daughter Janet fell and her leg was fractured at the neck of the femur.

'The orthopaedic surgeon who examined her every six months since he put a pin through the neck of the femur, tells me that he will have to operate again to make the hip a fixture. As Janet has suffered so much pain and handicap during the last four years, I am very reluctant to agree to this operation.

'Neither my husband nor I approve of the treatment Janet has received. I am a S.R.N. and know just how much some specialists care for their patients these days. No more are they treated as individuals but as a number on a card, herded into waiting-rooms to be earmarked like a lot of cattle.

'We believe in spiritual healing and I have read so much about the wonderful work done by Dr. Lang through your hands that I feel sure that with your help he would spiritually guide me into making the right decision, which is such an important one because it can affect the whole of the child's future, this child of God's. It is such a serious step for us to take alone, especially as my husband and I feel that through your help and our prayers it may not be necessary in six months' time for this operation to be done.

'The specialist wishes to fix the hip because, he says, the blood supply to the head of the femur has been severed. Please advise me what to do.'

Mr. Lang requested George Chapman to inform Mrs. Haines that distant healing for Janet had commenced on receipt of her letter and that he would be visiting the child during her sleep state, and hoped to help her sufficiently so that the planned operation would not be necessary. In the following month Mrs. Haines wrote again to George Chapman:

'Many thanks for your letter of instructions and I feel now that something will be achieved in six months' time and Janet will not have to have the operation performed.

'Each night at ten o'clock my husband and I stand in meditation beside the child's bed, so as to link up with Dr. Lang. Since distant healing from Dr. Lang began, we have felt the spirit presence round us and I have placed my hands on Janet's hip and leg as well. I feel the glow of spirit power all tingling, and warmth flows through my arms and into my hands, and a great power presses down on my head. It brings great peace with it too.

'Janet says the pain in the hip is much better and the hip does not fix now like it used to when she stood on it for too long. She used to have great difficulty in sitting or standing if she stayed too long in one position. She can also bend more easily. To me there does not seem so much deformity and the leg itself looks better. Thank God.

'Please convey my heartfelt thanks to Dr. Lang for visiting us, and to all the spirit helpers that come also, for everything that is being done for my child. We know that with God's help and power—if it be His will—all things are possible.'

Distant healing was given by Mr. Lang regularly and he and his assistants visited Janet during her sleep state so as to attend to her spirit body and eventually bring about a corresponding effect on her physical body. Mrs. Haines wrote about one of these spirit visits: 'My husband and my daughter Janet have both seen Dr. Lang and his band of spirit helpers round her bed. Janet received a most remarkable spirit operation during which her spirit body was completely detached from her physical body and her physical body was to all who saw it, materially, "dead", *no* pulse, *no* heart-beat, *nor* breathing—and I, with twenty-five years' nursing behind me, can vouch for that.

'From that night onwards, Janet's condition improved rapidly. The pain in her leg has greatly diminished and she can stand up or sit for much of the time without getting pain in the hip. I hope I am not too optimistic if I hope that the dreaded operation will not be necessary after all. I know of course the surgeon's verdict that unless I allow this child to have a fixation done to the hip she will be in constant pain, and become progressively worse as she gets older and eventually end up in a wheel-chair; but I also know that if it is God's will, spirit power will help her to recover.'

Then, in November of the same year, Mrs. Haines wrote once more to George Chapman:

'Last week I took Janet to the specialist for the six-monthly check-up at the hospital. Before he examined her he said she would have to go into hospital to have the fixation of the hip performed, and he repeated that he could see no other way of the bone building up because of the blood supply being severed. This meant that the bone was gradually wearing away at the neck of the femur, causing the pain she was getting. I let him talk because I somehow knew I would not have to make the decision—in fact I felt at peace with the whole world.

'Then, when the specialist examined Janet, he was quite astonished at the amount of mobility he was able to secure without any pain. He scratched his head in amazement and eventually said: "This is not possible, I must get it X-rayed." The X-ray showed that the pin had moved out and seemed to be floating in the fleshy part of the leg while the bone itself appeared to have started to build up again. Previously X-rays showed the pin in position and the bone tissues deteriorating.

'This latest X-ray completely baffled the specialist. I suppose he was on the defensive. In the end he said: "I don't know what has happened here; I'll have her in to see." I explained that we believed it was spiritual healing that had brought about the improvement. He pooh-poohed spiritual healing and said that he didn't wish to see her again till I decided to let him open up the leg. There we left him and Janet did not return to the hospital again.'

Four years later I discovered Janet's case history in George Chapman's records. but there was no further or recent report about her state of health. Had the surgeon been right after all, had an operation in hospital been performed since Mrs. Haines' last letter? I got in touch with the mother, and on December 12, 1964, she gave me the following answers:

'No operation was performed at the hospital after my last letter to Mr. Chapman in November 1960. In fact because of the specialist's atitude four years ago we haven't contacted him or the hospital authorities since. Janet has made remarkable progress. Apart from a slight shortening of the leg, and a little stiffness at times, neither of which worry her in any way, she is fine. She enjoys good health and a happy life. She can walk, dance, and do most things that other children do.

'We know that Dr. Lang and Mr. Chapman are still in spiritual contact with us, and with God's help Janet will be protected throughout the rest of her earthly life, living it normally and able to do as others do. One of the consequences of Dr. Lang's miraculous healing is that the child's whole personality has changed. She is loved by all who come in contact with her—some power emanates from her which we say is the Love of God who answered our prayers. She is always ready and willing to do *anyone* a kindness or favour and is a happy, lovable child, learning to live with the slight shortening of her leg, knowing she is in God's hands and still in the capable care of Dr. Lang.

'We have so much to thank them for, and once again I say: *If* it is God's will *all* things are possible.'

CHAPTER THIRTY-TWO

'Please help my little Sister!'

MRS. PAULINE PERRY, a laboratory technician of Swansea, was terribly worried. Not about herself or her own well-being, but because the life of Gwynneth, her thirteen-year-old sister, was in danger. She loved the child whose sweet personality enchanted everybody. Gwynneth was doomed to an early grave, and Pauline Perry was in despair. Anger too flooded through her—anger at the inability of medical science to save her young sister.

When things looked their blackest, Pauline heard about the spirit doctor William Lang. What she was told appeared fantastic. As someone engaged in a profession in which everything had to be proved, she couldn't accept the startling claims that were made. But what was there to lose? Her sister's life was slipping away in hospital, so why not try spirit distant healing even if it *was* something a good many people just brushed aside or scoffed at?

Pauline wrote at once to George Chapman. I quote her letters exactly as she wrote them, for they provide full details of a case that illustrates the remarkable success of yet another case of distant healing.

'Please help my little sister!' Mrs. Perry wrote on March 30, 1962. 'I hope you can give the child back her health although I cannot bring her to see you personally.

'My parents do not believe in these things and I have not told them about your healing powers, but it would be a wonderful triumph if Gwynneth could be healed. She is thirteen years of age and is at the moment at Morriston Hospital (Ward 2), Swansea, where she was taken after the collapse of a lung which has affected her heart.

'Since very early childhood, Gwynneth has suffered from severe attacks of asthma, and this, coupled with continual bronchitis, has now proved to be too much for her. My little sister has suffered so much pain and discomfort that she no longer wishes to live, which is an alarming and horrifying statement to hear from a child.

'*Please* will you work the miracle and give Gwynneth the gift of health that she may be as other children. She is so bright, normally a gay little chatterbox, frail and thin but exceptionally pretty. How empty the home is without her! My parents are heart-broken, especially my mother who is on the verge of a nervous breakdown through so many weary nights spent nursing Gwynneth.

'Mother's health is generally poor, blood pressure extremely low, and she is literally living on injections from the doctor, to stimulate her circulation. She is forty years of age, her whole system is fast wearing out, and her resistance and will to carry on are pathetically low. She is a broken and exhausted woman who seems to be shrinking before my very eyes.

'Please do something for them! I know that there are so many others much worse off, but these are my flesh and blood and I love them.'

On receipt of this letter, George Chapman immediately communicated its contents to Mr. Lang and distant healing commenced almost instantly. Mrs. Perry was asked to send a report regularly on the health of her mother and sister. In the following month she wrote:

'Here is the first report on the progress of my mother and my sister Gwynneth.

'My mother appears to be considerably improved, but puts this down to the fact that she has had two injections from the doctor. She is given them every month as a kind of energiser, but due to her anxiety for Gwynneth the doctor gave her two instead of the customary one.

'Gwynneth, according to the medical report, is improving slowly, but has developed a heavy cold. However, she is in high spirits and longing to leave the hospital. We have been told that the lung has collapsed again.

'You will, I am sure, be interested to hear that my parents now know of the treatment you have commenced, although, naturally, my young sister does not, and they are intensely curious.

'I had to tell them, due to the phenomenon of last Sunday night.

'Completely unaware of what was happening to both Gwynneth and my mother, the family went to bed as usual. They are solid folk, not given to flights of imagination and extremely wary of having anything to do with the world of spirits.

'My other sister, Janet, sleeping alone in the room which Gwynneth had previously shared, was getting into bed when she heard voices whispering at the foot of it. (She is nineteen years old and very straightforward.) Finding difficulty in putting her feet under the bed-clothes, she thought someone was sitting on the bed, and nervously switched on the light. The whispering stopped and she saw no one.

'About the same time, my mother, who sleeps in her own bed in the same room as my father, was trying to sleep, when she felt someone sit on the bed. There was a definite pressure and the bed subsided as though bearing extra weight. Then, as she lay there, she felt a hand, cool and gentle, touch her shoulder lightly, and then move to her head.

'Rather shaken, mother told father, and then Janet came into the room in a state of anxiety to explain her own experience.

'There are no animals in the house, and the family had not watched or heard anything morbid or unpalatable on the television or the radio. Thus, I told them about you, and they are greatly interested as to a possible link between the happenings I have described and the spirit doctors.

'Thank you for everything you are doing and I shall try my utmost to carry out your instructions.'

When I interviewed Mr. Lang about distant healing, I asked him if he had been concerned with the events at Swansea and he said: 'I wasn't there myself, but Basil and a colleague of his visited the house.' And how considerable the result of this visit by the spirit doctors turned out is revealed in a further letter from Mrs. Perry later that month.

'I am thrilled to tell you that Gwynneth seems to have been completely healed!' she reported. 'Since leaving hospital, she has had no more attacks and has never needed the oxygen cylinder beside her bed. She is livelier in spirit, happy, and although still painfully thin, abounding with energy.

'My mother still cannot sleep without the aid of sedatives, but she appears more restful in spirit and much calmer and happier She has not had any more injections from the doctor, but nevertheless seems to be far healthier.'

A fortnight later, on May 6, Mrs. Perry sent the following letter:

'Let me thank you again for your wonderful help in curing my young sister Gwynneth. She continues to improve and becomes stronger every day. The fluid in her lungs has dried up completely, much to the bafflement of doctors and hospital staff. Indeed, she is now riding her bicycle around and eating quite well. My sincere thanks to you and Dr. Lang.

'My mother looks a great deal healthier, but still takes her sleeping tablets through sheer habit. However, she has had no injections of late to tone up her circulation and pacify her nerves which is indeed a good sign.'

Then, on June 20, 1962, Mrs. Pauline Perry wrote this final communication to George Chapman:

'I think this will be my last letter of thanks to you, together with the medical report on my mother and sister.

'The two patients in question have progressed so amazingly that I think all will be well with them from now on, and it only remains for me to say once more that you have my deepest gratitude for your wonderful help.

'I do hope that you are as well as your ex-patient, my young sister Gwynneth. Thanks to you, she has not been troubled with asthma or any pulmonary complications since. May God abundantly bless you and thank Dr. Lang for working a miracle.'

This last letter was received nearly two and a half years ago and as far as I could tell the case was closed. But, was it not perhaps possible that there had been a relapse and Mrs. Perry had not written about it? It was imperative for me to find out the *present* state of health of Mrs. Perry's mother and sister, so I got in touch with her in December 1964.

'My mother's health has improved since she received distant healing,' Mrs. Perry told me. 'She has never been a robustly healthy person, but compared to what she was, I would say she is now in "much better shape".

'Gwynneth is now remarkably healthy and full of energy. Her

zest for living is quite remarkable. Occasionally she has a "tightness" in her chest, but those dreadful bouts of choking asthma are gone.

'She is always under medical care really, because of what happened to her in 1962, and her doctor is obviously ready for another attack. However, I am glad to say that he is still waiting! The fact remains that my young sister is healed, and no one can dispute that fact.'

CHAPTER THIRTY-THREE

The intricacy of Spirit Healing

HAVING QUESTIONED a considerable number of Mr. Lang's patients about their illnesses and experiences with the spirit doctor, and then tested their evidence, it was only natural that I should want to know exactly *how* spirit operations are performed and *how* the patient's spirit body is treated. I questioned Mr. Lang at length about it.

'The simplest answer to your question of how spirit healing actually works is: Spirit healing is healing from the spirit world and is given to a patient by spirit doctors,' Mr. Lang replied. 'The healing takes place upon the patient's spirit body which brings about a change in the physical body for the better. It is as simple as that.

'If I went into all the technical details you just would not be able to comprehend it—no one could *fully* conceive the intricacies of spirit surgery and treatment until he is in the spirit world himself and endowed with the understanding of spirit. Even then, unless one becomes a spirit doctor, one couldn't understand all the complex methods and techniques. So, I think, the best and easiest way to answer your question is to reiterate what I said a moment ago—spirit healing is healing *from* spirit, *through* spirit, *to* the spirit body of the patient, and thence to the physical body of the patient.'

'I agree that I would be unable to understand fully the intricacies of spirit surgery techniques, since I am an author and not a doctor,' I said. 'But couldn't you explain it in a way which would be understood by ordinary people?'

'I'll try,' Mr. Lang consented. After a moment's thought, he said: 'I think the best way to explain the *basic* conception of spirit healing is by making it clear that the healing vibrations that are used in spirit healing are of divine source—coming direct from God. They are precisely the same vibrations as were used by Jesus Christ—the greatest healer that ever lived!—and later by His disciples in the performance of healing miracles. These same vibrations were also used in the early days by the Sovereigns of this country when they exercised their divine power of healing but, as medical knowledge grew, the power reposing in them became dormant. To this day, exactly the same vibrations are being used by some clergymen of all denominations and religions and frequently bring about successful cures or improvements of various diseases. These clergymen, however, attribute their healing achievements to religion and do their utmost to conceal the fact that their successes are due actually to spirit healing.

'The use of healing vibrations to cure the sick is a science and not a religion. They form part of the natural laws of the Universe and should, in consequence, be used accordingly.

'When I—or any other spirit doctor—attend to a patient, I make full use of these healing vibrations. I draw healing power from spirit and this power passes through me to the spirit body of the ailing patient and thence to his physical body.'

'When I discussed your spirit operations with various people, and particularly with a doctor, I found that they refuse to accept the existence of an unseen spirit body even though they acknowledge your successes in overcoming incurable diseases,' I said.

'Well, I know that a good many people—and especially members of the medical profession—just will not accept the fact that there is a spirit body,' Mr. Lang said. 'People with a materialistic outlook cannot get it into their heads that besides having a physical body which they can see, they also have a spirit body which they can't see. But each and every person has a spirit body, this is undeniable.

'It would be easier for them to accept and understand if they could say: "When my life on earth is finished, I pass into the spirit world, and when I do so, I live in my spirit body which is the same as I inhabited on earth; and the only difference is the texture, and the fact that the physical body is mortal while the spirit body lives on after death." And if they advanced a step further and said: "I have a spirit body that the spirit doctor can either operate on or apply treatment to bring about changes; these changes will in due course transfer to my physical body and improve my physical condition," they would understand the overall working of spirit healing.

'I see for myself only too often how very difficult it is for some people—and particularly medical men—to really accept these things. For example, if I talk with some doctors who come to consult me—or with other intelligent and knowledgeable patients—about, say the brain, and say: "Well, you've got a brain, you have eight cranio* bones, we can part these and remove the tumour", they know what I'm talking about. But if I say: "You have a spirit body here which you can't see and I am going to perform an invisible and painless operation on it, remove the tumour, and by removing it from your spirit body, bring about a satisfactory change in your physical body", it's beyond them. They just say "yes" but don't really understand what I am saying. So, you see, one has to express one's self in simple terms.'

'Can you tell me how it is that you are able to give such a precise diagnosis of a patient's ailment, and how you operate on the spirit body?' was my next question.

'Well, as a preamble I should perhaps tell you that as a spirit doctor, I can see the spirit body which is invisible to you and most people. Thus, when I look upon a patient, I can see both his bodies—the physical and spirit body—simultaneously, I can also see the person's aura,† or reflected light, which is constantly moving and changing colour, and exists about two inches from the body. The aura consists of colour vibrations reflected by the organs of the body, which are constantly changing according to the state of their health. Each organ, when healthy, reflects a definite colour in the aura, but when the organ becomes diseased, or its condition deteriorates, the reflection changes colour. So, you see, by looking at a patient's aura, I know immediately the *overall* state of health which is of course of some diagnostic help.

'However, to diagnose a patient's trouble *precisely*, it is necessary to examine the body, because the reflection of the aura, as I said before, gives only an overall picture. Now, how I examine patients

* Cranio (kranion) = combining form denoting the cranium, the foetal head; cranial.

† The human aura was demonstrated and photographed by Dr. Kilner in 1913. Apart from spirit doctors (and other spirits) the aura can also be seen by people with very well-developed psychic faculties.

I needn't describe to you because you know this from your own experience, and you also know that I always examine the patient's *spirit* body. The reason I am able to give a precise diagnosis and detect conditions which earthly doctors and specialists cannot discover by physical examination, is due to my ability to examine the spirit body.

'But don't let it ever enter you head the reason for doctors and specialists sometimes being unable to diagnose correctly, or cure, some difficult disease is that they are incompetent or just don't care about their patients! The medical profession is a noble one and not to be needlessly attacked or criticised. It is my own profession and one which, after all, provided me with my education and knowledge. It was my passport for my return to earth as a spirit doctor working through my medium.

'The reason why some doctors are unable to diagnose, or cure, certain diseases is that earthly conditions, which govern the physical body, often hinder them in their sincere desire to heal. As a spirit doctor, I am in a privileged position, because earthly conditions do not interfere with my work. Attending to the spirit body, I can examine each organ with ease and am not handicapped by the skin and other tissues that cover the organs of the physical body. I am able to see and recognise at once what is wrong.

'This, I think, answers your question on how I diagnose. Now as to the next one—how I operate on the spirit body and so forth.

'If I need to operate on the spirit body, or give it any other form of treatment, I must draw it slightly away from the physical body so as to establish the healing vibrations with the spirit world—draw on the spirit power—so that the spirit body is in a proper condition to be attended to.

'Now, people—and perhaps you are one of them—don't really have a complete picture of the spirit body, and those who accept the fact that there is such a thing as an unseen spirit body, usually assume that it is within the physical body. This is, however, not so—the spirit body is, in fact, outside the physical body, wrapped round it, as it were, yet it can also contract into the physical body. But, although the spirit body is outside, it is essential to draw it forward slightly so that I can create the vibrations whereby it becomes "alive". You see, when the spirit body becomes "alive", those organs which were previously tiny, assume their right size, and we are able to operate or provide what treatment is advisable.

'I am not *always* performing operations. If I find, for instance, that a patient has a liver complaint which I can cure by giving him injections, I use an astra fluid which I inject into the organ of the spirit body. Such activities as I have so far described are all carried out, one must not forget, by Basil and my colleagues and assistants.'

'Are operations on the spirit body similar to those performed by surgeons in hospital?' I enquired.

'Well, yes, on the whole there is a similarity as far as the actual surgery is concerned,' Mr. Lang explained. 'Most of the spirit instruments are identical with those used in hospitals, but we use fewer instruments because the texture of the spirit body is different, and we are thus able to reach the site of the operation very quickly. A surgeon or theatre sister who watches me perform an operation knows what I am doing from the instruments I ask for and how I am using them, although they can't see the actual operation.'

I knew that this was so because several people with medical training had told me exactly the same when I interviewed them about their own cases; or cases which they had observed in Mr. Lang's consulting room.

I next asked Mr. Lang how it was that he, a noted *ophthalmic* surgeon during his lifetime, was now able to perform highly specialised operations in different fields of surgery?

'Oh, I am able to perform most operations because, you see, although I specialised in ophthalmology, I was also a general surgeon at the London Hospital at Whitechapel and I made a study of all forms of surgery,' Mr. Lang explained. 'But usually it's not just myself who is operating. For instance, over there just now is a group of my friends who actually worked with me at the hospital, and with them are also a number of Basil's contemporaries. Among them is David Little, Arnold Lawson, Adams, McEwen, and quite a few others.* Each of them is a specialist in his own field and has his own methods and technique, and we all work together as a team assisting each other.

* Some of the other surgeons in William Lang's team are: W. Pasteur, M.D., F.R.C.P.; Sidney Coupland, M.C., F.R.C.P.; Victor Bonney, M.D., M.S., B.SC., F.R.C.S.; W. Sampson Henley, M.D., M.S., F.R.C.S.; Sir John Bland-Sutton, F.R.C.S.; Sir R. Douglas Powell, Bart., K.C.V.O., M.D.; Sir W. T. Lister, etc. There is also a nursing staff, and the one in charge of it is Sister Ormand.

'If I have a patient, say with a grown exostosis,* then I may talk to one of my colleagues and ask him for his opinion. We generally have a consultation and I listen to what my colleagues say because they are specialised in particular fields. Now, if a very specialised operation needs to be performed, I prefer one of my colleagues to do it, but I do the talking to the patient and actively assist in the operation because I am the one working through a medium. My son Basil very often operates—he is a fine, a very fine surgeon.'

'When you perform your operations, you frequently flick your fingers. Did you do that as well when you were on earth?'

'Quite, quite. Of course the point was that if I worked with trained people they knew what I wanted just by the clicking of my fingers. The same now applies. If I want to start to perform eye surgery, for instance, I say "injection" and click my fingers, but afterwards I just click my fingers. I don't need to say anything, they know exactly what I want because they all are quite as good as—and even better than—I am. We are all equal—surgeons, sisters, and so on—there is no one higher or lower, we are a team.'

'In interviewing a considerable number of your patients, I discovered that some of them had noticed operation scars on their physical bodies—in fact I myself discovered a pink scar-like appearance on my own body,' I said. 'Can you tell me how these phenomena—light pink marks which look like scars and with pink dots which look like stitch marks but which are so smooth that the skin is not affected—come about?'

'I have explained to you that I always attend to the spirit body and that the operations I perform reflect upon the physical body and bring about the desired improvement or cure of the patient. I think this answers your question, because scars are part of operations.'

'But how is it then that some patients do not bear these marks on their bodies?' I asked.

'I think I am justified in saying that scars appear in every case, but the majority are so faint that the human eye cannot discern them. Certain patients, however, possess such very sensitive skins that the marks are clearly visible.'

* The most common benign tumour of the bone, usually seen as a cartilage-capped bony growth protruding from the surface.

'Can you enlighten me on the use of ectoplasm* for replacing damaged or diseased parts of the body?'

'Well, ectoplasm is a substance used from the medium's body—it's not from the spirit world—this is why I need a good medium,' Mr. Lang answered. 'When a patient, such as yourself, arrives, I make what I call a rod, and this rod joins you to my medium's body. I then draw up a certain amount of ectoplasm which I can mould.

'If a patient, for example, has a growth which is the cause of his ill health, I remove it by an operation and that is the end of it. The patient will in due course be cured. But, if a patient has a piece of diseased intestine, for instance, then I operate to remove it and replace it with ectoplasm, because the part is still vital to the human body. So you see, ectoplasm plays quite an important part in spirit surgery, but it is not something that is of universal and unlimited usage. Sometimes you hear people say that ectoplasm is used for this and that, but that's nonsense, it's just not so.'

'If, for one reason or other, an earthly surgeon cut off too much of an organ during an operation, could you replace that missing part with ectoplasm?' I asked.

'Yes, I attempt to do this, but it's not always successful, it depends on the circumstances and also on the individual patient. But I have had a fair number of patients in whose bodies I rebuilt missing parts in this way quite successfully. In fact, in some cases when patients went to the hospital for X-ray examinations after I had rebuilt a missing part in their bodies with ectoplasm, the X-rays showed that the previously missing parts had indeed "grown again".'

'Would you say that Spiritualists, people who implicitly believe in spirit healing, benefit more from your operations or treatment than others who have no faith in it but just hope for the best?'

'Not at all, it doesn't make any difference,' Mr. Lang stated with emphasis. 'It all depends on the person being "in tune", as I call it.

'Some of those who come to see me have no belief in anything at all, but intrinsically are good persons. I also get some who are,

* Ectoplasm is a protoplastic substance streaming out of the body of a medium; it is matter, invisible and intangible in the primary state but assuming vaporous liquid or solid condition in various stages of condensation. It often emits a smell. (The word ectoplasm originated from Professor Richet.)

inside themselves, evil. But I am not concerned with this, I am a spirit doctor here to help the sick. So I get them on the healing couch, talk to them and draw their spirit body away a little—as I explained to you earlier on. Even in the most difficult situation I manage to create an atmosphere which is calm and free from emotion, and as and when the patient is mentally and physically relaxed, and in a state to receive the treatment I need to give him, I start attending to his spirit body.

'I cannot stress it often enough that spirit healing has nothing whatsoever to do with faith or faith healing and is consequently available to everyone in need of healing. With spirit healing it is, in this respect, exactly the same as with medical treatment. A patient's personal beliefs or disbeliefs have nothing to do with the effectiveness of the treatment he receives from his own doctor or in hospital, and this applies to spirit healing. The only thing that helps spirit healing to bring about speedier results on the physical body is the patient's will to get better, but this is true of medicine generally.

'I think it is appropriate that I should mention the healing services which are from time to time attended and conducted by persons with strong religious convictions.

'During these services hymns are sung and fervent prayers offered for those members of the congregation in ill health. These proceedings are often carried out until an emotional state is built up and with it a certain amount of magnetic power. This power then passes into the bodies of the patients and, the store-house of energy being thus temporarily revitalised, the aura brightens and the patients feel somewhat better.

'The effect, however, is not lasting, and after a short while the patient relapses into his or her former state of ill health, but with the important difference that his or her mental state is worse than before. They do not understand the reason for their relapse, and if they are deeply religious they tend to become introspective. This leads them to question whether they have shown sufficient faith in God and they begin to ask themselves if they no longer enjoy His favour and have been deprived of His love and understanding. Most of them will doubt now that spiritual healing can restore their health, and in all probability may never seek its assistance again.

'In the circumstances which I have just described no healing has ever, in fact, taken place. The sick have merely been given a spiritual tonic which has had no lasting effect, because the illness has remained untouched. I do not mean to say that those churches, endeavouring to bring about spiritual healing by prayer, should give up trying to help the sick. But if they do not wish merely to scratch the surface of something they do not at present understand, they must seek a new approach to the problem and adopt the methods of spirit healing and train their members to be instruments of the Divine Powers as were Jesus Christ and His disciples.

'There are many people who have the latent gift of healing who could be trained to the services of the church and the medical profession. It is not the prerogative of the few, but many are unaware of such gifts having been bestowed on them. But if these people could enter the realm of spirit healing in the same way that my medium has done, then they could become available to many spirit doctors who are eager to work on earth in the same way as I do, by restoring health to the sick.

'Let me say that spirit healing is a science—a science of the Universe—and to achieve the results of which it is capable you must obey its laws. And, being a science, spirit healing requires no religious ceremony, invocation, or emotion. I wish to make it clear, however, that I pay due respect to those who, in a spirit of thankfulness to God, turn to hymns and prayers of praise for the benefits and blessings they hope to receive; but these things are not essential.

'If I say that prayers are not necessary for bringing about effective spirit healing, it is not to be assumed for one moment that spirit controls are not of God. We are all of God and I never commence a healing session without giving thanks to God for being allowed to return to earth, and also for the use of my medium.'

I enquired of Mr. Lang how he managed to visit the many thousands of patients who have come to him through George Chapman and regularly require distant healing.

'Oh, I just can't be in every place, that's quite impossible,' Mr. Lang replied. 'I visit of course a great many patients during their sleeping state, but I only visit those who I feel require my personal attention. Other patients are visited by my colleagues in spirit. It doesn't really matter to the patient whether it is myself, Basil, Lister, or any other spirit doctor who comes to visit him; the important thing is that he receives spirit healing and benefits from it.'

'How do you, or your spirit doctor colleagues, find the patients?'

'It's easy—but it's more correct to say that the patients find *me*. You see, when a patient is ill, he or she thinks of me and thus sends out a thought vibration which is very positive. Now, when it is received into the spirit world it's picked up by someone who then passes it on to me.

'Very often when a person feels very ill and wants me to attend to him as speedily as possible, I may be performing an operation or examining a patient here and cannot, consequently, receive the thought message. So, whoever picks up the vibration goes to help the patient, and then comes to tell me what's happened. As soon as I am free, they take me to wherever the patient is.'

'Would you say that distant healing is as effective as contact healing?'

'Oh, my goodness, no. Contact healing is far more successful. Let me explain. You come to see me here and I know I can help you, so I operate on you. Then I tell you I'm going to visit you during your sleep state and this I do. Now then, when I visit you during your sleep state I can attend to what needs to be done—because I operated on your spirit body during contact healing—and frequently I use healing rays; this is why people often see lights.

'Generally speaking, when a person writes for distant healing only—and is somebody with whom I have not established direct contact before—the results are not nearly as striking.

'Of course distant healing is of considerable importance. In many cases where the patient is very, very ill—maybe a young child or someone who is bedridden—and I know I can really do something, then help is very effective even if the patient has never experienced contact healing. But don't ever get the idea we can do away with contact healing and go over entirely to distant healing. Distant healing is, broadly speaking, just spirit treatment, while with contact healing I can perform *any* necessary operation and, being able to draw so much from the medium, I am able to use almost unlimited power from the spirit world.'

'Having investigated a number of your distant healing cases, I discovered that some of them resulted in truly miraculous cures.'

'Quite. Some patients we visit are very psychic, and when they are really at the lowest degree of consciousness we are able to draw their spirit bodies far enough away—into the spirit world, so to speak. I can then operate and give the patient such treatment as I do in contact healing. On occasions—while the medium is sleeping soundly in his normal rest—I can also use some of his power to supplement the treatment in these particular distant healing cases, and, if there is a strong psychic in the family, I can do much the same. This is why some cases of distant healing are as effective as contact healing. But you must always remember that these special cases are few and far between.'

'You would then advise anyone suffering from a serious illness to come for contact healing whenever possible?'

'Yes—if it is possible.'

'One of your patients told me that you have a secretary in the spirit world who keeps complete records of all your patients for you. Is that correct, and if so, is his name Hunt?'

'Yes, that is so. His name was originally John Hunter but by legal arrangement he changed it to Hunt. He was in fact a friend of mine during my life upon earth, and over here our friendship continues of course. Now, although I've said he's my secretary it's not quite correct because, in the first place, he gives me advice, considerable help, and also keeps my records in order.

'Thanks to dear Hunt, I know what's wrong with a patient as soon as he comes here, because, you see, while I attend to a patient, Hunt records everything that takes place during the consultation. Yesterday, for instance, a patient called Clark arrived, but Margaret couldn't remember anything about him because he hadn't been here for years. As soon as they opened the door, I was, however, able to say: "Oh, yes, I know you," and tell him all about his visit some years ago—because of Hunt's invaluable records.'

The conversation returned to spirit healing and Mr. Lang confirmed to me that he and his colleagues are able to cure almost any illness—provided it is not too late even for spirit healing. He mentioned his success with several victims of poliomyelitis by removing the deadly virus and preventing paralysis. He also furnished me with proof that he and his colleagues had managed to save victims of leukaemia.

'The word "incurable" which has long been in medical currency —and I suppose I myself have used it on certain occasions—is not always accurate,' Mr. Lang concluded. 'If I can judge a patient's life force—the spark, if you wish, the desire to get well—and the patient is determined to fight the illness, then of course I can help.

'It is of no use seeking out the help of a healer or doctor and expecting to play a passive role. A patient, and especially an "incurable" patient, should co-operate by his desire to get better.

'Broadly speaking, nothing is incurable—provided the patient seeks help when his health deteriorates and does not fight the help he is given.'

CHAPTER THIRTY-FOUR

Ever victorious?

IT WOULD be reasonable to assume that anyone reading this catalogue of success is likely to wonder if it is not inevitable. I asked William Lang if this could be said of his work.

'No. I do not perform miracles and I do not lead patients to believe that I can. When my spirit operations and treatment end in failure—and, unfortunately, this does happen from time to time, though, thank God, only rarely—it is due to the fact that even spirit doctors work within a framework of natural laws. Age must eventually takes its toll with every one. Those parts of the body that become worn out with age, cannot be entirely replaced. But in those cases, where I am able to recognise that the earthly life of a patient is approaching its end, I continue to do all I can to relieve suffering. I can still perform operations on their spirit bodies with ectoplasm, but this is only a temporary measure to secure some relief and comfort for them. When the earthly life is nearing its inevitable close we cannot prolong it, but we endeavour to make the passing into the spirit world as easy for the patient as we can.

'Another reason for spirit operations and treatment not being always successful is that some of the patients come to see me too late in the day. In these cases the disease—often caused by a dangerous virus infection—has already secured too devastating a grip on the patient. As a result, nothing that I can do is of any avail, that is in a permanent sense. No, spirit operations and spirit treatment are not *always* successful. But I would again like to emphasise that no disease is incurable, if a patient consults me in time.'

I also spoke with George Chapman on the same subject, and he told me very candidly that some people do not benefit at all from Mr. Lang's treatment. He recalled an instance which occurred seven years previously.

'The relatives of a patient who was in a large west country hospital asked me to see him there and to give him spirit healing,' he said. 'They told me that the surgeon in charge of the case had given permission. I was also told that there was an early history of pneumonia and removal of appendix, and that at that time the patient was thought to be suffering from a slipped disc. However, in an operation the surgeon had removed a cancerous abscess; later another operation had been performed in London for the removal of a duodenal ulcer. Just before I'd been asked to visit the hospital a further operation had been carried out to deal with conditions set in the liver and prostate gland. There was serious concern about the patient's condition and the hospital held out very little hope of recovery. The patient was in severe and constant pain, for which large dosages of morphia were being given.

'When I saw him in a private ward, it looked as if his end was very near. The hospital staff were very kind and co-operative and a nurse remained with the patient while I went into trance and Mr. Lang afterwards took over. Well of course he did everything he could to ease the poor man's pain, and he succeeded. The patient became more peaceful and at ease. Mr. Lang spoke to the nurse during the treatment, and to the patient's mother telling her what he was doing, and explaining to her that although her son was too far gone, it was possible to alleviate his suffering. The mother was so grateful you know. A few days later the man died peacefully.

'One afternoon, about a year after this incident, my wife received a telephone message to the effect that a child was in a very bad way in a large Midlands general hospital. The surgeon there had said he doubted if the child would last the night. And of course her mother and father were frantic. It upset me, because I love children, so, although the case seemed hopeless, I promised I would drive to the hospital immediately to enable Mr. Lang to do what he possibly could for the child. It was a dark night with heavy rain, and conditions were wretched.

'When I arrived at the hospital I learned that the child was suffering from leukaemia and was having a blood transfusion. I had to wait a long time in the depressing atmosphere of a waiting-room, doing my best to comfort the parents who were in despair. Contrary to what I had been given to understand, they had not obtained permission from the hospital authorities for my visit. This resulted in further delay but, when approached, the surgeon in charge readily gave his consent, and in fact watched Mr. Lang attending to the child.

'It was one o'clock when I left the hospital, but despite the depressing conditions of the journey home, I felt that even if the child could not be saved, we had done all we could. I wasn't able to get to the hospital again and distant healing was given instead. It was sad that this little child's life couldn't be saved. The call had come too late. The only thing that could be done was to make her last hours on earth as comfortable as possible.

'Both the contact and distant healing had the expected effect. Three weeks after my visit to the hospital the child was able to return home where she spent a few happy months free from pain, before passing peacefully into spirit.'

In a more cheerful vein George Chapman went on to tell me:

'Not all our visits to hospitals ended unhappily. Mr. O., for instance, wrote asking for distant healing for his wife, who was in hospital with cancer of the breast. He asked if I would see her there and give her contact healing. Permission for this was granted by the surgeon, so I went. William Lang decided it was necessary to perform some operations on the woman's spirit body, and when he eventually finished his surgery, he stated that she was now clear of cancer, and requested that the surgeon should confirm this.

'The surgeon re-examined the patient and because of doubt decided to obtain another opinion. The woman was seen by another specialist but he too was unable to express a definite opinion. The situation was explained to the husband who was asked if he would permit an exploratory operation to be performed in order that the surgeon could ascertain exactly what had taken place. The husband agreed, and after it had been done, it was stated that "it was a wrong diagnosis in the first place; there must have been just a small cyst which has cleared away".

'The patient was discharged from hospital three days later. This took place in February 1954, and the patient has been fit and well ever since.'

I asked Chapman if he could provide me with an overall percentage of failures.

'I'm afraid I don't know,' he replied. 'It is not easy for me to compile accurate records on the effect of William Lang's treatment, because I depend entirely on information from the patients. Every patient who comes here for contact healing, and those who receive distant healing, are asked to submit health reports regularly. As long as they do this I know to what extent the healing is successful. The trouble is, however, that most of them stop writing to me when they are fully recovered. But I have no means of knowing if the healing is lasting. It is of course true that when a patient experiences any sort of deterioration in health, he or she is quick to write for an appointment with Mr. Lang or for distant healing to be resumed; but this is no guarantee that those patients who have *not* communicated again with me since they last reported a complete cure of their complaint, *are* permanently cured.

'You yourself discovered that patients suddenly "fade out" when you examined my files. You saw that a lot of the patients' records are far from up-to-date, and that the last entry in many of them dates back to anything up to ten years, or even longer. I'd like to think that where a patient no longer informs me about his state of health that we've been able to cure him permanently. But how can one be sure? As a matter of fact, the only authentic evidence I have about patients experiencing lasting cures since they stopped writing to me, was furnished by yourself after you had them traced to their homes.

'If I wanted to keep all the case histories up-to-date so that I would know exactly what happened to them I'd have to employ a special clerical staff just for correspondence and filing work. And I, too, would have to give up a lot of time to it. As things stand, there just isn't enough time available for me to enable William Lang to see all the patients who ask for appointments. I have to try to fit them in at dates in the future and arrange that during the waiting time they receive distant healing. I consider it more important to spend what available time is left to me (after dealing with patients' health reports, etc.) by being in trance and enabling William Lang to help the sick, than keeping reliable post-treatment records.'

Under the circumstances, I'm afraid, I cannot provide an answer as to what proportion of failures there is among the enormous number of Mr. Lang's successes.

During my investigations I interviewed 153* Lang-Chapman ex-patients, and after the most searching enquiry into all the circumstances found that these men and women had been cured completely and lastingly by Mr. Lang—the majority of them many years ago.

Following upon the opinions expressed by Lang and Chapman as to whether spirit healing is always successful, I decided to seek the view of a medical man on the subject. The person best qualified to answer this question seemed to me to be Mr. S. G. Miron, L.D.S., R.C.S. (Eng.), because he is able to speak with authority both from the orthodox viewpoint and from personal knowledge of William Lang's achievements. I asked him point blank: 'As a researcher of William Lang's work, would you say his spirit operations are always successful?'

'No, I would not agree. I would say they were not more successful than ordinary operations in this phase of existence. The reasons, however, are far deeper and more obscure.

'I have been present at many operations in hospitals where the operation as a technical excercise was completely successful, but the patient died, for one reason or another. In some cases the actual cause of death was never fully established.

'Suffice to say, however, that the majority of cases that come before William Lang are those which have received little benefit from orthodox medical and surgical treatment, and many are very advanced cases. Yet I myself know of a number of cancer sufferers, regarded as hopeless cases, who have recovered and returned to normal health following William Lang's spirit healing.

'The purposes of spirit operations are manifold, but generally

* Some of these patients objected, for strictly personal reasons, to my publishing their names and addresses, but willingly gave me all the information I required about their medical history and the treatment and cure by Mr. Lang. They also allowed me to check and counter-check their tape-recorded statements. Some suggested I should just quote their initials. But as they were unwilling to be interrogated by other researchers if necessary, I decided not to include their cases in this book. I explained earlier that I intended to deal with *named* patients only who were willing to substantiate my enquiry into their cures. Being limited by space, the omission of those patients who wanted to remain anonymous served a two-fold purpose.

they do not differ from the operations performed by ordinary surgeons. Even where William Lang's spirit operations or treatment do not cure a seriously ill patient, I can say without hesitation—speaking from experience and thorough research of Lang's work—that the sufferer is helped tremendously, and greatly eased the passage into the next level of existence.'

During the many interviews I had with William Lang or George Chapman we often talked about the impossibility of giving all but a few new patients an appointment for an early consultation. 'Only if there is a cancellation can a new patient, whose case is urgent, be fitted in. Otherwise it means having to wait your turn, unfortunate as it is,' George Chapman told me.

'The real answer to the problem is the training of more mediums to work with those spirit doctors who are awaiting the day when they too can exercise their skill on earth in the same way as William Lang,' I said.

'This is true in respect to the principles of William Lang's activities as seen in the direct doctor-to-patient approach but it requires long training,' Chapman said. 'Remember how many years it took before the spirit world trained me before I became capable of working with William Lang?'

'Do you happen to know if mediums of your type are being trained now for future work with spirit doctors on this earth?'

'I don't know what sort of training is being given to healing mediums by the spirit people, but I dare say such efforts are being made because of what William Lang has said on various occasions,' Chapman replied. 'The only thing I can tell you for certain is that a trance medium and a non-trance healer are receiving training here at the Tuesday Free Clinic.'

'How is this training of the trance medium being done?'

'Well, I think you'd better ask my control. Anything I could tell you would only be second-hand because, as you know, while I am in trance I have no knowledge whatsoever of what is taking place here. William Lang can tell you much better because he is doing the training.'

I broached the question to the spirit doctor, and he gave me the following explanation:

'I have a lady student at the Tuesday Free Clinic, and she's a very promising prospect as a healing-medium. As a matter of fact, she is being trained to become her father's instrument and enable him to work in the same way as George enables me to work. You see, her father was a splendid doctor while he lived on this earth, and he's a dear friend of mine. He is waiting for the day when he'll be able to resume his healing work. He is anxious to set up his own spirit doctor practice with his daughter as medium at Hayes in Middlesex.'

'How is the training carried out?'

'I am only helping with it,' Mr. Lang corrected me. 'The actual *mediumistic* training is being done by the spirit people who have the necessary knowledge in this particular field—it's the same process as that employed with George when he was being prepared for becoming my instrument before I took control of his entranced body. However, in order to try to shorten the training period as much as possible, and enable her father to become a spirit doctor more speedily, the daughter receives here what you could call preliminary spirit surgery tuition. And while she is here, developing and getting to know her own healing powers, her father looks in and acquaints himself with our methods of healing, and also takes every opportunity to experiment in taking control of the body of his future instrument.'

'When do you think this lady will be sufficiently trained?'

'It's very difficult to say,' Mr. Lang replied diplomatically. 'The training period of a healing-medium—a medium such as George is —is a lengthy affair. But the young lady is making very promising progress.'

'As and when the day comes that this new spirit doctor will be able to work through his medium, will it mean that you and George are not as overworked as you are at present?'

'Well, yes. You see, there are many spirit non-trance healers in this country, and some of them are really outstanding with many successes to their credit. But many patients today are just not content with receiving healing and being cured by a healer through the agency of spirit power but who cannot talk to them as a doctor does and explain to them what's wrong with them. They like to speak with the spirit doctor, to ask him questions—as they do with earthly doctors and specialists—and this is why it is so important that as many healing-mediums as possible are trained, so that spirit doctors can work through them.'

'As far as you know, are there many healing-mediums being trained to serve as future instruments for spirit doctors who wish to return to earth?'

'A fair number are being trained but, of course, only *born* mediums can be developed for this special task. But, as times goes on, new healing-mediums will appear on the scene and more and more spirit doctors will be able to perform operations and treat all those sufferers who are in urgent need of help.'

'If the number of spirit doctors increase as time goes by, won't this affect the livelihood of the non-trance healers, many of whom, as you say, achieve remarkable successes with incurable diseases?'

'No, there can never be enough *good* healers. More and more people are turning for help to spirit healing. It is only too obvious that many more healers and spirit doctors are required.'

'If there is eventually a much denser network of spirit doctors and non-trance healers, will it affect the medical profession?'

'Good Lord, no! We are not competing with the medical profession, we are doing all we can to co-operate with them, in so far as they allow us to do so. At present, there are only comparatively few medical men who accept our co-operation; most doctors stubbornly refuse to acknowledge any successes brought about through spirit operations or healing. But when a vast body of spirit doctors and first-class non-trance healers are able to operate all over the country, and irrefutable proof of the efficacy of spirit healing is established beyond contradiction, the medical profession will revise their present hostile attitude and will eventually co-operate. And, then, humanity will benfit as it is entitled to—on the grand scale. Unnecessary suffering and premature deaths will become things of the past.

'Anyone who thinks in terms of competition between spirit healing and the medical profession has got hold of the wrong end of the stick. Let me sum it up this way:

'Spirit healing cures illnesses and brings comfort to the sick, but everyone must always recognise that the medical profession does this too. It is a fine profession and one which humanity could not do without. Surgeons, doctors and nurses give magnificent service to the sick all over the world. No healer should ever discourage a patient from attending a doctor—in fact he should always advise his patient to seek the help of the medical profession. Whenever possible, doctors should be told when their patients are receiving spirit healing. There should be the fullest co-operation between the two professions because each can learn much from the other. After all, modern scientific medicine owes much to its early forbears. And, in the main, spirit doctors who return to do healing work on earth were doctors during their earthly life span. So you see, though, broadly speaking, miles apart at present, spirit doctors and earthly doctors belong to the same profession—the profession whose noble aim it is to cure the sick.'

The passionate intensity with which Lang spoke revealed how greatly concerned he was, and is, with human welfare. It also indicated once again how strongly he feels on the subject of the abolition of barriers between orthodox medicine and spirit healing. Surely, these are sufficient reasons for the making of a great attempt to secure a unity that will assuredly benefit mankind.

EPILOGUE

WHEN I went to see William Lang on January 6, 1964, I drove to Aylesbury as a sceptic, but at the moment of writing fourteen months later, I am firmly convinced that the seemingly old white-coated gentleman who receives patients at St. Brides is indeed the spirit of the late William Lang, F.R.C.S., acting through his medium's body. I am equally convinced that, in the Aylesbury house, daily cures of a miraculous nature are brought about.

My conviction was bolstered by the stubborn and thorough investigation and research work I engaged in during the past twelve months. Naturally the first stirrings of belief came from my own experience in connection with my eyes, the sight of which is still steadily improving. But, as I pointed out at the beginning of this book, it is not my intention to try to convert anyone to my own way of thinking.

While working on the book, I have frequently talked with doctors and nurses about the cures claimed for William Lang. Many of them had come into contact in one way or another with the remarkable curative changes that occurred after patients sought help at Aylesbury. Some of them openly endorsed the fact that extraordinary cures of incurable diseases had indeed been brought about by the spirit doctor's operations and treatment. Another section, despite confrontation with authenticated evidence of cures, still insisted that the laws of nature could and must have been instrumental—this despite the overwhelming medical and mathematical odds against the possibility of it happening. And of course there were those who did not wish to commit themselves either way. They just said they were not convinced that the phenomena *had* or *had not* been caused by spirit healing. In all honesty I must confess that this latter group, the non-committal, made up the greatest numbers. It was also distinguished for its *consensus ad idem* on one particular point—all its members said that basically they were not too concerned about how the cures had happened, the main thing was that they had happened.

On frequent occasions I have also spoken with my friend Liam Nolan—a writer and a most critical and down-to earth man possessing what I consider to be a high degree of intelligence—about the Lang-Chapman partnership, their fabulous successes and, in particular, about the fantastic improvement of my own eyesight. We'd only met and become friends *after* William Lang had saved me from threatened blindness, so Nolan didn't know from personal observation how appallingly poor my vision had been before my visit to St. Brides.

I was aware of the fact that Nolan was far from convinced that the spirit doctor could bring about all the miraculous cures I'd told him about, he was too polite in the beginning to press any question or openly challenge anything I'd said. The glint of cynicism in his eyes, however, betrayed that he was far from accepting that the events of which I had spoken could be possible. It struck me that he thought I might have become a victim of self-delusion. As time went by and we continued discussing William Lang and his work, it became more obvious than ever that Nolan could not fathom how the sceptical and cynical journalist and writer he knew me to be could be taken in so completely by what could easily have been pretence or trickery. Of course he never dropped any remark that put it so bluntly, but I had a good idea of how his thoughts were running.

Then, one day when I was telling him about an especially striking example of Lang's skill which I had just investigated, I suggested to my writer friend that he should come with me to Aylesbury to meet the spirit doctor and his medium. He readily agreed. It didn't surprise me. I knew the kind of coldly analytical and perceptive mind he had, and I was fairly sure he'd say yes when I made the suggestion.

Our appointment with William Lang was for four o'clock in the afternoon—after the spirit doctor had attended to his last patient that day.

Liam Nolan sat opposite the doctor, scepticism and alertness written all over his face. I sat on the settee at the far side of the consulting room, watching the two and listening to the interrogation that my friend launched. As the meeting went on, the spirit doctor's polite sincerity began to have some effect on Nolan's semi-hostility. His approach became slightly friendlier, though he continued questioning the spirit doctor over a wide range of subjects. Once or twice his questions led Lang to rise from his chair and walk to a picture on a wall, and to a book-case.

The interview lasted about an hour.

After, when George Chapman regained consciousness, Nolan talked with him in a nonchalant way about Liverpool, Chapman's youth, work and many other topics. It was quite plain to me that he was keeping the conversation flowing, trying by astute probing and conversational gambits to make Chapman talk as much as possible. He had on occasions said to me that if a person talks long enough and freely enough you will get the key to his character. It seemed to me now that he was trying to pick similarities in speech between Chapman and Lang.

Later, when I was sitting next to Nolan as he drove his car along the A-413 towards London, I enquired what he thought about his meeting with the spirit doctor and his medium.

'I'm sorry to have to say this, Joe, but I am not at all convinced that the man in the white coat is William Lang, the surgeon,' he said.

'What about the marked differences in speech and mannerism between the man in the surgery and Chapman with whom you've just been drinking tea?' I asked.

'That doesn't convince me in the least. Anyone with a flair for acting and some talent could play the two roles quite convincingly. Vocal tricks aren't all that difficult you know.'

'I disagree,' I said, but did not pursue the issue and went on to my next question: 'What about the spirit doctor's vast medical knowledge which you ascertained to a certain extent when questioning him? George Chapman has no medical knowledge at all—he was a garage hand, a butcher, served with the R.A.F. during the war and ended up as a fireman before he became a full-time medium.'

'How do *you* know that Chapman has no medical knowledge?' he fired at me.

'I checked his background and ascertained that he had only an elementary school education. Besides, a number of trained people questioned him during his waking state about medical subjects and confirmed that he has no medical knowledge whatsoever.'

'All this could be a calculated act,' Nolan said. 'Supposing he had no higher school education, that doesn't say he's not intelligent. And it isn't all that difficult for a person with intelligence to pick up an impressive-sounding vocabulary of medical terms from an encyclopaedia, or from the medical reference books in a library. Especially if he wanted to do so badly enough.'

'Aren't you going a bit too far, Liam?'

'I don't think so, Joe. If, for some reason best known to himself, he wanted to create the impression that, in his consulting room, he is the spirit doctor Lang, but in his conscious state he is just an ordinary man, it would be the easiest thing in the world for him to say no, he knows nothing about medicine when he is acting George Chapman again.'

'Very well,' I said, 'let's assume that the claim about the spirit doctor is a fake—fraud if you wish . . .'

'I didn't say that,' Nolan interrupted me.

'I know. But let's assume that the whole thing *is* a fake, fraud, hocus-pocus, trickery, or whatever we wish to call it. What good would it do Chapman?'

'Well, there are two basic reasons why he might be doing it.'

'Namely?'

'Namely: *One*, money. *Two*, could be that he is genuinely interested in conning people into thinking they are getting better. I mean maybe there is the power motive—a sort of medical Will Rogers. Or deep human feeling for people who are sick and who, because of his power to convince them, reckon they're not so bad after all. Some people you know almost revel in the idea that they're not well.'

'Let's put the money motive aside for the moment,' I said, 'because I think I can effectively prove that it's non-existent. Let's take your second reason—that he's interested in, as you say, "conning" people into getting better, how does he do it? How, if there's no spirit doctor working through him?'

'I wouldn't have thought miracles were the sole preserve of spirit doctors,' he replied. 'After all over five hundred million faithful of the Roman Catholic Church have a pretty solid catalogue of miracles running back nearly two thousand years. And their belief is in God, and the saints. What about Lourdes? Even non-Christians and anti-Christians have been on the panels of doctors and investigators who have certified miraculous cures there. And they've done it. Christians might well say that the cures that happen at Aylesbury are acts of God. And could you say they are not?'

'No, but then both William Lang and George Chapman always reiterate that they pray to God for His help and that all healing comes from God. You don't disbelieve that miracles can happen?' I asked.

'As a Catholic, how could I?' he said. 'All I'm saying is that I'm not convinced that, if miracles happen at Aylesbury, they happen because William Lang supposedly controls George Chapman. And, furthermore, I'm still not sure that miracles are accomplished there. A genuine miracle is a pretty phenomenal thing you know, and takes a hell of a lot of proof. There's such a thing as auto-suggestion, and that's powerful in the right hands.'

We left it at that for a while, agreeing to disagree.

Some little time later I asked Nolan if he would help me with the book by editing it and, where necessary, rewriting any parts that needed such treatment. He agreed, and I was pleased for a number of reasons, not the least of which was my awareness that he would bring a balanced and objective mind to the subject. He would not be 'conned'.

As I gathered the material, travelling up and down the country with my tape-recorder, I fed it to my colleague. I refrained from asking him whether he had undergone any change of mind about William Lang. I wanted him to see all the evidence, read what the patients and the doctors had to say. It was some months before I tackled him again, by which time the book was near completion.

'What do you make of the Lang-Chapman healing successes now?' I enquired.

'I am still not a hundred per cent convinced that the man I met at Aylesbury is the spirit doctor he purports to be,' he said in a semi-apologetic tone.

'And what about the unique healing successes? Do you refute them too?'

'No, I don't refute then,' he said. 'The authenticated case histories would make that very hard to do. There seem to have been some astonishing things done, and I can't pretend to understand how. But it is still too much for me to accept that there is such a thing as an unseen spirit body and that Lang, through Chapman, does operations on it and succeeds. It's investing him with the powers of a God, and that I can't accept.'

'But you are prepared to accept that miracles do happen in some inexplicable way after people visit St. Brides, and that also George Chapman is in some strange manner involved?'

'I'm very reluctant to commit myself on it, Joe,' he said. 'Something akin to miracles seems to have occurred. Real miracles? I don't know. And what Chapman's part in the whole scheme of things is I'm not sure of either.

'But yes, I do agree that phenomena of a greater or lesser degree have been attendant upon George Chapman's visits to sick people, and their visits to him. I don't accept your explanation. I'm puzzled.'

'As far as I myself am concerned,' I said, 'I am convinced that it *is* William Lang who works through the mediumship of George Chapman, but—everybody is perfectly entitled to his own view and to accept or reject *my* personal belief.

'In my view the only important issue is the question of whether or not these healing results have in fact happened. I think they've been brought about through Lang-Chapman. I am convinced of this, but you and many other people may argue against it. I also happen to believe that the only ones who are qualified to make an authoritative statement about the effectiveness of William Lang's cures and healing successes are the numerous patients of his who experienced both orthodox medical and spirit healing.

'All those patients whose cases are published in this book are living people, and all of them can hardly be wrong. They are able and willing to testify to the great help and benefit they have received through spirit operations and treatment from William Lang, should the need arise. I don't think it entirely reasonable that any one person should dismiss outright all claims of the Lang-Chapman healing successes while there exist such a large body of people—patients and doctors and nurses—who can testify in favour of the "dead" surgeon and his medium.'

Liam Nolan agreed that the bulk of evidence was impressive and that to dismiss it lightly would be unreasonable.

The number of people from all walks of life—in this country and many others—who believe that spirit healing can help the sick and who consequently avail themselves of its unique possibilities, is steadily growing. So far as George Chapman and William Lang are concerned, the rapid increase of patients who request early consultations with the spirit doctor is so great that Chapman finds it most difficult to comply with their desire.

Despite this trend, and despite the fact that some doctors, consultant specialists and hospital authorities accept William Lang's successes, the medical profession as a whole will not accept, at the moment, spirit healing in any degree. Indeed, it was not uncommon that when a convincing case of a miraculous cure by William Lang of a so-called incurable was presented for investigation, some of the medical profession just wagged their heads and said in effect: 'No, we cannot accept this. There must have been a mistake in the diagnosis in the first place.'

In their persistence in refusing to accept evidence these ultra-orthodox members of the medical profession are, in a way, enemies of humanity because *without attempting to engage in any research*, they determinedly dismiss any possibility of healing that does not originate from orthodox medicine. Fortunately, however, not every member of the medical profession thinks and behaves on these 'closed shop' lines. But as long as the present 'official' attitude towards spirit healing prevails, most of them dare not openly express their views, nor can they engage in research for fear that they might be accused of 'unprofessional conduct'.

Is it not strange that scientists everywhere are vying with each other to establish links between the earth and the planets, yet no serious scientific investigations are being made into spirit healing—a matter eminently affecting everyone? To establish a link with George Chapman and William Lang might afford a scientific basis for many discoveries for healing the sick, and for assisting the medical profession.

Though neither George Chapman nor William Lang has ever claimed that the healing of any spectacular case has been the result of a miracle—indeed, both always emphasised very strongly to me, and to countless other people, that Lang does not perform miracles—miracles *do* happen at Aylesbury.

THE BALAAM TEXT FROM DEIR ‘ALLĀ

HARVARD SEMITIC MUSEUM

HARVARD SEMITIC MONOGRAPHS

edited by
Frank Moore Cross

Number 31

THE BALAAM TEXT FROM DEIR ‘ALLĀ

by
Jo Ann Hackett

Jo Ann Hackett

THE BALAAM TEXT FROM DEIR ʿALLĀ

Scholars Press
Chico, California

THE BALAAM TEXT FROM DEIR 'ALLĀ

Jo Ann Hackett

Scholars Press Edition 1984

Library of Congress Cataloging in Publication Data

Hackett, Jo Ann.
The Balaam Text from Deir 'Allā.

(Harvard Semitic monographs ; 31)
Bibliography: p.
1. Inscriptions, Aramaic—Jordan—Dayr 'Allā, Tall.
I. Title. II. Series.
PJ5208.J63H32 1984 492'.2 83-27125
ISBN 0-89130-723-0

Printed in the United States of America

PREFACE

My work on the Deir ʿAllā inscription could not have been completed without the assistance and encouragement of several individuals and organizations, and I would like to acknowledge their contributions.

The Mrs. Giles Whiting Foundation supported my final year of thesis work with their generous award. This fellowship made it possible for me to devote an entire year to my thesis without distraction, for which opportunity I am most grateful.

The Marion and Jasper Whiting Foundation awarded me the necessary travel money to go to Amman in the spring of 1979 and examine the plaster of the Deir ʿAllā inscription. My work would have suffered considerably without this experience, and I am indebted to the Foundation for giving me such an opportunity.

In Amman, my work was made immeasurably easier by the kindness of James and Susan Sauer and the American Center of Oriental Research, and by the cooperation and encouragement of Dr. Adnan Hadidi, Director of the Jordanian Department of Antiquities. The staff of the Amman Museum were always helpful and welcoming and, in fact, worked out the day-by-day details of my examination and photographing of the plaster. Finally, Gerrit van der Kooij took the time from a very busy schedule to discuss the inscription with me and to take me to Tell Deir ʿAllā so that I could see the excavation site. I owe a great deal to all of these people and would like to express my appreciation at this time.

In the summer of 1981, a research grant from the American Schools of Oriental Research made it possible for me to visit Amman a second time, to prepare for the publication of my dissertation. Again, the people at the Department of Antiquities and the Amman Museum were entirely helpful, and the American Center of Oriental Research, now headed by David and Linda McCreery, was the home base that made my work possible.

Many of the results of Chapter IV have appeared in "The Dialect of the Plaster Text from Tell Deir ʿAlla" in *Orientalia* 53 (1984). I am indebted to the Pontifical Biblical Institute for permission to use that material in the present volume.

An earlier version of this study was presented to Harvard University in 1980 as my doctoral thesis. Frank M. Cross was the adviser for my thesis. His warmth and good will were an encouragement to me throughout my tenure at Harvard, and his scholarly influence on me and on this study will be obvious at a glance.

P. Kyle McCarter, Jr., of the University of Virginia, kindly consented to be a member of my thesis committee because of his interest in the Deir ʿAllā inscription. His remarkable insight and constant good humor eased a good many of the problems I had in the course of my work.

Michael D. Coogan read diligently the several drafts of my thesis. His close scrutiny and seemingly endless patience made it possible for me to proceed with this work under otherwise frantic circumstances.

Though not on my original thesis committee, Thomas O. Lambdin gave of his time to help me improve this study, and John Huehnergard attempted, patiently, for hours on end, to remove many of the mistakes from the manuscript. To both of them, my respectful gratitude. Any errors remaining are, of course, my responsibility.

Jo Ann Hackett

Cambridge, Massachusetts
February 1984

TABLE OF CONTENTS

ABBREVIATIONS

ADAJ	*Annual of the Department of Antiquities of Jordan*
AJSL	*American Journal of Semitic Languages and Literatures*
Akk	Akkadian
Arb	Arabic
ATDA	J. Hoftijzer and G. van der Kooij, *Aramaic Texts from Deir ʿAlla*
AUSS	*Andrews University Seminary Studies*
BA	Biblical Aramaic
BA	*Biblical Archeologist*
BANE	*The Bible and the Ancient Near East: Essays in Honor of William Foxwell Albright*, ed. G. Ernest Wright
BASOR	*Bulletin of the American Schools of Oriental Research*
Bauer-Leander	Hans Bauer and Pontus Leander, *Historische Grammatik der hebräischen Sprache des Alten Testamentes*
BDB	Francis Brown, S. R. Driver, and Charles A. Briggs, *A Hebrew and English Lexicon of the Old Testament*
BH	Biblical Hebrew
BiOr	*Bibliotheca Orientalis*
Brockelmann	Carl Brockelmann, *Grundriss der vergleichenden Grammatik der semitischen Sprachen*, vol. I
C	the causative form of the verb
CAD	*The Assyrian Dictionary of the Oriental Institute of the University of Chicago*
CAH	*Cambridge Ancient History*
Caquot & Lemaire	André Caquot and André Lemaire, "Les textes araméens de Deir ʿAlla"

CBQ	*Catholic Biblical Quarterly*
CMHE	Frank Moore Cross, *Canaanite Myth and Hebrew Epic*
CTCA	Andrée Herdner, *Corpus des tablettes en cunéiformes alphabétiques*
D	the verbal conjugation in which the middle radical is doubled
Degen	Rainer Degen, *Altaramäische Grammatik*
DISO	Charles-F. Jean and Jacob Hoftijzer, *Dictionnaire des inscriptions sémitiques*
EA	J. A. Knudtzon, *Die El-Amarna-Tafeln*
EHO	Frank Moore Cross, Jr., and David Noel Freedman, *Early Hebrew Orthography*
Eth	Ethiopic
Fitzmyer	Joseph A. Fitzmyer, S.J., *The Aramaic Inscriptions of Sefîre*
Friedrich	Johannes Friedrich and Wolfgang Röllig, *Phönizisch-punische Grammatik*
G	the basic form of the verb
GAG	Wolfram von Soden, *Grundriss der akkadischen Grammatik*
Gardiner	Sir Alan Henderson Gardiner, *Egyptian Grammar*
GKC	*Gesenius' Hebrew Grammar*, ed. E. Kautzsch
Gt	the basic form of the verb with infixed *t*
Harris/*Dialects*	Zellig S. Harris, *Development of the Canaanite Dialects*
Harris/*Grammar*	Zellig S. Harris, *A Grammar of the Phoenician Language*
Hoftijzer	commentary on the Deir ʿAllā text by Jacob Hoftijzer, in *ATDA*, pp. 173-282
IEJ	*Israel Exploration Journal*
JA	Jewish Aramaic
Jastrow	Marcus Jastrow, *A Dictionary of the Targumim, the Talmud Babli and Yerushalmi, and the Midrashic Literature*

JBL	*Journal of Biblical Literature*
JNES	*Journal of Near Eastern Studies*
Joüon	Paul Joüon, S.J., *Grammaire de l'hêbreu biblique*
JSS	*Journal of Semitic Studies*
KAI	H. Donner and W. Röllig, *Kanaanäische und aramäische Inschriften* (3rd ed.)
van der Kooij	analysis of the Deir ʿAllā text by Gerrit van der Kooij, in *ATDA*, pp. 97-170
Lichtheim	Miriam Lichtheim, *Ancient Egyptian Literature*
McCarter	if cited with a page reference following in parentheses, the reference is to P. Kyle McCarter, Jr., "The Balaam Texts from Deir ʿAllā: The First Combination"; if cited in reference to Combination II, with no page number following, the reference is to a typescript of McCarter's work on Combination II, cited in n. 54 on p. 56
MH	Mishnaic Hebrew
N	the reflexive/medio-passive of the G
Payne Smith	Robert Payne Smith, *A Compendious Syriac Dictionary*
PEQ	*Palestine Exploration Quarterly*
PRU	*Le palais royal d'Ugarit*, vol. III, ed. Jean Nougayrol, and vol. V, ed. Charles Virolleaud
RB	*Revue Biblique*
tD	the D verb with prefixed *t*
tG	the G verb with prefixed *t*
Ug	Ugaritic
UT	Cyrus Gordon, *Ugaritic Textbook*
VT	*Vetus Testamentum*
Wright	William Wright, *Grammar of the Arabic Language*
ZDMG	*Zeitschrift der Deutschen Morgenländischen Gesellschaft*
ZDPV	*Zeitschrift des Deutschen Palästina-Vereins*

INTRODUCTION

The plaster text from Tell Deir ʿAllā was found in 1967 toward the end of the season when an Arab worker discovered a piece of plaster with writing on it, a piece that is part of what we now call the first combination.[1] This was not the first important epigraphic find to come out of the east Jordan Valley site. In 1964, two clay tablets were found inscribed in a script that is as yet unidentified.[2] The 1967 find, however, proved to be quite a long inscription in black and red ink. The surviving fragments were salvaged over the remaining weeks of the 1967 season.

The first announcement of the find by the excavator, H. J. Franken, identified the context of the inscription as the Persian period.[3] A photograph of a large part of the "second combination" was published at the same time, and on the basis of that photograph, several scholars objected to the dating on paleographic grounds. J. Naveh in 1967 identified the script as Aramaic, and suggested a date in the middle of the 8th century B.C.E. or even earlier.[4] F. M. Cross accepted this dating provisionally in 1969, but noted that the script at Deir ʿAllā shares several features with later Ammonite inscriptions, and, therefore, might have to be dated in a series outside the Aramaic.[5] Paul Lapp defended Franken's Persian period date in

---

[1] P. A. H. de Boer describes the circumstances of the find in his preface to *ATDA*, p. ix.

[2] See Franken, *ATDA*, p. 4; *VT* 14 (1964) 377-79; *VT* 15 (1965) 150-52. Albright thought the clay tablets were evidence of Sea Peoples' infiltration in the area and that the script should be compared to the Minoan Linear A and B tablets. See W. F. Albright, *CAH* II, 2, p. 510.

[3] *VT* 17 (1967) 480-81.

[4] *IEJ* 17 (1967) 256-58.

[5] *BASOR* 193 (1969) 14 n. 2.

1970 on the basis of the pottery finds.[6] Cross, however, continued to insist that the script was somewhat earlier than the Persian period, and in 1973 published his opinion that the script was, in fact, Ammonite and not Aramaic, and that it dated from the beginning of the 7th century B.C.E.[7] He expanded on his position in a 1975 article.[8]

In 1976 the entire corpus from Deir ʿAllā was published by J. Hoftijzer and G. van der Kooij in *Aramaic Texts from Deir ʿAlla*.[9] Van der Kooij contributed a paleographic analysis of the text, including a painstaking description of the difficult readings and traces, and Hoftijzer wrote the commentary and grammatical analysis. Various specialists, including van der Kooij, wrote sections on several aspects of the find, such as analyses of the plaster and ink. The first chapter, concerning the archaeological evidence, was written by Franken. The authors published color (and in some cases infra-red) photographs of the text. By the time of this publication, the Persian date for the text had been dropped. In his chapter on the archaeological evidence Franken states:

> Since the Phase M pottery was made shortly before the appearance of wheel-made pottery which on the basis of our present knowledge has to be dated sometime in the 7th century B.C., the Aramaic text may still have existed after the Assyrians invaded Palestine and the area of the Zerqa.[10]

Van der Kooij comes to a similar conclusion. He describes the script as Aramaic and dates it tentatively to 700 B.C.E., plus or minus twenty-five years.[11]

According to the *editio princeps* the plaster fragments were found in two major groupings within what is described as

---

[6] *VT* 20 (1970) 255.

[7] *BASOR* 212 (1973) 13-14, esp. n. 7.

[8] *AUSS* 13 (1975) 11-17.

[9] Leiden: E. J. Brill, 1976. Hereafter, references to van der Kooij's work or to Hoftijzer's commentary will be cited simply as "van der Kooij" or "Hoftijzer" plus a page number.

[10] *ATDA*, p. 12.

[11] *Ibid.*, p. 96.

a small "room."[12] Furthermore, the fact that the plaster in the areas which must be the edges of the inscription is thinner and curved backward suggests that the plaster was not attached directly to a wall, but rather was applied to an object, perhaps a stela, which was suspended from a wall.[13] One grouping was lying against the stump of a wall and, therefore, probably had not fallen from a great distance. The other grouping was several meters distant from this and the fragments of this grouping were in disarray. Consequently, the excavators propose that this second grouping fell from some distance and, further, that it had been situated higher up on the stela than the other grouping which was still close to the wall.[14] It is possible that the wall had originally separated the locations where the two groupings were found in 1967, although the excavators do not rule out a doorway between the two locations.[15] Since the destruction of this level at Deir ʿAllā was caused by an earthquake (or, more likely, two earthquakes[16]), it is possible that the wall and the stela on it collapsed violently and the rubble fell together. The stela could have broken in two (or more) large pieces. Since the wall was also collapsing, the distribution of the large pieces of the stela with reference to the former location of the wall need not be a problem. That is, the text could still have been written in one long column, even though pieces of the text were found on two sides of what was once the wall which supported the inscription and the object on which it was written.[17]

---

[12] *Ibid.*, p. 26.

[13] H. J. Franken and M. Ibrahim, *ADAJ* XXII (1977-78) 65-68.

[14] *Ibid.*, pp. 65-67.

[15] *Ibid.*, p. 65.

[16] *ATDA*, pp. 8-10. I.e., part of the text fell with the first earthquake and was burned. The remainder fell with the second shock and did not burn. These remaining fragments were found between wall fragments and were apparently protected.

[17] Or, it is possible that the two large groupings were written on two sides of a stela, or on two separate stelae, and were not part of a single long column. Van der Kooij (26) favors having only one object on which the text was written.

The grouping which fell close to the wall and which probably formed the lower part of the inscription is called Combination II in the *editio princeps*. The largest grouping of fragments which fell away from the wall and which probably comprised the top of the inscription is called Combination I. Van der Kooij arranged the remaining small fragments, which could not be fitted with certainty into the two large combinations, into thirteen other groupings,[18] including number XIV, which appears to be a drawing of a winged sphinx and which probably stood above and to the left of the beginning of the inscription.[19]

The complex of rooms which included the room in which the inscription stood has been described as a sanctuary, but with some hesitation.[20] The finds in the area include "weaving installations" (many loom weights), a goblet, and inscriptions on stone and pottery.[21] Two of the inscriptions are clearly Aramaic.[22] The floor of the room in which the inscription was probably located sloped to the middle, "forming a shallow round pit."[23] The roof was a mat of reed leaves.[24]

In the *editio princeps* Hoftijzer translated the first combination as a prophecy of Balaam in which a goddess is

---

[18]*ATDA*, pp. 146-47.

[19]*Ibid.*, p. 165. Van der Kooij's placement of this sphinx figure has recently been challenged by Gordon Hamilton of the Department of Near Eastern Languages and Civilizations at Harvard University (private communication). Hamilton has done long and careful studies of the placement of the remaining fragments, using copies of the original infra-red photographs and his own skill at photographic reproduction to study the edges of the fragments. He believes the sphinx should be placed above the inscription proper, precisely in the middle. References to Hamilton's work will be made elsewhere in this study.

[20]*ATDA*, pp. 12-13.

[21]*Ibid.*, pp. 4, 15.

[22]*Ibid.*, p. 267. See also the article in *BASOR* 239 by P. Kyle McCarter, Jr., which deals primarily with the first combination of the Deir ʿAllā text. Hereafter, the article is cited simply as "McCarter" plus page number.

[23]*ATDA*, pp. 9-10, 26.

[24]Franken and Ibrahim, *op. cit.* (n. 13), p. 65.

entreated not to destroy the land with fire as she has threatened to do, and in which people are warned of the seriousness of the destruction if they do not repent. He sees the second combination as a series of curses, probably spoken by Balaam, which his hearers reject.[25]

Since the initial publication of the text, several articles dealing with the inscription have appeared. In 1977, E. Hammershaimb published a discussion of the text, which, for the most part, follows the *ATDA* readings and interpretations and offers nothing new for our reading of the text.[26]

Also in 1977, A. Caquot and A. Lemaire published their suggestions for improved readings and translations.[27] Their interpretation of the inscription differed from Hoftijzer's in some respects. For instance, among other suggestions they have rearranged Combination I slightly (see below, p. 7) and they interpreted the second combination as referring to "youth" rather than as a series of curses dealing with "death" (a difference in translation of the word *ʿlm*).

H. Ringgren offered a short article with translation and commentary, in which he suggested the context of a royal birth, issuing from a sacred marriage. His interpretation was based on the appearance in Combination II of the term *nqr*, read as cognate to BH *nēṣer*, "shoot," and used in the same sense as *ṣēmaḥ* in Zech 3:8.[28]

H.-P. Müller has written two articles about the inscription, one in 1978 concentrating on the light shed on Hebrew Bible problems by the Deir ʿAllā text, and one in 1982, with useful bibliography, a transliteration, translation, and commentary, and a section, again, on connections between the

---

[25]Hoftijzer's commentary appears on pp. 183-282 of *ATDA*. See also his article in *BA* 39 (1976) 11-17.

[26]*Dansk Teologisk Tidsskrift* 40 (1977) 217-42.

[27]*Syria* 54 (1977) 189-208, hereafter cited simply as "Caquot and Lemaire" plus page number.

[28]*Religion och Bibel* 36 (1977) 85-89, esp. 88. Ringgren has apparently written a longer article about the Deir ʿAllā inscription for the I. L. Seeligmann *Festschrift*, but that work is not available to me at this time. See the citation in H.-P. Müller, *ZAW* 94 (1982) 214 n. 5.

Deir ʿAllā text and the Hebrew Bible Balaam narratives.[29]

In 1979, A. Rofé published a monograph on the Hebrew Bible Balaam traditions, which included an appendix on the Deir ʿAllā inscription.[30] Rofé offers his own transcription and commentary on the text, and suggests that the inscription concerns a severe drought, which the people of Balaam attempted to avert by setting up, on his advice, a house of sacred prostitution and a fertility cult. Rofé also proposes that the biblical Priestly source's Balaam traditions are based on the existence of this cult, which is a Midianite cult in P, and that the language of the inscription is Midianite.[31]

Also in 1979, G. Garbini presented his ideas about the Deir ʿAllā inscription.[32] He included in the article his negative evaluation of the *editio princeps*; notes on the difficulties in assigning the text to the Aramaic language family, suggesting a "new Northwest Semitic language" exhibiting connections with both Aramaic and Arabic;[33] and a transliteration, translation, and comments.

In 1982, H. and M. Weippert's article on Combination I of the inscription appeared.[34] Again we have a transliteration, translation, and commentary, with a particularly good representation of previous work by other scholars.

Several reviews of *ATDA* have appeared since 1976,[35] including one long review article by B. Levine,[36] in which he draws parallels between our inscription and texts which deal

---

[29] *ZDPV* 94 (1978) 56-67 and *ZAW* 94 (1982) 214-44.

[30] *The Book of Balaam (Numbers 22:2-24:25)* [Hebrew].

[31] *Ibid.*, p. 69.

[32] *Henoch* 1 (1979) 166-88.

[33] *Ibid.*, p. 170.

[34] *ZDPV* 98 (1982) 77-103.

[35] J. Fitzmyer in *CBQ* 40 (1978) 93-95; E. Puech in *RB* 85 (1978) 114-17; G. Wallis in *BiOr* 35 (1978) 316-17; J. Naveh in *IEJ* 29 (1979) 133-36; J. Greenfield in *JSS* 25 (1980) 248-52; S. Kaufman in *BASOR* 239 (1980) 71-74; M. Dahood in *Biblica* 62 (1981) 124-27.

[36] *JAOS* 101 (1981) 195-205.

with a descent into the underworld, especially the "Descent of Ishtar."

P. Kyle McCarter, Jr., has dealt extensively with the Deir ʿAllā text in several public lectures and has published his suggestions for the first combination in *BASOR*.[37] McCarter has contributed greatly to our understanding of the text. He suggests, for instance, that the change in ink color is made because the red-ink sections actually refer to the inscription itself, and he has discovered the logical pattern in the "birds" passage beginning in I, 7 (see my commentary on that section of Combination I). As will become obvious, the present work relies heavily on McCarter's analysis at several points.

In their 1977 article, Caquot and Lemaire (193) suggested that Fragments VIII (d) and XII (c) should belong together because the name *blʿm.brbʿr* could then be read. They also suggested that Fragments I (c) and (d) of the first combination should be moved up two lines, changing somewhat the readings of the initial section of Combination I. Caquot and Lemaire were correct in these two suggestions, as is now confirmed with my discovery of the proper position of the two fragments in question within the first combination. When Fragments VIII (d) and XII (c) are inserted within I (a), (c), and (d), and I (c) and (d) are moved up two lines, the traces fit together perfectly. This placement necessitates renumbering the lines and rearranging the fragments of Combination I in relation to one another, as Caquot and Lemaire suggested. (For specific details of the join, see below, p. 21.) This new arrangement is reflected in my transliteration and translation, below.

J. Hoftijzer's contribution to the *editio princeps* was extremely thorough. He provided numerous parallels to the literature of the Deir ʿAllā inscription and various suggestions for translation and understanding of the words through cognate languages. Van der Kooij's contribution was also done in much detail. He described fully and drew every letter and trace he could see in the texts, including those he identified through the use of a microscope, and attempted to distinguish between ink and dirt and other damages within the text. Because of the

[37] Cited above, n. 22.

mass of information included in *ATDA*, I have not tried to duplicate the work done there. In the situations where Hoftijzer has already cited other literature as parallel to a given phrase, I generally have not reiterated his suggestions in the present work. The same is true for van der Kooij's work with the readings. The present work does offer new readings and suggestions, however, while combining the improvements made by previous writers. Since the sense of the text has been changed considerably by new contributions, it has been necessary for me to offer an update of the grammar and syntax sections included in the *editio princeps*. I have had the opportunity to go to Amman and examine the texts first-hand, also with the help of a microscope, and have made a very few suggestions as to other possible readings.

Finally, I have attempted to look at the script and language of the Deir ʿAllā inscription in a different light from previous authors, in that I have not accepted the analysis of either as Aramaic. There are excellent arguments to be made that the script is not Aramaic, but is, rather, related to later Ammonite scripts. The language also is not simply a strange form of Aramaic, but is instead, I believe, related to the South Canaanite languages of the first millennium B.C.E. The evidence for the Canaanite classification of the language is considerable and should be given due consideration.

Thus the present work seeks to update the *editio princeps*, by incorporating the research of others, where that has seemed appropriate, and my own research on the text; it further offers alternative interpretations for difficulties of content, script, and language within the inscription.

Chapter I

THE SCRIPT OF THE DEIR ʻALLĀ TEXT

As was explained on pages 1-2 of the Introduction, the script of the Deir ʻAllā text has been a matter of dispute from the beginning. Most scholars have maintained that the script can be dated within the Aramaic series, although the use of that series for dating has generally resulted in an earlier date for the inscription than that finally decided upon by the excavators.[1] We saw that van der Kooij, however, dated the script within the Aramaic series at ca. 700 B.C.E.[2] As was stated before, Cross suggested dating the inscription ca. 700 B.C.E. on the basis of the Ammonite series.[3] McCarter (50) has suggested yet another alternative. While agreeing with Cross that the Deir ʻAllā script is in line with the tradition represented in the Ammonite inscriptions of the early sixth century, he prefers to call the script "Gileadite" rather than "Ammonite." He argues that this script tradition probably is not the *Ammonite* national script, as was previously thought, since we now have evidence of this tradition from the Deir ʻAllā inscription, and in his opinion, the language of that inscription is not Ammonite, but Aramaic. Therefore, "Ammonite national script" would be too narrow a term for this script tradition.

The controversy over this script arises from the difficulty in distinguishing between a script that is basically Aramaic but shows a certain influence from "Ammonite" sources, and a genuine script tradition that has deviated from the Aramaic and exhibits homogeneous characteristics that are not present in the Aramaic script from the same period. Cross has

---

[1]See above, Introduction, p. 1 and nn. 4 and 5.

[2]See above, p. 2 and n. 11.

[3]See above, pp. 1 and 2 and nn. 5, 7, and 8.

argued, and I agree, that the Ammonite inscriptions from the early sixth century have deviated from Aramaic to such a degree that they represent a true alternative to the Aramaic script tradition, an alternative whose peculiar characteristics are consistent and can be enumerated and recognized. Furthermore, the idiosyncrasies (to use McCarter's term) in the Deir ʿAllā script are sufficiently similar to forms in the Ammonite script to align the Deir ʿAllā script with the Ammonite tradition, regardless of the other dissimilarities with Ammonite inscriptions. With additional evidence of the spread of this script tradition, we may need to rename it, as McCarter suggests, but for the present I will continue to use the term "Ammonite."

What follows is a detailed analysis of the letters of the Deir ʿAllā inscription, with comparison to the Aramaic cursive and lapidary scripts and to the Ammonite inscriptions. The appendix to this study contains two script charts: one of several Aramaic inscriptions; and one of the scripts from inscriptions found in Ammon.

ʾAlep

The *ʾalep* in the Deir ʿAllā script is archaic. It is made with two bars coming to a point on the left and the downstroke cutting through the bars to the right of their joining.[4] This *ʾalep* is to be distinguished from the star *ʾalep* which appears in Aramaic cursive in the 7th century (e.g., the Assur Ostracon). In the Ammonite series this archaic *ʾalep* is kept even in the latest cursive (Heshbon Ostracon XI), with the possible exception of Heshbon Ostracon IV. The star *ʾalep* is made with a check on the right side of the downstroke and a left bar made as a separate stroke from the check. The *ʾalep* in Heshbon Ostracon IV resembles the star *ʾalep* but still we seem to have only two bars. Here, however, the lower bar does not connect with the upper to the left of the downstroke, making this a more developed form. In the Ammonite series, this archaic *ʾalep* is kept even into the 6th century, as opposed to the Aramaic series (the Saqqarah Papyrus, for instance, and even more developed in Heshbon Ostraca I and II). The *ʾalep* at

---

[4]Van der Kooij (60) suggests this also.

Deir ʿAllā shows the tendency to keep the archaic form rather than a tendency toward the star *ʾalep*.

Bet

The *bet* is one of the most notable letters of the Deir ʿAllā script because it is still entirely closed at the top. In the Aramaic series, the *bet* is open as early as with the Nimrud Ostracon in the 8th century. Even in the Ammonite series, the *bet* is open in all the other inscriptions. We must go back to the Nineveh lion weights in the middle of the 8th century to find the period when the *bet* was still closed in the Aramaic series. Thus the *bet* at Deir ʿAllā either dates the text to the 8th century, or else points to a separate development from the corresponding Aramaic series.

Gimel

The *gimel* at Deir ʿAllā is the shape of an inverted "*V*," with the right leg slightly longer than the left. It is of no interest in the dating of the script.

Dalet

dalet, like *bet*, is of interest because its top is still closed. Unlike *bet*, however, the *dalet* remained closed, so far as we know, throughout the Ammonite series. One *dalet* in the Tell Sīrān inscription is slightly open, but the model is still clearly a closed top. This is, again, distinct from the Aramaic series where the *dalet* is open already with the Nimrud Ostracon in the 8th century.

He

There is some variety in the writing of *he* at Deir ʿAllā, but two forms predominate. These are the two represented on the chart, with the *s*-shaped tick either standing free, or else extending off the thin left-hand downstroke. It should be noted, however, that in at least one case, in II, 8, we find a very archaic three-barred *he*. This letter occurs in a damaged section and it is possible that the original letter did not have this shape at all; on close examination, however, the letter seems clear enough, so I am including it in the discussion here (although I have not included it in the script chart.) At first glance, the *he* at Deir ʿAllā resembles the *he* of the Aramaic cursive of the 7th century (see the Assur Ostracon and Saqqarah Papyrus). The more curved form of the Deir ʿAllā *he*, however (the one on the right in the script chart), and the *he* from Tell Sīrān imply a different development from the Aramaic. The left downstroke of the Deir ʿAllā *he* is not simply a straight or curved stroke off the horizontal, but is rather an *s*-shaped stroke. This *s* shape is also probably the origin of the Tell Sīrān *he* with its two downstrokes and added vertical on the left, and of the typical *he* of Ammonite seals (𐤄) with its two downstrokes. If the scribe made the horizontals of the *s* fairly long so that they connected with the downstroke on the right, an entirely new form of two-stroke *he* could be created.[5] Unfortunately, there are no more *he*'s in the Ammonite series for comparison.

Waw

The *waw* at Deir ʿAllā and on Heshbon Ostracon IV looks very much like the *waw* in the Aramaic series in the 8th and 7th centuries and is not useful in dating beyond that range.

Zayin

The *zayin* at Deir ʿAllā shows the *z* shape which appeared sporadically in Aramaic in the 8th century, eventually developing into a straight, slanted line by the time of the Assur Ostracon. The *zayin* in the first handwriting from the Nimrud Ostracon is the closest *zayin* we have to our Deir ʿAllā form, but compared to this, the Deir ʿAllā *zayin* is sometimes rather long. At any rate, this still decidedly *z*-shaped *zayin* has not at all developed into the simple slanted line that is the norm for Aramaic cursive in the 7th century.

Ḥet

In the Aramaic series, the two-bar *ḥet* gave way to the one-bar *ḥet* in the 8th century (see the Nimrud Ostracon, Assur Ostracon, and even one form on the Hamath bricks). At Deir ʿAllā, however, we find not only the old two-bar *ḥet*, but even three-bar *ḥet*'s,[6] which were standard in Aramaic lapidary till the beginning of the 8th century. Tell Sīrān also preserves the two-bar *ḥet* all the way into the 6th century in the Ammonite series. Heshbon Ostraca IV and XI have a form of one-bar *ḥet*,

---

[5] I am indebted to F. M. Cross for these observations.

[6] Van der Kooij (63) sees the three-bar *ḥet* as the model.

but it is a form which is not at all like the one-bar *ḥet*'s in the Aramaic series. It appears to be a sort of backward *N* and must be related to one of the forms found at Deir ʿAllā (on the left in the script chart) rather than to the development of *ḥet* outside the Ammonite series. Thus, one *ḥet* at Deir ʿAllā is a much older form than we would expect if comparing strictly with the Aramaic series, and another provides a link with the later *ḥet*'s in Ammonite cursive which cannot be established within the Aramaic series.

Ṭet

The *ṭet* at Deir ʿAllā is quite unlike the *ṭet*'s found in Aramaic cursive of the 7th century (see the Assur Ostracon and the Saqqarah Papyrus). The *ṭet* at Deir ʿAllā is closer in form to the *ṭet* on the Amman Citadel inscription or the Bir-Rakib inscription than to the *ṭet* in the Aramaic cursive series. The top has opened at Deir ʿAllā, but the cross-bar goes from upper left to lower right, unlike the *ṭet*'s of the Assur Ostracon and Saqqarah Papyrus.

Yod

The *yod* at Deir ʿAllā is very similar to the *zayin*. It is, however, more elongated than the *zayin* and less slanted. And, of course, the tick on the left identifies it as a *yod*. The *yod* at Deir ʿAllā preserves the older form of *yod* with its "*2*"-shaped base and a tick to the left. This older *yod* survives in all the Ammonite cursive inscriptions, even down into the 6th century. In the Aramaic cursive series, however, the *yod* develops, beginning in the 8th century, into a straight slanted line with another line, usually slanting downward, leading off from the middle of the left side of the main downstroke. The second handwriting from Nimrud shows the beginnings of this kind of development. The Deir ʿAllā *yod* does not exhibit this tendency at all. The *yod* at Deir ʿAllā is sometimes quite small in relation to the other letters in the script. This seems to be an idiosyncrasy of the scribe and is not the case in other Ammonite or Aramaic scripts. Thus, the *yod* at Deir ʿAllā does not seem to be following the tendency of the Aramaic cursive and fits in better with the Ammonite series.

Kap

The *kap* is the first letter we have come to that exhibits the very long, graceful tail that is so characteristic of the Deir ʿAllā script. The downstroke slants to the left with a triangular-shaped head on the upper left-hand side of the downstroke. Many of the *kap*'s at Deir ʿAllā do not show a deliberate tick down off this triangle (see II, 3, or II, 9, for instance), unlike the *kap*'s in the Aramaic series, which preserve the second stroke of the older shape of *kap*, as can be seen in the Hamath bricks or the Nineveh lion weights. Thus, the model form of the head of the *kap* at Deir ʿAllā was simply a triangle. It was made in a two-stroke motion, of course, which sometimes left a tick to the bottom. Such a triangular head was the norm for the Ammonite scripts, as especially is evident in the Tell Sīrān script.

Lamed

The *lamed* does not change much throughout the Aramaic or Ammonite series and so is not valuable for dating or identification of the script. It should be noted, however, that the *lamed* at Deir ʿAllā is consistently written well above the line.

Mem

mem and *nun*, like *kap*, have long, fairly thin tails in the Deir ʿAllā script. The *mem* is notable, however, because of its archaic form. The rather shallow zigzag head of the Deir ʿAllā *mem* marks it off completely from the development of the Aramaic cursive series. In Aramaic cursive, already in the first handwriting from the Nimrud Ostracon, we see evidence of the development of *mem* away from the zigzag head into a head consisting of a curved line with a straight vertical line drawn through it. This is the direction of the development of *mem* in Aramaic cursive from the Assur Ostracon on. Furthermore, even the zigzag *mem*'s of the Nimrud Ostracon and the Nineveh lion weights show a tendency for the head to slant downward to the right, while the head of the *mem* at Deir ʿAllā is horizontal. In the Ammonite series, this horizontal, curvy, zigzag-headed *mem* is the norm throughout the series, even down into the 6th century. The common Aramaic cursive *mem* never shows up in the Ammonite script. Again in this case, the Deir ʿAllā script is more in line with the development of the Ammonite script than with the Aramaic cursive.

Nun

nun at Deir ʿAllā, as has been said, also has the distinctive flowing downstroke. *nun*, like *lamed*, shows little change in the time span with which we are concerned, and so is of little use for dating. It should be pointed out, however, that the *nun* at Deir ʿAllā never exhibits a tendency to develop into a straight line as is the case with the Aramaic cursive even as early as the Nimrud Ostracon. This tendency shows up in the Ammonite series later on, as well, but not until the Tell Sīrān bottle. At Deir ʿAllā, the *nun* always exhibits a large curve for the head that curves back up before it is attached to the downstroke.

Samek

The clearest *samek*'s in the inscription can be found on the infra-red photographs of Fragment V (q), Plate 13 in *ATDA*. *samek* at Deir ʿAllā clearly is still made with three distinct strokes for the head and has not developed into the zigzag *samek*, seen already in the Nimrud Ostracon, which becomes the norm for Aramaic cursive.

ʿAyin

The *ʿayin* at Deir ʿAllā, like the *bet* and *dalet*, is distinctive because it is still closed at the top. *ʿayin* is open already in the Aramaic cursive as early as the Nineveh lion weights in the early 8th century. It remains open after that. In the Ammonite series, on the other hand, the *ʿayin* is still closed in Heshbon Ostracon IV in the late 7th or beginning of the 6th century. Even at Tell Sīrān there are still closed *ʿayin*'s, although the opening of the *ʿayin* has begun by this time. The *ʿayin* at Deir ʿAllā forces us either to date the text in the early-/mid-8th century, or to recognize a development outside that of the Aramaic scripts.

Pe

The *pe* at Deir ʿAllā is another letter with a long thin tail slanting downward to the left. The *pe* occurs so seldom, however, that it is of little use in dating. The Deir ʿAllā *pe* is very similar to the *pe*'s from the Assur Ostracon and the Saqqarah Papyrus.

Ṣade

The *ṣade* at Deir ʿAllā resembles most closely the *ṣade* of the Amman Citadel inscription.[7] The downstroke with a curved stroke off the upper right part of the downstroke, or perhaps with two curved strokes coming together at the upper right-hand side of the downstroke, is unlike the usual downstroke with zigzag stroke off the upper right, which we find in the Aramaic series as well as the Tell Sīrān bottle. Therefore, the Deir ʿAllā *ṣade* can be compared only to the Citadel inscription, which is usually described as Aramaic lapidary. It is interesting that the odd forms of both *ṭet* and *ṣade* are paralleled in this inscription from the same area as the later Ammonite inscriptions. Perhaps a local variant of the Aramaic script was in its beginning stages even as far back as the Citadel inscription.

Qop

The *qop* at Deir ʿAllā is a development from the earlier Aramaic lapidary *qop*, which was a circle with a downstroke passing through the circle at the bottom. The Aramaic cursive series developed this old *qop* in two major directions. On the one hand, we find the circle developing into two semi-circles, usually open at the top (there is one such *qop* on the Nineveh lion weights and on the Assur clay-tablets), while the standard *qop* in the 7th and 6th centuries took a different direction, that of the downstroke with an *s*-shaped curve to the top and upper right side of the downstroke (another *qop* in the Nineveh lion weights, the Assur Ostracon, Saqqarah Papyrus). The *qop* at Deir ʿAllā is open at the top and is clearly not developing

---

[7] Although in the photograph of the Amman Citadel inscription published by S. Horn in *BASOR* 193 (1969) 3, the *ṣade* appears to have an extra stroke downwards, connecting the two strokes off to the right, this extra stroke probably does not exist, as was pointed out to me by van der Kooij. There is a small chip out of the letter at this point, which is almost as long as the distance between the two right-hand strokes. Close examination of the inscription indicates that this chip may have been unintentional. At any rate, the shadow on the photograph is misleading.

into the *s*-shaped top. The head was apparently drawn in two strokes, however, and is not simply an open circle (see I, 13, the infra-red photograph on Plate 10 of *ATDA*; II, 11, and II, 12, Plate 11, where the two arms of the *qop*'s are obviously not aligned). The fact, however, that so many of the *qop*'s are drawn as if the two arms were extensions of each other (I, 16, Plate 3 of *ATDA*; II, 5, Plate 4; II, 14, Plate 11) suggests that the open circle was still the model form. The open circle does not, however, connect with the top of the downstroke, as in the *qop*'s in Panammû or Bir-Rakib. With this letter, as with others, the relationship with the older Aramaic form is clear, but the development may have diverged from the normal Aramaic cursive lines. The only other *qop* we have at present from the Ammonite cursive series has developed along the same lines as the Deir ʿAllā *qop*. At Tell Sīrān in the 6th century we find *qop* written as an open circle with a downstroke.

Reš

Like *bet*, *dalet*, and *ʿayin*, *reš* is closed at the top, whereas *reš* in the Aramaic cursive is open from the time of the Nimrud Ostracon on. In the Ammonite series the *reš* is still closed at Tell Sīrān, but on Heshbon Ostracon XI from about the same time, the *reš* is open. Still, a closed *reš* is in evidence in the Ammonite series much later than in the Aramaic.

Šin

The *šin* at Deir ʿAllā is an archaic form, but the *šin* in the Aramaic and in the Ammonite series does not develop significantly in the 8th-6th centuries, and so is a poor letter for dating purposes.

Taw

For the most part the *taw* at Deir ʿAllā resembles the *taw*'s of both the Aramaic and the Ammonite cursive series, except that the left cross-bar of the *taw* at Deir ʿAllā is rather elongated and the right cross-bar always crosses and breaks through the left at the top. The cross-bar also breaks through sporadically in the Aramaic series, but usually in the 8th-7th centuries, the right bar either does not break through or else the left bar is not so long as the one in the Deir ʿAllā *taw*. Seldom do we find both together. We should note that the *taw*'s of Tell Sīrān and

Heshbon Ostracon XI are similar to the one at Deir ʿAllā, although at Tell Sīrān it is the right cross-bar that is elongated.[8]

Conclusions

We have seen that several of the letters in the Deir ʿAllā script are archaic enough to call for an 8th-century date: *ʾalep*, *bet*, *dalet*, *zayin*, *ḥet*, *yod*, *mem*, *ʿayin*, and *reš*. On the other hand, several letters show developments beyond 8th-century Aramaic, yet different from the 7th-century Aramaic cursive: the archaic *ʾalep* instead of a star *ʾalep*; the *he* with its *s*-shaped left leg; the elongated *zayin*; the backward *N* form of the *ḥet*; the triangular-headed *kap*; the horizontal head of the *mem* and *nun*; the head of the *qop*; and the *taw* with both a long left downstroke and the right stroke breaking through. Moreover, many of these archaic features and unusual developments exhibit similarities with the series of Ammonite cursive inscriptions: the archaic *ʾalep*; the closed *dalet*; the unusual *he*; both the two-bar and the backward *N*-shaped *ḥet*; the older form of *yod*; the triangular-headed *kap*; the horizontal zigzag *mem*; the closed *ʿayin*; the open-circle *qop*; the closed *reš*; and the long *X*-shaped *taw*. In view of all this evidence it is safe to propose that the script of the Deir ʿAllā text is our earliest example of the same script which is used for several Ammonite inscriptions. The similarities of this script with early 8th-century Aramaic cursive must be significant in dating not the script, but rather the point at which this Ammonite script diverged from mainline Aramaic, as Cross has suggested.[9] The script at Deir ʿAllā has preserved several features that were common to Aramaic cursive in the 8th century, but has developed several others in a new direction. The fact that so many archaic features are preserved, however, points to a date for the script that is not far removed from the mid-8th century. The remainder of the Ammonite series that is so far

---

[8] Many of the letters on the Tell Sīrān bottle lean more to the right than we would expect, probably because of the difficulty of writing on such a tiny, curved surface.

[9] *BASOR* 212 (1973) 13.

in evidence shows a much greater development than the Deir ʿAllā script, and all dates from the late 7th/early 6th century. Therefore, a date for the Deir ʿAllā script at the beginning of the 7th century will not be far from correct.

Chapter II

THE TEXT

A. *Introduction*

The text that is presented here is based primarily on G. van der Kooij's work as detailed on pages 99-167 of *ATDA*. In a few instances, I have suggested possibilities that differ from his suggestions, based on my own work with the text in the Amman Museum.

As was mentioned in the Introduction (p. 7), I have rearranged the fragments of Combination I, and have inserted two small fragments within that combination. I have inserted Fragment VIII (d) between Fragments I (a) and I (d) so that the tail of the *m* in Fragment VIII (d) is in line with the end of the tail visible above line 5 of Fragment I (d). Fragment XII (c) is inserted to the left of Fragment VIII (d) so that the bottom of the *l* and the tail of the *n* visible in line 5 of Fragment I (d) are in line with the top of the *l* and *n* in Fragment XII (c), and so that the bottom of the *h* and *s* (?) visible on the top of Fragment XII (c) are in line with the tops of the *h* and *s* (?) from line 3 of Fragment I (a). This placement necessarily involves shifting Fragment I (c) up two lines, because of the obvious correspondences between I (d) and I (c). For instance, *wyʾ* at the end of line 4 of I (d) should be continued by *mr* at the beginning of line 5 of I (c), and so on. I have renumbered the lines according to this new arrangement, and unless otherwise specified, all line numbers quoted in the present study are based on the new numbering.

As has been stated before, the text is written in black ink, with the exception of three extant red-ink sections. The rubrics are indicated in the commentary, but not in the transliteration. Red ink sections include: the beginning of the text in I, 1, through the first occurrence of *ʾlhn* in line 1; *ypʿl* in line I, 2, through --*ʿt* at the end of line 2; *ldʿt* at the beginning of II, 17, through *mlqh* in line 17. Word dividers are used consistently in the text, with a few exceptions which will be noted in the commentary. There is no indication of the ends of sentences. It may be that large sections were set off, because we have in Fragment V (q) the letters *kšd* plus a word divider, and there is apparently nothing written directly to the left of the word divider. It is not possible, however, to place this fragment within either major combination, so the reason for the apparent blank space remains unknown.

B. Methodology for Vocalization and Representation of Consonants

Methodological guidelines are provided here in the hope that they, along with the cognates listed in the glossary, will make clear the reasons for a given vocalization. In the transliteration I have represented the consonants in the inscription exactly as they are represented in the orthography; however, in the vocalization, which follows the transliteration, each word is vocalized in its earliest recoverable form. In the vocalization, then, I have represented the consonants in their assumed Proto-Semitic forms. In general, furthermore, the only vowels I have used are *a*, *i*, *u*, *ā*, *ī*, and *ū*; however, in words where **-iyu* has contracted (or where **-iyu* dropped the final vowel and **-iy* contracted) and the resulting vowel is marked by a *h* as *mater*, I have vocalized with *e*. When such a word occurs in the construct state, I have vocalized *ē*. (The Hebrew forms suggest this difference; e.g., *śādeh*, cs. *śədēh*.)

I have not assumed that the Canaanite shift was operative in this dialect. There is no internal evidence, of course, for the shift, so I have opted here again to vocalize the earlier form. If the shift had taken place in this dialect, all vowels /*ā*/ would be pronounced [ō].

In using the earliest possible form of a word, I do not believe I am reproducing the pronunciation current at Deir ʿAllā in 700 B.C.E. I have tried, however, to present pronounceable, identifiable forms in order to facilitate reading the text, without choosing between later Aramaic and Hebrew vocalizations, so as not to prejudge the classification of this dialect. In three cases, this was not possible. The different vocalizations of the III-*W*/*Y* second and third person plural verbs in Hebrew and Aramaic cannot be represented without bias. They arise from different results of the collapsing of the **-ayū* triphthong. There is also a difference in the vowel that precedes the 3 m. sg. suffix *-h* on singular nouns and prepositions. Finally, the G passive participle is **qatūl* in Hebrew and **qatīl* in Aramaic. (A similar problem arises with stative verbs: sometimes **qatul* in Hebrew, but **qatil* in Aramaic.)

In the case of the third-weak verbs, I have opted for the Hebrew vocalization. I will argue in a later chapter that the verbal system of this inscription more closely resembles South Canaanite than it does Aramaic. This resemblance, of course, does not necessarily indicate the manner in which triphthongs might have been resolved in the dialect of this text; it is simply a basis for making an inevitable choice.

The choice for the vowel preceding the 3 m. sg. suffix is somewhat easier. Aramaic is peculiar in preferring **-ihī̆* over **-uhū̆* as its base for this suffix. **-uhū̆* is by far the more common form in Semitic languages, and that is the one I have used.

I have opted for **qatūl* over **qatīl* for the G passive participle, on the basis of Hebrew **qatūl* (vs. Aramaic **qatīl*; cf. also Arb **maqtūl* and Eth **qetūl*).

If the vocalization of any given verb can be discerned from comparative evidence, I have, of course, followed that evidence, instead of any theoretical model. Where comparative evidence is lacking or inconclusive, I have assumed that the G imperfects of transitive and intransitive active verbs were originally **yaqtul* and **yaqtil*, respectively, and that those of stative verbs were originally **yiqtal* (i.e., I have assumed that the "Barth-Ginsberg Law" had operated in this dialect). II- and III-Guttural verbs are vocalized on the **yiqtal* model. III-*W*/*Y* verbs are vocalized on the **yaqtil* model, unless, again, cognates argue for another vocalization.

I have assumed the vocalization of the G infinitive construct to be **qutul*, following Brockelmann (§122) and Bauer-Leander (§43b). I have vocalized the G infinitive absolute as **qatāl*, based on the Hebrew infinitive absolute and the Akkadian infinitive. I have vocalized all G imperatives according to comparative evidence, or as *qv_1tv_1l, where v_1 is the theme vowel of the imperfect. (See Brockelmann, §258, for all the possibilities.)

Since broken plurals for "segholate" nouns (original **qatl*, **qitl*, and **qutl*) seem to have operated in both Hebrew and Aramaic, I have vocalized the plurals of such nouns in this inscription as broken plurals.

Concerning the 2 and 3 m. pl. suffixes *-km* and *-hm*, I have presented a vocalization as close to the original as the orthography will allow. Assuming the original suffixes (m. and f.) to have been **-kum(ŭ̄)* and **-kin(na)*, **-hum(ŭ̄)* and **-hin(na)*, Hebrew and Aramaic seem to have leveled through either the consonants or the vowels of the original feminine forms. Hebrew keeps the **m*/**n* contrast, but levels through the **i* vowel. Aramaic keeps the **u*/**i* contrast, but eventually levels through the **n*. I have vocalized *-km* and *-hm*, therefore, with the original **u* vowel, and have assumed the anceps vowel to have disappeared, since there is no *mater*. There are no f. pl. suffixes in the extant text.

Matres lectionis are indicated in the vocalization as follows: *w* and *y* as *matres* for final *ū* and *ī*, respectively, are indicated by a circumflex over the *u* or *i* (*û*, *î*); *h* as a *mater* for *e*, *ē*, or *ā*, is simply included in the vocalization in parentheses. I have avoided the use of *shewa* entirely, so that occasionally a vowel is added (*v*) which cannot be deduced from comparative evidence.

In the transliteration, a reading that is uncertain is written with a small circle over the letter in question. Reconstructions are enclosed in brackets. The vocalization is based on the consonants put forth in the transliteration; again, reconstructions are enclosed in brackets.

Cognates in the Canaanite and Aramaic dialects are included in the glossary for each word in the text (except the common Semitic roots). Occasionally reference to Akkadian, Arabic, or Ethiopic is necessary, and when it is, those cognates are listed also.

C. *Transliteration of the Text*

Combination I

ʾlwh

1 [VACAT]*spr*[.*bl‘m.brb‘*]*r.ʾš.ḥz̊h.ʾlhn̊*[.]*hʾ*[.]*wyʾtw.ʾlhn.blylh.ẘyḥz.mḥ̊zh*

2 *km̊šʾ.ʾl.wyʾmrw.l*[*bl‘*]*m.brb‘r.kh.yp‘l*[.]*ʾ.ʾḥrʾh.ʾš.lr*[ ]*‘t*[.]

3 *wyqm.bl‘m.mn.mḥr*[.]*l̊.y*[ ]*.mn.*[ ]*s̊h.wlyk̊*[*l.l* .]*wbk*

4 *h.ybkh.wy‘l.‘mh.ʾlẘh.*[*wyʾmrw.l*]*h̊*[.]*bl‘m.brb‘r.lm.tṣm.ẘtbkh.wyʾ*

5 *mr.lhm.šb̊w.ʾḥwkm.mh.šd̊*[*yn.p‘lw.*]*wlkw.rʾw.p‘lt.ʾl̊hn.ʾl*[*h*]*n.ʾ̊tyḥdw.*

6 *wnṣbw.šdyn.mw‘d.wʾm̊rw.lš*[.]*tpry.skry.šmyn.b‘bky.šm.ḥšk.wʾl.n*

7 *gh.‘l̊m.wʾ̊*[*l.*]*s̊krky.thby.ḥt*[*m.*]*b̊.ḥšk.wʾl*[.]*thgy.‘d.‘lm.ky.ss‘gr.ḥr*

8 *pt.n̊šr.wql̊.rḥm̊n.y‘nh.ḥ̊*[*sd.* .]*b̊ny.nḥṣ.wṣrh.ʾprḥy.ʾnph.drr.nšrt.*

9 *ywn.wṣpr*[.]*yn.*[ ]*.mṭh.bʾšr.rḥln.yybl.ḥṭr.ʾrnbn.ʾklw.*

10 [ ]*ʾ̊b̊.ḥpš*[ ]*.štyw.ḥmr.wqb‘n.šm‘w.mwsr̊.gry.š*

11 [*‘l.* .]*lḥkmn.yqḥk.w‘nyh.rqḥt.mr.wkhnh.*

12 [.]*lnšʾ.ʾzr.qrn.ḥšb.ḥšb.wḥšb.ḥ*

13 [*šb.* .]*wšm‘w.ḥršn̊*[.]*mn.rḥq*[.]

14 [.]*s̊kl.ḥzw.qqn.šgr.w‘štr.l*

15 [ ]*̊nmr.ḥnyṣ.hqrqt.bn*

16 [*y.*]*mšn.ʾz̊rn.w‘yn.*

Combination II

1 [ ]

2 *h.lšd̊*[ ]

3 *rn.ʾkl--*[ ]

4 *ʿlmh.rwy.ddn.k--*[ ]

5 *lḧ̊.lm.nqr.wmdr.kl.rṭb̊*[ ]

6 *yrwy.ʾl.yʿb̊r̊.ʾl.byt.ʿlmn.by*[*t.*]

7 *byt.lyʿl.hlk.wlyʿl.ḥtn.šm.byt*[.]

8 *wrmh.mn̊.gdš.mn.pḥzy.bny.ʾš.wmn.šqy-*[ ]

bk

9 [ ]*ly.hlʿṣh.lytʿṣ.ʾwlmlkh.lytmlk.yšb̊.-*[ ]

10 *n.m*[ ]*bn̊̊.tksn.lbš.ḥd.hn.tšnʾn.yʾnš.hn.t*[ ]

11 *ʾšm*[. .]*tḥt.rʾšk.tškb.mškby.ʿlmyk.lḥlq.l-*[ ]

12 *ʾd̊-.r̊k̊*[ ]*h.blbbm̊.nʾnḥ.nqr.blbbh̊.nʾnḥ̊.*[*nqr*?]

13 *bt.šmh.mlkn.yḥz̊ẘ.*[ ]*t̊̊.lysbm̊*[.]*yqḥ.mwt.ʿl.rḥm.wʿl--*[ ]

14 [ ]*ʿl*[ ]*-r.m̊ẘt̊.šmh.kb-*[ ]*ḥ.yk̊n̊.lbb.nqr.šh̊.ky.ʾth.l-*[ ]

15 *lqṣh.š*[ ]*wzlp̊̊.gdr*[.]*ṭ̊š̊*[ ]*šʾlt.mlk.ssh*[.]*wš*[ʾ]*l*[*t.*]

16 *h.*[ ]*ḥz̊n.r̊ḥq*[ ]*mk.šʾltk.lm.-*[ ]

17 *ldʿt.s̊pr.dbr.lʿmh̊.ʿl.lšn.lk.m̊špṭ.wmlqh̊̊.ʾmr*[ ]

18 *wl̊nšty.lmlk*[ ]

D. Vocalization of the Text

Combination I

(1) [VACAT] sipr [bilʿam birbuʿu]r ʾaš ḥāzē(h) ʾilāhīn huʾ
way-yaʾtû ʾilawh ʾilāhīn ba-laylah way-yaḥz maḥze(h)

(2) ka-maśśaʾ ʾil way-yaʾmurû la-[bilʿa]m birbuʿur kāh yipʿal
[ ]ʾ ʾaḫarʾah ʾaš LR[ ]ʿT

(3) way-yaqum bilʿam min maḫar [ ] L.Y [ ] min
[ ] SH wa-lā-yak*v*[l la-] wa-bakā

(4) (h) yabke(h) way-yaʿl ʿammuh ʾilawh [way-yaʾmurû la-]h
bilʿam birbuʿur lam taṣūm wa-tabke(h) way-yaʾ

(5) mur la-hum θibû ʾaḥawwikum mah θadda[yyīn paʿalû] wa-likû
riʾû puʿullāt ʾilāhīn ʾilā[hī]n ʾityaḥḥidû

(6) wa-niṣṣabû θaddayyīn mawʿid wa-ʾamarû la-Š[ ] tupurî
sukurî šamayīn ba-ǵabkî śām ḥušk wa-ʾal nu

(7) gh ʿālam wa-ʾi[l] sikrikî tihabî ḫāta[m]b ḥušk wa-ʾal
tahgî ʿad ʿālam kî sūsʿagūr ḥarra

(8) pat nišr wa-qāl raḫamīn yaǵne(h) ḥ*v*[sīd] banay NḤṢ
wa-ṣarā(h) ʾipruḫay ʾanapā(h) d*v*r*v*r naššarat

(9) yawn wa-ṣippar [ ] YN [ ] maṭṭe(h) ba-ʾaθr
raḫilīn yayubbal ḫuṭr ʾarnabīn akalû

(10) [ǯi]ʾb ḤPŠ [ ] šatiyû ḫamr waǯ̣abuʿīn
šamaʿû mawsar gūray θ*v*

(11) [ʿ*v*l] la-ḥak(k)*v*mīn yiǯ̣ḥak wa-ʿanīyā(h)
raqaḥat murr wa-kāhinā(h)

(12) [ ] la-naśīʾ ʾizār qūrīn ḥašūb
ḥašab wa-ḥāšib ḥa

(13) [šub] wa-šamaʿû ḫ*v*r(r)*v*šīn
min raḥ(ḥ)*v*q

(14) [ ] sakal ḥazû ǯ*v̄*qān šigr
wa-ʿaθtar L

(15) [ ] namir ḫunayṣ haḏriqat bana

(16) [y] (?)

Combination II

(4) ǵalmuh rawî dādīn [

(5) (?) lam niḏr wa-madūr kāl raṭīb [

(6) yirway ʼil yaʻbur ʼil bayt ʻālamīn bay[t

(7) bayt lā-yaʻl hālik wa-lā-yaʻl ḫatan θam bayt [

(8) wa-rimmā(h) min gadīš min pāḫizay banay ʼīš wa-min-šāqay[

(9) --LY ha-la-ʻiθā(h) bak lā-yittaʻaθ ʼaw-la-milkā(h) lā-yitmalik yāθib [

(10) (?) takassīnn lubūš ḥad hin tiśna'inn yiʼnaθ hin tv[

(11) ʼaśīm [ ] taḥt rvʼšak tiškab miškabay ʻālamayk la-ḫuluq la-[

(12) (?) (?) ba-libabam niʼnaḫ niḏr ba-libabuh niʼnaḫ [niḏr (?)

(13) (?) (?) yiqqaḥ mawt ǵūl raḥm wa-ǵūl [

(14) (?) (?) libab niḏr šahā(h) kî ʼatā(h) la-[

(15) la-qiṣṣuh (?) (?) [

(16) (?) (?) (?) [

(17) la-daʻt sipr dabbar la-ʻammuh ʻal lvš(š)ān lak miθpaṭ wa-malqe(h) (?) [

(18) wa-lā-ništay (?) [

E. Translation

Combination I

The account of [Balaam, son of Beo]r, who was a seer of the gods. The gods came to him in the night, and he saw a vision (2) like an oracle of El. Then they said to [Balaa]m, son of Beor: "Thus he will do/make [ ] hereafter (?), which [ ]." (3) And Balaam arose the next day [ ] from [ ] but he was not ab[le *to*] and he wept (4) grievously. And his people came up to him [*and said to*] him, "Balaam, son of Beor, why are you fasting and crying?" And he sa(5)id to them: "Sit down! I will tell you what the Šadda[yyin *have done*.] Now, come, see the works of the gods! The g[o]ds gathered together; (6) the Šaddayyin took their places as the assembly. And they said to Š[ ]: "Sew up, bolt up the heavens in your cloud, ordaining darkness instead of (7) eternal light! And put the dark [se]al on your bolt, and do not remove it forever! For the swift re(8)proaches the griffin-vulture and the voice of vultures sings out. The *st[ork*] the young of the NḤṢ-bird (?) and claws up young herons. The swallow tears at (9) the dove and the sparrow [ ] the rod, and instead of the ewes, it is the staff that is led. Hares eat (10) [*a wo*]*lf* (?) [ ] drink wine and hyenas give heed to chastisement. The whelps of the *f*(11)[*ox*] laughs at the wise. And the poor woman prepares myrrh while the priestess (12) [ ] for the prince, a tattered loincloth. The respected one (now) respects (others) and the one who gave respect is (now) re(13)[spected.] and the deaf hear from afar. (14) [*and the ? of* (?)] a fool see visions. The constraint of fertility (lit.: "offspring") (15) [ ] the leopard. The piglet chases the you(16)[ng of] (?) . . . . "

Combination II

(4) his boy, full of love [ ]

(5) (?) "Why are/do the scion and the firepit containing foliage [. . . ?" ". . . *so that*]

(6) El will be satisfied. Let him go (lit.: "cross over") to

the House of Eternity, the hou[se]

(7) the house where the traveler does not rise and the bridegroom does not rise, the house [. . ." ". . .]

(8) and the worm from the tomb, from those who have arisen among human beings, and from the graves of [. . ."]

(9) [ ] "As for counsel, is it not you with whom he will take counsel; or for advice, will he not ask advice from one residing [. . . ?]

(10) [ ] You will cover him with one garment. If you are unkind to him (lit.: "hate him"), he will falter. If you [. . ."]

(11) "I will put [ ] under your head. You will lie down on your eternal bed to perish [. . ."]

(12) [ ] to themselves (lit.: "in their heart"). The scion sighs to himself (lit.: "in his heart"). [*The scion* (?)] sighs [ ]

(13) [ ] Death will take the newborn child, the suckling [ ]

(14) [ ] (?) [ ] (?) The heart of the scion is weak for he goes to [ ]

(15) to his end [ ] (?) [ ]

(16) [ ] (?) [ ] (?) [ ]

(17) to make known (lit.: "to know") the account he spoke to his people orally (lit.: "by tongue"), your judgment and your punishment." (?) [" . . .]

(18) and we will not drink. (?) [. . . . "]

F. Commentary

Combination I

Line 1.

[VACAT]*spr*[.*blʿm.brbʿ*]*r.ʾš̆.ḥz̊h.ʾlhn̊*[.]*hʾ*[.] This announcement of the text to follow is written almost entirely in red ink (all but the final *hʾ*).[1] The name of Balaam son of Beor is

[1]Gordon Hamilton (see p. 4, n. 19) has argued convincingly that the variation in ink color need not be taken into account in problems of syntax. He notes that the rubric in I, 2, begins at the same point in the line where the rubric in I, 1, leaves

the obvious restoration in view of his mention in lines 2, 3, and 4 of the first combination.

spr. The *r* is fairly certain. The preceding letter is either *m*, *p*, or *k*. Caquot and Lemaire assume *p* and restore *spr*. McCarter restores *ʾmry*. Once again, I believe Hamilton has found the solution, by placing Fragment III (h) above and to the right of the long tail and the *r*. He reads III (h) as the tops of a *s* and a *p*, and thus completes the word *spr*.

ʾš. In context, this word may be read as the Canaanite relative pronoun,[2] or as *ʾīš*, the common word for "man."[3] The sense of the passage is best served by reading *ʾš* as the relative pronoun, and *hʾ* (in black ink) as a copula completing the relative clause.[4] As was mentioned in n. 1 of this section, I believe there is no problem here with the change in ink color.

ḥ̊zh. G active participle, m. sg. cs., of *ḥzh*. The *h* *mater* indicates the **-iy* ending has contracted, as was explained above, p. 22.

(Black ink)

hʾ. Van der Kooij read *hʾwyʾtw* with no word divider. The

---

off. Thus, the red-ink sections in Combination I need not be complete statements in themselves, but instead simply extend approximately half-way across the line in which they are written. Cross (private communication), and Fitzmyer, Naveh, Levine, and Greenfield (in review articles of *ATDA* [see p. 6, n. 35]) all agree in ignoring the ink color.

[2]For *ʾš*, see Harris/*Grammar*, pp. 54-55, 82; "$\check{s}_1$" in *DISO*, pp. 285-86. As Harris points out, *ʾš* must be related to Akkadian *ša* and Hebrew *š*-, not to Hebrew *ʾăšer*, which is from **ʾaθr*. At some point this *š*- or *ša* relative must have acquired a prosthetic *ʾalep* and probably lost the short final vowel.

[3]For *ʾīš* plus a word indicating a function, see Hoftijzer (184).

[4]Cross (private communication) and Fitzmyer (*CBQ* 40 [1978] 94-95) also suggest this interpretation. For the relative pronoun followed by a third person independent pronoun, see KAI 43:4-5; and, e.g., Gen 9:3; Lev 11:26; Num 9:13. The personal pronoun follows the relative immediately in these passages; for the order in our text, cf. several negative relative clauses in BH (e.g., Gen 7:2; 17:12; Deut 17:15). Sefîre III, 8, *kl zy rḥm hʾ ly*, has the pronoun in the middle of the relative clause.

text is damaged at this point, however, and there may have been a word divider at one time. At any rate, the letters must be read as two words: *h'* and *wy'tw*. *h'* can be read as the pronoun *hu'* or as "behold."[5] As was indicated above (under *'š*), I prefer to read *hu'* as a copula, connected with the preceding description of Balaam as seer of the gods and specifically related to the relative *'š*.

wy'tw. Converted imperfect, 3 m. pl., from the root **'tw*.[6] (The root is well known in Aramaic and Hebrew. The *w* is supplied by Ugaritic and Ethiopic.)

'lwh. This word apparently was left out of the text by mistake and inserted above the line at a later time. The *-wh* 3 m. sg. suffix on plural nouns and certain prepositions is well known from Aramaic.[7] The suffix is discussed briefly in Chapter 4, pp. 115-16.

blylh. I have vocalized as if the final *h* is not a *mater lectionis*, but is rather the "adverbial" or "directive" *h*. I have assumed arbitrarily that adverbial *h* is still consonantal at this point.[8]

---

[5]Caquot and Lemaire (194) and McCarter (52) opt for "behold."

[6]I have vocalized the *waw* consecutives in this text with doubled *y*. This is an arbitrary decision, based on BH. It is in BH that we have our first vocalized *waw* consecutives.

[7]See *EHO*, p. 29, #68; and Fitzmyer, p. 31.

[8]The *h* on *lylh* is open to several interpretations. It may be that this *h* is a *mater* for *ê*, from a diphthong contracted from a reduplicated root **laylay* (see Fitzmyer, pp. 38-39), although this is unlikely since diphthongs do not contract in this dialect. It may be that the *h* is a vestige of the adverbial *h*. (The penultimate accent in Hebrew would support this view.) Even here, however, there are two possibilities. We know that locative *h* was consonantal in Ug, but we do not know whether there was a short vowel following the *h* (**-ah* or **-ahv*). If there were a final vowel, it would have dropped off when final short vowels were lost. At some point, to judge from later Hebrew and Aramaic evidence, the final *h* was no longer pronounced and the preceding *a* vowel was lengthened. This left the vestigial *h* as a *mater* for the *-ā* ending. We do not know when this change took place. Later in Aramaic, an *'* *mater* is

ẘyḥz.mḥ̊zh. This ending for line 1 is supplied by another of Hamilton's placements of fragments. He has added here Fragments V (e) and XV (c), which addition makes for a smooth and felicitous completion of the line.

Line 2.

kmš̊ʾ. The restoration here differs from that of Caquot and Lemaire, and of McCarter. In both articles, the suggested restoration is *kmlyʾ*. Both restorations are feasible on paleographic grounds. The lacuna is large enough to contain two small letters, such as *l* and *y*, or one large letter. *š* is large enough, and is often written rather high on the line. (See, for example, the height of *š* as opposed to *m* in I, 10, and II, 11.)[9] The restoration *kmlyʾ* identifies the *ʾalep* as the Aramaic emphatic ending, but the emphatic ending does not appear in any unambiguous context in this text.[10] Thus, the reconstruction of the emphatic here is risky, even though the spacing makes it possible. I prefer to consider the *ʾalep* part of a root III-ʾ, and *maśśaʾ ʾil*, "an oracle of El," is a fitting phrase in context, satisfying the sense of the text and the requirements of the spacing and traces.

yʾmrw. I have vocalized *yaʾmurû*, because this is probably the early form of the word.[11]

[blʿ]m.brbʿr. The restoration of Balaam's name is based on the occurrence of the name in line 4, and on his full name

---

also used. I have chosen to vocalize this inscription as if the *h* is still consonantal, because that is the earliest situation possible after the loss of final short vowels.

[9]This restoration was suggested to me independently by A. Rofé and F. M. Cross, and E. Puech argued convincingly that the paleography of this inscription will allow for a *š* in this location. See now Rofé (cited in n. 30, p. 6, above), p. 61.

[10]Hoftijzer identifies this *ʾalep* as the definite article also, although the placement of the fragments in *ATDA* gave rise to a different reading than that mentioned above. See *ATDA*, pp. 188-89.

[11]We assume that in Hebrew, **yaʾmur* > **yā(ʾ)mur* > **yō(ʾ)mur*. Then **yō(ʾ)mur* > *yō(ʾ)mar* by a process of dissimilation. (See Bauer-Leander, §53c.)

in the Hebrew Bible, where he is referred to as "son of Beor." In fact, in rearranging the fragments of this combination, I placed Fragments I (c) and I (a) in position relative to each other according to the amount of space between *l* "to" and the rest of Balaam's name. (See p. 21, above, for a discussion of the arrangement of the fragments.) The vocalization *bir* has long been established from Assyrian materials.[12]

kh.ypʿl.[ ]ʾ.ʾḥrʾh.ʾš.lr[ ]ʿt This mostly red-ink section is the text of a direct speech by the gods to Balaam, if I am correct in restoring only Balaam's name in the lacuna before *brbʿr*. McCarter (49) has suggested that the rubrics deal with the inscription itself, and that this proclamation allows for the setting up of the inscription.

kh. Similar arguments can be made for the *h* in *kh* (and *mh*, below, in I, 5) as for the *h* in *lylh* (see n. 8 above). It is either consonantal (from **kah* or **kaha*), or it is a *mater* for *ā*. In *kh*, however, there is no proof that the *h* was ever a part of the word, since *kh* does not occur in earlier materials. *kh* "thus" can be read either as associated with what has come before, or as associated with what comes after it. E.g., "they said to Balaam thus: 'He/It will make/do...'" or "they said to Balaam: 'Thus he/it will make/do...'" (again, ignoring the variation in ink color). As the beginning of an oracle from the gods, the latter seems preferable. Cf. the common BH *kō(h) ʾāmar YHWH*.

ypʿl.[ ]ʾ. I read *ypʿl* as a unit,[13] and, therefore, most likely a third-person verbal form. If the proposed connection with *kh* is accepted (see directly above, under *kh*), in the context of a speech from the gods to Balaam, *kh ypʿl* should mean "thus he will make/do," although in such a broken context,

---

[12] W. F. Albright, *AJSL* 44 (1927-28) 33.

[13] Hoftijzer (187-88) divides the word after the ʿ and proposes a noun *ypʿ* meaning "fire" from the root *ypʿ*. It should be pointed out that the original reading of these letters was somewhat difficult (see van der Kooij, 102). I found the ink too faded at this point for further comment.

there are other possibilities ("thus it will be made/done," "thus let it be made/done," "thus let him make/do"). Unfortunately, the second word cannot be read. The third (?) letter is an *'alep*; the second (?) appears to be *g*, *l*, or *ṭ*. The first is almost entirely obliterated. If McCarter is correct, we would expect a word that means "inscription" or a word that describes the stela or other foundation for an inscription. None of the possibilities fits the tracings, however.

'ḥr'h. Hoftijzer (186-87) interpreted this word as built upon a root *ḥr'* meaning "to burn." Caquot and Lemaire (194-95) and McCarter (52) suggested that the root was *'ḥr*, "after." McCarter compares this word with BH *hā́lǝ'āh*, "further on," and suggests that *'ḥr'* is the emphatic state of *'ḥr* and that the *-h* is an adverbial ending; the combination would mean "hereafter." Given the analogy with Hebrew *hā́lǝ'āh*, however, it is not necessary to interpret this *'alep* as an emphatic ending, and, as I argued above in connection with *kmš'* earlier in this line, it is risky to posit an emphatic *'alep* in a troublesome situation since there are no clear emphatics elsewhere. I agree with the comparison to *hā́lǝ'āh* and with the translation "hereafter," but prefer to explain the *'alep* here as something other than the Aramaic emphatic ending. Whatever the reason might be for the *'alep* in *hā́lǝ'āh*, it is surely not an Aramaic emphatic. We do not expect an internal emphatic in any case. Thus, I have vocalized *'aḥar*, "after," plus *'*, plus *-ah* according to the pattern for adverbial *h*.

'š. Like the *'š* in line 1, this word can be interpreted in a number of ways. Besides the relative pronoun and "man," it might also mean "fire." There is simply not enough of the context left to be certain. Hoftijzer translated "fire" in keeping with his translation of *'ḥr'h* as "I want to kindle" (cohortative). Caquot and Lemaire and McCarter opt for "man" or "someone." I prefer the relative pronoun before the preposition (or negative) *l-*, but this suggestion is extremely tenuous.

lr[ ]*'t*. Again, there is no certain translation since there is so much missing from these words. If McCarter is correct, and the gods are declaring that something should be set up to preserve the words of their night message to Balaam, then these letters might represent the order to display something that Balaam has heard. Note that there is a trace of a long tail in red ink, next to the *ʿayin* of *-ʿt*, so that the last letter in the break should be *k*, *m*, *n*, *p*, or *t*.[14]

We would be happier with an interpretation of this communication if it could explain the reaction Balaam exhibits after his visit from the gods. There is obviously nothing in the "message" as I have presented it that would upset Balaam as much as he is upset later in the narrative. We must assume that the content of the actual vision was not spelled out this early in the narrative of our text. The gods made it possible for Balaam to have a vision so upsetting to him that he was moved to fast and to cry uncontrollably (see below), but that information is not the topic of this direct speech section written mostly in red ink. In fact, it would be very surprising if such a short section contained the entire content of their message. Rather, we assume that Balaam's vision is the one referred to at the end of line 1, and that the direct message reported in I, 2, is a final admonition of some sort. The full story is not revealed to us until Balaam relates the message to his people, beginning in line I, 6.

Line 3.

wyqm.blʿm.mn.mḥr. Notice the *waw* consecutive, and the fact that Balaam's name is spelled out for the first time. The entire phrase serves to emphasize the fact that Balaam received his message at night, while lying down, asleep. (Cf. Num 22: 8-13, 19-21, where Balaam receives communication from Elohim at night. The verb *wyqm* is used there also in vv. 13 and 21, to describe Balaam's action the next morning.)

There must have been some mention in the following words of Balaam's refusal to eat, since his fasting is remarked upon later in the text. The insertion of Fragment VIII (d) allows us to read *y*[ ]*.mn*, then a break. Following the break we read

---

[14]See McCarter (51-52). He restores *lr*[*ʾt.zy.šm*]*ʿt*, and translates, "so that what you have heard may be seen."

s̊h.lyk/m[ ]. One letter toward the end of this new break has a long tail. I have chosen to read *lyk̊*[*l*], "he was not able."[15]

Lines 3/4.

wbkh.ybkh. The obvious interpretation of this phrase is that it is an infinitive absolute plus a finite verb of the root *bkh*, coupled for emphasis. In the infinitive the *h mater* here is used for *-ā*. The finite verb has a *h* as *mater* also, indicating in this case an *e* vowel from **-iy*.

wyʿl.ʿmh.ʾlẘh. The translation of this phrase hinges on the change from *ʾlqh* of the *editio princeps* to *ʾlwh*. This change was suggested to me by McCarter, and an examination of the plaster indicated that it was a reasonable reading.[16] This relieves us of the troublesome "Eliqah," a personal name which Hoftijzer and Caquot and Lemaire had to use. Once the third word is established as "to him," it is easy to read the second word as "his people." I have translated the verb as a form of the root *ʿlh*. *ʿll* is also possible, of course. If the root is *ʿlh*, the short form of the imperfect is what we would expect with a *waw* consecutive.

ʿmh. I have vocalized with *-uh* as the pronominal suffix. (For *-uh* instead of *-ih*, see p. 23, above.) It is possible that the anceps vowel should be kept at the end of this word. For reasons the presence of an anceps vowel may be suspected, see the discussion of *tšnʾn* in II, 10.[17]

---

[15]McCarter (51-52) restores *lyk*[*l.lʾkl*] "[he] could not [eat]." Hamilton may be correct, however, that the long tail toward the end of the break must go with the final letter of any reconstructed word (private communication), so that *ʾkl* would be difficult here.

[16]Note that van der Kooij (105) described the right arm of the "*q*" as being nearly in line with the bottom stroke. In fact, it appears to be the upper extension of the vertical stroke, and must be part of a *w* with an unusually high right stroke.

[17]As with the adverbial *h* (see n. 8, above), it is impossible to determine whether the *h* here (if there is no anceps vowel following) is consonantal or a vestige retained as a *mater*. Presumably, **-uhū/*-ihī* > **-uh/*-ih*, and eventually > *-ō(h)/-ē(h)*. Again, we do not know when the *h* became quiescent.

ʾlẘh. See the earlier discussion of this word under I, 1.

Presumably we may restore a phrase before our next visible ink which indicates that Balaam's people spoke to him, asking him the questions that follow.

lm.tṣm.ẘtbkh. *lm* has been translated as an Aramaic particle indicating direct speech.[18] I think it is more likely that this word is an interrogative, "why?" like Ugaritic *lm*, represented in Hebrew by *lā́mmāh*, and in Aramaic by *ləmā*.[19]

ẘtbkh. The traces revealed by the new arrangement of the fragments indicate a letter plus word divider before *tbkh*, rather than simply a word divider, as in *ATDA*. *w* fits the traces.

Lines 4/5.

wyʾmr.lhm. Note again the *waw* consecutive in obvious past tense narrative. Note also that the m. pl. pronominal suffix ends in *m*, as in Canaanite languages and in early Aramaic material.[20]

Line 5.

š̊bw. Pl. m. imperative from the root *yšb*. (This form is known from Hebrew and Old Aramaic.)

ʾḥwkm. 1 c. sg. D imperfect from the root *ḥwh*, plus 2 m. pl. objective suffix. The suffix ends in *m*, as did the third person suffix directly above. The *a* vowel of the prefix is assumed from Ugaritic evidence of the first person D imperfect verbs (*UT* §9.35).

mh.šd̊[yn.pʿlw]. As was noted above under *kh*, the *h* in *mh*

---

[18]Hoftijzer (222, n. 105), in reference to II, 5; McCarter (53). Caquot and Lemaire (194) reconstruct *l[m]h* and translate "why?".

[19]We would assume, then, that the Ugaritic *lm* represented **lamă*, with the vowel dropping off in the dialect of our text, but retained and lengthened in Hebrew and Aramaic.

[20]See Degen, §36, p. 55; or Segert, §§5.1.3.4.3 and 5.1.3.4.5, pp. 173-74.

may or may not be a *mater lectionis*.[21] I have restored the end of this phrase in a way that is suitable to the context and the spacing.[22] *šdyn* is the obvious restoration for the first word, since this group of gods is mentioned in the next line as part of Balaam's revelations.[23] (See below, p. 40, on the vocalization.) The verb could be any one of a number of possibilities, *pʿl* or *ʾmr*, for instance. The choice is arbitrary.

wlkw.rʾw.pʿlt.ʾlh̊n. Here Balaam invites his people to learn of the scene he has witnessed in the Divine Council. The rest of the first combination is a description of what was done and said in this meeting.[24]

rʾw. In context, this must be a plural imperative. *šbw* and *lkw* before it are pl. imperatives. The root is *rʾh*, a root unknown in Aramaic, but common in Hebrew, of course. For the significance of the occurrence of *rʾh* (and *lkw*) in this text, see the discussion in the dialect section, pp. 121-23, below.

pʿlt. For the vocalization, cf. Akk *qutull(at)* forms (*GAG* §55q).

ʾl[h]n.ʾ̊tyḥdw. This is actually the first phrase in Balaam's description to his people of what he saw. McCarter (53) suggested restoring the *h* in *ʾlhn*, even though there is no trace of the letter in the text. There is, however, a large enough break at this point to demand a letter to fill it.

---

[21]Unlike *kh*, however, we do have evidence from Ugaritic for this word. The *h* is used consistently on *mh* at Ugarit. Note, however, the discussion of *lm* in n. 19. In Hebrew and Aramaic, *lmh/ʾ* is analyzed as *l* + *mh/mʾ*, "for what" = "why." If the same analysis is applied to Ugaritic *lm*, then *mh* in combination with a preposition can be written simply *m*. Thus, *m* may have been a biform of *mh*, even at Ugarit.

[22]McCarter (51, 53) proposes the same restoration.

[23]Hoftijzer restores *šəgar* here in accordance with his belief that a goddess *šəgar* appears in the inscription. See his discussion on pp. 273-74, and my commentary on I, 14, below.

[24]The *h* of *ʾlhn* is not visible in the drawing of the *editio princeps*, but there are slight traces of a letter in this space on the plaster.

ʾtyḥdw. The verb *yḥd* occurs in the tD in MH and in Aramaic, meaning "to be alone with, to be closeted with."[25] Here, the meaning must be something to do with gathering together. (See below, p. 119, for a discussion of the reading *ʾ* here, and of the *ʾalep*-preformative in this text.)

Line 6.

wnṣbw.šdyn.mwʿd. The first word is most reasonably translated as a m. pl. perfect verb of the N conjugation. As has been pointed out, the N fits the context better than any other possibility.[26] There is at least one other N form within this inscription (II, 12 bis), so we should not be surprised to find one here. The word is vocalized according to the N in Hebrew. (See the discussion of the N in this inscription, on p. 117, below.) Psalm 82:1 is perhaps the best analogy to our phrase. Hoftijzer (193) has gathered considerable evidence for the interpretation of *mwʿd* as an adverbial accusative, "in an assembly," or "as an assembly," without the use of a preposition. Reading these words along with the previous phrase, we have a description of all the gods gathering together, with "*šdyn*" apparently the appellation of the gods who stand as the council.[27] I have vocalized *šdyn* following the vocalization of biblical Šadday, El Šadday (assuming *-ay* < **-ayyu*), as the simplest and most direct solution.

ʾtyḥdw wnṣbw . . . wʾmrw lš[ ] We notice immediately that the use of the *waw* consecutive, which is clear with several imperfects early in the inscription, is not extended in lines 5/6 to the perfect. The first verb in this series is a perfect, and the two following must also be past tense verbs. Hence, the *waw* is non-converting. It is not necessary for the *waw* consecutive plus imperfect to be used every time there is a need for a past tense, of course. Within BH, *waw* plus a

---

[25]Jastrow, p. 573.

[26]See Hoftijzer (192); McCarter (54); cf. Caquot and Lemaire (196), where the word is translated as G, "to set up."

[27]It would seem that *šdyn* is the name applied to the gods who make up this council of El. An excursus, pp. 85-89, will discuss their relationship with the *ʾlhn* and with El Šadday.

perfect is not necessarily the equivalent of an imperfect, although it usually is. (See Joüon §155c.)

š[ ]. It is particularly frustrating that the name of the major deity to whom the *šdyn* speak is not clearly represented on the recovered fragments. We know that the deity is female (the following words are f. sg. imperatives) and that her name begins with *š*/*ś*. Hoftijzer (272-74) proposes that the word *šgr* found in I, 14, is the name of the goddess. He points to the association in this text of *šgr* with *ʿštr* (the god ʿAštar, according to Hoftijzer), and to the fact that these words are associated in the Hebrew Bible and at Ugarit. While at Ugarit *šgr* occurs in a list of divine names,[28] the occurrences of *šgr* and *ʿštrt* in the Hebrew Bible are best translated "young" or "offspring" (BDB 800, 993). In I, 14, of our inscription, *šgr* and *ʿštr* occur in a series of phrases, most of which have to do with the animal kingdom. Even though our inscription is badly broken at that point, the BH usage of the terms fits better with our text than the possibility of two divine names occurring in such a context. (See under I, 14, for interpretation.)

Caquot and Lemaire (196-97) argued that *šgr* is not suitable as the goddess in this inscription and suggested Šamaš instead. They point out that the goddess in question would have to have great cosmic powers in order to carry out what is requested of her, and that the sun is considered feminine at Ugarit. McCarter (53-54) argued that the sun goddess would not likely be the one to obscure the light in the sky, and that the sun's "dark cloud" (*ʿb*) has no obvious referent. He suggested instead the personified underworld, "Sheol," as a possibility for our goddess. While McCarter's arguments are good, the sun goddess may still be the best candidate for the goddess in this inscription. The phrase in I, 6/7, "ordaining darkness *and not* light," is the key. It implies that the goddess in question does have the power to ordain light, and that, in fact, that is her normal function. Apparently the unnatural darkening of the sky is an appropriate divine punishment for an

---

[28] In Jean Nougayrol, *et al.*, *Ugaritica V*, 9 reverse, p. 584.

unacceptable situation on earth. As a response to sin in the Hebrew Bible, Yahweh often declares that he will darken the sun and moon (Joel 2:10, 3:4, 4:15; Amos 8:9; Mic 3:6), and once (Ezek 32:7) he says he will cover the sun with a cloud. Thus, it is possible that in the Deir ʿAllā text, the sky is to be darkened because of the upheaval of nature reported in the last half of the first combination (see commentary on lines I, 7, and following), and that the goddess who is asked to darken the sky is one who normally (or "perpetually" or "eternally") gives light, i.e., the sun goddess, a great and powerful deity whose name begins with *š*.

(If, however, my suggestion for interpreting II, 7, is correct, which suggestion implies a male sun deity, a sun goddess would not be appropriate in this context.)

Finally, another possibility suggests itself, namely Šala, a goddess of Hurrian origin, usually pictured in Mesopotamia along with the storm god Adad, and now also known (also in association with Adad) from the Tell Fakhariyeh inscription. A storm goddess would be reasonable here, since her "dark cloud" is referred to later in the line, but one would expect a better-known goddess for the central deity in our text.

tpry.skry.šmyn.bʿbky. The first two letters of the first word offer some problems. Van der Kooij (110) explains that the small fragment on which the tops of the letters are situated was turned nearly 180° from its correct position when it was placed with the rest of the text. It was felt that the fragment belonged in this location, but the position was unknown. It was later discovered that turning the fragment 180° would mean, probably, that the traces on the small fragment and the traces (two long tails) on the larger fragment with which it belongs would fit together. It also seemed probable that the plaster edges would make a good fit. Unfortunately, the fragments had been set in position, more or less permanently, before this discovery was made, so the theory cannot be tested easily. Although the head of the *t* is no longer discernible, the second letter is most probably the head of a *p*, so I have accepted van der Kooij's reading of the letters themselves. Although there is clear ink at the beginning of the small fragment, I could not see the word divider that van der Koiij reports on the small fragment or on the larger fragment. There is some ink on the left side of the small fragment, but it is difficult to decide what its relation might be to the following *r*, if the fragment were rotated. So I choose to ignore the possibility of a word divider, as did Caquot and Lemaire and McCarter. (Even on van der Kooij's drawing there is no complete word divider, merely some extra ink in a small space between the *p* and the *r*.)[29]

tpry.skry. Read both as f. sg. G imperatives. Note the asyndetic construction, as above in line 5, *lkw r'w*.

šmyn. Read as m. pl., *šamayīn*. (See GKC §88d.)

bʿbky. The *-ky* suffix is 2 f. sg., *-kī*. The long form of this suffix is known from a few forms in the Hebrew Bible, from Qumran, and from Imperial Aramaic (see Segert §5.1.3.2).

Lines 6/7

šm.ḥšk.w'l.ngh.ʿl̊m. Read *šm* as G infinitive absolute from the middle-weak root *śym*. (The word is vocalized according to the Hebrew infinitive absolute of middle-weak verbs.) This word has generally been interpreted as *šam*, "there."[30] This, however, makes for awkward syntax in the words that follow, since the use of *'al* with a noun is rare. Hoftijzer (196) notes the only instance in Hebrew Bible in Prov 12:28. McCarter (51) has taken a more reasonable line, assuming the phrase means "there let there be darkness and no light," with the ellipsis of the verb "to be," as in 2 Sam 1:21. Even this, however, is less satisfactory than assuming the ellipsis of a verb after *'al* that is actually present earlier in the sentence.

---

[29] McCarter has suggested (private communication) that the "head" of the *p* could be connected with the following *r* to give a *q*, if only the fragment were nudged upward. This seems possible to me. On examining the plaster, my only reservation in accepting the reading *tp* was that the trace on the fragment seemed too large to be the head of a *p* (i.e., reading it as the arm of a *q* is a real possibility).

[30] See Hoftijzer (179 and 195); Caquot and Lemaire (197, although they mention the possibility of a verb form from the root *śym*); McCarter (51).

Interpreting *šm* as a verb from the root *śym* gives a smoother reading. It cannot be an imperative, like *tpry* and *skry*, as the f. sg. imperatives have *-y* endings (for *-ī*). We know, however, that the infinitive absolute can substitute for the imperative.[31] Another possibility is to interpret the infinitive as a gerund connecting this phrase with the previous one, "ordaining darkness. . . ." In either case, the *ʾal* is now connected with a verbal form and does not negate a noun.

ʿl̊m. The reading of this word is difficult. Van der Kooij (106) sees a *ṭ* instead of *l*, but this gives a word that is unknown outside this inscription, unless we assume a lapse in the usual phonology.[32] Consequently, other readings have been suggested for the unclear middle letter. Caquot and Lemaire (197) suggest a *d* and give Arabic *ʿadam*, "nothing," as cognate. They assume, however, that this word must parallel *ḥšk*, which assumption is, I think, incorrect. McCarter reads *ʿlm* and sees the word in connection with *ngh* before it (54). After looking at the plaster, I think this is the most likely reading, and the one that makes the most sense.[33] Even this reading is not without difficulties. The word *ʿlm*, "eternity," is well known, of course, but may sound awkward at this point in the inscription. It may be used here to emphasize the fact that *Šmš* generally and always gives light and not darkness, to point up that what is being asked of her here is unusual. McCarter's translation "perpetual" fits this interpretation.[34]

---

[31]GKC §113z, bb; W. L. Moran, *BANE*, pp. 69-70.

[32]This is Hoftijzer's explanation, i.e., in this one case, *θ̣ > *ṭ*, rather than > *ṣ* (197, 284).

[33]In my opinion this cannot be a *ṭ*. The ink that van der Kooij sees as the point of the right arm of the *ṭ* and the middle stroke of the *ṭ* is actually part of one stroke, written from upper right to lower left. This ink must be from the lower part of the downstroke of the *l* because the stroke is quite wide at this point. The ink that van der Kooij sees as the upper right arm of the *ṭ* would then be the upstroke of the *l*.

[34]Concerning this word, note the use of *šmš ʿlm* at Karaṭepe (A III, 19), *šamaš dārītum* at Amarna (*EA* 155:6, 47), and *špš ʿlm* at Ugarit (*PRU* V, 8, 7).

Line 7.

wʾ̊[l.]s̊krky.thby.ḥt[m.]b̊.ḥšk. *ʾalep* is a good possibility for the letter following *w* (see van der Kooij, 106), and a small letter like *l* must follow.[35] In fact, nearly everyone restores these two letters,[36] but the word has always been interpreted as the negative, like the preceding *ʾl*. I have translated instead the word "to" and have connected this preposition with the verb *thby* further on in the line to read "you will give to" in the sense of "putting" or "placing on." (See, e.g., *ntn ʾl* in 1 Sam 6:8.)

The word after *ʾl* could be *skrky* or *smrky* (van der Kooij, 107) although the traces seem to me to fit *k* better than *m*. *skr* is more likely anyway since it could then be related to the verb *skry* above. I have vocalized the word according to Akkadian *sikru*, "closure," with *i* before *-kī* dictated by vowel harmony.

In the next break, I accept McCarter's restoration (51, 54) of *m* after *ḥt*. His suggestion of *ʿ* before the faint *b* of the next visible ink is also possible, but there is no room for his word *ʿl* before *ʿb* as I have rearranged the fragments. Consequently, the phrase might be rendered "the seal of the cloud of darkness," or better, "the dark cloud's seal." The *b* of *ʿb* is, however, not at all certain (van der Kooij, 112), and it could be that another word entirely stood in the break. The gist of the phrase is still that the goddess is being told to put a (dark) seal on her "bolt" in the heavens, a "bolt" that may be the cloud itself, or something applied to the cloud.

thby. This must be the rare imperfect (or jussive; see the next paragraph) of the verb *yhb*, known from Aramaic and Hebrew (in Hebrew in the imperative only), which means "to give, place, put." Although in later Aramaic the imperfect of *ntn* (*ytn*) is always used for the imperfect of *yhb*, the proper imperfect is known from Old Aramaic inscriptions (as Sefîre I B

---

[35]Although van der Kooij is dubious about *l*, he does not rule it out (107).

[36]E.g., Hoftijzer (173); Caquot and Lemaire (196); McCarter (51).

38, for instance; see *DISO* 105 for other possibilities). In this case, the imperfect/jussive is being used as a substitute for the earlier imperatives.

Note that in an Aramaic dialect, we would expect a final -*n* on the 2 f. sg. imperfect. If this dialect followed that rule, *thby* (and *thgy* below) would be jussive. We have no clear case of a 2 f. sg. imperfect within this inscription, however (i.e., a form that must be imperfect, with no suspicion that it might be jussive), so it is impossible to know whether this dialect employed the long form of the 2 f. sg. imperfect, and consequently, whether *thby* and *thgy* are jussive or imperfect. (I do not interpret *tksn* and *tšn*ʾ*n* in II, 10, as 2 f. sg. imperfect. These words have been given varying interpretations. See the discussion below, on pp. 65-66.)

*w*ʾ*l.thgy.*ʿ*d.*ʿ*lm.* I think McCarter (54) is correct that the verb here must be cognate to the rare Hebrew *hgh* II (BDB 212), "remove," rather than *hgh* I meaning "to murmur," etc. ʾ*l* plus the imperfect (or jussive; see the paragraph directly above) is used here in the usual sense of a prohibition.

Lines 7/8.

*ky.ss*ʿ*gr.ḥrpt.n̊šr.wql̊.rḥm̊n.y*ʿ*nh.* At this point we begin a long series of phrases beginning with "because," which serves to give the reason for such drastic action on the part of the gods. McCarter has given the best explanation for these phrases (58-59), and these first two offer the key. That the swift, a tiny bird, should reproach the griffin-vulture, and that voiceless vultures should sing, is an unnatural situation. Nature seems to be turned upside-down. This whole series of statements describes a state in which people, animals, even inanimate objects are no longer conforming to normal, natural patterns. This is the reason the gods are petitioning the goddess to seal up the heavens, to provide darkness (on earth) rather than light. It is a catastrophic situation that has caused such disfavor in the heavens.

The use of the reversal of the natural order as a sign of catastrophe is known from other literature as well. In the course of the commentary, reference will be made especially to Egyptian literature, where the resemblance to our text is often remarkable. This principle of uncharacteristic actions will guide my translation of the rest of the first combination.[37]

The forms of the verbs in this section are ambiguous. We might well have perfects, imperfects, and participles present. I have translated them as if they represent durative or habitual action, but this interpretation has been questioned (see n. 37, below).

ssʿgr. Written as one word in our text, this bird is known from the Hebrew Bible. The name has been given various explanations, however. Once, it is written as if two separate birds: Jer 8:7, *wəsûs* (Kt) *wəʿāgûr*; once, written as two words, but with no intervening *waw*: Isa 38:14, *kəsûs ʿāgûr*. Whatever the origin of this name, it is now clear that *ʿgr* is a part of the name of one bird, and not another bird name (cf. BDB 723). Here it is treated as f. sg. (see directly below).

ḥrpt. I have vocalized as a 3 f. sg. perfect D verb. (*ḥrp* occurs most often in the D in BH.) For evidence that the 3 f. sg. perfect retained the -*t* in this dialect, see *nšrt* in I, 8, most likely a D verb, and therefore a perfect rather than a participle; or better *hqrqt* in I, 15, with no context, but unlikely to be anything other than a C 3 f. sg. perfect. (*ḥrpt* is not in itself evidence of this phenomenon, since it is possible, though unlikely, that it could be a G f. sg. participle.)

yʿnh. I have interpreted this verb as a 3 m. sg. G imperfect of *ʿnh*, "to sing" (BDB 777 and Jastrow *ʿnh* I, 1093).

Line 8.

ḥ̊[sd. .]b̊ny.nḥṣ.wṣrh.ʾprḥy.ʾnph. We must interpret the first part of the phrase by referring to the second part, which is complete.

---

[37]Both R. Clifford and J. Milgrom have suggested (private communication) that the series of phrases following *ky* can also be interpreted as themselves a curse that the gods are proclaiming for the earth. In this case, the cause of the gods' anger would presumably not be apparent in the extant text. While this interpretation has strong biblical foundation (e.g., Isa 3:4-5, 24), the syntax of our text demands, in my opinion, that the force of the *ky* is to give the reasons behind the drastic request for darkness.

ʾnph. We know this bird from the Hebrew Bible. *ʾănāpāh* is listed in Lev 11:19 and Deut 14:18 as an unclean bird, possibly a heron.

ʾpr̦hy. This noun is m. pl. cs. of *ʾpr̦h*, from the root *pr̦h* with prosthetic *ʾalep*. This word is also known from the Hebrew Bible: *ʾeprōḥîm*, with the meaning "young ones."

ṣrh. This word must be a 3 m. sg. perfect verb from a third-weak root *ṣrh*. The 3 f. sg. perfect ends in *-t* in this inscription, as we saw in *ḥrpt* above. Hoftijzer translates the word as a noun from the root *ṣrr*, "distress, trouble," but the parallelism between *bny nḥ̣ṣ̣* (to be discussed below) and *ʾpr̦ḥy ʾnph* argues for the division of the phrase as I have made it, and the sense is best served by some verb at this point. Caquot and Lemaire read *d* instead of *r* and translate "owl" as in Sefîre I A 33. But the traces of the long tail of the *r* are definitely visible on the plaster (see also van der Kooij, 113). Aramaic *ṣərê*, meaning "to split, tear open" (Jastrow 1301), or better, Syriac *ṣrā*, "to mangle (with claws or knives)" (Payne Smith 483), is perfect. (McCarter has opted for the same translation, 51, 55).

Thus, the second part of this section says that some animal (m. sg.) mangled the young of the heron (with claws). I assume the first part to be parallel with this in meaning.

b̊ny.nḥ̣ṣ̣. I have restored *b* here (which van der Kooij lists as a possibility, 113) because *bny* corresponds perfectly with *ʾprḥy* in the second part of this sentence. It is probably the young of some bird that is spoken of. Unfortunately, we have no exact cognates for *nḥ̣ṣ̣*. (Modern Arabic *ḥawṣal*, "pelican," might be a clue to the meaning of *nḥ̣ṣ̣*.) Thus, the lacuna must contain the name of the animal that has mangled the young herons and done something (something violent, we assume) to the young of the *nḥ̣ṣ̣*. The only letter preserved is a *ḥ*. There is room for four or five more letters in the gap. McCarter (51, 55, 58) suggests restoring *ḥsd*, "stork," in spite of its feminine gender in Hebrew, because of its similarity to the heron, and because it is known to be a gentle bird. Therefore, its ripping up of the young of similar birds would be an unnatural action.

Lines 8/9.

drr.nšrt.ywn.wṣpr[.]

drr. *dərôr* (BDB 204) is a swallow in the Hebrew Bible and, as noted by BDB, is used in simile for quiet, peace, security in Ps 84:4. The word is feminine in Hebrew.

nšrt. Read as 3 f. sg. D perfect from a root *nšr*, which in MH means "to tear, lacerate" (transitive) in the D (Jastrow 942). McCarter (51, 55) also reads the verb; Hoftijzer (204) translates this word as a collective feminine noun ("birds of prey") as a part of a list rather than of a sentence.

ywn. Read "dove" with Caquot and Lemaire (198-99) and McCarter (51, 55), as against Hoftijzer's "marsh." We need another bird name at this point.

ṣpr. The word should mean something more specific than "bird" in this situation. The Arabic cognate *ʿuṣfūr* means "sparrow," and Hebrew *ṣippōr* denotes "sparrow" in some instances (e.g., Ps 84:4; Prov 26:2).

Thus, in this sentence, the peaceful swallow has torn into the dove and the sparrow has done something which we suppose was equally alien to its usual character. The rest of the sentence is broken completely, except perhaps for the *yn* of the next visible ink, but this is not helpful.

Line 9.

[ ]*.mṭh.bʾšr.rḥln.yybl.ḥṭr.* Again, McCarter's key to these phrases is helpful here. He reads the second part of this phrase, "instead of ewes the stick is driven along" (51, 55). That is to say, the stick, which normally drives the ewes, is now being driven along itself, reading *yybl* as D passive. We can suggest, then, that in the first half of the phrase (with about six letters missing) we have a description in which some animals normally led by a staff, *mṭh*, are now leading it.

Lines 9/10.

ʾrnbn.ʾklw.[ ]*ʾ̊b̊.ḥpš*[ ]. Van der Kooij reads *ʾrnbn. ʾklw.-ḥd/b* (108), but no word *-ḥd* or *-ḥb* seems to make sense in this context.[38] I can see no traces in the photographs on Plates 2 and 9 of *ATDA* that demand a *ḥ* here and would suggest reading an *ʾ* instead, plus *b*, and would propose that a *z* (< *ḏ) stood in the break. This reading, [*z*(?)]*ʾb*, gives good sense as the wolf, under normal circumstances, would be expected to eat the hares.

ḥpš[ ]. *ḥpš* can be read as "free" or as a word from the root *ḥpś*, "to seek." Furthermore, in MH and JA there is a word *ḥippûśît* meaning, "beetle," which might be more appropriate in the context, since it is at least an animal. For that reason, Arabic *ḫuffāš*, "bat," should also be considered.

Line 10.

štyw.ḥmr. "(They) have drunk wine." There is unfortunately too much space (15 or 16 letters) between these two words and the phrase preceding them concerning eating to suggest that they are part of the same pair of phrases.[39]

štyw. The *y* of this originally third-*Y* verb is kept here. The vocalization *šatiyû* is based on evidence from cognates. (Note the cognates included in the glossary.)

Lines 10/11.

wqbʿn.šmʿw.mwsr̊.gry.š[*ʿl*.]

qbʿn. In this word we have our first example in the extant text of *q* representing *ḏ̣. This word is most easily translated as cognate to MH *ṣābû*^{a}*ʿ* and Arabic *ḍabuʿ*, "hyena." There is a Hebrew word *qubbāʿat* meaning "cup" which might be appropriate since *štyw* has just preceded this word, but it is difficult to understand how the sentence would be translated if that is the meaning. "They drank wine and cups" is less satisfactory to me than the translation I have offered.

Hoftijzer (209-11) has given a completely different translation of this word and the entire phrase, but he was not working on the assumption that McCarter proposed and that I am

---

[38]See McCarter (55). He suggests -*ḥd* is the name of a food that hares do not normally eat.

[39]*Pace* Hoftijzer (207).

following (interpreting this section as a series of reversals). This assumption narrows considerably the possibilities for a given phrase.

mwsr. This is a nominal form from the root *ysr*, originally **wsr*. It resembles closely BH *mûsār*, but in this inscription, internal long *ū* is never represented by a *mater*. Medial *aw* is, however (e.g., *ʾlwh* for *ʾilawh*), so the word in question must have been *mawsar*.

I assume that these two phrases constitute a pair. The first must have contained reference to some one or group not normally noted for their gregarious behavior, who are now drinking wine. McCarter suggests Nazirites (58). At the same time, hyenas, who are famed for irreverence ("laughing hyenas"), are here described as paying attention to chastisement. The "hyenas" phrase is probably complete at this point. The unnatural situation has already been expressed. I assume that *gry* is the beginning of the next pair of phrases.

gry.š[ʿl.] *gry* is m. pl. cs. from the root *gwr*, cognate to Hebrew *gûr*, "whelp, young." Caquot and Lemaire (200, n. 8) give the same translation. They propose the restoration *š[ʿl]* for the second word, cognate to Hebrew *šûʿāl*, "fox," and this is a reasonable choice.

Line 11.

lḥkmn.yqḥk. *yqḥk* is best explained by translating it from a root *ḍ̈ḥk*, "to laugh." This root has undergone several changes in the various Semitic languages (see the cognates listed in the glossary). Our word is the equivalent, in Deir ʿAllā orthography, of the Arabic.

For the phrase *ḍ̈ḥk l*, "to laugh at," see Gen 21:6.

wʿnh.rqḥt.mr.wkhnh.[ ] The first word must be a f. sg. substantive from a third-weak root *ʿnh*. The second is either the f. sg. G perfect verb or the f. sg. G participle, both ending in *-t*. Of all the possibilities, *ʿnh*, "poor, humble" (BDB 776), is the best in the context of an unusual action. Myrrh was a precious substance, which was prepared by careful mixing (*rqḥ*). A poor woman probably could not afford myrrh.[40] The mention of the priestess at the beginning of the next phrase was perhaps meant as a contrast between a woman of some means and a poor woman.

ʿnyh. This word should be compared to BH *ʿănîyāh*, from an original **qatīl* formation of a third-weak root.[41]

Line 12

lnšʾ.ʾzr.qrn. Several possibilities suggest themselves for this combination of words, including the possibility that they are not all part of the same phrase. But since the next four words seem to form a unit (see below) I assume that these three are the end of a pair of phrases. *nśʾ* as a verb can mean "to lift, bear (or wear)," and the nominal form *nāśîʾ* is taken from this root. *nšʾ* can mean "to lend on interest" or "to beguile," but it is difficult to imagine what the relation of such a verb to *ʾzr* might be. *qrn* might be related to BH *qîr*, "wall" (although the plural is *qîrôt*), or to BH *ṣar* from an original root **ḏ̣rr*, "adversary." There is also *qeren*, "horn."

McCarter translates "to the one who wears a girdle *of threads*" (51, 56), with reference to the rare biblical word *qûr*, "thread." He points to Arabic *qwr*, which can mean "to coil," and *qawr*, "snake," and interprets this girdle of threads as a sturdy garment (private communication).

I have used McCarter's translation "threads," but have interpreted the phrase differently. The text is broken here, but it is possible to imagine what this phrase might have been. In the Egyptian "Admonitions of Ipuwer," a work with many similarities to this "birds" section, there are several phrases in which the reversal of the fortunes of the wealthy is described in terms of the change in their clothing. "Lo, ---------- noblewomen, / Their bodies suffer in rags."[42] "See, those who

---

[40]Hoftijzer (212-13) interprets *ʿnyh*, *rqḥt mr*, and *khnh* as a list of cultic functions. As before, the principle McCarter has outlined seems preferable as a key to translation.

[41]See Joüon §96Dc.

[42]Lichtheim, vol. 1, p. 152.

owned robes are in rags, / He who did not weave for himself owns fine linen."[43] In line with these phrases from Ipuwer, a garment "of threads" could mean one "hanging in threads" and, therefore, "tattered." In our context, a prince wearing a tattered loincloth would have been paralleled by a description of a poor man wearing fine clothes.[44]

Lines 12/13.

ḥšb.ḥšb.wḥšb.ḥ[šb.] Again, we must look to McCarter's translation. He has made sense out of this grouping by interpreting these words as a series of active and passive verbs and participles (56). Interpreting *ḥšb* with the sense "to esteem, value, respect," and using the principle of uncharacteristic action, he translates, "the esteemed esteems and the esteemer is esteemed." That is, the one who is normally held in respect is now giving out his respect to others, and the one who normally respects another is now being respected himself.[45] The words are vocalized as G passive participle, 3 m. sg. perfect active, active participle, and 3 m. sg. perfect passive.

Line 13.

wšmʿw.ḥršn̊[.]mn.rḥq[.] This is one of the phrases that fits most obviously into McCarter's scheme. *ḥršn* here is cognate to BH *ḥērēš*, "deaf."

Line 14.

s̊kl.hzw.qqn.šgr.wʿštr.l[ ] This is the most perplexing grouping in the entire first combination. There is one difficulty in reading (the first letter may be *w* or *s*), and the word *qqn* can be interpreted in several ways, especially since the *q* can represent two different sounds in this inscription.

---

[43] *Ibid.*, p. 156.

[44] M. Coogan has reminded me that this phrase is also reminiscent of the Song of Hannah, 1 Sam 2:1-10. In verse 8 it is said that Yahweh raises a poor man from the dust to sit with princes.

[45] Again, Egyptian parallels are striking: "He who gave orders takes orders" from "The Complaints of Khakheperre-Sonb," Lichtheim, vol. 1, p. 148; "One salutes him who saluted" from "The Prophecies of Neferti," Lichtheim, vol. 1, p. 143.

Finally, *ḥzw* must be dealt with, in terms of its orthography and its meaning.

Caquot and Lemaire and McCarter do not divide the grouping; they translate from *wkl* to *wʿštr* as a unit.[46] Hoftijzer (218-19) divides the phrase as I do, but he translates the first phrase "and they suffered oppression" and the second as two divine names.

I think the key to the translation is the meaning of the verb *ḥzh*. Already in this inscription we have seen *ḥzh* and *rʾh* used in different senses. *rʾh* seems to be the normal word "to see" (I, 5), while *ḥzh* is used of Balaam's function as prophet (I, 1). If the contrast between these verbs is consistent, then *ḥzw* here should have to do with seeing visions rather than simply "seeing." It would be appropriately ironic for a fool (*skl*) to be having visions. Van der Kooij suggests *s* as well as *w* for our first letter, but then rejects it (117). The stance of the letter looks much more like *s* than *w*, however (see Plate 3 of *ATDA*). Thus, I have opted for *skl*.

ḥzw is probably a m. pl. perfect G verb. It is conceivable that it is singular, but not likely.[47] If it is plural, then, there must have been a m. pl. noun in construct with *skl* (perhaps something like "the children of" a fool).

qqn has no obvious translation, although there are in BH *qāṣîn*, from **qḏy*, meaning "chief," and the root *ṣwq* (*ṣwq* I, BDB 847, *ṣ* < **ḏ̣*), having to do with restraint. It is also not obvious whether *qqn* goes with what precedes it or with what follows it. However, the mention of *šgr* and *ʿštr* in the present context probably has something to do with failure to produce offspring and the concept of "constraint" would, therefore, fit

---

[46] Caquot and Lemaire (201-02): "Et tous voient restreint le croit des bovins et des ovins. . . ." McCarter (51-52, 56): "and everyone has seen *those things that decree* offspring and young."

[47] *ḥzh* was a III-*W* verb originally (note *ḥezwā* in BA). We might interpret *ḥzw* as sg. with the *w* remaining (i.e., *ḥazaw*), but there are no extant examples of G sg. verbs ending in *-aw* in Canaanite or Aramaic of this period. The one example at Sefîre (*rqw*) is D imperative in *-iw* (see Fitzmyer, pp. 109-10). The two examples in the Mesha stela (*wyʿnw* and *ʾʿnw*) are also D verbs in *-iw* (see *EHO*, p. 37).

well here (i.e., a noun from the root *ṣwq* I, plus afformative -*n*). Thus I have chosen to interpret the fool's seeing visions as a unit in itself, to divide the phrases at that point, and to translate *qqn* with the words that follow it.[48]

Again, the "Admonitions of Ipuwer" offers parallels. "Lo, women are barren, none conceive."[49] "Gone is the abundance of children."[50]

Line 15.

nmr. This word is cognate to Hebrew *nāmēr*, "leopard." Since the next three words are probably the beginning of another phrase, this word must have stood at the end of a pair, now lost. It is possible that there was a *l* before *nmr* (see van der Kooij, 118).

Lines 15/16.

ḥnyṣ.hqrqt.bn[*y*.] *ḥnyṣ* is a diminutive of the *qutayl* formation[51] and must be considered feminine singular here (see next word).

hqrqt. The only possible interpretation of this word is as 3 f. sg. C perfect from original **ḏ̣rq*, known to us from Sefîre *qrq*, "to flee," and Syriac *ʿrq*. In the C this verb means "to cause to flee, to banish." This phrase must refer to a piglet chasing the young of some animal that would normally chase it. It is not clear why the verb should be feminine.[52] To my knowledge diminutives are nowhere considered feminine by signification.[53]

---

[48]See above, p. 41, for a discussion of the meaning of *šgr* and *ʿštr*.

[49]Lichtheim, vol. 1, p. 151.

[50]*Ibid*., p. 154. Both these examples deal with human reproduction, but the idea is the same.

[51]See GKC §86gN.

[52]Hoftijzer (219-20) assumes the feminine verb *hqrqt* refers to *šgr*, the goddess of the inscription in his interpretation.

[53]Another possibility is to redivide the words, making the *h* of the C form go instead with *ḥnyṣ*. Then we would have a feminine diminutive and a G or a D verb, also feminine. But,

There is little else that can be read in the first combination. We might read *ʾzrn* in line 16, "girdles" or "those who wear girdles." The word *ʿyn*, "eye" or "fountain" probably stood at the end of line 16, but the context is too broken for comment.

Combination II

The first three lines of the second combination do not yield sufficient information for interpretation. Thus, the commentary will begin with line 4.

Line 4.

ʿlmh.rwy.ddn. I have interpreted *ʿlmh* as "his young man," i.e., "his son." Several alternatives are possible, of course. Caquot and Lemaire (202) and McCarter[54] translate the entire phrase, "Young woman, drink your fill of love!" which is certainly possible within the orthography of our text. Hoftijzer (221) translates *ʿlmh* as "a girl," but sees the next word as a m. pl. cs. participle, which is, I think, less likely. If is to be translated "young woman," the f. sg. imperative agreeing with "young woman" is preferable. It is also possible that *ʿlmh* is from another root *ʿlm*, and refers to "eternity."

rwy. This word is from the root *rwy*, (*rawiya*, *yirwā* in Arabic). Consequently *rwy* should not be the perfect 3 m. sg. of the verb, as the reflex of **-iy* is normally represented by *h* as *mater* in this text. Since I have translated the first word in the line "his son," I prefer to see this phrase as a description of the child just mentioned, and to interpret the *y* as if the word is a **qatīl* adjective (see the discussion of *ʿnyh* in I, 11). Hoftijzer has pointed out (221) that the root is known together with the plural of *dd*, meaning the abstract "love," from the Hebrew Bible (Prov 7:18 and perhaps 5:19). There the implications are of sexual love.

---

unfortunately, the word divider is clear, and the *h* is written very close to the following *q*.

[54]McCarter has kindly provided me with a sketch of his unpublished suggestions for the second combination, to which I refer throughout my treatment here.

Line 5.

l̊h̊.lm.nqr.wmdr.kl.rṭb̊[ ] This is a difficult passage because the readings are far from secure. Van der Kooij reads the first two letters as *lh* plus a word divider (121). The *h*, however, does not resemble any of the other *h*'s in the inscription. The legs of this *h* appear to be two straight lines from upper left to lower right, whereas the more common form for this inscription shows the left leg to be somewhat *s*-shaped, and the right leg to curve down to a point. The word divider is also unusual in that it is rather large and curved for a word divider. It should perhaps be connected to the left leg of the "*h*" to form a *r* or *q*, but this leaves the "right leg" without an obvious interpretation. Another difficulty with this passage is that the readings as they stand do not make sense. It is awkward to begin a question (or any direct statement) with "the scion (or "shoot") and the pit," or some such, without a following verb.[55] I am convinced that we are reading incorrectly here, but have not been able to interpret the traces at the beginning of the line in any meaningful way. Because I cannot find a better solution, I have left the readings as van der Kooij gives them.

lm. If the readings are to be left as we have them, I would read "why?" here, as in I, 4.

nqr. Hoftijzer (237) translates "blinded one," but a more suitable translation is "sprout" or "scion," assuming the *q* to represent *ʒ̣, and comparing the word with Hebrew *nēṣer*.[56] This is the key word for the several interpretations of the second combination (see below, pp. 75-85).

mdr. This word has been compared with Syriac *medrā* by previous commentators, and has been translated "soil" or "earth."

---

[55]McCarter has suggested a *casus pendens* construction: "As for the sprout, the soil/pit contains moisture/foliage. . . ." This is a reasonable solution with the present readings. So much of this line is missing that its context is difficult to determine.

[56]Caquot and Lemaire have seen this already (202), and McCarter uses this translation as well (51).

(*medr* is the common Ethiopic term for "earth," as well.) An alternate possibility is that the word is derived from the root *dwr* with the meaning "circular." In Isa 30:33 we find the Hebrew word *mədûrāh* used to describe part of a tophet or child sacrifice precinct. The word is feminine in BH and feminine in the sg. in MH, but the pl. cs. in MH is *mədûrê*.

The analysis of the syntax of this line is by no means certain. Unless the first four letters plus word divider can be re-read and interpreted as a verb, we have a direct speech which begins with a question word, followed by a noun joined to another noun.

kl. The position and meaning of *kl* are difficult. Whether the phrase *mdr kl rṭb* means "fire-pit, all *of it* green twigs" or "soil, all *of it* moist," we would expect a suffix on the *kl*. Caquot and Lemaire translate *kl* as an adverb, "entirely" (203), but I know of no comparable use of *kl* in Hebrew or Aramaic. Therefore, I have not translated *kl* as "all," but rather as a participle from the rare root *kwl*, meaning "to contain or enclose."[57]

rṭb̊. The *b* is fairly certain. This word generally means "moist," but is also used of young plants or wood, and in MH is extended to mean simply "foliage."[58]

Line 6.

yrwy.ʾl.yʿbr̊.̊ʾl.byt.ʿlmn.by[*t.*] The identification of the last letter in the third word is crucial here.[59] The letter appears to be *r* in the photographs, rather than *d*, but there is much brown dirt below the letter on the plaster, and only a tiny trace of what might have been the longer tail of the *r* is visible now.

If the letter is *d*, I believe the word should be translated

---

[57] Note the use of a participle in the familiar *ʾereṣ zābat ḥālāb ûdəbaš*.

[58] Jastrow (1470-71), *rṭb Hiphil* (2) and *rəṭîbāh*.

[59] *ATDA* transcribes *wyʿbd* on p. 174, but van der Kooij makes no mention of a *w* (121). There is no *w* on the plaster, nor is there room for one.

"he will serve" and the rest of the sentence would be "the god of the house of eternity (the underworld)." Hoftijzer translates "El will make graves," but this is a difficult phrase to fit into an overall scheme, as Hoftijzer admits (223-25). Caquot and Lemaire interpret *ʿlmn* as having to do with youth, and *ʾl* as the plural demonstrative, "he will make these things (for) the house of young people," but the phrase *byt ʿlm* is well enough established as an expression for the grave that we must be dealing with death here.[60]

I do not agree with van der Kooij that there is no word divider between *yʿbd/r* and *ʾl*.[61] It was the absence of a word divider that was the obstacle to translating *ʾl* as a preposition (Hoftijzer, 223). I have read a word divider here and have chosen to read the *d/r* as *r*. It is a possible reading, and the one that gives the best sense. So the last part of the line reads "he will cross over to the grave/underworld/house of eternity." This leaves us with *yrwy ʾl* at the beginning of the line. The verb *yrwy* should not be a D or C verb (*pace* Hoftijzer, 223-24) because, again, the reflex of the ending would be written with *h* as *mater*. In the G, however, as was pointed out before, this verb was originally conjugated as a stative verb. Thus, *yrwy* must be read as a *yiqtal* imperfect (or jussive), where the **-ay* ending was kept.

Caquot and Lemaire translate *ʾl* "with these" (203), but two other alternatives are more appealing. *ʾl* here might be a reference to the high god El. *yrwy ʾl* would then mean "El will be sated."[62] I think it is most likely that this phrase is

---

[60]Jastrow, *ʿlm* III, pp. 1084-85.

[61]There seems to be a small trace of ink above and to the left of the head of the *d/r*. This could not be the trace of a part of the following *ʾalep* about which van der Kooij warns (121). He argues that there is no surface damage at this point, so a word divider should be visible if it had been there. The ink I see is rather high on the line, however, so it may still be simply an odd word divider. There is certainly room between the *d/r* and *ʾ* for a word divider. These letters are spaced rather far apart, in fact.

[62]Note line 12 of the Mesha inscription, where Mesha reports killing people for the "satisfaction" (*ryt*) of Chemosh and Moab.

part of a purpose clause:[63] something must be done *in order that* El will be satisfied. *yʿbr* could then be read "let him pass over." It is just as likely, however, that this *ʾl* represents the negative *ʾal*, and that *ʾl yʿbr* go together: "let him *not* cross over."[64] In this case also *yrwy* would belong to a phrase that began in the preceding break.

Line 7.

byt.lyʿl.hlk.wlyʿl.ḥtn.šm.byt[We seem to have a continuation here of the description of the underworld or the grave that was begun in line 6, "the house of eternity, the house of . . . the house where the traveler does not rise, the house where the bridegroom does not rise, the house . . . ." The phrase ending with *šm*, then, consists of a noun modified by a relative clause of the type discussed in GKC §155i. (Gesenius points to Jer 2:6, another such phrase ending in *šm*.) According to GKC §155b, a relative clause that modifies a noun, as in this case, is often written without the relative pronoun in Hebrew. The *šm* in this phrase functions as a resumptive adverb.

See Hoftijzer (225-26) for examples of desolation described as places where no traveler passes through, and for a justification of the translation "bridegroom" (instead of "father-in-law," "son-in-law"). It is also true that biblical parallels indicate that "no bridegroom" suggests no joy and that that is an appropriate description of the grave. I think a better point to be made, however, is that everyone enters the grave, but no one comes back.[65] Consequently, I have translated as if the verb in question is *ʿlh*, "to go up," in the short imperfect after negative *l-*.[66] The short form is necessary because

---

[63]See GKC §107q.

[64]McCarter reads this *ʾl* as the negative.

[65]Cf. the etymology for Belial noted by Cross and Freedman in *Studies in Ancient Yahwistic Poetry*, p. 143, n. 6, as "*bal(i) yaʿl(e) = (place from which) none arises, a euphemism for Hades or Sheol." Akkadian *erṣet lā târi* (*CAD*, "*E*," p. 308) is an expression for the underworld in a similar phrase.

[66]The short form of the imperfect is the norm after the negative *lam* in Arabic (Wright, I, §362ff.), and the short form

we would expect a *mater* in the long form of the imperfect of a third-weak verb in this dialect.

We can look to Ps 19:5b-6 for a further possibility. In this psalm, Šemeš is described as "coming forth like a bridegroom from his canopy, running the course joyously like a warrior." The sun here, then, is seen as one who comes forth (presumably *rising*) and runs the course (of the sky). It is possible that our text employs a well-known metaphor for the sun (bridegroom who rises and travels) to describe the underworld as a place where the sun does not rise and, therefore, never shines, i.e., a place of perpetual darkness. This interpretation at least offers an explanation of the otherwise rather strange juxtaposition of "traveler" and "bridegroom" in our passage.

McCarter agrees with Hoftijzer that this line is a description of the grave as a place where one does not receive visitors, i.e., that it is meant to be a description of some of the unpleasantries of the grave. Caquot and Lemaire offer a completely different translation (203). Since they do not believe it is the grave that is spoken of here, but rather something to do with youth, they reject the translation of *lyʿl* as "not entering" or "not returning," and see instead some relationship to the root *yʿl* which, in the C, means "to be useful" in Hebrew. Thus they propose that this is a house that exists "for the use of" the traveler and the bridegroom. *šm*, then, is translated "the name of," and the name appears to be "the house." Rofé suggests here that the house "for the use of a guest and a bridegroom" is a house of sacred prostitution.[67]

Line 8.

wrmh.mn̊gdš.mn.pḥzy.bny.ʾš.wmn.šqy-[ ] This line has received two basic interpretations, the differences depending on the presuppositions of the commentators. Hoftijzer (226-28) and McCarter have seen references to the grave here, while Caquot and Lemaire (203-04), in line with their own

---

occurs after *lōʾ* several times in the Hebrew Bible (see GKC §§109d, 72r).

[67] A. Rofé, *op. cit.* (cited above, p. 6, n. 30), p. 68.

interpretation, have suggested alternate translations for some words that give a more uplifting tone to this phrase.

rmh. This word can be interpreted in several ways: as from the root *rwm*, or the root *rmh*, with the addition of a 3 m. sg. pronominal suffix; as a word for "height" or "pride"; or as the noun meaning "worm." I have chosen to translate "worm," as did Hoftijzer and McCarter, because of the association of worms with death and decay. Caquot and Lemaire translate from the root *rwm*, interpreting *rmh* as a feminine participle, "rising up."

mn.̊*gdš*. It is questionable whether there is a word divider between these two words. Van der Kooij submits that there is not (122), but there seems to be a trace of ink under the brown dirt to the upper right of the *g*. It would not be serious if there were no word divider here since the words are closely related. Still, we expect one in this inscription.

gdš is the key word for interpreting this line in terms of someone's dying. Hoftijzer and McCarter read "grave" here, cognate to Hebrew and Aramaic *gādîš*. Caquot and Lemaire, however, compare the word to Syriac *gedšā* and translate "misfortune." Thus, they give these three words a much more optimistic interpretation, "rising up from misfortune," as opposed to "a worm (or vermin) from the grave," which I prefer as a translation here.

mn.pḥzy.bny.ʾš. The translation of this phrase revolves around the word(s) represented by *pḥzy*. Hoftijzer, Caquot and Lemaire, and McCarter have offered three different translations here. I will suggest a fourth.

Hoftijzer reads *pḥzy* as cognate to Arabic *faḫiḏ* "tribe" or "clan," and suggests that this phrase was the beginning of a new curse indicating that the people would be driven away from the tribes of humanity (*bny ʾš*). ("Driven away" is restored.) Caquot and Lemaire use the more obvious translation of *pḥz* as "insolence" and translate "rising up from . . . the insolent ones among men."

McCarter (59, n. 3) divides *pḥzy* into *pḥ* and *zy*, "the bird-trap for human beings," reading *zy* as a determinative pronoun. There is no word divider between the *ḥ* and the *z*, but the space between them is somewhat larger than the normal space between two letters in the same word in this inscription, which fact might argue in favor of McCarter's interpretation.[68]

There is still another alternative. F. M. Cross has pointed out (private communication) that the root *pḥz*, which usually means "to be wanton, reckless" in Hebrew and Aramaic, is known also from 4QSam[b] as a synonym for *qwm*. In 1 Sam 20:34, where MT has *wyqm yhwntn mʿm hšlḥn*, 4QSam[b] reads *wypḥz ywntn mʿl hšlḥn*. Apparently *pḥz* can be used of impulsive action in the sense of jumping up or rising quickly, as well as of wantonness. In our inscription, *pḥzy* could be a participle, m. pl. cs., and would speak of those who rise up (from the underworld) among human beings. For *bny ʾš* as an expression for humanity in general, see Pss 4:3, 49:3, 62:10; Lam 3:33. (See also below, p. 83, another suggestion of McCarter's for *pḥzy bny ʾš*.)

mn.šqy-[ ] Van der Kooij (122) reads a probable *y* as the last visible letter in this line. There is a word *šāqā* in Syriac with the meaning "mound of earth, a sarcophagus" (Payne Smith 593). McCarter has chosen this word as cognate (although he does not read the *y*), and sees four expressions in this line that point to the grave: a worm, the grave itself, the "bird-trap" for human beings (as a symbolic description of the grave), and a sarcophagus, but if the *y* at the end of the word is the correct reading, *šqy* must be a m. pl. cs. Even though the word is feminine in Syriac, the pl. has the masculine ending *-ē*.

Hoftijzer reads *šq* as cognate to Aramaic *šûq*, "street" or "market-place," and translates *šqy* as "places of . . . ," i.e., a location from which Balaam's hearers will be driven away, according to his reconstruction discussed above. Caquot and Lemaire do not offer a translation of this word.

---

[68] I am, however, disturbed by the use of *zy* here. There are many other examples of nouns in genitival relationship in this inscription and in no case is the determinative pronoun utilized. Furthermore, if I am correct that *ʾš* is the relative pronoun in I, 1, then *zy* would not be used here. (See above, p. 31.)

Line 9.

hlʿṣh.bk.lytʿṣ.ʾwlmlkh.lytmlk.yšb-[ ] (The second word, *bk*, was omitted by the scribe and, like *ʾlwh* in I, 1, is written above the line.)

h. . . ʾw. The *h* here is interrogative, continued by *ʾw*, "or." (Hoftijzer, 229-30, interprets the *h* here as asseverative, and does not feel that a question is indicated.)

lʿṣh. . . lmlkh. *l* in both cases is topicalizing: "*as for* counsel. . . *as for* advice." *mlk* for "advice" is never feminine elsewhere. *mlkh* might mean "his advice," but the suffix is not expected here, and in view of the parallel *ʿṣh* (without suffix) is probably not correct. It is simpler to propose that the word has the feminine ending commonly found on abstract nouns.

ytʿṣ. This word is probably to be derived from a root *ʿwṣ*, a biform of the more common *yʿṣ*. The root occurs in JA (strangely, with a *ṣ*) and in the Hebrew Bible (twice, in Judg 19:30 and Isa 8:10). If the root had been *yʿṣ*, we would expect the initial *y* to show up in the tG or tD, using Hebrew and Aramaic as models. (There is an exception, however, if the word were a Gt of *yʿṣ*, modeled after the Arabic 8th form, in which case the vocalization would still be *yittaʿaṣ*.)

The Aramaic tG of a root *ʿwṣ* would be *yittəʿaṣ* < **yittaʿaṣ*, and that is the basis of my vocalization. The tD of such a form would show a *y* as the middle radical. The tG is rare in Hebrew; the tD of a middle-weak root takes the *Hithpolel* form.

In MH and JA, the tD of *yʿṣ/ṭ* plus *b*- means "to consult with," "to ask advice of."

ytmlk. *mlk* in the tG (or tD) can be used in JA to mean "to ask advice of" without a preposition. (The vocalization assumes this form is tG, as *ytʿṣ* above.) The fact that a preposition is unnecessary is important here, because in a line where a scribe carefully went back and inserted above the line the necessary *bk* to complete the meaning of *ytʿṣ*, there is no corresponding prepositional phrase to complete *ytmlk*. This must mean that the words that follow *ytmlk* indicate from whom advice will be asked. *yšb* could be a participle, which would have been in construct with the word that followed it, now lost. Hoftijzer (180) and McCarter supply "you" at the end of this phrase, to parallel *bk* in the preceding phrase, while Caquot and Lemaire (204) translate simply "Will he (not) deliberate?" Hoftijzer does not translate *yšb-*; McCarter reads *yšbq* (see van der Kooij, 123) and translates "he will depart."

bk.lytʿṣ. . . lytmlk. According to my interpretation, the verbs in this rhetorical question are presented in the negative because the answer expected is "yes."

Line 10.

tksn.lbš.ḥd. Caquot and Lemaire (204) read *mšgb.mtksn. . .* in this line, but the traces are so faint that this suggestion is tentative, to say the least. I believe the line makes better sense as van der Kooij read it, and will not attempt to fill in the blanks preceding *tksn*.

tksn. This word is best interpreted as 2 m. sg. D imperfect of the root *ksh*, with a 3 m. sg. object suffix attached. (See directly below under *tšnʾn* for the reasoning.)

hn.tšnʾn.yʾnš.hn.t[ ] This is clearly a conditional sentence, and the switch to third person in the apodosis explains the *-n* suffix on *tšnʾn* (and, by extension, on *tksn*).

hn (= "if") is known from Aramaic *hēn*, and Hebrew *hēn* and *hinnēh* are also used to mean "if." Hoftijzer interprets *tšnʾn* and *tksn* as 2 m. sg. imperfect plus energic *-n* (297-98). The forms are more easily explained as either f. sg. or pl. imperfect, in which case we have suddenly switched to speaking in terms of a woman or a number of women, or 2 m. sg. imperfect plus a pronominal suffix. Caquot and Lemaire choose the latter, but they find the first person suffix (sg. or pl.) in *-n* (204). The singular would surely be *-ny* in our orthography, however. The first person pl. suffix is a possibility (cf. Syriac *-an*), although here also we would expect a longer suffix, either *-nā(h)* or *-nû*. Even if the form is possibly first person, the sentences make less sense if the verbs are so translated: "You will cover *us* with one cloth. If you hate *us*, *he* will grow weak." It is much better to assume that the *-n* is the 3 m. sg.

object suffix. "You will cover *him* with a cloth. If you are hateful toward *him*, *he* will be weak." (In each case, *tšn'n* is translated from the root *śn'*, "to hate.")

The addition of energic *n* before an object suffix is well known, both in Hebrew and Aramaic, but the suffix is added to different forms of the energic in the two languages. Arabic exhibits both a long and a short form of the energic, *-an* and *-anna*.[69] The Aramaic forms must arise from the addition of the longer form of the energic to the imperfect verb. This leaves a vowel between the *n* and the suffix. In the case of the 3 m. sg. suffix, it is always written *-nh*. In Hebrew, however, the suffix *-hŭ* is added to the short energic form, giving **-inhŭ*, which assimilates to **-innŭ*.[70] Since we have only the *-n* suffix here, a similar development must have occurred, but accompanied by the loss of the anceps vowel (since there is no *mater*).

Hoftijzer's translation differs somewhat from mine (180, 231-33). As was noted above, he does not see an object suffix on the two 2 m. sg. verbs. He also does not read a conditional sentence beginning with *hn*, but rather a "whether. . . or" sequence for *hn*. . . *hn*. Finally, he interprets the *y* of *y'nš* as a vocative and reads, "oh men." "You are hated (or: you hate), oh men," is seen as another curse directed at Balaam's people.

Caquot and Lemaire (204-05) read "those who are covered with one cloth" according to their transcription of the first part of the line, reported above. They do read the second half as a conditional sentence, but because of their interpretation of the object suffix, their translation is quite different from mine: "If you hate me (or us), he will restore friendship . . . ," translating *'nš* as cognate to Arabic *'anisa*, "to be friendly."

McCarter's translation is along the same lines as the one I have offered, but he reads the *-n*'s as energics without suffix, the "him" being understood in both cases.

---

[69] Wright, I, p. 61.

[70] Note also the Ugaritic *-n* which alternates with *-nh* (*UT* Grammar §6.17).

Line 11.

ʾšm[. .]*tḥt.rʾšk*. Hoftijzer (233-35) and Caquot and Lemaire (205) find difficulties with this phrase. Hoftijzer does not translate the first word. Caquot and Lemaire read the first word *ʾšt*, but do not translate ("woman"?). McCarter reads *ʾš*, "someone," presumably the subject of the sentence that follows the break. In fact, the sentence makes sense as it stands, even with a word missing. *ʾšm* is the first person sg. imperfect from the root *śym*, "I will put." The "you" being addressed here is the same person as the one who is apparently about to die in the second half of the line. Something (some sort of pillow?) is to be put under someone's head when he lies down (*tškb*).

Hoftijzer would prefer to divide the line into parts of two curses, although he finds difficulty with the phrase "under your head" in the context of a curse (235). His other alternative is to translate *tḥt* as a verb form from *ḥtt*, reading "she will smash your head." I prefer my own reading in the context of some sort of ritual, even though the exact nature of the ritual cannot be determined from this general sentence. It is clear from what follows, however, that someone is about to die.

tškb.mškby.ʿlmyk.lḥlq.l-[ ] Caquot and Lemaire (205) read *mškby ʿlmyk* as having to do with youth, but the phrase should be compared to *byt ʿlmn* in line 6, which has more definite parallels with language surrounding death. The root *škb* and the noun *mškb* have sexual implications, as well, but the subject matter of this inscription appears to be death rather than rejuvenation. It is not a problem that *mškby* is plural; see Hoftijzer, 233. For the plural form of *ʿlmyk*, compare *ʿlmn* in line 6.

In the context of death, *lḥlq* can more easily be translated "to perish" than "for a portion" or the like. Hoftijzer (234) gives both translations, and then points out that *ḥlq* with the meaning "to perish" is attested in Ugaritic, Akkadian, Ethiopic, Arabic, and BH (Isa 57:6). The only objection to this translation is that it is a bit abrupt in a sentence that is apparently addressed to the person who is to die. Perhaps the remainder of the line contained some words intended to soothe or soften the impact of this phrase.

Line 12.

blbbm̊. Van der Kooij and Caquot and Lemaire transcribe *blbb.mn*. Van der Kooij (126-27) and Hoftijzer (236) both discuss the problem of the *mn* here. There is a trace of a word divider after *blbb*, then a *n* was written, and later a *m* was written in much the same place, which covered over part of the *n*. Given the fact that the first letter in the following word is *n*, the most logical solution seems to me to be that the scribe made a mistake in ending *blbb* without a suffix. The scribe wrote the word divider and the *n* of *nʾnḥ*, then realized the mistake and went back to write a *m* in its proper place next to the final *b* of *blbb*. In so doing, the scribe wrote over part of the incorrect *n*, intentionally. *blbbm* means "in their heart(s)," and refers perhaps to all the people watching the ceremony. It could be the end of a sentence describing their grief. (It is also possible that the *m* in this case is actually a *k*: see van der Kooij, 127. In that case, the sentence probably would still be addressed to the dying person, like the line before.) If my interpretation is correct, it not only explains the odd set of signs following *blbb*, but it also rids us of the difficulties in translation caused by *mn*, "whoever," at this point.[71]

nʾnḥ.nqr.blbbh̊. When we remove the *mn* from consideration, we are left with a sentence in understandable order. This phrase must be a description of the doomed person's reaction to what is happening to him. "The sprout sighs" is perhaps too weak a translation, but the idea to be gotten across is that he is grieved by his situation. This is perhaps what the words after the second *nʾnḥ* conveyed.[72]

---

[71]Hoftijzer gives possibilities (237-38) as do Caquot and Lemaire (205), but both solutions are rather awkward.

[72]At this point, Caquot and Lemaire (205) suggest in passing a connection between the use of *nqr* here and *ṣmḥ* or *šrš* in child sacrifice texts.

Line 13.

bt.šmh.mlkn.yḥzw. If the readings *bt* and *šmh* are correct, they are open to several interpretations. *šmh* could mean "thither" or "his name" or some form of the verb *śym* with suffix, or even "destruction" (Hoftijzer's choice, 240). The last two letters of *yḥzw* are mere traces. If the readings are correct, the obvious translation is "kings will see,"[73] but this makes no sense in context. It is possible that *mlk* in *mlkn* has something to do with the *mlk* that is found in child sacrifice texts to refer to the child.[74] Or perhaps *mlkn* refers to the gods as kings.

lyšbm. Van der Kooij discusses these letters on p. 128. He reads *lyš.bmyqḥ.* I think the word divider he sees between *š* and *b*, however, is dirt rather than ink. One might also read *n* instead of *m*. The reading is difficult, but I can see only one curve below the crack that slices through this letter, and only one tip above. There is so much damage above the *y* of the next word that it is impossible to tell if a word divider might have been there, but I assume there was.

I read this word as a C imperfect, 3 m. sg. (or pl.? "the gods"?), with 3 m. pl. suffix, and negative *l-* prefixed. The

---

[73] This would mean that the dialect of this inscription does not use the long imperfect with *-n* ending on 2 or 3 m. pl. verbs (unless *yḥzw* can be jussive). The reading is difficult here, but there are no traces of an *n* (van der Kooij, 127-28). The only other possibilities for a long imperfect in *-n* are better explained as f. pl. or as sg. imperfects with a 3 m. sg. object suffix. *tksn* and *tšn'n* in II, 10, are the latter. *tṭpn*, which occurs twice in the broken latter part of Combination II (lines 35 and 36), is most probably a third-person form, and, therefore, 3 f. pl. *ydh.tṣmqn* occurs in the fragmentary Combination X (d). It is tempting to translate "his hands will wither," but we would expect the *-wh* suffix on the dual form. Even if the translation is correct, the verb would be 3 f. pl., and the *-n* is to be expected. However, the context is so broken that we cannot break a basic rule about suffixal form because of the "sense" of the passage. There are thus several alternatives for translating *tṣmqn*, but it would seem that a 2 m. pl. is one of the least likely, especially with a sg. imperative following.

[74] The classic treatment of *mlk* as a term for the sacrificial victim is, of course, Otto Eissfeldt, *Molk als Opferbegriff im Punischen und Hebräischen und das Ende des Gottes Moloch.*

root is *šwb*. For the causative of this root with the meaning "restore from the dead," see Job 33:30, and especially 2 Sam 12:23. If *n* could be read instead of *m* (i.e., another 3 m. sg. suffix in -*n*), the phrase would refer to the dying person himself.

yqḥ.mwt.ʿl.rḥm. Dividing the words in this fashion gives us a fairly straightforward sentence. The interpretation of *ʿl rḥm* is difficult, however. *ʿl* is properly a suckling.[75] Therefore, *ʿl rḥm* could mean "the suckling child of the slave-woman," or it could refer to the suckling child *just out of* the womb, i.e., a newborn child, which is the translation I prefer.[76]

No two commentators have read this line the same way, so interpretations vary greatly from one to the other. There is very little that can be said about the beginning of the line. Hoftijzer (238) divides *lyš*, *bm*, and *yqḥ* into three separate words. He translates *lyš* as "lion," and points to biblical scenes of impending doom where lions are mentioned. For *bm*, he reads "Why?" and suggests that at this point Balaam is asking a rhetorical question concerning the fate that is about to befall his people.

Caquot and Lemaire (206) re-read the *q* as *r*, and propose a word *rḥmwt*, "tenderness," doing away with the death theme altogether. They further propose to read *lyš* as a passive participle from the root *lwš*, and translate "kneaded with waters (*bmy*) of tenderness." This translation suffers from the orthographic difficulty of reading the *w* in the ending -*wt*, presumably feminine plural, of *rḥmwt*. The *w* should not appear in this text.

McCarter accepts the switch from *q* to *r*, but reads *bmy rḥ*

---

[75]See *KAI* 61A2, 98.2, 99.2 (all three *bʿl*; F. M. Cross [private communication] believes the *b* is *bet essentiae*, "consisting of"). In addition, Cross reads *KAI* 163.3 as *ʿl trbt* rather than *KAI*'s *d/šl trbt*.

[76]See below, pp. 80-85, for a possible interpretation of Combination II that would involve child sacrifice, specifically, p. 82 for evidence that most of the children sacrificed at Sousse and Carthage were newborns.

as "in the scented waters," thus avoiding the orthographic difficulty. He ties *lyš* to *mwt* and interprets the phrase to say there is *no* death for the womb, etc. He proposes an alternate reading, however, which is essentially the same as the one I have proposed, beginning with *yqḥ*. In a text that has been concerned largely with death, the best translation would seem to be the one that speaks of the death of a newborn child.

Line 14.

[ ]-*r.m̊ẘt̊.šmh*. Of the many traces that can be noted at the beginning of this line, the possibility of reading *mwt*[77] appeals to me here. Presumably a verb of action preceded *mwt* and *šmh* completes that verb.

kb-[ ]*ḥ.yk̊n̊.lbb.nqr.šhh.ky.ʾth.l*-[ ] Van der Kooij reads *ykn* tentatively (130) before *lbb*. Even if this reading is correct, it is difficult, since we do not have the words that preceded *ykn*, to know where the sentences break. I have chosen to keep *lbb* and *nqr* together because *lbb* has no pronominal suffix. It is easier to translate "the heart of the scion" than to make sense of "the heart" or "a heart" without further specification. This leaves the verb *šhh* to describe the action of the heart. *šhh* in JA means "to pause or delay" and in Syriac "to be weary, worn out." It may be the equivalent of Hebrew *šʾh*, "to crash into ruins."

This phrase is a problem in the other treatments of the text as well. McCarter, however, varies slightly from the usual attempts in that he translates *ʾth* as "you" and ties the sense of this phrase into the expression at the end of line 10. In line 10 someone is warned that he must take care of the sprout. Here McCarter believes that someone is being reprimanded for not nurturing the sprout and thereby causing him to languish.

Note that we have another scribal error here. The second *h* in *šhh* was left out initially and was later squeezed in above the line.

---

[77]Van der Kooij (129).

Line 15.

lqṣh. The *h* in this word is either a *mater* or a pronominal suffix. In either case the word probably means "end." Both forms are attested in Hebrew: *qāṣeh* or *qāṣāh* (both from *qṣh*) if the *h* is a *mater*; *qēṣ* (from *qṣṣ*) if the *h* is a suffix. *qēṣ* is also attested for JA. I have chosen to translate "to his end," assuming this word is connected distantly with "going to" which is the last readable phrase in the preceding line.

Van der Kooij reads several letters following *lqṣh*, but they are ambiguous and any translation is risky. Hoftijzer's suggestion (243) to read *gdr ṭš* as "a plastered wall" is not impossible, however, especially considering the fact that our text is written on plaster.[78]

š'lt.mlk.ssh.wš[']*l*[*t.*] The first two words are open to several interpretations. The first word can be a noun or a verb. As a noun, it would be f. sg. cs., meaning "the request of/for." As a verb, it would be G perfect, 1 sg., 2 m. sg., or 3 f. sg. (although the 1 sg. would probably have a *-ty* ending). The second word, *mlk*, is also ambiguous. If it means simply "king," we are at a loss to know why a king is introduced here, as in line 13. It could be a reference to a divine king, or even to Molech, the god to whom children were sacrificed.[79] Finally, *mlk* could refer to the *mulk*-sacrifice itself, if it is present in this inscription. (See the discussion below, pp. 80-85.)

Van der Kooij (132) reads *ssh* for our third word and Plate 11 of *ATDA* shows his reading to be probable, although in context it is difficult to understand the reference to a mare.

---

[78]Caquot and Lemaire (207) also discuss this possibility, but they are not convinced. McCarter has recently suggested (private communication) that the entire phrase reads *wzlp.gdr. ṭš*[.]*b* . . . , "And smear/he smeared a wall with plaster." This reading appeals to me because I have always read the letter after *wzl* as *p* (cf. van der Kooij, 131). This nice translation, however, had not occurred to me.

[79]See 2 Kgs 34:10; Jer 32:35; Lev 18:21, 20:2, 3, 4. It may be that there was never a god Molech, that all these occurrences refer to the *mulk* sacrifice. See Eissfeldt, *op. cit.* (cited in n. 74), pp. 36-40.

The same word appears to occur in Fragment V (q), however, so it is possible that a mare (or "his horse"?) has a role in the narrative that we simply do not understand at the present.

Line 16.

[ ]*ḥz̊n.r̊ḥq*[ ] The readings are very difficult, but these words could mean "a distant (i.e., long-ago) vision."

š'ltk.lm. We have the same problems here with *š'lt* as in line 16. It can be either a noun or a verb, this time with pronominal suffix. *lm* implies that the next words are direct speech, probably a question (see I, 4). If there is a question, the answer is probably to be found in the rubric that follows. (See further under line 17.)

Line 17. (Red ink)

ld't.s̊pr.dbr.l'm̊h.'l.lšn. McCarter used this phrase as the key to his suggestion for the meaning of the red-ink sections (see above, p. 34). By reading *s* instead of *w* in the second word, and by using van der Kooij's alternate *m* instead of *n* in *l'mh*, he can make perfect sense of this phrase. I checked the reading *s* in the second word against the plaster and it is, I think, a better reading than *w*.

Thus, we may have another phrase concerning the inscription itself. As McCarter has pointed out, *'l lšn* is to be contrasted with the written form of the story within the inscription.

lk.m̊špṭ.wmlq̊h. Van der Kooij reads *nšpṭ*, but admits that the *n* is damaged (136). This phrase will only make sense if we read *nšpṭ* and *nlqh*, or *mšpṭ* and *mlqh* (both *n*'s or both *m*'s). The *m* of *mlqh* is fairly clear (see Plate 5 of *ATDA*), so I assume the damaged letter before *špṭ* is the one to be changed. I interpret *lk* as the genitive use of *l*, i.e., "your," plus m. sg. suffix. Van der Kooij (136) prefers the reading *mlqh* to Hoftijzer's *mlqb*. *mlqh* is "punishment, chastisement" (MH and JA *malqût*). The root is *lqh*.[80] Thus, "your judgment and your

---

[80] I have vocalized masculine *-eh*, as in other *m*-preformative nouns from third-weak roots: see Hebrew *mar'eh*, *ma'ăśeh*, *ma'ăleh*, etc., and *maṭṭeh* in I, 9, of this inscription.

punishment" must be the object of *ldʿt*, as is *spr*. The purpose of the inscription is to portray what Balaam said orally, and to threaten punishment for the readers of the inscription.

Although I have followed McCarter's suggestion as to the sense of the line, he chose to read *nšpṭ.wnlqh*, "Come, let us judge and render a verdict!" Caquot and Lemaire also read *n*'s in both words, and they transcribe *spr* instead of *wpr* (207).

This is the end of the rubric. There is one more word visible on the line, *ʾmr*, which is written in black ink.

Line 18.

wl̊nšty.lmlk[ ] I would not divide the word after *wln*, as van der Kooij has done (although cautiously, 136). The purpose of these words is obscure, but we can read the first as a 1 pl. verb, imperfect or jussive, from *šty*. Perhaps now it is the people to whom Balaam's message was addressed who are speaking, offering to abstain from eating and drinking, although the reason is unknown.

McCarter reads ʿ instead of *l* here, and translates *wʿnšty* as a 1 sg. perfect verb from the root *ʿnš*, "to punish" or "to fine."

lmlk[ ] We cannot read what followed these four letters, so I would suggest interpreting *lnšty* as the end of a sentence and *lmlk*, with topicalizing *l*, as the beginning of another.

McCarter reads the entire phrase "And I have punished kings . . . ," assuming that Balaam is the speaker again.

There are literally hundreds of traces on the remaining lines of the second combination, but almost none of them in sufficient quantity for meaning. The only exception I will note is lines 35 and 36. These lines begin with phrases that must mean that rain and dew dripped down on earth in abundance, signaling the return of fertility. (See below, p. 80.)

Interpretations

We have in the first combination a rather typical Divine Council scene in which the seer, Balaam, has been given access to the meeting of the council, and then reports on that meeting to his people. (On the make-up of the council and the role of the Šaddayyin, see the excursus on pp. 85-89.) The gods are upset by the unnatural developments on earth and ask a goddess to withhold light from earth as punishment. The upheaval in nature is described in a series of phrases that remind us of biblical materials such as Isa 34 (and 35); the withdrawal of the sun's light as punishment is also a biblical theme, as McCarter has pointed out (58). The reversal of the natural order has even more striking parallels, however, in some Egyptian literature, such as "The Admonitions of Ipuwer," "The Prophecies of Neferti," and "The Complaints of Khakheperre-Sonb,"[81] where we find line after line of situations that are reversed from their normal state. Among other things, we read of the rich becoming poor and the poor having untold luxuries; of animals behaving contrary to their nature; of wealthy and esteemed persons who are no longer respected and are treated badly by underlings. In "The Prophecies of Neferti," we even read that the sun god Re will withdraw from humankind because of all this perversity in nature.

---

[81]Lichtheim, vol. 1, pp. 139-63. The validity of my use of this Egyptian material as helpful in interpreting the Deir ʿAllā text may be questioned. The Deir ʿAllā text is far removed from the Egyptian texts in time and, probably, in context. This is especially a problem since it is traditional for Egyptologists to interpret these works as deriving from specific historical calamities, in particular the unrest of the First Intermediate Period. This view no longer holds sway, however. Lichtheim's summary of the dispute (vol. 1, pp. 149-50) ends: "In sum, the *Admonitions of Ipuwer* has not only no bearing whatever on the long past First Intermediate Period, it also does not derive from any other historical situation. It is the last, fullest, most exaggerated and hence least successful, composition on the theme 'order versus chaos.'" Thus we may treat the Egyptian material as exemplars of a particular genre that need not be tied to a specific time and place, so that these materials may be used as a valid aid in interpreting this section of our text.

It seems, therefore, that the upheaval described here and the reactions of the gods are not out of line with other Ancient Near Eastern literature. The people of Balaam would be distressed (as Balaam was) at this constant darkness and at the loss of fertility which the lack of sunlight implies. At this point we must confront the question of whether the first and second combinations are two parts of the same narrative. It should be pointed out that the scribe is most certainly the same in both combinations. As was discussed above (pp. 2-4), archaeological evidence does not allow for any certainty about the situation of the texts before the wall was destroyed. What we call Combination I and Combination II may have been the top and bottom of a single column (and, therefore, we suppose, a single narrative), or they may have been situated on two separate objects, side by side. In the latter case, the two combinations may represent two entirely different narratives.

Hoftijzer expresses uncertainty about whether the text stood all in one column (270), but he concludes that there must have been at least two separate stories within the inscription, and perhaps more, because of the blank space following *kšd* in V (q) 2 and because of the introduction of Balaam's name in Fragment VIII (d) 2, which, he feels, should be placed below this blank space visible in Fragment V. If this placement were correct, Fragment VIII (d) would be outside the scope of the first story about Balaam, told in Combination I (269). Hoftijzer believes, however, that the second combination deals with Balaam also, whether or not Fragment VIII is a part of the same story as the rest of Combination II (270).

While I agree with Hoftijzer that both combinations probably deal with Balaam, I cannot accept his arguments that the two combinations are probably unrelated because of the placement of fragments. First of all, we have seen that the fragment with Balaam's name on it, Fragment VIII (d), should be placed near the beginning of Combination I.[82] In light of this unexpected (but surely correct) placement of two fragments within the first combination, I do not think that the possible original location of Combination V, and the unexplained blank

[82]See above, p. 21.

space in V (q), are convincing arguments that there was a clear break between Combinations I and II. Moreover, I believe that both combinations have to do with Balaam in some way, because of the mention of "his people" in II, 17 (McCarter's reading), and in view of the use of *spr* in the same line, possibly a reference to *spr* in I, 1. I think the rubric in II, 17, indicates that we are still dealing with the same situation as was described at the beginning of the first combination, where the text is described as *spr* [*blʿm brbʿ*]*r*, and where Balaam is seen to disclose his vision to "his people." It should be noted, however, that Balaam's name is nowhere present in the extant portions of Combination II, and the scene seems to have shifted considerably. The content of Combination II is a matter of considerable debate, but the context is clearly not the same as the rather straightforward narrative of the first combination.

Hoftijzer's interpretation of the second combination can be considered aside from the question of the continuity or discontinuity of this combination with the first. He relies heavily on the biblical picture of Balaam as one who delivers curses (270). This was true as well of his interpretation of the second half of Combination I (most of which I have not used in the present study because I feel McCarter's interpretation is far more suitable). While Hoftijzer analyzed those final lines in Combination I as appeals by Balaam for conversion, interpreting such words as *šmʿw* and *ʾklw* as plural imperatives addressed to Balaam's people, he sees the second combination as a series of curses and a description of impending doom, which Balaam's hearers reject in II, 17 (280).

Caquot and Lemaire also addressed themselves to the relationship between Combinations I and II. They agreed with Hoftijzer that the final lines of Combination I were an announcement of impending doom, but they see Combination II in a more hopeful light and describe it as "foreign" to the tone of the first combination (203). Their interpretation rests largely on their translation of the words *nqr* and *ʿlm*. Hoftijzer has translated *nqr* as "a blinded one" in the context of a curse, and *ʿlm* as having to do with death. Caquot and Lemaire suggested that the *q* in *nqr* may have represented *ʒ̣, and that the word was cognate with Hebrew *nḗṣer*, "sprout" or "branch." They translate *ʿlm* as "youth" and see, therefore, a much brighter context for Combination II, one in which references are made to rejuvenation and sexual pleasures, rather than the gloomy world of death and physical hardship of Hoftijzer's translation.

Although McCarter's *BASOR* article deals primarily with the first combination, he has worked with the second combination also, and has presented his results at several public lectures.[83] McCarter's approach is quite different from the two previous interpretations. He also interprets *nqr* as "sprout" and maintains that the word is being used metaphorically. He believes that it describes a person in terms of a "shoot" or "branch." He has considered possible connections between our text and the various descriptions of "Adonis gardens," but feels that this type of text would have no obvious connection with the first combination. The Adonis gardens approach relies especially on the references in II, 5 and 6, to a sprout, possibly to moist soil, to drinking one's fill (of the moisture from the soil, presumably), and to the attempts to keep the sprout alive which McCarter sees in lines 6 and 10. These elements can be compared to the classical descriptions of Adonis gardens[84] and to the reference in Isa 17:10-11, which disclose a practice of setting out shoots in shallow soil and nurturing them so that they grow quickly, within days. But the shallow soil does not allow firm rooting, so that the shoots wither very quickly. The garden is thought to represent the body of Adonis,[85] and is said to have been placed on his bier during the annual ceremony of mourning for the dead god.[86] There are some striking resemblances in our text to several of these details. Even though McCarter would not present the Adonis gardens approach as his final solution to the second combination,

---

[83]See above, p. 56, n. 54.

[84]See esp. the summary in de Vaux, "Sur quelques rapports entre Adonis et Osiris," *Bible et Orient*, pp. 379-405; T. K. Cheyne in P. Haupt, ed., *Isaiah* in *The Sacred Books of the Old and New Testaments*, p. 146; J. G. Frazer, *The Golden Bough*, V.

[85]De Vaux, *op. cit.* (cited in n. 84), p. 383.

[86]*Ibid.*, p. 380.

he has made several interesting and useful suggestions in conjunction with his exploration of that approach, and I will present them here as one possibility for interpretation.

"Young woman, drink your fill of love!" (McCarter's translation of II, 4) might be a reference to the ceremony surrounding the planting of the Adonis gardens. It was traditionally females who planted the gardens and who mourned the dead god. The mention of a sprout in line 5 can be seen as an obvious allusion to the sprouting of the plants in the Adonis garden, especially since the plants never developed beyond the sprouting stage. Further in line 5, there is a possible reference to moist soil (*mdr kl rṭb*). While Hoftijzer and Caquot and Lemaire also translate "soil" here, the Adonis garden is the interpretation that really finds a place for that translation within a general scheme. The mention of the soil for sprouting is an obvious possibility within an Adonis gardens text, and we know that these gardens were well watered and carefully nurtured so that the plants would sprout within a matter of days.

In line 6, McCarter would interpret *yrwy* as "let (the sprout) drink his fill," an allusion to the moist soil mentioned in line 5. Furthermore, he would read the first *ʾl* as a negative, as was pointed out above, in the commentary on that line. The use of the negative is crucial. The Adonis gardens represented the god himself, and although the gardens obviously did wither and die, it was considered a tragedy. In that case, it would be understandable to have here an expression of pleading that the sprout/god not be made to pass over into death. Skipping to line 7, we might suggest a similar interpretation. In the context of an Adonis gardens text, these expressions for the grave could represent the state from which the women tending the gardens are anxious to preserve the sprout/god. Line 9 might be a similar plea for the preservation of the god. McCarter has read two questions and two negative statements, i.e., "Is it for counsel? He will not take counsel with you." He relates these phrases to the similar ones in Psalms (30:10 and 119:175, for example) where the point is made that the supplicant can only praise Yahweh while alive. If the sprout/god dies, he cannot be of help to his people.

Line 10 might be interpreted in terms of nurturing the garden. The person addressed is probably male, as McCarter notes, although we would expect a female in the context of nurturing the garden. Still the need for nurturing is apparently expressed and the gender is ambiguous in these forms. The cloth that is mentioned might even be a shroud, since the garden is symbolic of the body of the dying god.

Another line of interpretation has been suggested to me by F. M. Cross. In several Punic and neo-Punic texts, a child is referred to as a *ṣēmaḥ*.[87] *ṣēmaḥ*, of course, also means "sprout" and in the Hebrew Bible, both *nēṣer* and *ṣēmaḥ* are used to speak of a scion, of the line of David, for instance (*nēṣer* in Isa 11:1; *ṣēmaḥ* in Jer 23:5, 33:15). In the context of child sacrifice, the "sprout" is the child who is the victim of the sacrifice, or, at least, the one for whom substitution is made. In this case, then, the "sprout" actually would be a human being, rather than a plant that is used as a metaphor for a person or god, as in McCarter's interpretation.

One advantage that the child sacrifice approach has is that it can be tied in nicely with the first combination. We know of situations where child sacrifice was performed in a crisis situation as a means of averting the crisis. (One thinks immediately of the sacrifice of Mesha's first-born in 2 Kgs 3 in order to break the siege against him by Israel, Judah, and Edom.) The first combination of the Deir ʿAllā text is a description of a crisis of monumental proportions. Perhaps the break between the first and second combinations contained an account of the failure of fertility and the universal darkness, with the suggestion made, perhaps by Balaam or by the gods themselves, that the sacrifice of a child would appease the gods and remedy the situation. Two of the few translatable phrases at the end of the second combination seem to describe the return of fertility. In lines 35 and 36 we read *tṭpn šr* and *tṭpn ṭl*, "they (f. pl.) will drip with heavy rain" and "they will drip with dew." ("They" are perhaps clouds, *ʿābôt* in Hebrew.)

---

[87]See *KAI* 43.11, 162.2, and 163.3. 162 and 163 are neo-Punic child sacrifice texts.

In the interest of presenting child sacrifice as another possible line of interpretation, at this point I will summarize briefly what we know about the neo-Punic rituals of child sacrifice. In an unpublished Harvard University dissertation, P. Mosca has compiled all of the classical references to Phoenician-Punic child sacrifice.[88] At times these references conflict, but a broad outline of the practice can be set out as follows:

1. The sacrifices were made to Kronos (= El).

2. The sacrifices were institutionalized in a cult, but are also reported to have been the response to severe civic crises (sometimes in these cases with outlandish numbers of victims).

3. The sacrificial victims were burned. There is conflicting evidence as to whether the child's throat was cut beforehand, or whether he or she was burned alive.

4. The children were not necessarily always male or first-born, but they were generally children of noble families. On occasion there were substitutes, either of animals, or of children of poor families who were bought for the purpose.

5. There was in Carthage a bronze statue of Kronos with arms extended palms up, but sloping downward. The children were placed into the arms of Kronos, whence they rolled down into a pit filled with fire.

6. The parents were expected at least to show no negative reaction as they stood on watching the sacrifice, and according to one source,[89] they offered their children freely, comforting them so that they would not cry.

7. The sacrifice was accompanied by loud music, presumably to drown out the screams of the children.

Mosca also compiled archaeological, medical, and epigraphic evidence pertaining to child sacrifice. The sacrificial precincts are described by Mosca, following Moscati, as "unroofed sacred areas which were enclosed by means of walls and in which

---

[88] P. G. Mosca, "Child Sacrifice in Canaanite and Israelite Religion."

[89] Tertullian, *Apology*, IX 2-4, quoted on p. 20 of Mosca (cited in n. 88).

were placed urns containing the calcined remains of children and small animals."[90] Mosca summarizes a medical study of the bones in urns taken from Carthage and Sousse, which concluded that the children were overwhelmingly newborn infants.[91] It should be pointed out that, as far as I know, there is no evidence of massive infant burials at Deir ʿAllā, and I am not suggesting that the "sanctuary" at Deir ʿAllā was a sacrificial precinct. There is no evidence to support such an assertion. That fact does not exclude the possibility, however, that a text dealing with child sacrifice was displayed in the area.

According to this interpretation, then, the second combination would begin with a description of the child who is to be sacrificed, the "sprout" (= "scion"), and a further description of the child's fate. In such a broken context as we have in line 4 it is impossible to say what is meant that someone is "drunk with love," but if it is the scion who is spoken of, it may mean that he was well-loved by his family (and hence a greater sacrifice).[92]

As was pointed out above (pp. 57-58), *mdr* in II, 5, may refer to the fire-pit of the tophet precinct, rather than to the soil. Mosca quotes de Vaux and argues that the *mədûrāh* of Isa 30:33 is not a pyre or a heap of wood (BDB 190 and Jastrow 733), but rather a pit that is made "deep and wide."[93] He relates this word to the mention of a fire-pit under the statue of Kronos at Carthage.[94] Even though there is a gender problem

---

[90]Mosca (cited in n. 88), p. 39.

[91]*Ibid.*, pp. 51-53. He cites the unpublished doctoral thesis of Dr. Jean Richard, "Etude médico-légale des urnes sacrificielles puniques et leur contenu" (Institut Médico-Légal de Lille, 1961).

[92]Mosca (cited in n. 88), p. 16, quotes Philo of Byblus (preserved in Eusebius' *Praeparatio Evangelica* Bk. I.10.40c) that the child to be sacrificed was the "best-loved" of the rulers' children. McCarter has urged, however, that *rwy ddn* must refer to sexual love and would therefore be inappropriate as a description of a family's attachment to a child (private communication).

[93]Mosca (cited in n. 88), p. 214; for the reference to de Vaux, see his n. 195.

[94]See above, p. 81.

since our word is masculine, the occurrence of such a similar word in a child sacrifice context in the Hebrew Bible cannot be overlooked. (If *mdr* is "fire-pit," *rṭb* later in the same line must carry the more developed meaning "foliage." If the wood in the pit is to be used for fire, the "moist" connotation is not appropriate.)

In line 6, where the Adonis gardens interpretation suggested that *'l y'br* represented a plea that the sprout not die, the child sacrifice context might be better served by assuming *yrwy* and *'l* go together, and that "passing over into the grave" was seen as a necessary fate for the child in order for El to be "satisfied."

Next, there would seem to be some conversation, presumably between the child's parents and the person (or god) recommending the sacrifice, concerning the best way to approach the child to calm his fears. Line 8 might represent part of that conversation if it can be interpreted as part of an attempt by the parents to guard their child from the grave. Or, it is possible that the parents, even though they have agreed to the sacrifice, would still like to avoid for the child the more terrifying aspects of dying: the vermin from the grave, and the unnatural beings who have arisen from the grave. (Here, McCarter has suggested an alternative translation for *pḥzy bny 'š* that would tie it more closely to the child sacrifice context. *bny 'š* may not be an expression for human beings at all, but rather a similar phrase to the one that is used in Job 5:7, to mean flames, i.e., "children of fire." In that case, *pḥzy bny 'š* would mean "those who leap up from the flames.")

It is tempting in line 9 to see in the words *mlkh* and *ytmlk* something to do with the *mulk* sacrifice, or perhaps the connotations of promising or vowing that the root *mlk* has in Syriac. In close conjunction with the words *'ṣh* and *yt'ṣ*, however, it is difficult to avoid the more common meaning of advising that *mlk* has in the reflexive in Aramaic and later Hebrew. I have translated each phrase as if the entire phrase is a question: "As for counsel, is it not you with whom he will take counsel? . . ." F. M. Cross has suggested (private communication) that if this translation is correct, we would expect the people to be asking advice of a deity or deities.

My own tentative suggestion concerns the "conversation" interpretation. We might see here an attempt on someone's part to persuade the father of the child[95] that his son will comply with the ritual as long as the father agrees, that the child will turn to the parent for advice. In this case, we can understand why *bk* is presumably inserted before the verb *lytʿṣ*. The prepositional phrase is placed *before* the verb to emphasize the father's role as the obvious one to whom the child will turn.

Arguing along the same lines, the word *yšb*, which should be the direct object of *ytmlk* according to my interpretation,[96] might represent someone who "lives with" the child, someone under his own roof, in other words. The next letter seems to be *q* or *r*, however, and no suitable word beginning with one of those letters comes to mind.

Line 10 also fits nicely into the context of child sacrifice. Covering the child with a cloth could be some aspect of the ritual. As in the case of the Adonis garden, the possibility of a shroud comes to mind. The second half of the line could be interpreted as instructions to the parent as to how to treat the child so that he will be less frightened or reluctant.[97]

Following this line, we might have a first-person account of what the father or mother says to the child (line 11), and perhaps the parents' reactions "in their hearts" (*blbbm* in line 12). It may be that the attitude of the "sprout" is even mentioned in two places (lines 12 and 14), apparently as the ceremony is taking place. The use of the word *mlk* in lines 15 and 18 may also be a reference to the *mulk* sacrifice, although in context this is difficult to prove.

If this interpretation is correct, our text is unusual in its apparent lack of judgment on the sacrifice. It would have to originate with a group for whom child sacrifice was an

---

[95] *-k* rather than *-ky* is presumably masculine.

[96] See above, pp. 64-65.

[97] See above, p. 81, where evidence is cited from classical sources that indicates that this actually happened in cases of child sacrifice.

accepted practice, and this text might have served as a sort of justification for a continued ritual of child sacrifice.

As should be obvious at this point, the broken lines that make up the extant portion of Combination II are ambiguous enough to admit wide-ranging interpretations. There are, however, certain elements of the text which seem relatively secure to me. I find it impossible to avoid the language of death and the grave in this text, so that I do not agree with the interpretation set forth by Caquot and Lemaire. I also have translated *nqr* as "sprout" or "scion," however, just as they did. The language of this portion of the text seems too concrete to allow for a "metaphorical" interpretation, such as McCarter has argued for in the past (although it is possible that this concrete language simply serves to heighten the metaphor, to emphasize that the sprout does indeed represent a sentient being as well as a form of vegetation). If the concrete language may be taken literally, however, it is possible to suggest, on the basis of II, 13, that the person being referred to is, in fact, a child. Lines 10 and 11 suggest to me some form of ritual, and I assume that it is this ritual, whatever it may be, that binds together the broken phrases that we have to work with in Combination II of our text.

Excursus: the Šaddayyīn

One of the most fascinating aspects of the text from Deir ʿAllā is the mention of a group of gods called *šdyn*, the *Šaddayyīn*. (On the vocalization, see above, p. 40.) One is immediately reminded, of course, of *Šadday* as an epithet of El in the Hebrew Bible, and the appearance here of the *Šaddayyīn*, in a non-Israelite text, gives us a broader base from which to interpret this epithet. Our first task will be to determine the position of the *Šaddayyīn* in the text at hand.

According to my translation of I, 2, and II, 6, the chief god at Deir ʿAllā was El. We are not surprised to find a group of gods under him, called *ʾlhn*, who gather together in the council (I, 5) and who act as intermediaries between the council and the human prophet Balaam (I, 1 and 2). Balaam reports to his people that a divine council was called together and that the *Šaddayyīn* took their places in the assembly. It is not immediately obvious who these *Šaddayyīn* are, whether they are identical to the *ʾIlāhīn* or whether they form a separate group within the larger group of gods. All we can say with certainty at this point is that the *Šaddayyīn* are gods, that they are included in the council of El (and apparently have some authority there since their demands were presumably met), and that they concern themselves with human events.

šdyn and *ʾlhn*, however, are used in statements in lines 5 and 6 that are parallel, if not in the same sense as "poetic" parallelism, at least in statements describing the same event with the simple interchange of *šdyn* and *ʾlhn*. In line 5, "the works of the *ʾIlāhīn*" is used to describe something we know to have been done by the *Šaddayyīn*, since according to line 6, it is the *Šaddayyīn* who made the demands on the goddess. This leads us to suspect that the statement in lines 5/6, "the *ʾIlāhīn* gathered together / the *Šaddayyīn* stood as the assembly," is also a statement of parallel events. If so, we may conclude simply that *ʾIlāhīn* is the generic term for "gods," as we would expect, and that "the gods" as they stand in the council of El, as envisioned in this inscription, carried the additional appellative *Šaddayyīn*.

We have seen that the *Šaddayyīn* are actively concerned with happenings on earth and are capable of taking effective action to influence the human situation. The *Šaddayyīn* are horrified by the reversal of nature they have observed on earth and seek to punish the earth for its perversity. The shutting up of the heavens means not only darkness, of course, but absence of rain and, therefore, fertility as well. This sort of watchfulness is exactly what the gods of the council of El are lacking in Psalm 82, and it is for this reason that they are upbraided by El.

It is these same gods (if *ʾIlāhīn* and *Šaddayyīn* can be equated) who come to Balaam in a dream to inform him, and therefore his people, of the coming disaster and the reasons for it. We have, then, a vivid picture of the workings of the council of El, and of the prophet as the intermediary who is privy to the divine decisions and who makes them known to the people.

The existence of a group of gods known as *Šaddayyīn*, who are the high gods who meet in the council of El, can shed some light on the epithet *Šadday* given to El in the Hebrew Bible. We need not look at *Šadday* as an isolated epithet of El that simply describes his origin as a mountain god.[98] While the etymological considerations are not changed by this new text, it is clear that *Šadday* has wider implications than the etymological ones. If the gods in the council were known at some time and place as *Šaddayyīn*, there is good reason to suspect that *Šadday* is applied as an epithet of El in his position as chief of the council. We may also speculate that the association of the council with mountains is an obvious development from the fact that the council is generally described as meeting on a mountain.[99]

There are other examples in the Ancient Near East of a god whose name, in the plural, signifies a whole group of gods. In the Hebrew Bible, of course, *ʾĕlōhîm* can be used as a plural to mean simply "the gods." At Ugarit, the gods in El's assembly are called *ʾlm*, and there is another group of gods called *ʾlnym*, "gods" or "divinities," but their function is not clear. Also at Ugarit we find Kothar (or Kothar wa-Hasis) and Rpʾ as well as the groups of gods, *kθrt* and *rpʾum*. There is no concrete evidence that either Rpʾ or Kothar was the chief of the group that bears his name, but *ʾlm* is used at Ugarit to refer to El's assembly (*pḫr ʾlm*) and *ʾĕlōhîm* in the Bible can be used in the same way (Psalm 82, for instance). In summary, since El and *Šadday* can be used to refer to the same deity in the Hebrew Bible, and since we now have a text where *šdyn* and *ʾlhn* are used interchangeably when referring to "the gods" in the council of El, it is reasonable to suggest that *Šadday* was the epithet applied to El as head of the council in the region where the gods in that council were known as *šdyn*. It is no coincidence, then, that Balaam identifies himself in Num 24:4, 16 as the man who sees the vision of *Šadday*.

---

[98]On this problem, see especially W. F. Albright, *JBL* 54 (1935) 180-93; *CMHE*, pp. 52-60; M. Weippert, *ZDMG* n.s. 36 (1961) 42-62.

[99]McCarter (57) comes to the same conclusion.

There may be some trace of the *Šaddayyīn* remaining in the Hebrew Bible. In Deut 32:17 we read that there was a time when the Israelites sacrificed to *šdym* (*šēdîm*) and not to *ʾĕlōah*, and in Ps 106:37, the same *šdym* are mentioned, but this time in reference to child sacrifice. We read in vv. 35 and 36 that the Israelites mingled among the nations instead of destroying them, and that they served their idols. Then, in vs. 37, we have *way-yizbəḥû ʾet-bənêhem wə-ʾet-bənôtêhem laš-šēdîm*. The usual etymology of *šēd* from Akkadian *šēdu* is less than satisfactory, even though long-standing: *šēd* was taken to mean "demon" already by the time of Mishnaic Hebrew. Akkadian *šēdu* is generally a protective spirit, however, and only means "demon" with the addition of *lemnu*. In the biblical context, moreover, the *šdym* are identified as *gods* of foreigners. It is possible that *šdym* originally referred to the same gods who are found in the Deir ʿAllā text. This would mean that the *y* was originally consonantal, and only later interpreted as a *mater*. At some point, perhaps the significance of the *Šaddayyîm* was forgotten, or perhaps the association of these gods with child sacrifice was frowned upon in light of the similarity between their name and the epithet of El, *Šadday*. At any rate, by rabbinical times, the meaning "demon" was firmly established.

The occurrence of *šdym* in Ps 106 is especially interesting since a few verses earlier, in vs. 28, we find a reference to the Baal-Peor incident where the people's yoking themselves to Baal-Peor is described as "eating the sacrifices of the dead."[100] Although Balaam is not mentioned in Ps 106, he is described in Num 31:16 as the person who was responsible for the Israelites' participation in the incident at Baal-Peor. These references are widely separated in the Bible, but the fact remains that there are vestiges preserved of a tradition that links Balaam to sacrifices of the dead, and of another (?) tradition that asserts that the Israelites at one time offered

---

[100]Marvin Pope pointed out to me the implicit connection between Balaam and sacrifices of the dead, on the basis of Ps 106, and Robert Good brought to my attention that *šdym* was also present in this psalm.

their children to foreign gods called *šdym*. It is surely no coincidence that we now have a text that may link child sacrifice with Balaam and the gods he serves, the *šdyn*.

Chapter III

GRAMMAR

A. *Phonology*

Most of the consonants in this inscription represent only one Proto-Semitic phoneme. There are five exceptions:

(1) *ḥ* represents both **ḥ* and **ḫ*. Examples of words with **ḫ*: *ʾḥrʾh*, I, 2; *mḥr*, I, 3; *ḥt*[*m*]?, I, 7; *rḥmn*, I, 8; *ʾprḥy*, I, 8; *rḥln*, I, 9; *ḥṭr*, I, 9; *ḥmr*, I, 10; *ḥršn*, I, 13; *ḥnyṣ*, I, 15; *ḥtn*, II, 7; *pḥzy*?, II, 8; *lḥlq*, II, 11; *nʾnḥ*, II, 12 bis.

(2) *ʿ* represents both **ʿ* and **ǵ*. Examples of words with **ǵ*: *bʿbky*, I, 6; *yʿnh*, I, 8; *ʿlmh*?, II, 4; *ʿl*, II, 13 bis.

(3) *ṣ* represents both **ṣ* and **θ̣*. Examples of words with **θ̣*: *hlʿṣh*, II, 9; *lytʿṣ*, II, 9.

(4) *q* represents both **q* and **ʒ̣*. Examples of words with **ʒ̣*: *qbʿn*, I, 10; *yqḥk*, I, 11; *qqn*?, I, 14; *hqrqt*, I, 15; *nqr*, II, 5, 12, 14.

(5) *š* represents **š*, **ś*, and **θ*. Examples of words with **ś*: *mš̊ʾ*?, I, 2; *šm*, I, 6; *ḥpš*[*t*]?, I, 10; *lnšʾ*, I, 12. Examples of words with **θ*: *š̊bw*, I, 5; *šd̊*[*yn*], I, 5; *šdyn*, I, 6; *bʾšr*, I, 9; *š*[*ʿl*]?, I, 10/11; *ʿštr*, I, 14; *šm*, II, 7; *yšb*?, II, 9; *yʾnš*?, II, 10; *šmh*?, II, 13, 14; *lyšbm*?, II, 13; *m̊špṭ*, II, 17.

B. *Orthography*

(1) Final *î* represented by *y*:
tpry tupurî (I, 6); *skry* sukurî (I, 6); *bʿbky* ba-ǵabkî (I, 6); *sk̊rky* sikrikî? (I, 7); *thby* tihabî (I, 7); *thgy* tahgî (I, 7); *ky* kî (I, 7; II, 14); *rwy* rawî? (II, 4).

(2) Final *û* represented by *w*:
wyʾtw way-ya'tû (I, 1); *wyʾmrw* way-ya'murû (I, 2); *šbw* θibû (I, 5); *wlkw* wa-likû (I, 5); *rʾw* ri'û (I, 5); *ʾ̊tyḥdw* 'ityaḥḥidû (I, 5); *wnṣbw* wa-niṣṣabû (I, 6); *wʾmrw* wa-'amarû (I, 6); *ʾklw* 'akalû (I, 9); *štyw* šatiyû (I, 10); *šmʿw* šamaʿû (I, 10, 13); *ḥzw* ḥazû (I, 14); *yḥz̊ẘ*? yiḥzû? (II, 13).

(3) Final *ā* represented by *h*:
bkh bakā(h) (I, 3/4); *ṣrh* ṣarā(h) (I, 8); *ʾnph* 'anapā(h) (I, 8); *ʿnyh* ʿanīyā(h) (I, 11); *wkhnh* wa-kāhinā(h) (I, 11); *rmh* rimmā(h) (II, 8); *hlʿṣh* ha-la-ʿiθ̣ā(h) (II, 9); *ʾwlmlkh* 'aw-la-milkā(h) (II, 9); *šhh* šahā(h) (II, 14); *ʾth* 'atā(h) (II, 14); *ssh* sūsā(h)? (II, 15).

(4) Final *e*/*ē* represented by *h*:
ḥz̊h ḥāzē(h) (I, 1); *mḥ̊zh* maḥze(h) (I, 1); *ybkh* yabke(h) (I, 4); *tbkh* tabke(h) (I, 4); *yʿnh* yaĝne(h) (I, 8); *mṭh* maṭṭe(h) (I, 9); *mlqh̊*? malqe(h)? (II, 17).

(5) Final *ay* represented by *y*:
bny banay (I, 8 *b̊ny*; II, 8); *ʾprḥy* 'ipruḫay (I, 8); *gry* gūray (I, 10); *yrwy* yirway (II, 6); *pḥzy* pāḫizay? (II, 8); *mškby* miškabay (II, 11); *wlnšty*? wa-lā-ništay? (II, 18).

(6) Final *aw* represented by *w*:
this would apply only to the plurals of III-*W*/*Y* verbs, if they should be vocalized -*aw* rather than -*û* (see above, pp. 22-23).

(7) Medial *ay* (diphthong) represented by *y*:
blylh ba-laylah? (I, 1); *ḥnyṣ* ḫunayṣ (I, 15); *wʿyn*? wa-ʿayn? (I, 16); *byt* bayt (II, 6 bis, once *by*[*t*], 7 bis); *ʿlmyk* ʿālamayk (II, 11).

(8) Medial *aw* (diphthong) represented by *w*:
ʾlwh 'ilawh (I, 1, 4); *mwʿd* mawʿid (I, 6); *ywn* yawn (I, 9); *mwsr* mawsar (I, 10); *ʾwlmlkh* 'aw-la-milkā(h) (II, 9); *mwt* mawt (II, 13, 14 *m̊ẘt̊*).

(9) Medial *ī* is never represented by a *mater*:
ʾlhn ʾilāhīn (I, 1 bis, 5 bis, once *ʾl[h]n*); *šdyn* θaddayyīn (I, 5 *šd̊[yn]*, 6); *šmyn* šamayīn (I, 6); *rḥmn* raḫamīn (I, 8); *rḥln* raḫilīn (I, 9); *ʾrnbn* ʾarnabīn (I, 9); *wqbʿn* wa-ð̣abuʿīn (I, 10); *lḥkmn* la-ḥak(k)*ʊ*mīn (I, 11); *lnšʾ* la-naśīʾ? (I, 12); *qrn* qūrīn? (I, 12); *ḥršn* ḫ*ʊ*r(r)*ʊ*šīn (I, 13); *ddn* dādīn (II, 4); *ʿlmn* ʿālamīn (II, 6); *gdš* gadīš (II, 8); *ʾš* ʾīš (II, 8); *ʾšm* ʾaśīm (II, 11); *lyšbm*? lā-yaθībim? (II, 13).

(10) Medial *ū* is never represented by a *mater*:
tṣm taṣūm (I, 4); *ssʿgr* sūsʿagūr (I, 7); *gry* gūray (I, 10); *qrn* qūrīn? (I, 12); *ḥšb* ḥašūb (I, 12); *ʿl* ġūl (II, 13 bis); *ssh* sūsā(h)? (II, 15).

(11) Medial *ā* is never represented by a *mater*:
ḥz̊h ḥāzē(h) (I, 1); *ʾlhn* ʾilāhīn (I, 1 bis, 5 bis, once *ʾl[h]n*); *pʿlt* puʿullāt (if plural) (I, 5); *šm* śām (I, 6); *ʿlm* ʿālam (I, 7 bis, once *ʿl̊m*); *wql* wa-qāl (I, 8); *wṣpr* wa-ṣippār (I, 9); *wkhnh* wa-kāhinā(h) (I, 11); *ʾzr* ʾizār? (I, 12); *wḥšb* wa-ḥāšib (I, 12); *ddn* dādīn (II, 4); *kl* kāl? (II, 5); *ʿlmn* ʿālamīn (II, 6); *lyʿl* lā-yaʿl (II, 7 bis); *hlk* hālik (II, 7); *pḥzy* pāḫizay? (II, 8); *lytʿṣ* lā-yittaʿaθ̣ (II, 9); *lytmlk* lā-yitmalik (II, 9); *ʿlmyk* ʿālamayk (II, 11); *lšn* l*ʊ*š(š)ān (II, 17).

(12) *h* is consonantal and not a *mater* in the following words:
ʾlwh ʾilawh (I, 1, 4); *blylh* ba-laylah? (I, 1); *kh* kāh? (I, 2); *ʾḥrʾh* ʾaḫarʾah? (I, 2); *ʿmh* ʿammuh (I, 4; II, 17); *mh* mah? (I, 5); *ʿlmh* ġalmuh? (II, 4); *blbbh* ba-libabuh (II, 12); *šmh* θammah? (II, 13, 14); *lqṣh* la-qiṣṣuh? (II, 15).

C. Morphology

1. Pronouns

a. Personal

Independent: 3 m. sg. *hʾ* (I, 1)

Suffixal:

on singular nouns:

2 m. sg.: *rʾšk* (II, 11); *šʾltk*? (II, 16).

2 f. sg.: *bʿbky* (I, 6); *sk̊rky* (I, 7).

3 m. sg.: *ʿmh* (I, 4; II, 17); *ʿlmh*? (II, 4); *blbbh* (II, 12); *lqṣh*? (II, 15).

on plural nouns: 2 m. sg. *ʿlmyk* (II, 11).

on "singular" prepositions:

2 m. sg.: *bk* (II, 9); *lk*? (II, 17).

3 m. sg.: [*l*]*h̊* (I, 4).

3 m. pl.: *lhm* (I, 5).

on "plural" prepositions:

3 m. sg. *ʾlwh* (I, 1, 4).

on verbs:

2 m. pl.: *ʾḥwkm* (I, 5).

3 m. sg.: *tksn* (II, 10); *tšnʾn* (II, 10).

3 m. pl.: *lyšbm*? (II, 13).

b. Relative: *ʾš* (I, 1, 2?).

c. Indefinite: *mh* (I, 5).

2. Nouns and adjectives

m. sg. abs.: *lylh* (I, 1); *mḥzh* (I, 1); *mḥr* (I, 3); *mwʿd* (I, 6); *ḥšk* (I, 6, 7); *ʿlm* (I, 7 bis); *ḥ*[*sd*]? (I, 8); *nšr* (I, 8); *ywn* (I, 9); *ṣpr* (I, 9); *mṭh* (I, 9); *ḥṭr* (I, 9); [*z*]*ʾ̊b̊*? (I, 10); *ḥmr* (I, 10); *mwsr* (I, 10); *š*[*ʿl*]? (I, 10/11); *mr* (I, 11); *nšʾ* (I, 12); *rḥq* (I, 13); *skl* (I, 14); *šgr* (I, 14); *ʿštr* (I, 14); *nmr* (I, 15); *ʿyn*? (I, 16); *nqr* (II, 5, 12, 14); *rwy*? (II, 4); *mdr* (II, 5); *rṭb* (II, 5); *byt* (II, 7 bis); *hlk* (II, 7); *ḥtn* (II, 7); *gdš* (II, 8); *ʾš* (II, 8); *lbš* (II, 10); *ḥd* (II, 10); *mwt* (II, 13, 14); *rḥm* (II, 13); *g̊dr*? (II, 15); *ṭ̊š̊*? (II, 15); *mlk* (II, 15, 18); *ḥzn*? (II, 16); *rḥq*? (II, 16); *spr* (II, 17); *lšn* (II, 17; may be fem.); *mšpṭ* (II, 17); *mlqḥ̊*? (II, 17).

m. sg. cs.: *spr* (I, 1); *br* (I, 1 [*br*], 2, 4); *mš̊ʾ* (I, 2); *ngh* (I, 6/7); *ḥt*[*m*] (I, 7); *ql* (I, 8); *ʾzr* (I, 12); *qqn*? (I, 14); *ʿyn*? (I, 16); *byt* (II, 6 bis, once *by*[*t*]); *ʿl* (II, 13); *lbb* (II, 14).

m. sg. with suffix: *ʿmh* (I, 4; II, 17); *ʿbky* (I, 6); *ʿlmh*? (II, 4); *rʾšk* (II, 11); *lbbm* (II, 12); *lbbh* (II, 12); *qṣh*? (II, 15).

f. sg. abs.: *ss*ʿ*gr* (I, 7); ʾ*nph* (I, 8); *drr* (I, 8); ʿ*nyh* (I, 11); *khnh* (I, 11); *ḥnyṣ*? (I, 15); *rmh*? (II, 8); ʿ*ṣh* (II, 9); *mlkh* (II, 9).

f. sg. cs.: *š*ʾ*lt*? (II, 15 bis, once *š*[ʾ]*l*[*t*]).

f. sg. with suffix: *š*ʾ*ltk*? (II, 16).

m. pl. abs.: ʾ*lhn* (I, 1 bis, 5 bis, once ʾ*l*[*h*]*n*); *šdyn* (I, 5 *šd̊*[*yn*], 6); *šmyn* (I, 6); *rḥmn* (I, 8); *rḥln* (I, 9); ʾ*rnbn* (I, 9); *qb*ʿ*n* (I, 10); *ḥkmn* (I, 11); *ḥršn* (I, 13); ʾ*zrn* (I, 16); *ddn* (II, 4); ʿ*lmn* (II, 6); *mlkn*? (II, 13).

m. pl. cs.: *bny* (I, 8 *b̊ny*, 15 *bn*[*y*]; II, 8); ʾ*prḥy* (I, 8); *šqy*? (II, 8); *mškby* (II, 11).

m. pl. with suffix: ʿ*lmyk* (II, 11).

f. pl. cs.: *p*ʿ*lt* (I, 5), if plural.

3. Verbs

a. Strong Verb

(1) G active perfect

3 m. sg.: *zlp̊*? (II, 15).

(2) G active imperfect

2 m. sg.: *tškb* (II, 11).

(3) G imperative

f. sg.: *tpry* (I, 6); *skry* (I, 6).

(4) tG imperfect

3 m. sg.: *ytmlk* (II, 9), unless tD.

(5) D active perfect

3 m. sg.: *dbr* (II, 17).

(6) C active perfect

3 f. sg.: *hqrqt* (I, 15).

b. I-*N*

(1) N perfect

3 m. pl.: *nṣbw* (I, 6).

(2) D active perfect

3 f. sg.: *nšrt* (I, 8).

c. I-Guttural

(1) G active perfect

3 m. sg.: *ḥšb* (I, 12)

3 m. pl.: *ḥzw* (I, 14).

(2) G active imperfect

2 f. sg.: *thgy* (I, 7), unless jussive.

3 m. sg.: *yʿnh* (I, 8); *yʿbr* (II, 6), unless jussive.

3 m. sg. jussive: *yʿl* (II, 7 bis).

3 m. sg. converted: *wyḥz* (I, 1); *wyʿl* (I, 3).

3 m. pl.: *yḥz̊ẘ*? (II, 13).

(3) G infinitive

cs.: *ḥlq* (II, 11).

(4) G active participle

m. sg. abs.: *ḥšb* (I, 12).

m. sg. cs.: *ḥzh* (I, 1).

(5) G passive perfect

3 m. sg.: *ḥ[šb]* (I, 12)

(6) G passive participle

m. sg. abs.: *ḥšb* (I, 12).

(7) tG imperfect

3 m. sg.: *ytʿṣ* (II, 9).

(8) D active perfect

3 f. sg.: *ḥrpt* (I, 7/8).

(8) D active imperfect

1 sg. with suffix: *'ḥwkm* (I, 5).

d. I-*Y*

(1) G active perfect

3 m. sg.: *yk[l]*? (I, 3).

(2) G active imperfect

2 f. sg.: *thby* (I, 7), unless jussive.

(3) G imperative

m. pl.: *šbw* (I, 5).

(4) G infinitive

cs.: *dʿt* (II, 17).

(5) G active participle

m. sg. (cs.?): *yšb*? (II, 9).

(6) D passive imperfect

3 m. sg.: *yybl* (I, 9).

(7) tD perfect

3 m. pl.: *'̊tyḥdw* (I, 5).

e. I-ʾ

(1) G active perfect

3 m. sg.: *ʾth* (II, 14); *ʾmr*? (II, 17).

3 m. pl.: *ʾmrw* (I, 6); *ʾklw* (I, 9).

(2) G active imperfect

3 m. sg.: *yʾnš* (II, 10).

3 m. sg. converted: *wyʾmr* (I, 4/5).

3 m. pl. converted: *wyʾtw* (I, 1); *wyʾmrw* (I, 2).

(3) N perfect

3 m. sg.: *nʾnḥ* (II, 12 bis).

f. II-Guttural

(1) G active perfect

3 m. sg.: *šhh* (II, 14).

(2) G active imperfect

2 f. sg.: *thby* (I, 7), unless jussive.

3 m. sg.: *ypʿl* (I, 2), unless jussive or passive; *yqḥk* (I, 11).

(3) G imperative

m. pl.: *rʾw* (I, 5).

(4) G active participle

f. sg. abs.: *khnh* (I, 11).

m. pl. cs.: *pḥzy*? (II, 8).

(5) tD perfect

3 m. pl.: *ʾ̊tyḥdw* (I, 5).

g. II-*W*

(1) G active imperfect

2 m. sg.: *tṣm* (I, 4).

3 m. sg. converted: *wyqm* (I, 3).

(2) G active participle

m. sg. abs.: *kl*? (II, 5).

(3) tG active imperfect

3 m. sg.: *ytʿṣ* (II, 9).

(4) C active imperfect

3 m. sg. with suffix: *yšbm*? (II, 13).

h. II-*Y*

(1) G active imperfect

1 sg.: *ʾšm* (II, 11).

(2) G infinitive

abs.: *šm* (I, 6).

i. III-Guttural

(1) G active perfect

3 f. sg.: *rqḥt* (I, 11), unless G active participle, f. sg.

3 m. pl.: *šmʿw* (I, 10, 13).

(2) G active imperfect

2 m. sg. with suffix: *tšnʾn* (II, 10).

3 m. sg.: *yqḥ* (II, 13).

(3) G infinitive

cs.: *dʿt* (II, 17).

(4) N perfect

3 m. sg.: *nʾnḥ* (II, 12 bis).

j. III-*W*/*Y*

(1) G active perfect

3 m. sg.: *ṣrh* (I, 8); *šhh* (II, 14); *ʾth* (II, 14).

3 m. pl.: *štyw* (I, 10); *ḥzw* (I, 14).

(2) G active imperfect

1 pl.: *nšty*? (II, 18).

2 m. sg.: *tbkh* (I, 4).

2 f. sg.: *thgy* (I, 7), unless jussive.

3 m. sg.: *ybkh* (I, 4); *yʿnh* (I, 8); *yrwy* (II, 6), unless jussive.

3 m. sg. converted: *wyḥz* (I, 1); *wyʿl* (I, 4).

3 m. sg. jussive: *yʿl* (II, 7 bis)

3 m. pl.: *yḥz̊ẘ*? (II, 13).

3 m. pl. converted: *wyʾtw* (I, 1).

(3) G imperative

m. pl.: *rʾw* (I, 5).

(4) G infinitive

abs.: *bkh* (I, 3/4).

(5) G active participle

m. sg. cs.: *ḥzh* (I, 1).

(6) D active imperfect
1 sg. with suffix: *'ḥwkm* (I, 5).
2 m. sg. with suffix: *tksn* (II, 10).

k. Doubly Weak
(1) I-Guttural and II-*W*: *yt'ṣ* (II,9).
(2) I-Guttural and III-*W/Y*: *ḥzh* (I, 1); *wyḥz* (I, 1); *wy'l* (I, 4); *'ḥwkm* (I, 5); *thgy* (I, 7); *y'nh* (I, 8); *ḥzw* (I, 14); *y'l* (II, 7 bis); *yḥz̊ẘ?* (II, 13).
(3) I-*Y* and II-Guttural: *thby* (I, 7); *'̊tyḥdw* (I, 5).
(4) I-*Y* and III-Guttural: *d't* (II, 17).
(5) I-' and III-Guttural: *n'nḥ* (II, 12 bis).
(6) I-' and III-*W/Y*: *wy'tw* (I, 1); *'th* (II, 14).
(7) II-Guttural and III-*W/Y*: *r'w* (I, 5); *šhh* (II, 14).

l. Other
(1) *hlk*
G imperative, m. pl.: *lkw* (I, 5).
G active participle, m. sg.: *hlk* (II, 7).
(2) *lqḥ*
G active imperfect, 3 m. sg.: *yqḥ* (II, 13).

4. Adverbs and Particles
a. Negative *'l*
(1) preceding an imperfect (or jussive; prohibition): *'l thgy* (I, 7).
(2) with following imperfect omitted (prohibition): *w'l* (*tšmy* omitted) *ngh 'lm* (I, 7/8).
b. Negative *l* (always prefixed to verb; simple negation):
(1) preceding a perfect: *wlyk[l]* (I, 3).
(2) preceding an imperfect: *lyt'ṣ* (II, 9); *lytmlk* (II, 9); *lyšbm?* (II, 13); *lnšty?* (II, 18).
(3) preceding a jussive: *ly'l* (II, 7 bis).
c. Adverbial *h*: *blylh?* (I, 1); *'ḥr'h?* (I, 2); *šmh?* (II, 13, 14).
d. *šm*
(1) "there": (II, 7).
(2) *šmh* ("thither")?: (II, 13, 14).
e. *kh* ("thus"): (I, 2).

f. *ʾḥrʾh* ("afterwards, hereafter"): (I, 2).
g. *lm* ("why"): (I, 4; II, 5?, 16?).
h. Interrogative *h-*: *hlʿṣh* (II, 9).

5. Prepositions
 a. *ʾl* "to"
  (1) with pronoun suffixed: *ʾlwh* (I, 1, 4).
  (2) preceding a noun: *ʾl s̊krky* (I, 7); *ʾl byt* (II, 6).
 b. *b-* "in": *blylh* (I, 1); *bʿbky* (I, 6); *bk* (II, 9); *blbhm* (II, 12); *blbbh* (II, 12).
 c. *bʾšr* "in the place of, instead of": *bʾšr rḥln* (I, 9).
 d. *k-* "like": *kms̊ʾ* (I, 2).
 e. *l-*
  (1) "to" directional: *ʾth l*[ ]? (II, 14); *lqṣh*? (II, 15).
  (2) "to" dative: *l*[*blʿ*]*m* (I, 2); *wyʾmr lhm* (I, 5); *wʾmrw lš*[ ] (I, 6); *lḥkmn yqḥk* (idiomatic use with the verb) (I, 11); *lnšʾ*? (I, 12); *lʿmh* (II, 17); *lk mšpṭ*? (II, 17).
  (3) "to" expressing purpose: *lḥlq* (II, 11); *ldʿt* (II, 17).
  (4) "as for" topicalizing: *hlʿṣh* (II, 9); *ʾwlmlkh* (II, 9); *lmlk*? (II, 18).
 f. *mn* (*min*)
  (1) "from": *mn* [ ]? (I, 3); *mn rḥq* (I, 13); *mn gdš* (II, 13); *mn pḥzy* (II, 13); *mn šqy*[ ] (II, 13).
  (2) of time "after": *mn mḥr* "on the morrow" (I, 3).
 g. *ʿd* "until": *ʿd ʿlm* (I, 7).
 h. *tḥt* "under": *tḥt rʾšk* (II, 11).

6. Conjunctions
 a. *ʾw* "or": *ʾwlmlkh* (II, 19), continuing an interrogative sequence.
 b. *hn* "if": *hn tšnʾn* (II, 10); *hn t*[ ] (II, 10).
 c. *ky* "for": *ky ssʿgr ḥrpt* (I, 7); *ky ʾth l*[ ] (II, 14).
 d. *w-*
  (1) converting, with imperfect verbs: *wyʾtw* (I, 1); *wyḥz* (I, 1); *wyʾmrw* (I, 2); *wyqm* (I, 3); *wyʿl* (I, 4); *wyʾmr* (I, 4/5).

(2) non-converting, continuing a verbal sequence
with the perfect: *wnṣbw* (I, 6); *w'mrw* (I, 6); *wṣrh* (I, 8); *wšm'w* (I, 13); *wzlp̊*? (II, 15).
with infinitive absolute plus finite verb: *wbkh ybkh* (I, 3/4).
with imperative: *wlkw* (I, 5).
with imperfect: *ẘtbkh*? (I, 4).
with a negative: *wlyk[l]*? (I, 3); *w'l* (*tšmy*) (I, 6); *w'l thgy* (I, 7); *wly'l* (II, 7); *wlnšty*? (II, 18).

(3) other occurrences of *w*-: prefixed to a noun in *wql* (I, 8); *wṣpr* (I, 9); *wqb'n* (I, 10); *w'nyh* (I, 11); *wkhnh* (I, 11); *wḥšb* (I, 12); *w'štr* (I, 14); *w'yn*? (I, 16); *wmdr* (II, 5); *wrmh* (II, 8); *w'l* (II, 13); *wš'lt*? (II, 15); *wmlqh̊*? (II, 17); prefixed to a preposition in *ẘ'[l]* (I, 7); *wmn* (II, 8).

D. Syntax

1. Pronouns

a. Personal

Independent: there is only one example of an independent pronoun, *h'*, in I, 1. Here it functions as a copula, completing a relative clause.

Suffixal: these pronouns generally occur on nouns, expressing a genitival relationship, or on prepositions. In four cases a pronominal suffix occurs on a verb as object suffix. Three times it is the accusative object: *tksn* "you will cover him" (II, 10); *tšn'n* "(if) you hate him" (II, 10); *lyšbm* "he will not restore them" (?) (II, 13). In one case, it is the dative object: *'ḥwkm* "I will tell you" (I, 5).

b. Relative: the relative pronoun *'š* is found in I, 1: *'š ḥzh 'lhn h'* "who was a seer of the gods." It is perhaps also present in *'š lr[ ]'t*, in I, 2, but the context is too broken for comment. See further under *mh* directly below.

c. Indefinite: *mh* is used in I, 5, as a relative pronoun in an indirect question: *ʾḥwkm mh šd̊[yn*] "I will tell you what the Šadda[yyin]" (have done? have said?).

d. Numeral: only one numeral appears in this text, *ḥd*, "one," in *lbš ḥd* (II, 10). In the context, the phrase can be translated "a cloth" or "one cloth."

2. Nouns and adjectives

a. Nouns in apposition to each other: *brbʿr* is in apposition to *blʿm* in I, 1 [*brbʿ*]*r*, 2, 4. *by*[*t*] (II, 6) . . . *byt* . . . *byt* (II, 7) may be in apposition to *byt* in II, 6.

b. Construct chains:

spr [*blʿm*] (I, 1); [*brbʿ*]*r* (I, 1); *ḥzh ʾlhn* (I, 1); *ms̊ʾ ʾl* (I, 2); *brbʿr* (I, 2, 4); *pʿlt ʾlhn* (I, 5); *ngh ʿl̊m* (I, 6/7); *ḥt*[*m*]*b̊ ḥšk*? (I, 7); *ql rḥmn* (I, 8); *b̊ny nḥṣ* (I, 8); *ʾprḥy ʾnph* (I, 8); *gry š*[*ʿl*]? (I, 10/11); *ʾzr qrn*? (I, 12); [ ] *skl*? (I, 14); *bn*[*y*]? (I, 15/16); *rwy ddn*? (II, 4); *byt ʿlmn* (II, 6); *pḥzy bny ʾš* (II, 8); *mškby ʿlmyk* (II, 11); *ʿl rḥm* (II, 13); *lbb nqr* (II, 14); *šʾlt mlk*? (II, 15).

c. Noun or construct chain as predicate of a nominal clause:

ḥzh ʾlhn (I, 1).

d. Noun or construct chain as title or announcement:

spr [*blʿm brbʿ*]*r* (I, 1).

e. Noun or construct chain as subject of a verbal sentence:

ʾlhn (I, 1); *blʿm* (I, 3); *ʿmh* (I, 4); *šd̊*[*yn*] (I, 5); *ʾl*[*h*]*n* (I, 5: the second *ʾlhn* in the line); *šdyn* (I, 6); *ssʿgr* (I, 7); *ql rḥmn* (I, 8); *drr* (I, 8); *ṣpr* (I, 9); *ḥṭr* (I, 9); *ʾrnbn* (I, 9); *qbʿn* (I, 10); *gry š*[*ʿl*]? (I, 10/11); *ʿnyh* (I, 11); *khnh* (I, 11); *ḥšb* (I, 12 bis); *ḥršn* (I, 13); [ ] *skl*? (I, 14); *qqn šgr wʿštr*? (I, 14); *ḥnyṣ*? (I, 15); *ʾl* (II, 6);

hlk (II, 7); *ḥtn* (II, 7); *nqr* (II, 11); *mlkn*? (II, 13); *mwt* (II, 13, 14?); *lbb nqr* (II, 14); *šʾlt mlk*? (II, 15).

f. Noun or construct chain as direct object of a verb: *mḥzh* (I, 1); *pʿlt ʾlhn* (I, 5); *šmyn* (I, 6); *ḥšk* (I, 6); *ngh ʿlm* (I, 6/7); *ḥt*[*m*]*b̊ ḥšk*? (I, 7); *nšr* (I, 8); *b̊ny nḥṣ* (I, 8); *ʾprḥy ʾnph* (I, 8); *ywn* (I, 9); [*z*]*ʾ̊b̊*? (I, 10); *ḥmr* (I, 10); *mwsr* (I, 10); *mr* (I, 11); *bn*[*y*]? (I, 15/16); *rṭb* (II, 5); *mškby ʿlmyk* (II, 11); *ʿl rḥm* (II, 13); *g̊dr*? (II, 15); *spr* (II, 17).

g. Noun or construct chain as the object of a preposition: *lylh* (I, 1); *mš̊ʾ ʾl* (I, 2); [*blʿ*]*m* (I, 2); *mḥr* (I, 3); *š*[ ] (I, 6); *ʿbky* (I, 6); *s̊ḳrky* (I, 7); *ʿlm* (I, 7); *rḥln* (I, 9); *ḥkmn* (I, 11); *nšʾ* (I, 12); *rḥq* (I, 13); *nmr*? (I, 15); *byt ʿlmn* (II, 6); *by*[*t*]? (II, 6); *byt*? (II, 7); *gdš* (II, 8); *pḥzy bny ʾš* (II, 8); *šqy*? (II, 8); *ʿṣh* (II, 9); *mlkh* (II, 9); *rʾšk* (II, 11); *lbbm* (II, 12); *lbbh* (II, 12); *qṣh* (II, 15); *ʿmh* (II, 17); *lšn* (II, 17); *mlk*? (II, 18).

h. Noun and construct chain as vocative: *blʿm brbʿr* (I, 4).

i. Noun used as adverb: *mwʿd* (I, 6) "as an assembly"; *lbš ḥd* (II, 9) "with one garment"; *ṭ̊š̊*? "with plaster" ? (II, 15).

3. Verbs

There are six (seven?) subordinate clauses in the text: *ʾš ḥzh ʾlhn hʾ* in I, 1; (*ʾš lr*[ ]*ʿt* in I, 2 ?); *mh šd̊*[*yn*] in I, 5; *byt lyʿl hlk* in II, 7; *hn tšnʾn yʾnš* in II, 10; *ky ʾth l*[ ] in II, 14; and *spr dbr lʿmh* in II, 17. Since these are only six or seven, all verbal uses described below will be those in main clauses unless otherwise specified. Because the "birds" section of Combination I begins with *ky*, the entire section could be considered subordinate to the preceding imperatives. This is unlikely, however, and the uses of the verbs included in that section do not seem to be affected by the *ky*, so they will also be treated as if they are verbs in main clauses.

It should also be noted that, with a very few exceptions, the verbs in the first combination refer to the past or present, and the verbs in the second combination refer to the future.

a. The Perfect

The perfect verbs in the text can be interpreted to refer to past time, with the following exceptions: the verbs in the "birds" section (I, 7 ff.) may all describe "habitual" or "durative" actions; *nʾnḥ* (II, 12 bis), *šhh* (II, 14), and *ʾth* (II, 14, in a subordinate clause), may refer to the present if this part of the text is a description of an actual ritual.

b. The Imperfect

The majority of occurrences of the imperfect refer to the future, including the one occurrence within a subordinate clause, *tšnʾn* in II, 10. The exceptions and qualifications follow.

(1) In three cases, the "imperfect" may actually be a jussive:
 (a) *ypʿl* (I, 2);
 (b) *ʾl thgy* (I, 7);
 (c) (substituting for the imperative) *thby* (I, 7).

(2) Several imperfects probably have a durative function, i.e., they describe an action that is or was *being* done: *wbkh ybkh* (I, 3/4); *tṣm* (I, 4); *tbkh* (I, 4); *yʿnh* (I, 8); *yybl* (I, 9); *yqḥk* (I, 11).

c. The Converted Imperfect

The converted imperfects in the text refer to the past.

d. The Participle

(1) Most participles in this text are used as substantives, including both the active and passive participles of *ḥšb*. *khnh* (I, 11), *ḥšb* (I, 12, both active and passive), and *hlk* (II, 7) are subjects of verbal sentences. *ḥzh* (I, 1) is the predicate of a nominal clause.

(2) *kl* (II, 5), if interpreted correctly, acts as a verb as well as an adjective in that it takes as its object *rṭb*, but must be seen to modify *mdr*.

e. The Imperative

The five imperatives in this text are used to express commands.

f. The Infinitive

(1) There are two infinitives absolute in this text, *bkh* (I, 3/4) and *šm* (I, 6). *bkh* precedes a finite verb from the same root to intensify the description of crying. *šm* occurs after a phrase containing two imperatives to continue the commands (or requests) to the goddess.

(2) *ḥlq* (II, 11) and *dʿt* (II, 17) are infinitives construct of *ḥlq* and *ydʿ* and are used, preceded by *l*-, to express purpose.

4. Adverbs and Particles

Most of the adverbs and particles in this text do not need comment here, but a word should be said concerning the use of the negatives. In previous translations, *šm* in I, 6, has not been interpreted as a verb, and so, the use of *ʾl* following *šm* was not clear. Interpreting *šm* as a volitive form does away with the need to find obscure functions for *ʾl*. It is used simply in a prohibition following a volitive form, where the prohibition expresses the exact opposite from the volitive form. It is understandable, therefore, that the verb is not repeated in the prohibition.

5. Prepositions

See the *Morphology* section, where the prepositions are classified according to their use.

6. Conjunctions (see *Morphology* for the contexts of the occurrences of *w*-)

a. *w*- is the most common conjunction in this text, and is most often used to coordinate equivalent main verbal clauses, or a main verbal clause and an adversative clause (e.g., *šm ḥšk wʾl ngh ʿlm* in I, 6/7). This clause-coordinating function is accomplished by prefixing *w-* to verbs (or negative particles), nouns, and (once) a preposition (I, 7).

b. Sometimes *w-* is used to coordinate equivalent nouns or prepositional phrases: *šgr wʿštr* (I, 14); *nqr wmdr*? (II, 5); *mn pḥzy bny ʾš wmn šqy* (II, 8); *ʿl rḥm wʿl* [ ] (II, 14) is probably coordination of construct phrases; *šʾlt mlk ssh wšʾlt*? (II, 15); *mšpṭ wmlqḥ*? (II, 17).

c. Once *ʾw* is used to coordinate two equal verbal clauses: II, 9.

d. Relative clauses generally occur without conjunctions in this text: *byt lyʿl hlk* (II, 7), "the house (where) the traveler does not come up"; *spr dbr lʿmh* (II, 17), "the message (that) he spoke to his people." One exception occurs in I, 1: *ʾš ḥzh ʾlhn hʾ*, "who was a seer of the gods." Another possible occurrence of the relative *ʾš* is in I, 2: *ypʿl* [ ]*ʾ ʾḥrʾh ʾš lr*[ ]*ʿt*. *ʾš*, however, can be interpreted as other than the relative pronoun here (see above, p. 35).

e. There is one complete conditional sentence and the beginning of another in II, 10: *hn tšnʾn yʾnš* and *hn t*[ ], "if you are unkind to him, he will falter. If you . . . ." The verb is imperfect in both the protasis and the apodosis.

f. *ky*, "for, because," introduces the long series of phrases that runs from the last part of I, 7, to the end of the extant portion of the first combination. These phrases describe the upheaval of the natural order on earth and in that sense represent an extended causal expression.

g. *ky* also introduces an incomplete clause in II, 14, which is perhaps a causal construction: *šhh ky ʾth l*[ ].

h. *mh* is used once as an indefinite relative pronoun: *šbw 'ḥwkm mh šd̊[yn*] (I, 5), "Sit down! I will tell you what the Šadda[yyin]" (have done? have said?).

i. Most of the imperative sequences in the text are asyndetic. Therefore, the phrase directly above in (h) may mean, "Sit down *that* I *may* tell you . . . ." Likewise, there is no *w* between *lkw* and *r'w* in I, 5, or between *tpry* and *skry* in I, 6. There is a *w* preceding *lkw* in line 5, but this may be simply a means of continuing the narrative.

j. The clauses beginning with *w*- prefixed to a non-verb do not seem to be particularly disjunctive, with the exception of *w* plus negative *'l* or *l*-, in which case, of course, the second clause is adversative. The *w* in many of the clauses beginning with *w* plus a noun could conceivably be translated "while" or "but." This is especially true of those clauses in the "birds" section.

Chapter IV

THE DIALECT

Introduction

The plaster text from Deir ʿAllā has generally been published as Aramaic, with due restrictions on the definition because of the unusual features of the text. The most compelling factor in the decision to place this text alongside the known Old Aramaic inscriptions is the phonology. There are several features of the text, however, that are commonly designated South Canaanite. Thus one might argue that the Aramaic designation for the Deir ʿAllā inscription has been proposed too hastily and must be reconsidered.

In light of the small amount of material included in this inscription, and of the unusual nature of the combination of features, the classification of the Deir ʿAllā inscription can become a matter of definitions. If, by definition, no Canaanite dialect may represent *ð̣ by *q*, then our dialect is, by definition, not Canaanite. Phonology, however, should not be an absolute determining factor. Other considerations must be made for the verbal system (morphology and syntax), for pronominal suffixes, vocabulary, etc., in the classification of this dialect.[1]

No one feature can determine the classification of a dialect, because any linguistic feature (or bundle of features) can, in theory, spread beyond the territory of the language with which it is identified, into other speech-areas. L. Bloomfield gave the classic statement of this situation in his explanation of the wave-hypothesis.

> Different linguistic changes may spread, like waves, over a speech-area, and each change

[1]For an example of this type of approach, see I. J. Gelb, *Syro-Mesopotamian Studies* I/1, May 1977, pp. 3-30. Cf. E. Ullendorff's review of the article in *JSS* 23 (1978) 151-54.

> may be carried out over a part of the area that does not coincide with the part covered by an earlier change. The result of successive waves will be a network of isoglosses.[2]
>
> The comparative method presupposes clear-cut splitting off of successive branches, but the inconsistent partial similarities show us that later changes may spread across the isoglosses left by earlier changes; that resemblance between neighboring languages may be due to the disappearance of intermediate dialects (wave-theory); and that languages already in some respects differentiated may make like changes.[3]

Thus, it is not the appearance in our text of any one feature or cluster of isoglosses, but rather the importance one assigns to the isoglosses, that is crucial. It is the choice of criteria and the ordering of those criteria that may determine the category into which the dialect must fall, and this is an area that linguists find difficult to legislate in general terms. R. Anttila does give a few suggestions in his discussion of the wave theory.

> In theory, all isoglosses are equally important, but, for defining purposes, some must be regarded as more fundamental than others. Unique relics are particularly interesting. . . . If relics can be used to define general characteristics, certain innovations give footholds for relative chronology. . . . But, of course, there is always the danger that an innovation might be as old as the protolanguage. In such cases the relative chronology would be wrong, but it would still serve as a characterization of the dialect against others.[4]

It would seem, then, that unique relics and shared innovations are significant features to note among the isoglosses that a dialect may share with a larger grouping. At this point we will examine the various features of the Deir ʿAllā dialect that show a relationship with Aramaic or with South Canaanite,

---

[2]L. Bloomfield, *Language*, p. 317.

[3]*Ibid.*, p. 318.

[4]R. Anttila, *An Introduction to Historical and Comparative Linguistics*, p. 306.

in an effort to determine whether the overall picture exhibits more (and more important) isoglosses with one language or another.

Phonology of the Deir ʿAllā Text

In several places in this inscription, we find words in which a *q* is best interpreted as representing the reflex of Proto-Semitic *ʒ̣: *qbʿn*, I, 10; *yqḥk*, I, 11; *qqn*, I, 14; *hqrqt*, I, 15; *nqr*, II, 5, 12. This is the only place where the known Old Aramaic texts and the known first millennium South Canaanite inscriptions differ in their phonology, the South Canaanite representing *ʒ̣ by *ṣ* and the Old Aramaic utilizing *q* for this phoneme. That is to say, as early as the Ugaritic texts, *ʒ̣ had fallen together with **ṣ* in Canaanite, and is represented by *ṣ*,[5] while the merging of *ʒ̣ with *ʿ which we find in later Aramaic (BA, JA, Syriac, e.g.) has not yet taken place in the Old Aramaic inscriptions. *ʒ̣ is represented by *q* in these inscriptions, which fact indicates that *q* was the letter in the Phoenician alphabet that most closely approximated the pronunciation of this consonant by Aramaic speakers in this period. This could mean that the original sound was still being produced, or else that the merging of *ʒ̣ with *ʿ was already in process, with the *q* representing an intermediate stage.

As was mentioned above, we also find *ʒ̣ represented by *q* in the Deir ʿAllā inscription. As is the case with Aramaic, this does not mean that *ʒ̣ had merged with **q* in the dialect of this inscription. We know of no Semitic language where *ʒ̣ merged with **q*. Thus, the writing with *q* does not really tell us how the phoneme was being pronounced at Deir ʿAllā, just as it does not tell us how it was pronounced in the Old Aramaic inscriptions. We do not even know whether this phoneme was tending toward a merger with *ʿ at Deir ʿAllā, as it was in Aramaic, or whether it was to follow a different course altogether. It should be stressed that the representation of *ʒ̣ as *q* in the Deir ʿAllā inscription and in the Old Aramaic

---

[5]In *CTCA* 12, *ʒ̣ is represented by θ̣. See Harris/*Dialects*, p. 35 and n. 18.

inscriptions is not proof of a merger common to both Aramaic and the dialect of the Deir ʿAllā inscription. It is not a merger at all. Thus, it is incorrect to maintain that the phonology of the Deir ʿAllā inscription is the same as the phonology of the Old Aramaic inscriptions. In fact, we cannot be sure of the exact phonology of either dialect. We can only say that at Deir ʿAllā, the same graphemes are used to represent the reflexes of Proto-Semitic consonants as are used in the Old Aramaic inscriptions.

The phonology of the Deir ʿAllā inscription, then, is ambiguous. It represents a possible link with the Old Aramaic inscriptions, but we can say no more than that from the evidence.

The Old Aramaic inscriptions are themselves an example of the necessity of appealing to a complex of features rather than appealing merely to phonology in order to arrive at a classification. Their phonological representation is closer to South Canaanite than to later Aramaic, differing from South Canaanite only in the representation of *ḏ̣ by *q* rather than by *ṣ*. Other distinctive features, however, such as the emphatic *ʾalep* and the *zy* relative pronoun, must be taken into account, and they argue strongly that those inscriptions represent an early form of the Aramaic language.[6]

Moreover, it can be pointed out that neither the South Canaanite material nor the Aramaic material is strictly uniform in its phonology. Biblical Hebrew, for instance, apparently preserved the distinction between *š and *ś, while the two had early fallen together in Ugaritic and Phoenician.[7] Hebrew shares this preservation with the Old Aramaic inscriptions.[8] Thus, there is one phonological isogloss linking Biblical Hebrew and the Old Aramaic inscriptions, that separates Hebrew from the

---

[6]See the discussion of the problems of classification of these inscriptions in *EHO*, pp. 22-23.

[7]Harris/*Dialects*, pp. 33-35.

[8]*ś is represented with the *š* sign in the Old Aramaic inscriptions, but with *s* in Syriac. Since *ś, then, was not progressing toward a merger with *š, we must assume that, as in Hebrew, the *š* sign in the Old Aramaic inscriptions was being used to represent two phonemes, and that the distinction between *š and *ś was still being kept.

other Canaanite languages about which we know this information. Likewise, within Aramaic we find phonological changes from one region to another, such as the tendency in the Nerab inscriptions not to have two emphatic consonants in the same word.[9] Thus, even within the Aramaic dialects, the representation of Proto-Semitic consonants is not strictly uniform.

Writing System

As was explained in Chapter 2, paleographic analysis of this text has produced mixed results. Some scholars have interpreted the writing system as Aramaic and other as an offshoot of Aramaic, in line with the later Ammonite inscriptions. Although the writing system of the Deir ʿAllā inscription derives from the Aramaic script, it should be noted that this is not a comment on the *language* of the text, but rather a vestige of scribal training at some point in history. The script of the Ammonite inscriptions from the Amman citadel and from Tell Sīrān, and of several of the ostraca from Ḥesbān, is derived from Aramaic, but the language of those inscriptions is Canaanite. The Kilamuwa inscription is another example of such mixing. The script of the inscription is Aramaic, but the language is Phoenician.

Definite Article

The direction of the development of a definite article would, of course, be a decisive factor in a classification of the language of this text. I.e., we would like to know whether the definite article was developing toward a final *-āʾ* or prefixed *ha-*, or toward some other alternative. Unfortunately, there is no clear instance of any definite article in this inscription. Hoftijzer's only clear case of the Aramaic emphatic ending (*wbmšktʾ*, 188-89) disappears with the new arrangement of the fragments. Others have translated the emphatic ending in several words in the first combination, but in each case the ending is either reconstructed, or it can be explained without reference to the emphatic *ʾalep*

---

[9]See, for example, J. Greenfield, *JNES* 37 (1978) 95.

ending.[10] There is still no clear-cut example of an Aramaic emphatic ending in this text.[11]

There is also no example of the usual South Canaanite definite article *h*-. The safest approach to this problem is to submit that we have no identifiable definite article anywhere in this inscription. It is possible that the dialect represented here is in an intermediate stage of development of a definite article, perhaps as outlined by T. O. Lambdin.[12] It is also possible that we are dealing with an isolated dialect, which simply did not develop a definite article. McCarter (50-51) has suggested that this text represents a "literary" dialect, or at least an archaizing dialect, which eschews the use of a definite article as does biblical poetry. His suggestion is made with due reserve, as we have no other comparable "literary" material from this period with which to judge our inscription.

Relative Pronoun

The discovery of a relative pronoun in our text also would be an important factor in the classification of the dialect. Here again the results are unsatisfactory. McCarter has identified the relative pronoun *zy* in II, 8, but I have not interpreted the text in the same way. (See my discussion on p. 63, n. 68.[13]) I have translated *ʾš* as the relative pronoun in I, 1, and perhaps in I, 2. If that translation is correct, this feature would place the dialect of the Deir ʿAllā text in line with Phoenician usage, and with the Ammonite dialect of

---

[10]See above in the commentary on *kmšʾ* (I, 2) and *ʾḥrʾh* (I, 2). Caquot and Lemaire (195) also reconstruct *gdʾ*, "fortune," for the damaged second word in the rubric in I, 2.

[11]The existence of the emphatic *ʾalep* on two other inscriptions found in the same level as this text has been cited as evidence that in the common language at Deir ʿAllā, a dialect of Aramaic was spoken. See Hoftijzer (267) and McCarter (50-51).

[12]T. O. Lambdin, in Hans Goedicke, ed., *Near Eastern Studies in Honor of William Foxwell Albright*, pp. 315-33.

[13]*zy* also occurs on the two inscriptions with emphatic *ʾalep* mentioned above in n. 11.

the same general time period (*'š* is used in line 6 of Heshbon Ostracon IV).

Noun Morphology

The only pertinent fact here is that the masculine plural absolute noun ends in *-n*. This is a regular feature of Aramaic, of course. The *-n* ending on the masculine plural noun is no obstacle to classifying this dialect as South Canaanite, however. One need only turn to Moabite to find a South Canaanite language with *-n* masculine plurals. Later Hebrew, of course, also employs *-n* plurals.

Pronominal Suffixes

There are four pronominal suffixes that are of interest to us here:

1. The 3 m. sg. suffix on plural nouns and some prepositions is *-wh* (*'lwh*, I, 1, 4; probably *kpwh*, IX [a] 3).

2. The 2 m. pl. objective suffix on an imperfect verb is *-km* (*'ḥwkm*, I, 5).

3. The 3 m. pl. suffix with the preposition *l-* is *-hm* (*lhm*, I, 5).

4. The 3 m. sg. accusative suffix on an imperfect verb is *-n* (*tksn* and *tšn'n* in II, 10).

#1 is, of course, the expected 3 m. sg. suffix on plural nouns in Aramaic and never in Canaanite. #2, #3, and #4 follow the Canaanite pattern, but #2 and #3, *-km* and *-hm*, are written regularly in *m* rather than *n* in the Old Aramaic inscriptions and Imperial Aramaic, and occasionally in BA.

#4 would seem important in that Aramaic never shows *-n* alone as the 3 m. sg. verbal suffix. The energic *n* on the imperfect with suffix is common in Old Aramaic, Imperial Aramaic, BA, and JA, but the suffix is always written *-nh*. The difference between the Aramaic suffix *-nh* and the Hebrew suffix where the *h* assimilates to the *n*, giving *-innû*, is probably simply the use of the long and short forms of the energic. The suffix in this inscription, then, actually represents the choice of the short energic form in this situation. As we saw above (65-66), it is possible for one language to utilize both the short and the long forms of the energic, so this suffix is in fact probably not a significant factor in our analysis of the dialect.

#1, the *-wh* suffix on plural masculine nouns and the preposition *ʾl*, is as yet unknown in a Canaanite inscription. This suffix has been described as *-aw* reduced from **-ayhū*, plus the addition of a secondary *h*.[14] This explanation of the formation of the suffix has not been particularly satisfying, however, in that the source of the secondary suffix is somewhat problematic. Nevertheless, this addition, if it is such, apparently did not take place in previously known Canaanite texts, so that the appearance of the *-wh* suffix in this text is actually the strongest argument for the Aramaic classification of the text. This discussion is aimed at demonstrating, however, that the evidence toward South Canaanite outweighs this one factor.

Orthography

The text is written with final *matres lectionis* to mark long vowels, but there are no medial *matres*. (See the section on orthography above, pp. 91-93.) There are several instances of *y*'s and *w*'s in medial positions. In one case, the *w* is consonantal (*ʾḥwkm*, I, 5); in the other instances, the orthography is evidence that diphthongs have not contracted. The orthography of this inscription conforms to that of some Aramaic and some South Canaanite dialects in 700 B.C.E. Medial *matres* occur in the inscription from Tell Fakhariyeh,[15] but otherwise are not expected in Aramaic this early, and diphthongs are not contracted in any Old Aramaic inscriptions. Judahite Hebrew in the first half of the first millennium B.C.E. also does not contract diphthongs, and utilizes final but not medial *matres*.[16] Diphthongs are uncontracted in some forms in the Mesha inscription as well. The evidence from Ammonite material is mixed: *ywmt* in line 7 of the Tell Sīrān inscription indicates an uncontracted *aw*, but *yn* ("wine") in Heshbon Ostracon IV (lines

---

[14] *EHO*, p. 29, #68.

[15] See now Abou-Assaf, A., P. Bordreuil, and A. R. Millard, *La statue de Tell Fekherye*, pp. 23, 40-42.

[16] *EHO*, p. 57.

7 and 8) is evidence of contraction of *ay*. (Perhaps contraction of *aw* and *ay* need not occur at the same time.)

Verbal System

The verbal system of the Deir ʿAllā text provides the strongest arguments in favor of a South Canaanite classification for the dialect. Several aspects of the system enter into the discussion.

1) N conjugation. In two instances, verbs beginning with *n* are most easily translated as examples of an N reflexive conjugation: *nṣbw*, I, 6; *nʾnḥ*, II, 12 bis. This is one of the most damaging forms for the thesis that the dialect of the Deir ʿAllā inscription is a form of Old Aramaic. The N conjugation is not attested in any known Aramaic.[17] It is possible, but not likely, that the apparent N verbs in this inscription were borrowings, since neither root (*nṣb* or *ʾnḥ*) occurs in the G in Hebrew. Such an explanation might be used as a last resort.

Furthermore, since the N conjugation was a part of the Proto-Semitic system (it occurs in languages as far apart as Arabic and Akkadian, as well as the other Northwest Semitic languages--Hebrew, Phoenician,[18] and probably Ugaritic[19]), we must assume that it fell out of use in Aramaic at some point, when the tG took over its functions.[20] It is possible, therefore, that some early form of Aramaic did employ an N conjugation, but we would expect a genuine N verb in an Aramaic inscription as late as 700 B.C.E. only if the dialect of the inscription were extremely conservative, and had retained the N centuries longer than any known Aramaic. This is, of course, not likely.

---

[17]Segert §5.6.7.3.7 discusses the form *nšht* (in Text 15:10 in A. E. Cowley, *Aramaic Papyri of the Fifth Century B.C.*), which he calls a *Nifʿal*, but he believes it to be a Phoenicianism.

[18]See Harris/*Grammar*, p. 42.

[19]See *UT* Grammar §9.34.

[20]The tG is known already in the Sefîre inscriptions, where it is used as a passive.

2) Long form of the 3 m. pl. imperfect without *-n*. In II, 13, we have (if the reading is correct) *mlkn.yḥzw*. The context here is difficult; both the reading and interpretation of *mlkn.yḥzw* are ambiguous enough to prevent us from placing much emphasis on this verb as an example of any particular feature. If *yḥzw* is functioning here as an imperfect rather than as a jussive, however, it represents another distinction from the Old Aramaic inscriptions.

3) G infinitive with no preformative *m-*. We have such infinitives in *bkh* (I, 3/4), *šm* (I, 6), *ḥlq* (II, 11), and *dʿt* (II, 17). The G infinitive in later Aramaic always has preformative *m-*. The evidence from Old Aramaic is mixed: there are several forms from Sefîre and from the Panammû inscriptions that are G infinitives without the preformative;[21] but the Aramaic from Tell Fakhariyeh has several *m*-preformative G infinitives.[22] The Deir ʿAllā forms are, of course, the expected forms in South Canaanite.

4) *waw* consecutive. *waw* plus an imperfect verb represents a past tense in several instances: *wyḥz* (I, 1); *wyʾtw* (I, 1); *wyʾmrw* (I, 2); *wyqm* (I, 3); *wyʿl* (I, 4); *wyʾmr* (I, 4/5). Although examples of *waw* consecutive appear in the Zakkur inscription, it is not used in later Aramaic. The Zakkur forms are usually described as archaizing or Canaanizing. As R. Degen[23] and T. O. Lambdin (private communication) have pointed out, since we have the contrast in Old Aramaic between the short form and long form of the imperfect, the conditions for a frozen *waw* consecutive form existed in Aramaic as well. This cannot be demonstrated with certainty, however. Although the form does not seem to have been current in Aramaic at the time, it was apparently understood by the author (and presumably the readers) of the Zakkur inscription, either because they knew enough Canaanite to make sense of certain formulas, or because the

---

[21]See Fitzmyer, pp. 40, 109-10 (commentary on *lḥzyh* and *rqh trqhm*).

[22]Lines 7, 9, 10, and 14. See A. Abou-Assaf (cited in n. 15 above), pp. 23, 31, 55.

[23]Degen, in n. 21 on pp. 114-15, gives a large sampling of scholarly opinions on the *waw* consecutive in the Zakkur text.

waw consecutive was familiar from an older form of their own language, and survived in certain formulas or archaizing contexts. It should be pointed out that the *waw* consecutives at Deir ʿAllā, unlike their context in the Zakkur inscription, are used in what seems to be narrative prose, as simple past tense forms. This is precisely what we would expect for a South Canaanite dialect.

5) I-*W* infinitive construct with -*t*. In II, 17, we have the form *dʿt* from the root **wdʿ*. We do not have this form with -*t* in any Old Aramaic inscriptions, but no I-*W* infinitives are extant in the Old Aramaic inscriptions. It is not known what this form would have looked like in Aramaic before the introduction of the *m*-preformative G infinitive (see #3 above). We might speculate that without a preformative, the I-*W* G infinitive would have been felt to be too short (as in Hebrew) and some addition could have been made. There is, however, no evidence in any Aramaic that would lead us to expect a G infinitive in -*t*.

6) Infinitive absolute plus finite verb. This combination occurs in *bkh.ybkh* (I, 3/4). This is well known in South Canaanite, but is unusual in Aramaic. It does occur at Sefîre in several contexts, and in the Nerab inscriptions. It is also known from Jewish Aramaic.

7) *ʾalep*-preformative for the tD perfect. This apparently occurs in *ʾtyḥdw* in I, 5. The *ʾalep*-preformative is common in Aramaic, but is known in the Canaanite languages only in Ugaritic.[24] This issue is made even more difficult by the fact that *hqrqt* in I, 15, if I have translated correctly, is a causative with a *h*-preformative. The *h* in *hqrqt* is clear; the *ʾ* in *ʾtyḥdw* is not, although van der Kooij was certain of the reading (110). The infra-red photograph on Plate 10 of *ATDA* shows the traces of the letter, but they are still not entirely clear. That plaster is now lost. Thus, if all the readings are correct, there is a confusion in the form of the preformative. Such a confusion occurs at Sefîre,[25] but is unusual and perhaps should call the readings into question.

---

[24] *UT* Grammar §9.33.

[25] Fitzmyer, p. 157.

With the exception of the confusion in preformatives just discussed, then, the verbal system of the Deir ʿAllā inscription provides strong evidence that the dialect is closer to South Canaanite than to Aramaic. Although several of the features are possible in an Aramaic context, the combination of features as the regular narrative pattern is unknown in Aramaic. The lack of a definite article contributes to the artificial or literary language hypothesis, but this is not a necessary construct. The forms which, in Aramaic, might be called "archaizing," are used correctly and consistently in this inscription; moreover, they are not limited to any special section of the inscription. While the *waw* consecutives may not be used outside the narrative at the beginning, the N forms and the I-*W* infinitive with -*t* are.

Each of these forms may have existed at one time as regular Aramaic forms, but it would be most unlikely to find all of them as regular forms in an inscription that dates to 700 B.C.E. There is no difficulty, however, in identifying any or all of these forms in a South Canaanite inscription of that date, with the possible (and perhaps misread) exception of *ʾtyḥdw* in I, 5.

Vocabulary

There are several lexical items in this text that are generally construed as either "Canaanite" or "Aramaic." Theoretically, the entire Semitic lexicon was available to any given dialect or language, but in fact, many words have dropped out of use in the known South Canaanite and Aramaic materials. Even this fact does not exclude their being retained for rare use. It is usually difficult to distinguish the retention of rare but indigenous lexical items from valid borrowings. In the time period with which we are concerned, the scarcity of material dictates an even more cautious attitude toward categorizing any given lexical item as predominantly "Canaanite" or "Aramaic." To say that a word or root "does not occur" in one language or the other may simply mean that it has *not yet* occurred, or that it has dropped out by the time of our more extensive materials.

Words or forms that are more common in Aramaic include:

ʾth, I, 1; II, 14: occurs in BH in poetry, both early and late.

br, I, 1, 2, 4: occurs in the Phoenician inscription of Kilamuwa within Kilamuwa's name, "Kilamuwa, son of *ḤYʾ*."

yhb, I, 7: the verb occurs in BH only in the imperative.

ṣrh, I, 8: occurs only in JA and Syriac.

ywn, I, 9: as "dove," this noun has the feminine marker everywhere except in Syriac.

ybl, I, 10: the only certain occurrence of the D of this verb is in Syriac.

ḥnyṣ, I, 15: only in Syriac with these root letters. In BH, JA, and MH, we find words from the root letters *ḥṣr*. It is possible that these are all related, however, since in Ugaritic we find both *ḫṣr* and *ḫnṣr*, and in Akkadian we have *ḫumṣiru*.

qrq, I, 15: does not occur in a Canaanite language.

mlk, II, 9: occurs only once in the Hebrew Bible with the meaning "to advise."

ḥd, II, 10: occurs once in the Hebrew Bible instead of the usual *ʾḥd*.[26]

Words or forms that are more common in Canaanite include:

ʾš, possibly the relative pronoun in I, 1, 2: does not occur as the relative pronoun in Aramaic.

pʿl, I, 2: nominal forms appear in JA and Syriac, but the root is used as a verb only in Syriac. The usual Aramaic equivalent is *ʿbd*.

lm, I, 4; II, 5?, 16?: this short form for "why?" occurs elsewhere only in Ugaritic.

lkw, I, 5: the imperative of *hlk* is never *lk* in Aramaic.

rʾh, I, 5: does not occur in Aramaic.

hgh, I, 7: does not occur in Aramaic. (It is quite rare in BH.) The related root *ygh* does occur in the C in Syriac.

ssʿgr, I, 7: the combination nevers occurs in Aramaic, although the first "word" occurs in JA as *sûsyā*.

---

[26]The form also occurs in Punic, but only after *w*, probably because of the elision of the *ʾ* between *w* and *ḥ* (Friedrich, p. 243).

rḥm, I, 8: as "vulture," never occurs in Aramaic.

drr, I, 8: does not occur in Aramaic.

mṭh, I, 9: does not occur in Aramaic.

qr, I, 12: as "thread," does not occur in Aramaic.

ʿštr, I, 15: as "offspring," does not occur in Aramaic.

nqr, II, 5, 12, 14: as "sprout," does not occur in Aramaic.

ʾnš, II, 10: as "to be weak," does not occur in Aramaic.

dbr, II, 17: as "to speak," does not occur in Aramaic.

mšpṭ, II, 17: the noun does not occur in Aramaic, although the verbal root does.

As was stated above, arguments from vocabulary are somewhat risky during this time period. Still, it is possible to evaluate what evidence we have. While it is unusual to find *br* (instead of *bn*),[27] *yhb* (instead of *ntn/ytn*), and *ḥd* (instead of *ʾḥd*) in a South Canaanite inscription, it would be far more surprising to find *rʾh* or *dbr* (with the meaning "to speak") in an Aramaic inscription. Furthermore, the imperative *lkw* from *hlk* is a development unknown in Aramaic.

T. O. Lambdin has pointed out (private communication) that a study of vocabulary would be more instructive if we could identify specialized meanings for given terms, meanings that are developed within one language for a root which, although shared by other languages, does not develop a particular specialized meaning in those other languages. This would be an instance of "shared innovation." There are only two possible cases of such specialization in our text.

ḥzh vs. *rʾh*. Whereas in Aramaic the verb *ḥzh* is the common verb "to see," in BH *rʾh* is the common verb of seeing and *ḥzh* is generally reserved for seeing in terms of having visions. The contrast in the first combination between the use of *rʾh* for common "seeing" (I, 5) and the use of the root *ḥzh* three times in I, 1, to identify Balaam as a "seer," and to describe his

---

[27]The use of *br* instead of *bn* perhaps can be explained by the fact that it is used only within Balaam's name. This is the same situation as that of the *br* used in the Kilamuwa inscription, and may be simply the proper rendering of Balaam's name. Cf. also the biblical frozen form *bənô bəʿōr* in Num 24:3, 15.

seeing a vision, offers this same distinction.

dbr. *dbr* in the D is a common verb for speaking in Hebrew and Phoenician, but the verb is used almost nowhere outside of South Canaanite with this meaning.

With due caution for the problems involved in utilizing vocabulary to distinguish between languages, the vocabulary of this inscription must be said to support the South Canaanite designation for the dialect rather than the Aramaic.

Conclusions

In conclusion, it is clear that too much emphasis has been placed, in most previous publications concerning this text, on the classification of the dialect as Aramaic. To conclude that this is an Aramaic inscription is to admit as Aramaic syntactical and lexical items which, while not unthinkable, are otherwise unknown to us in any form of Aramaic. On the other hand, the alternative is to posit a South Canaanite inscription in which *ḏ̣ is represented as *q* and in which a suffix -*wh* has developed.

The flux within phonological systems in this period is well documented and has not been, traditionally, sufficient grounds for classification of a dialect. We have seen that the consonant representation in question does not reflect an actual merger in either Old Aramaic or the dialect of the Deir ʿAllā text, so that the issue is less important as an element in classification. Furthermore, without the evidence from the Hebrew Bible, we would not expect to find a Canaanite language in the first millennium that still distinguished between *š* and *ś*. Thus, we know that such isolated preservations (or, at least, non-mergers) did occur in Canaanite.

In the total picture, the consonant representation is outweighed by several features that argue strongly for a classification for our text that is closer to South Canaanite. In particular, the verbal system has a decidedly Canaanite flavor, with the N conjugation, the I-*W* G infinitive with -*t*, and the *waw* consecutive used several times.

In terms of "shared innovations" or "unique relics," the features that Anttila suggests are the most important isoglosses in terms of classification (see above, p. 110), our evidence is scanty. It was mentioned above that the treatment of *ḥzh* and *r'h* may suggest a peculiar shading to the meanings of these words that does not exist in Aramaic, and that *dbr*, meaning "to speak," is rare enough to demand attention, and is unknown in Aramaic. Likewise, *lkw* as the (plural) imperative for *hlk* is unknown outside of Canaanite. The N conjugation, while hardly a *unique* relic, is, however, a relic of the Proto-Semitic system that did not survive in any known Aramaic. The use of a form in *-t*, without the initial *w*, as the G infinitive for I-*W* verbs, is, as far as we know, a Canaanite innovation.

The emphatic *'alep* does not occur in the text, but neither does any other definite article, as far as we can read securely, so this element is not a factor in the classification. On the other hand, *'š*, a Canaanite relative pronoun, appears to be used in I, 1, and possibly I, 2. Finally, although the 3 m. sg. pronominal suffix on the preposition *'l* is the characteristically Aramaic *-wh*, several of the lexical items that have been mentioned exhibit developments that took place only outside Aramaic dialects, as far as we know. Taken together, these points suggest that if a choice must be made between South Canaanite and Aramaic, South Canaanite dialects are considerably closer to the dialect of our text than is any known Aramaic.

SUMMARY

To summarize, we have seen that the Deir ʿAllā text reports a prophecy of Balaam which he received from the gods and which concerned a meeting of the Divine Council in which the gods expressed their displeasure over the unnatural state of affairs on earth. Further on, the text reports some ritual dealing with death, which is, I think, related to the meeting of the gods described earlier. I have presented evidence that the script of the inscription is related to the script of the later Ammonite inscriptions, and that the dialect is more closely related to the South Canaanite dialects of the first half of the first millennium B.C.E. than to Aramaic.

It is perhaps the most fascinating aspect of the Deir ʿAllā inscription that it is a Transjordanian inscription, written by a non-Israelite group, which focuses on Balaam son of Beor who was in the Hebrew Bible, of course, a prophet of a non-Israelite people who lived in that area east of the Jordan. This new inscription serves to authenticate the Balaam traditions in the Hebrew Bible to the extent that the bare facts of his existence are the same in each case. Balaam is included in the text with virtually no introduction. This fact implies that his name was well known to the people to whom the inscription was addressed, so we may infer that his was a tradition of long standing.

In an excursus, I have noted the biblical traditions of Balaam's connections with the high god Šadday (and perhaps the *Šaddayyîm*), and with a cult of the dead. I argue there that the people at Deir ʿAllā shared this tradition, or at least held traditions of the same prophet Balaam that were quite similar to those found in the Hebrew Bible.

GLOSSARY

Verbs are G unless marked otherwise. Uncertain readings are noted when that is essential.

ʾw- ("or"): II, 9.

ʾzr ("loincloth"): *ʾzr*, I, 12; *ʾz̊rn*?, I, 16. (BH and MH *ʾēzôr*; JA *ʾezôrā*.)

ʾḥr ("after"): *ʾḥrʾh*, I, 2. (BH and MH *ʾaḥar*; BA *ʾaḥărê*; JA *ʾăḥôrê*.)

ʾkl ("to eat"): *ʾkl*?, II, 3; *ʾklw*, I, 9.

ʾl ("god"): *ʾl*, I, 2; II, 6; *ʾlhn*, I, 1 bis, 5 bis. (BH and MH *ʾēl*; plural: BH and MH *ʾĕlōhîm*; BA and JA *ʾĕlāhîn*; Syr *ʾalāhīn*.)

ʾl ("to"): *ʾl*, II, 6; *ʾ̊[l]*, I, 7; *ʾlwh*, I, 1, 4. (BH and MH *ʾēl*; the suffix is vocalized according to BA and JA *-ôhî* and Syr *-aw(h)y*.)

ʾl ("not"): I, 6, 7.

ʾmr ("to say"): *ʾmr*?, II, 17; *ʾmrw*, I, 6; *wyʾmr*, I, 4/5; *wyʾmrw*, I, 2. (BH *ʾāmar*, *yō(ʾ)mar*; BA *ʾămar*, *yē(ʾ)mar*; JA *ʾămar*, *yêmar*; Syr *ʾemar*, *nē(ʾ)mar*.)

ʾnḥ ("to sigh"): N *nʾnḥ*, II, 12 bis.

ʾnph ("heron"): I, 8. (BH *ʾănāpāh*; Syr *ʾanpā*.)

ʾnš ("to be weak"): *yʾnš*, II, 10. (BH *ʾnš*; Akk *enēšu*; Arb *ʾnθ*?.)

ʾprḥ ("sprout, young"): *ʾprḥy*, I, 8. (BH *ʾeprōaḥ*; MH *ʾeprôaḥ*; JA *ʾeprôḥā*.)

ʾrnb ("hare"): *ʾrnbn*, I, 9. (BH and MH *ʾarnébet*; JA *ʾarnabtā*, *ʾarnəbā*; Syr *ʾarnbā*.)

ʾš (relative pronoun): I, 1, 2?. (Phn and Ammonite *ʾš*.)

ʾš ("man, human being"): II, 8. (BH and MH *ʾîš*.)

ʾšr ("that, which"): *bʾšr*, I, 9. (BH and MH *ʾăšer*; BA *ʾătar*; JA *ʾatrā*; Syr *ʾatar*, *ʾatrā*; Akk *ʾašar*, from *ʾašru*.)

ʾth ("to come, go"): *ʾth*, II, 14?; *wyʾtw*, I, 1. (BH *ʾātāh*, *yeʾĕteh*, *way-yaʾt*; JA *ʾătā*, *yêtê*; Syr *ʾetā*, *nē(ʾ)tē*.)

b- (preposition; "in"): I, 1, 6; II, 9, 12 bis.

bʾšr: see *ʾšr*.

byt ("house"): *byt*, II, 6, 7 bis; *by[t]*, II, 6. (BH and MH *báyit*; BA *baytā*; JA *bêtā*; Syr *baytā*.)

bkh ("to cry"): *ybkh*, I, 4; *ẘtbkh*, I, 4; *bkh* (inf. abs.), I, 3/4.

blʿm (PN): *blʿm*, I, 3, 4; *[blʿ]m*, I, 2; *[blʿm]*, I, 1. (BH and MH *bilʿām*.)

bʿr (PN, name of Balaam's father): *bʿr*, I, 2, 4; *[bʿ]r*, I, 1. (BH *bəʿôr* or *bəʿōr*. The *qutul* vocalization follows the Septuagint transliteration of *sədōm* [the same basic form as *bəʿōr*] as *Sodoma*.)

br ("son"): *br*, I, 2, 4; *[br]*, I, 1; *bny*, I, 8; II, 8; *bn[y]*, I, 15/16. (The vocalization *bir* is known from Aramean personal names transcribed in Assyrian as *bir*, e.g., Bir-Dadda, Bir-Atar. See p. 34, n. 12, for reference. Plural: BH and MH *bānîm*, *bənê*; BA and JA *bənê*; Syr *bnay*.)

gdr? ("wall"): *g̊dr*, II, 15. (BH *gādēr*; MH *gādêr*; JA *gādêrā*.)

gdš ("grave"): II, 8. (BH, MH, and JA *gādîš*; Syr *gdīšā*; cf. Arb *jadaθ*.)

gr ("whelp"): *gry*, I, 10. (BH and MH *gûr*; JA *gûrā*.)

dbr ("to speak"): D *dbr*, II, 17.

dd ("love"): *ddn*, II, 4. (BH and MH *dôdîm*.)

dwr: see *mdr*.

drr ("swallow"): I, 8. (BH and MH *dərôr*.)

h- (interrogative particle): II, 9.

hʾ ("he"): I, 1, used as copula. (BH, BA, MH, and JA *hûʾ*; Syr *hū*.)

hgh ("to remove"): *thgy*, I, 7.

hlk ("to walk, go"): *lkw* (m. pl. imperative), I, 5; *hlk* (m. sg. active participle), II, 7. (Imperative: BH and MH *lēk*.)

hn ("if"): II, 10 bis. (BH, BA, MH, and JA *hēn*.)

w- ("and"): I, 1 bis, 2, 3 ter, 4 ter, 5, 6 ter, 7 bis, 8 bis, 9, 10, 11 bis, 12, 13, 14, 16; II, 5, 7, 8 bis, 13, 15 bis, 17, 18.

zʾb? ("wolf"): *[z]ʾ̊b̊*, I, 10. (BH *zəʾēb*; JA *dêbā*; Arb *ðiʾb*.)

zlp? ("to spread"): *zlp̊?*, II, 15. (MH and JA *zlp*.)

ḥd ("one"): II, 10. (BA, JA, and Syr *ḥad*.)

ḥwh ("to tell"): *ʾḥwkm*, I, 5. (The root occurs in the D in BH, BA, MH, JA, and Syr.)

ḥzh ("to see visions"): *ḥzw*, I, 14; *ẘyḥz*, I, 1; *yḥz̊ẘ?*, II, 13; *ḥzh* (m. sg. active participle), I, 1. (BH *ḥāzāh*, *yeḥĕzeh*; JA *ḥəzā*, *yiḥzê*; Syr *ḥzā*, *neḥzē*.) See also *ḥzn*, *mḥzh*.

ḥzn? ("vision"): *ḥzn*, II, 16. (BH and MH *ḥāzôn*.)

ḥṭr ("staff"): I, 9. (BH *ḥṓṭer*; JA *ḥôṭer*, *ḥuṭrā*; Syr *ḥuṭrā*.)

ḥkm ("wise"): *ḥkmn*, I, 11. (BH and MH *ḥākām*; BA and JA *ḥakkîm*; Syr *ḥakkim*; Arb *ḥakam*, *ḥakîm*.)

ḥlq ("to perish"): *ḥlq* (inf. cs.), II, 11.

ḥmr ("wine"): I, 10. (BH *ḥḗmer*, *ḥā́mer* in pause; BA *ḥămar*; JA and Syr *ḥamrā*.)

ḥnyṣ ("piglet"): I, 15. (Ug *ḫzr/ḫnzr*; BH and MH *ḥăzîr*; JA *ḥăzîrā*; Syr *ḥnayṣā*; Akk *ḫumṣiru*.)

ḥsd? ("stork"): *ḥ[sd]*, I, 8. (BH and MH *ḥăsîdāh*.)

ḥpš (?): I, 10.

ḥrp ("to reproach"): D (probably) *ḥrpt*, I, 7/8.

ḥrš ("deaf"): *ḥršn*, I, 13. (BH and MH *ḥērēš*; JA *ḥaršā*, *ḥêršā*; Syr *ḥreš*.)

ḥšb ("to respect"): *ḥšb* (m. sg. passive participle, 3 m. sg. active perfect, m. sg. active participle), I, 12; *ḥ[šb]* (3 m. sg. passive perfect), I, 12/13.

ḥšk ("darkness"): I, 6, 7. (BH and MH *ḥṓšek*; BA *ḥăšôk*; JA and Syr *ḥeškā*.)

ḥtm ("seal"): *ḥt[m]*, I, 7. (BH *ḥō/ôtām*; MH *ḥôtām*; JA *ḥôtāmā*; Syr *ḥātmā*.)

ḥtn ("bridegroom"): II, 7. (BH and MH *ḥātān*; JA and Syr *ḥatnā*; JA *ḥătānā*.)

ṭwš ("plaster"): *ṭš̊̊*, II, 15. (MH, JA, and Syr *ṭwš*, "to smear.")

ṭl ("dew"): II, 36. (BH, MH, and BA *ṭal*; JA and Syr *ṭallā*.)

ybl ("to drive, lead"): D passive *yybl*, I, 9. (The root occurs in Syr in the D, and in BH, BA, MH, and JA in the C.)

ydʿ ("to know"): *dʿt* (inf. cs.), II, 17. (BH *dáʿat*, *daʿtî*.)

yhb ("to give, put"): *thby*, I, 7.

ywn ("dove"): I, 9. (BH and MH *yônāh*; JA *yônətā*; Syr *yawnā*.)

yḥd ("to be united"): tD *ʾtyḥ̊dw*, I, 5. (MH *hityaḥēd*; JA *ʾityaḥēd*.)

ykl? ("to be able"): *yk̊*[*l*] (perfect), I. 3. (BH and MH *yākōl*, *yûkal*; BA *yəkil*, *yûkal*; JA *yəkêl*, *yikkôl*.)

ysr: see *mwsr*.

yʿd: see *mwʿd*.

yʿṣ: see *ʿwṣ*, *ʿṣh*.

yšb ("to sit, dwell"): *šb̊w* (m. pl. imperative), I, 5; *yšb*? (m. sg. participle), II, 9. (Imperative: BH and MH *šēb*; JA *tib*; Syr *teb*.)

k- ("like"): I, 2.

kh ("thus"): I, 2. (BH and MH *kōh*; BA *kāh*; JA *kā*, *kāh*; Syr *kā*.)

khnh ("priestess"): I, 11. ("Priest" is vocalized as a participle in BH, BA, MH, JA, and Syr.)

kwl ("to contain"): *kl* (m. sg. participle), II, 5.

kwn? ("to be prepared"): N? *yk̊n̊*, II, 14.

ky (conjunction; "because"): I, 7; II, 14.

ksh ("to cover"): D *tksn*, II, 10. (Most commonly D in BH, MH, and JA.)

l- (preposition): ("to," directional) II, 14?, 15; ("to," dative) I, 2, 5, 6, 11, 12?; II, 17 bis; ("to," purpose) I, 2?; II, 11, 17; ("as for," topicalizing) II, 9 bis, 18?.

l- ("not"): I, 3; II, 7 bis, 9 bis, 13?, 18?.

lbb ("heart"): II, 12 bis, 14. (BH and MH *lēbāb*; BA *ləbab*; JA *ləbābā*/*libəbā*.)

lbš ("garment"): II, 10. (BH, BA, MH, and JA *ləbûš*; Syr *lbūšā*; Akk *lubūšu*.)

lylh ("night"): I, 1. (BH and MH *láylāh*; BA and JA *lêlā*; Syr *lēlyā*.)

lm ("why?"): I, 4; II, 5?, 16?. (Ug *lm*; BA and MH *lā́mmāh*; BA *ləmāh*; JA *ləmā*; Syr *lmā*.)

lqh: see *mlqh*.

lqḥ ("to take"): *yqḥ*, II, 13.

lšn ("tongue"): II, 17. (BH and MH *lāšôn*; BA *liššān*; JA *lišānā*; Syr *leššānā*; Arb *lisān*.)

mdr ("fire-pit"? "soil"?): II, 5. (BH *mədûrāh* "pit"; MH *mədûrāh*, *mədûrê* "pit"; or Eth *medr*, Syr *medrā* "earth.")

mh ("what"): I, 5. (BH and BA *māh*; MH and JA *māh*, *mah*; Syr *mā*.)

mwsr ("chastisement"): I, 10. (BH *mōsār* [once]; BH and MH *mûsār*.)

mwʿd ("assembly"): I, 6. (BH, MH, and JA *môʿēd*; Syr *mawʿād*.)

mwt ("death"): II, 13; *m̊ẘt̊*, II, 14. (BH and MH *mā́wet*; BA and JA *môt*; Syr *mawtā*.)

mḥzh ("vision"): I, 1. (BH *maḥăzeh*.)

mḥr ("morrow"): I, 3. (BH and MH *māḥār*; JA *məḥar*; Syr *mḥār*.)

mṭh ("rod"): I, 9. (BH and MH *maṭṭeh*.)

mlk ("to advise"): tG (tD?) *ytmlk*, II, 9. (BH and MH, N = "to counsel"; Akk *malāku* = "to counsel"; JA tG and tD, Syr tG and tD = "to ask advice of.") See also *mlkh*.

mlk ("king"? "*mulk* sacrifice"?): *mlk*, II, 15, 18; *mlkn*, II, 13.

mlkh ("advice"): II, 9. (JA *mēlak*; Syr *mlek*, *melkā*.)

mlqh ("punishment"): *mlqh̊*, II, 17. (No exact cognates; the root *lqh* exists in MH and JA. MH has *malqût*.)

mn (preposition): ("from") I, 3?, 13; II, 8 ter; (of time "after") I, 3.

mr ("myrrh"): I, 11. (BH and MH *mōr*/*môr*; JA *môr*, *mûrā*; Syr *murrā*.)

mšʾ ("oracle"): *mš̊ʾ*, I, 2. (BH and MH *maśśāʾ*.)

mškb ("bed, couch"): I, 11. (BH and MH *miškāb*; BA *miškab*; JA *miškəbā*; Syr *maškabtā*.)

mšn? (?): I, 16.

mšpṭ ("judgment"): II, 17. (BH and MH *mišpāṭ*.)

ngh ("light"): I, 6/7. (BH, MH, and BA *nōgah*; JA *nāghā*, *nôghā*; Syr *nughā*.)

nḥṣ (?; a bird): I, 8.

nṭh: see *mṭh*.

nṭp ("to drip"): *ṭṭpn*, II, 35, 36.

nmr ("leopard"): I, 15. (BH and MH *nāmēr*; BA and JA *nəmar*; JA *nimrā*; Syr *nemrā*; Arb *namir*.)

nṣb ("to stand"): N *nṣbw*, I, 6.

nqr ("sprout"): II, 5, 12, 14. (BH and MH *nḗṣer*; Arb *nḍr*.)

nšʾ ("prince"): I, 12. (BH and MH *nāśîʾ*; JA *nəśîʾ*/*nəsîʾ*.) See *mšʾ* from the same root.

nšr ("to tear"): D *nšrt*, I, 8. (MH *nšr* D; JA *nšr* G [intransitive].)

nšr ("griffin-vulture"): I, 8. (BH and MH *nḗšer*; BA *nəšar*; JA *nəšar*, *nišrā*; Syr *nešrā*.)

skl ("fool"): *s̊kl*, I, 14. (BH *sākāl*; JA and Syr *saklā*.)

skr ("to bolt"): *skry* (f. sg. imperative), I, 6. See also *skr* directly below.

skr ("bolt"): *sk̊rky*, I, 7. (Akk *sikru*.)

ssh ("mare"?): II, 15. (BH *sûsāh*; JA *sûsyā*.)

ssʿgr ("swift"): I, 7. (BH *sûs* and *ʿāgûr*; JA *sûsyā*.)

spr ("account, narrative"): I, 1; II, 17. (BH and MH *sḗper*, *siprî*; BA *səpar*; JA *siprā*; Syr *seprā*.)

ʿb ("cloud"): *bʿbky*, I, 6. (BH and MH *ʿāb*; JA *ʿêbā*; Syr *ʿaybā*, *ʿābā*.)

ʿbr ("to pass over"): *yʿbr̊*, II, 6. (BH *yaʿăbōr*; MH *yeʿĕbôr*; JA *yiʿbar*; Syr *neʿbar*.)

ʿd ("until"): I, 7.

ʿwl: see *ʿl* "suckling."

ʿwṣ ("to counsel"): tD *ytʿṣ*, II, 9. (BH *ʿwṣ*.) See also *ʿṣh*.

ʿyn? ("eye"? "fountain"?): I, 16.

ʿl ("upon"): II, 17.

ʿl ("suckling"): II, 13 bis. (BH and JA *ʿûl*; Syr *ʿūlā*; Arb *ǵyl*.)

ʿlh ("to go up"): *wyʿl*, I, 4; *lyʿl*, II, 7 bis. (BH short imperfect is *yắʿal*.)

ʿlm ("eternity"): *ʿlm*, I, 7 bis (once *ʿl̊m*); *ʿlmn*, II, 6; *ʿlmyk*, II, 11. (BH, MH *ʿôlām*; BA *ʿālam*; JA, Syr *ʿālmā*.)

ʿlm ("young boy"?): *ʿlmh*, II, 4. (BH and MH *ʿélem*, *ʿā́lem* in pause; JA *ʿûlêm*; Syr *ʿlaymā*; Arb *ǵilma[t]*.)

ʿm ("people"): *ʿmh*, I, 4; II, 17. (Note BH *ʿammî* and JA *ʿammā*.)

ʿnh ("to sing"): *yʿnh*, I, 8. (BH, MH, and JA G and D.)

ʿnyh ("poor woman"): I, 11. (BH and MH *ʿănīyāh*; BA *ʿănāyīn*; JA *ʿanyā*; Syr *ʿanwāyā*.)

ʿṣh ("counsel"): II, 9. (BH and MH *ʿēṣāh*; BA *ʿēṭā*; JA *ʿēṭā*.)

ʿštr ("offspring"): I, 14. (Ug [*PRU* III, p. 242] *aš-tar-a-bi*; BH *ʿaštārôt*.)

pḥz ("to rise"): *pḥzy* (m. pl. cs. participle), II, 8.

pʿl ("to make"): *ypʿl*, I, 2. See also *pʿlh*.

pʿlh ("work, deed"): *pʿlt*, I, 5. (BH *pəʿullāh*; MH *pəʿûllāh*; JA *pəʿûltā*.)

prḥ: see *ʾprḥ*.

ṣwm ("to fast"): *tṣm*, I, 4. (BH *ṣām*, *yāṣūm*; Syr *ṣām*, *nṣūm*.)

ṣpr ("sparrow"): I, 9. (BH *ṣippō/ôr*; BA *ṣippar*; MH *ṣippôr*; JA *ṣippar/ṣippôr*; Syr *ṣepprā*.)

ṣrh ("to claw"): I, 8. (JA *ṣərā*; Syr *ṣrā*.)

qbʿ ("hyena"): *qbʿn*, I, 10. (BH and MH *ṣəbôʿîm*; MH *ṣābûaʿ*; Syr *ʾapʿā*; Arb *ḍabuʿ*.)

qwm ("to rise"): *wyqm*, I, 3. (BH converted imperfect is *way-yā́qom*.)

qḥk ("to laugh"): *yqḥk*, I, 11. (Ug *θḥq*; Ug, BH, and MH *ṣḥq*; BH and MH *śḥq*; Syr *gḥk*; Arb *ḍḥk*; Eth *šḥq*.)

ql ("voice"): I, 8. (BH *qô/ōl*; BA *qāl*; MH *qôl*; JA and Syr *qālā*.)

qṣ? ("end"): *qṣh*, II, 15. (BH and MH *qēṣ*, *qiṣṣô*; JA *qēṣ*, *qiṣṣā*.)

qqn ("constraint"?): I, 14. (BH *ṣwq*; Arb *ḍāqa*.)

qr? ("thread"?): *qrn*, I, 12. (BH *qûr*.)

qrq ("to flee"): C *hqrqt*, I, 15. (JA and Syr *ʿrq*; Old Aramaic and Imperial Aramaic *qrq* [in the G, "to flee"].)

rʾh ("to see"): *rʾw*, I, 5.

rʾš ("head"): *rʾšk*, II, 11. (Ug *rʾiš*; BH, MH, and JA *rō(ʾ)š*; BA and JA *rē(ʾ)š*; Syr *rēšā*.)

rwh ("to drink one's fill, to be satisfied"): *yrwy*, II, 6. (BH *rāwāh*, *yirweh*; Arb *rawiya*, *yirwā*.) See also *rwy*.

rwy ("full"?): II, 4. (BH *rāweh*; JA *rəwê*, *rəwā*; MH *rāwāh*.)

rḥl ("ewe"): *rḥln*, I, 9. (BH and MH *rāḥēl*; JA *raḥlā*, *rəḥēlā*.)

rḥm ("vulture"): *rḥmn*, I, 8. (BH and MH *rāḥām*.)

rḥm ("womb"): II, 13. (BH and MH *rêḥem*, *raḥmāh*; BH *ráḥam*; BA *raḥămīn*; JA and Syr *raḥmā*.)

rḥq ("afar, distant"): I, 13; *r̊ḥq*?, II, 16. (BH and MH *rāḥôq*; BH *rāḥōq*; BA *rəḥîq*; MH *rāḥîq*; Syr *raḥḥīq*.)

rṭb ("foliage"? "moist"?): *rṭb̊*, II, 5. (JA *rəṭîbāh*, *raṭṭîb*. The root is the same in BH, MH, and Syr.)

rmh ("worm"?): II, 8. BH and MH *rimmāh*; Syr *remmtā*.)

rqḥ ("to mix perfume"): *rqḥt*, I, 11.

šʾlh? ("request"): *šʾlt*, II, 15 bis (once *š*[*ʾ*]*l*[*t*]); *šʾltk*, II, 16. (BH and MH *šəʾēlāh*; JA *šəʾēltā*.)

šgr ("offspring"): I, 14. (BH and MH *šéger*; JA *šigrā*.)

šdy (appellative for group of gods): *šdyn*, I, 6; *šd̊*[*yn*], I, 5. (BH, MH, and JA *šadday*. If from a word for "breast," *š* < *θ: BH *šad*; JA *taddā*.)

šhh ("to pause, be weary"): II, 14. (BH *šʾh*?; MH, JA, and Syr *šhh*/*ʾ*/*y*.)

šwb? ("to return"?): C *yšbm*?, II, 13.

šym ("to put, ordain"): *ʾšm*, II, 11; *šm* (inf. abs.), I, 6. (BH *śwm*/*śym*; JA *swm*/*sym*.)

škb ("to lie down"): *tškb*, II, 11. (BH *šākab*, *yiškab*; Syr *škab*, *neškab*.) See also *mškb*.

šm ("there"): II, 7. (BH and MH *šām*; JA *tām*.)

šmh ("thither"?): II, 13, 14. (BH *šā́mmāh*.)

šmyn ("heavens"): I, 6.

šmʿ ("to hear"): *šmʿw*, I, 10; *wšmʿw*, I, 13.

šnʾ ("to hate"): *tšnʾn*, II, 10. (BH *śnʾ*; JA *sənê*.)

šʿl? ("fox"): *š*[*ʿl*], I, 10/11. (BH *šûʿāl*; JA *taʿal*; Syr *tʿel*, *taʿlā*; Arb *θuʿāl*.)

špṭ: see *mšpṭ*.

šq? ("sepulchre"?): *šqy?*, II, 8. (Syr *šāqā*.)

šr ("heavy rain"): II, 35. (Arb *θarr*, "abounding in water.")

šth ("to drink"): *štyw*, I, 10; *nšty?*, II, 18. (BH and MH *šātāh*, *yišteh*; BA *'ištīw* [pl.], *yištôn* [pl.]; JA *šətî*, *yištê*; Syr *'eštī*, *neštē*; Eth *satya*, *yestay*.)

tḥt ("under"): II, 11. (BH, MH, and JA *táḥat*; BA and JA *təḥôt*; Syr *taḥt/tḥut/tḥet*.)

tpr ("to sew up"): *tpry* (f. sg. imperative), I, 6.

SELECTED BIBLIOGRAPHY

Abou-Assaf, Ali, Pierre Bordreuil, and Alan R. Millard. *La statue de Tell Fekherye et son inscription bilingue assyro-araméenne*. Paris: Editions Recherche sur les civilisations, 1982.

Albright, William F. "The Name of Bildad the Shuhite." *AJSL* 44 (1927-28) 31-36.

__________. "The Names Shadday and Abram." *JBL* 54 (1935) 180-93.

__________. "The Oracles of Balaam." *JBL* 63 (1944) 207-33.

__________. "Syria, the Philistines, and Phoenicia" (Chapter XXXIII). *CAH* II, 2.

Anttila, Raimo. *An Introduction to Historical Linguistics*. New York: Macmillan, 1972.

The Assyrian Dictionary of the Oriental Institute of the University of Chicago, ed. A. Leo Oppenheim, *et al.* Chicago: The Oriental Institute, 1956- .

Attridge, Harold W., and Robert A. Oden. *De Dea Syria*. Missoula, MT: Scholars Press, 1976.

Avigad, N. "Ammonite and Moabite Seals." *Near Eastern Archaeology in the Twentieth Century: Essays in Honor of Nelson Glueck*, ed. J. A. Sanders. Garden City, NY: Doubleday, 1970. Pages 284-95 and Plate 30.

__________. "An Ammonite Seal." *IEJ* 2 (1952) 163-64.

__________. "Seals of Exiles." *IEJ* 15 (1965) 222-29.

__________. "Two Ammonite Seals Depicting the *Dea Nutrix*." *BASOR* 225 (1977) 63-66.

Bauer, Hans, and Pontus Leander. *Historische Grammatik der hebräischen Sprache des Alten Testamentes*. Hildesheim: Georg Olms Verlagsbuchhandlung, 1965.

Bloomfield, Leonard. *Language*. New York: Henry Holt & Co., 1933.

Brockelmann, Carl. *Grundriss der vergleichenden Grammatik der semitischen Sprachen*. 2 vols. Berlin: Reuther & Reichard, 1908-13.

Brown, Francis, with S. R. Driver and Charles A. Briggs. *Hebrew and English Lexicon of the Old Testament.* Oxford: Clarendon Press, 1974.

The Cambridge Ancient History, 3rd ed., ed. I. E. S. Edwards, *et al.* Cambridge: University Press, 1975.

Caquot, André, and André Lemaire. "Les textes araméens de Deir ʿAlla." *Syria* 54 (1977) 189-208.

Cheyne, T. K. *Isaiah.* In *The Sacred Books of the Old and New Testaments,* ed. Paul Haupt. New York: Dodd, Mead & Co., 1898.

Cowley, A. E. *Aramaic Papyri of the Fifth Century B.C.* Oxford: Clarendon Press, 1923.

Cross, Frank Moore. "Ammonite Ostraca from Heshbon." *AUSS* XIII (1975) 1-20 and Pl. I-II.

__________. *Canaanite Myth and Hebrew Epic.* Cambridge, MA: Harvard University Press, 1973.

__________. "Epigraphic Notes on the Ammān Citadel Inscription." *BASOR* 193 (1969) 13-19.

__________. "Heshbon Ostracon II." *AUSS* XI (1973) 126-31.

__________. "Heshbon Ostracon XI." *AUSS* XIV (1976) 145-48.

__________. "Leaves from an Epigraphist's Notebook." *CBQ* 36 (1974) 486-94.

__________. "Notes on the Ammonite Inscription from Tell Sīrān." *BASOR* 212 (1973) 12-15.

__________, and David Noel Freedman. *Early Hebrew Orthography.* New Haven: American Oriental Society, 1952.

____________________. *Studies in Ancient Yahwistic Poetry.* Missoula, MT: Scholars Press, 1975.

Dahood, Mitchell. Review of *ATDA* in *Biblica* 62 (1981) 124-27.

Degen, Rainer. *Altaramäische Grammatik.* Wiesbaden: Deutsche Morgenländische Gesellschaft, 1969.

Donner H., and W. Röllig. *Kanaanäische und aramäische Inschriften.* 3rd ed. Wiesbaden: Harrassowitz, 1971.

Eissfeldt, Otto. *Molk als Opferbegriff im Punischen und Hebräischen und das Ende des Gottes Moloch.* Halle: Max Niemeyer, 1935.

Fitzmyer, Joseph A., S. J. *The Aramaic Inscriptions of Sefîre.* Rome: Pontifical Biblical Institute, 1967.

__________. Review of *ATDA* in *CBQ* 40 (1978) 93-95.

Franken, H. J. "Clay Tablets from Deir ʿAlla, Jordan." *VT* 14 (1964) 377-79.

__________. "The Excavations at Deir ʿAllā in Jordan." *VT* 10 (1960) 386-93.

__________. "The Excavations at Deir ʿAllā in Jordan." *VT* 11 (1961) 361-72.

__________. "The Excavations at Deir ʿAlla in Jordan: 3rd Season." *VT* 12 (1962) 378-82.

__________. "A Note on How the Deir ʿAlla Tablets Were Written." *VT* 15 (1965) 150-52.

__________. "The Stratigraphic Context of the Clay Tablets Found at Deir ʿAlla." *PEQ* 96 (1964) 73-78.

__________. "Texts from the Persian Period from Tell Deir ʿAllā." *VT* 17 (1967) 480-81.

__________, and Moawiya M. Ibrahim. "Two Seasons of Excavations at Tell Deir ʿAlla, 1976-1978." *ADAJ* XXII (1977-78) 57-79.

Frazer, Sir James George. *The Golden Bough*. London: Macmillan & Co., 1955.

Friedrich, Johannes, and Wolfgang Röllig. *Phönizisch-punische Grammatik*. 2nd ed. Rome: Pontifical Biblical Institute, 1970.

Garbini, Giovanni. "L'iscrizione di Balaam Bar-Beor." *Henoch* 1 (1979) 166-88.

Gardiner, Sir Alan Henderson. *Egyptian Grammar*. 3rd ed., rev. Oxford: Oxford University Press, 1973.

Gelb, I. J. "Thoughts About Ibla." *Syro-Mesopotamian Studies* 1/1 (1977) 3-30.

Gesenius' Hebrew Grammar, ed. E. Kautzsch. A. E. Cowley, trans. 2nd English ed. Oxford: Clarendon Press, 1910.

Gordon, Cyrus. *Ugaritic Textbook*. Rome: Pontifical Biblical Institute, 1965.

Greenfield, Jonas C. "The Dialects of Early Aramaic." *JNES* 37 (1978) 93-99.

__________. Review of *ATDA* in *JSS* 25 (1980) 248-52.

Hammershaimb, E. "De aramaiske indskrifter fra udgravningerne i Deir ʿAllā." *Dansk Teologisk Tidsskrift* 40 (1977) 217-42.

Harris, Zellig S. *Development of the Canaanite Dialects*. New Haven: American Oriental Society, 1939.

__________. *A Grammar of the Phoenician Language*. New Haven: American Oriental Society, 1936.

Herdner, Andrée. *Corpus des tablettes en cunéiformes alphabétiques*. Paris: Imprimerie Nationale, 1963.

Herr, Larry G. *The Scripts of Ancient Northwest Semitic Seals*. Missoula, MT: Scholars Press, 1978.

Hoftijzer, Jacob. "The Prophet Balaam in a 6th Century Aramaic Inscription." *BA* 39 (1976) 11-17.

__________, and G. van der Kooij. *Aramaic Texts from Deir ʿAlla*. Leiden: E. J. Brill, 1976.

Horn, Siegfried H. "The Ammān Citadel Inscription." *BASOR* 193 (1969) 2-13.

Jastrow, Marcus. *A Dictionary of the Targumim, the Talmud Babli and Yerushalmi, and the Midrashic Literature*. New York: Pardes Publishing House, Inc., 1950.

Jean, Charles-F., and Jacob Hoftijzer. *Dictionnaire des inscriptions sémitiques de l'ouest*. Leiden: E. J. Brill, 1965.

Joüon, Paul, S. J. *Grammaire de l'hébreu biblique*. Rome: Pontifical Biblical Institute, 1923.

Kaufman, Stephen A. "The Aramaic Texts from Deir ʿAllā." *BASOR* 239 (1980) 71-74.

Knudtzon, J. A. *Die El-Amarna-Tafeln*. Leipzig: J. C. Hinrichs, 1915. Reprinted, Aalen: Otto Zeller, 1964.

Lambdin, Thomas O. *Introduction to Biblical Hebrew*. New York: Charles Scribner's Sons, 1971.

__________. *Introduction to Classical Ethiopic (Geʿez)*. Missoula, MT: Scholars Press, 1978.

__________. "The Junctural Origin of the West Semitic Definite Article." In *Near Eastern Studies in Honor of William Foxwell Albright*, ed. Hans Goedicke. Baltimore: The Johns Hopkins University Press, 1971. Pages 315-33.

Lane, Edward William. *An Arabic English Dictionary*. New York: Frederick Ungar Publishing Co., 1955-56.

Lapp, Paul W. "The Tell Deir ʿAllā Challenge to Palestinian Archaeology" (review of *Excavations at Tell Deir ʿAllā I*, by H. J. Franken). *VT* 20 (1970) 243-56.

Levine, Baruch. "The Deir ʿAlla Plaster Inscriptions." *JAOS* 101 (1981) 195-205.

Lichtheim, Miriam. *Ancient Egyptian Literature*. 3 vols. Berkeley, CA: University of California Press, 1973-80.

McCarter, P. Kyle, Jr. "The Balaam Texts from Deir ʿAllā: The First Combination." *BASOR* 239 (1980) 49-60.

Moran, William L. "The Hebrew Language in Its Northwest Semitic Background." In *The Bible and the Ancient Near East: Essays in Honor of William Foxwell Albright*, ed. G. Ernest Wright. Garden City, NY: Anchor Books, 1965.

Mosca, Paul G. "Child Sacrifice in Canaanite and Israelite Religion." Harvard University Ph.D. thesis, 1975.

Müller, Hans-Peter. "Die aramäische Inschrift von Deir ʿAllā und die älteren Bileamsprüche." *ZAW* 94 (1982) 214-44.

__________. "Einige alttestamentliche Probleme zur aramäischen Inschrift von *Dēr ʿAllā*." *ZDPV* 94 (1978) 56-67.

Naveh, Joseph. "The Date of the Deir ʿAllā Inscription in Aramaic Script." *IEJ* 17 (1967) 256-58.

__________. *The Development of the Aramaic Script*. Proceedings of the Israel Academy of Sciences and Humanities, Vol. V, no. 1. Jerusalem, 1970.

__________. Review of *ATDA* in *IEJ* 29 (1979) 133-36.

Nougayrol, Jean. *Le palais royal d'Ugarit*, vol. III. Paris: Imprimerie Nationale, 1955.

__________, *et al. Ugaritica V*. Paris: Geuthner, 1968.

Payne Smith, Robert, ed. *A Compendious Syriac Dictionary*. Oxford: Clarendon Press, 1903.

Puech, Emil. Review of *ATDA* in *RB* 85 (1978) 114-17.

Ringgren, Helmer. "Bileam och inskriften från Deir ʿAlla." *Religion och Bibel* 36 (1977) 85-89.

Rofé, Alexander. *The Book of Balaam (Numbers 22:2-24:25)*. Jerusalem: Simor Ltd., 1979 [Hebrew].

Segert, Stanislav. *Altaramäische Grammatik*. Leipzig: Verlag Enzyklopädie, 1975.

von Soden, Wolfram. *Akkadisches Handwörterbuch*. Wiesbaden: Harrassowitz, 1965-81.

__________. *Grundriss der akkadischen Grammatik*. Rome: Pontifical Biblical Institute, 1952.

Thompson, Henry O., and Fawzi Zayadine. "The Tell Siran Inscription." *BASOR* 212 (1973) 5-12.

Ullendorff, Edward. Review of I. J. Gelb, "Thoughts about Ibla" in *JSS* 23 (1978) 151-54.

Vattioni, Francesco. "I sigilli ebraici." *Biblica* 50 (1969) 357-88.

de Vaux, Roland. "Sur quelques rapports entre Adonis et Osiris." *Bible et Orient*. Paris: Editions du Cerf, 1967. Pages 379-405.

Virolleaud, Charles. *Le palais royal d'Ugarit*, vol. V. Paris: Imprimerie Nationale, 1965.

Wallis, G. Review of *ATDA* in *BiOr* 35 (1978) 316-17.

Wehr, Hans. *A Dictionary of Modern Written Arabic*, ed. J. Milton Cowan. Ithaca, NY: Cornell University Press, 1961.

Weippert, Helga and Manfred. "Die 'Bileam'-Inschrift von *Tell Dēr ʿAllā*." *ZDPV* 98 (1982) 77-103.

Weippert, Manfred. "Erwägungen zur Etymologie des Gottesnames ʾEl Šaddaj." *ZDMG* n.s. 36 (1961) 42-62.

Wright, William. *Grammar of the Arabic Language*. 2 vols. 3rd ed, rev., by W. Robertson Smith and M. H. de Goeje. Cambridge: Cambridge University Press, 1971.

Zayadine, Fawzi. "Note sur l'inscription de la statue d'Amman." *Syria* 51 (1974) 129-36.

APPENDIX

SCRIPT CHARTS

CHART I

ARAMAIC CURSIVE SCRIPTS

1 & 2. Nimrud Ostracon, two handwritings, late 8th century

J. B. Segal, "An Aramaic Ostracon from Nimrud," *Iraq* XIX (1957) 139-45.

3. Assur Ostracon, mid-7th century

M. Lidzbarski, *Altaramäische Urkunden aus Assur* (Leipzig: Hinrichs, 1921) 5-15.

4. Saqqarah Papyrus, ca. 600

A. Dupont-Sommer, "Un papyrus araméen d'époque saïte découvert à Saqqarah," *Semitica* I (1948) 43-68, pl. opp. p. 68.

5. Starcky Tablet, 571/70

J. Starcky, "Une tablette araméenne de l'an 34 de Nabuchodonosor," *Syria* XXXVII (1960) 99-115.

CHART II

SCRIPTS FROM INSCRIPTIONS FOUND IN AMMON

1. Amman Citadel inscription, ca. 850, Aramaic lapidary

   Siegfried H. Horn, "The Ammān Citadel Inscription," *BASOR* 193 (1969) 2-13.

2. Deir ʿAllā plaster inscription, ca. 700

   J. Hoftijzer and G. van der Kooij, *Aramaic Texts from Deir ʿAlla* (Leiden: E. J. Brill, 1976).

3. Heshbon Ostracon IV, ca. 600, Ammonite cursive

   Frank M. Cross, "Ammonite Ostraca from Heshbon," *AUSS* 13 (1975) 1-20.

4. Tell Sīrān inscription, ca. 575, Ammonite cursive

   Henry O. Thompson and Fawzi Zayadine, "The Tell Siran Inscription," *BASOR* 212 (1973) 5-11.

5. Heshbon Ostracon XI, ca. 575, Ammonite cursive

   Frank M. Cross, "Heshbon Ostracon XI," *AUSS* 14 (1976) 145-48.

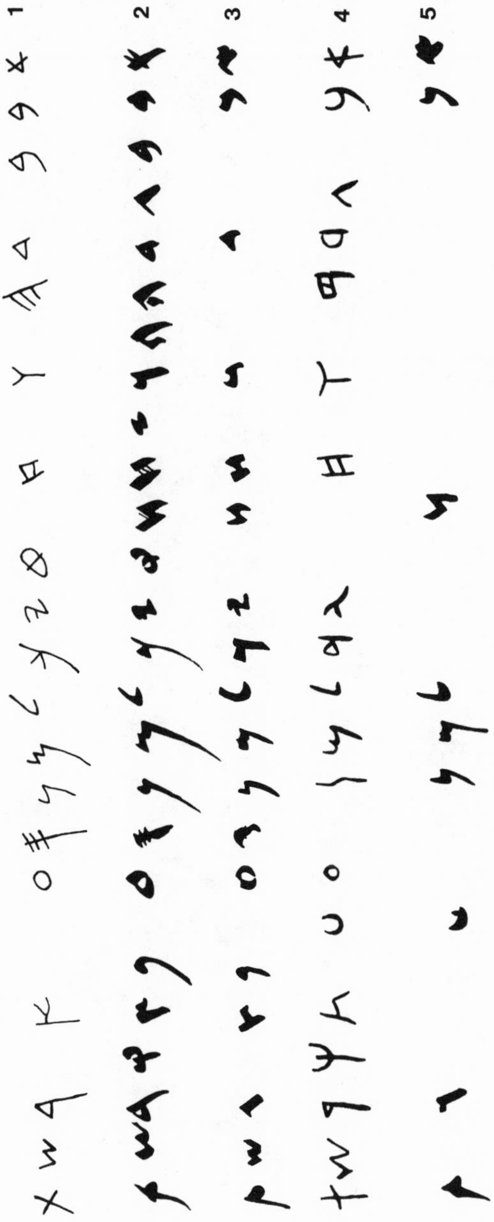
1
2
3
4
5